The Dispensation of the Báb

BORIS HANDAL

Author publications

El Concurso en Lo Alto. PROPACEB, Lima. Peru. 1985.

Eve Nicklin: She of the Brave Heart. CreateSpace, 2011.

The Khamsis: a Cradle of True Gold. IngramSpark. 2020.

Mirza Mehdi, Ghusn-i-Athar ("میرزا مهدی غصن اطهر"). IngramSpark. 2022.

Mírzá Mihdí: La Rama Mas Pura. Editorial Bahá'í de España, 2019.

Mírzá Mihdí: The Purest Branch. George Ronald, Oxford. 2017.

Muḥammad: Profeta de Dios. Editorial Bahá'í of Peru. 2005.

A Trilogy of Consecration: The Courier, the Historian and the Missionary. IngramSpark. 2020.

Varqá and Rúḥu'lláh: 101 Stories of Bravery on the Move. IngramSpark. 2020.

Quddús: The First in Rank, forthcoming.

The Dispensation of the Báb

BORIS HANDAL

Published: First Edition October 2023
Boris Handal

The Dispensation of the Báb

ISBN: 978-0-6458963-0-5 (print)
The Dispensation of the Báb

ISBN: 978-0-6458963-1-2 (e-book)
The Dispensation of the Báb

If His Holiness the Báb had not manifested love for mankind, surely he would not have offered his breast for a thousand bullets.

'Abdu'l-Bahá

To my daughter, Camelia Handal

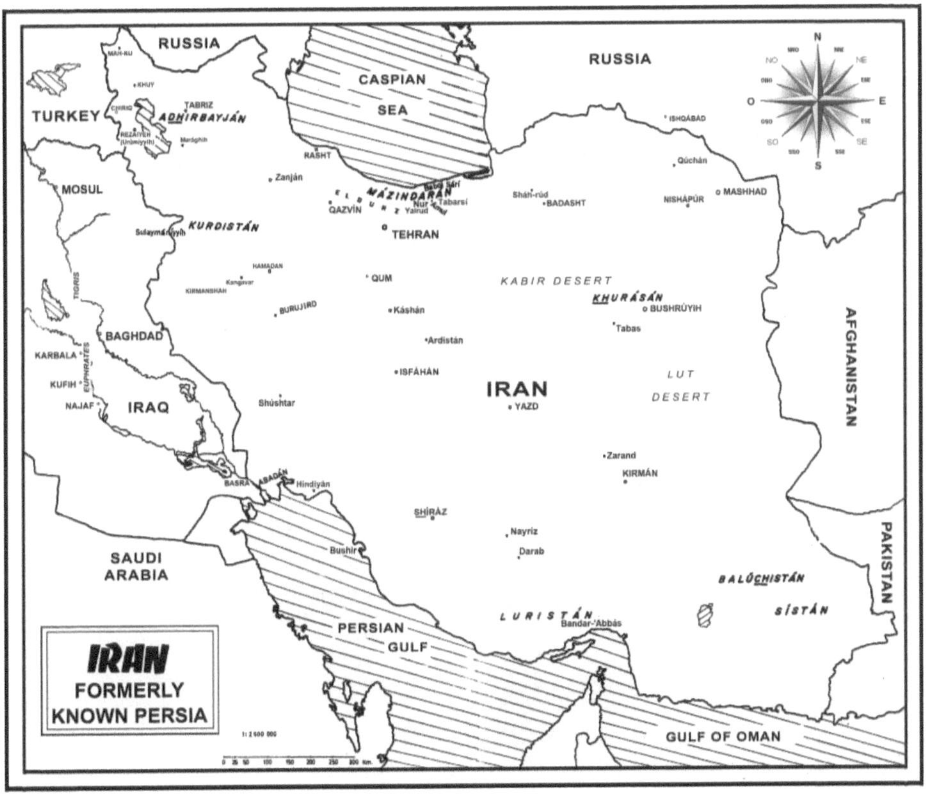

Figure 1: Map of Iran (by Pedro Donaires)

Acknowledgments

My gratitude goes to the Universal House of Justice for their continuous guidance throughout the writing project as well as to the Research Department of the Bahá'í World Centre.

This book would not have been possible without the exceptional editorial assistance of Dr Felicity Rawlings Sanaei, Dr Melanie Lotfali, Dr Vafa Lalehzari and Nur Mihrshahi. Similarly, I am thankful to Dr Khazeh Fananapazir, Adib Masumian and Qudrat Motallebi for their expert help with the Persian texts. I also would like to thank Farzad Naziri and Professor Bijan Samali for assistance with reading the Writings of the Báb in the original languages.

I also would like to express my gratitude to Washington Araújo, Dr Iraj Ayman, Michael Day, Dr Moojan Momen, Dr Siyamak Zabihi-Moghaddam, Dr Christopher Buck, Dr Stephen Lambden, Dr Grover Gonzales, Dr Necati Alkan and Dr Armin Eschraghi for their assistance with translations, historical research, responding to my queries or general commentary.

In particular, I would like to thank Michael W. Thomas and Dr Yvonne I. Woźniak for their amazing and careful work editing the manuscript and getting it ready for publication.

The beautiful illustration depicting the Máh-Kú fortress for the book cover was kindly provided by Jane MacMillan. The map of Iran was professionally designed by Pedro Donaires. The images for the book were kindly provided by the Audio-Visual Department of the Bahá'í World Centre. I also would like to express my gratefulness to the National Spiritual Assembly of the Bahá'ís of Australia for passing review of the manuscript.

Likewise, I am grateful to Dr Nader Saiedi for his scholarly advice and for generously allowing use of his provisional translations. I owe heartfelt gratitude to the Association of Bahá'í Studies in North America for their permission to include the provisional translations from the *Gate of the Heart* and to the publisher George Ronald for their copyright consent to include passages from *Selections from the Writings of E. G. Browne on the Bábí and Bahá'í Religions.* My special thanks also to David Palermo for sharing his compilation of authorized and provisional translations of the Writings of the Báb as well as for his comments on the manuscript.

Finally, my gratitude goes to my wife Parvin for her patient Farsi lessons during the past thirty-five years enabling me to understand in many colours the superlative beauty of the Writings of the Báb in the original languages.

To all those mentioned above, I offer my heartfelt gratitude.

Boris Handal
Sydney, Australia

Contents

Acknowledgments **ix**
Illustrations **xvii**
Glossary **xix**
Brief chronology of the life of the Báb **xxi**
Foreword **xxiii**
Preface **xxvii**
Bahá'í Romanization of Persian and Arabic terms **xxxii**
Introduction **1**
Announced by all Messengers 1
When the West looks East 2
The Promised One has come 4
A new religion—the Bábí Faith 5
Symbolism in previous prophecies 10
Claims of the Báb 12
The Bábí-Bahá'í Faith 13
Survey of the teachings of the Báb 14
Part I Divine Revelation **17**
1 God and His Creation **18**
Essence of God 18
The Primal Will 20
The Word of God 22
Creation 23
Seven stages of creation 24
2 God and His Manifestations **35**
The Primal Will and the Manifestations of God 35
The two stations of the Manifestations of God 37
Recognizing the Manifestations of God 40
The progressive revelation of God to humanity 43
The great Day of God and the Resurrection 45
Reaching towards the presence of God 47
3 Divine annunciations **49**
Mission of the Báb 49
Salmán the Persian 50
The Báb and John the Baptist 51
The Báb and Jesus 52

4 The Báb as a Manifestation of God **57**
The Báb as a Person 57
First intimations of the station of the Báb 62
The nature of the Revelation of the Báb 64
The spiritual substance of the Báb in mystical terms 67
5 Verses of the Báb **69**
Verses, signs and miracles 69
The abundance of His Revelation 72
The Writings of the Báb 75
6 Qayyúmu'l-Asmá and the Persian Bayán **79**
Qayyúmu'l-Asmá' 79
Persian Bayán 83
The Bayán and Him Whom God shall make manifest 87
Structure of the Bayán 90
The Writings of the Báb while incarcerated in Máh-Kú 90
7 The Faith of the Báb **95**
The purpose of the Faith of the Báb 95
The act of conversion 98
Bahá'u'lláh on the greatness of the Faith of the Báb 99
'Abdu'l-Bahá on the greatness of the Faith of the Báb 101
Shoghi Effendi on the greatness of the Faith of the Báb 102
8 The universal declaration of the Báb **104**
Muḥammad Sháh 104
Ḥájí Mírzá Áqásí 110
'Abdu'l-Majid and Najíb Páshá 111
Sovereigns 111
Persian religious leaders 112
Religious leaders 113
Muslims 113
People of the West 114
Mankind 114
9 Opposition to the Faith of the Báb **117**
Persecution of believers 117
Excuses for rejecting the Báb 119
Persecution of the Báb by Muslims 122
Belief in the concept of finality in Islam 122
Divine assistance promised during persecutions 123

Part II: The heavenly treasury of the Báb 126
10 Virtues, spiritual and mystical principles 127
Personal ethics 127
Spiritual principles and mystical themes 134
11 Individual and community exhortations 150
Exhortations in relation to oneself 150
Other individual ordinances 153
Some prohibitions 159
12 Societal organization 162
Exhortations pertaining to community life
and social development 162
Badí' Calendar 164
13 Some prayers and invocations 167
Devotions and worship 167
Prayers 167
Invocations 170
14 Messages of the Báb for His family 172
To His male relatives 172
To His female relatives 173
His mother, Fáṭimih Bagum 173
His wife, Khadíjih Bagum 173
His father, Siyyid Muḥammad Riḍá 174
Regarding His son, Aḥmad 174
The Afnán as celebrated by Bahá'u'lláh 175
Part III The Bábí and Bahá'í Revelations 177
15 He Whom God shall make Manifest: His station and influence 178
Greatness of Him Whom God shall make Manifest 180
Writings of Bahá'u'lláh compared to the Bayán 182
The station of Bahá'u'lláh 183
Proof and testimony of Him Whom God shall make Manifest 186
Praise for the station of Him Whom God shall make Manifest 187
Period between the two Revelations 188
16 He Whom God shall make Manifest: Believing and accepting 201
Believing in Him Whom God shall make Manifest 201
Station of the believer accepting
Him Whom God shall make Manifest 202
Recognizing Him Whom God shall make Manifest 203

Bábís converting to the Faith of
Him Whom God shall make Manifest 204
Veils hindering recognition of Bahá'u'lláh 206
Encouragement of certain predispositions toward
Him Whom God shall make Manifest 210
Discouragement of certain attitudes and behaviours towards
Him Whom God shall make Manifest 213
Promoting the cause of Him Whom God shall make Manifest 214
17 Progressive Revelation—Divine Laws 219
Evolvement of religious laws from one dispensation to the next 220
Evolvement of religious laws within each Revelation 223
Messianic expectations about the Qá'im 224
Implementation of the laws of the Báb 226
Nature of religious laws in the Bábí-Bahá'í Faith 228
Response of Bahá'u'lláh to the laws of the Bayán 230
18 Transition from the Bábí to the Bahá'í Faith 234
Renewed interest in Babism 234
The Báb as a new force in human development 235
The Shrine of the Báb 236
Growth of the Bábí-Bahá'í Faith 238
The life of Bahá'u'lláh 238
The relevance of the teachings of the Báb to a modern world 240
Part IV The laws of the Báb 242
19 Abrogation of Jewish, Christian and Islamic laws whose annulment is confirmed by Bahá'u'lláh 243
Jewish laws 243
Christian laws 246
Islamic laws 246
20 Bábí laws abrogated by Bahá'u'lláh 253
Death penalty 257
Payment of a fine for causing sadness 258
Travel restrictions 259
Destruction of books 259
Shaving of heads 260
Waging of holy war 260
Prohibition against "reading certain books" 262
Religious shrines 263
Prostrations for obligatory prayer 263

Laws regarding Him Whom God shall make Manifest 264
21 Bábí laws modified and/or confirmed by Bahá'u'lláh 267
Major spiritual laws 267
Laws of personal status 270
Burial, Ḥuqúqu'lláh and pilgrimage 275
22 Some Bábí ordinances not discussed in the Kitáb-i-Aqdas 282
Use of ringstones 282
Talismans and gematria 283
Tobacco 284
New personal salutations 284
Tattoos 285
Facing the sun and moon 286
Appendix: Best-known works of the Báb 291
Bibliography 293
Index 301
About the Author 305

Illustrations

1. Map of Iran (by Pedro Donaires)
2. The shop which was used by the Báb during His days in Bú<u>sh</u>ihr.
3. Site of the Kázirán gate, entrance to the city to <u>Sh</u>íráz.
4. The market-street of Vakíl, <u>Sh</u>íráz
5. Masjid-i-Vakíl where the Báb addressed the congregation, <u>Sh</u>íráz—Entrance door
6. View of the Masjid-i-Vakíl, <u>Sh</u>íráz—Section of the interior
7. View of the pulpit in the Masjid-i-Vakíl, <u>Sh</u>íráz from where the Báb addressed the congregation
8. Room (left hand side) where the Báb was born
9. View of the House of the Báb where He declared His Missions—Entrance
10. The Báb's sitting room
11. The room used by the mother of the Báb—Fáṭimih Begum
12. Bedchamber of the Báb
13. View of the upper room of the House of the Báb in <u>Sh</u>íráz where He declared His Mission
14. View of the upper room of the House of the Báb in <u>Sh</u>íráz where He declared His Mission
15. View of the upper room of the House of the Báb in <u>Sh</u>íráz where He declared His Mission
16. Orange tree planted by the Báb in the courtyard of His House
17. View of the Masjid-i-Jum'ih in Iṣfahán where the Báb prayed
18. View of the Masjid-i-Jum'ih in Iṣfahán and the pulpit in front of which the Báb prayed
19. Castle of Máh-Kú, 1930's
20. Ruins of the Fortress of Máh-Kú
21. Ruins of Máh-Kú, 1930's
22. Castle of Máh-Kú, 1930's
23. The Castle of Máh-Kú
24. Castle of Máh-Kú
25. Corner marked X showing where the Báb was bastinadoed in Tabríz
26. The Fortress of <u>Ch</u>ihríq
27. The Barrack-square in Tabríz where the Báb was martyred in 1850
28. The Tabríz Barrack Square
29. Facsimile of the Báb's Tablet to "Him Who will be Made Manifest (Bahá'u'lláh)
30. The Báb's Tablet to the First Letter of the Living
31. The Báb's letter to His wife, <u>Kh</u>adíjih Bagum
32. Calligraphic exercise of the Báb written before He was ten years old
33. Tablet by the Báb in His own handwriting (1)
34. Tablet by the Báb in His own handwriting (2)
35. Tablet by the Báb in His own handwriting (3)
36. Trading accounts in the handwriting of the Báb, March 1840

37. Tablet by the Báb in His own handwriting (4)
38. A printed version of the Persian Bayán (British Museum)
39. Mírzá Taqí Khán, The Amír Kabír
40. Muḥammad Sháh
41. Ḥájí Mírzá Áqásí
42. Dr William Cormick (1822–1877) who once treated the Báb
43. Dress worn under the jubbih, worn by the Báb
44. Cloth worn by the Báb when circumambulating the Ka'bih
45. Green silk robe worn by the Báb
46. Robe of the Báb (1)
47. Robe of the Báb (2)
48. A coat of the Báb
49. Sandals of the Báb
50. Relics of the Báb—beads
51. Relics of the Báb—the Qur'án
52. A ring belonging to the Báb
53. The Báb's brazier and samovar
54. Some Relics of the Báb (1)
55. Some Relics of the Báb (2)
56. Some relics of the Báb (3)
57. Cap worn by the Báb
58. A signet ring of the Báb
59. The Marriage Certificate of the Báb
60. A crystal Persian tea glass and china saucer with rose luster flowers belonging to the Báb
61. A small wool money purse which belonged to the Báb
62. Pocket Qur'án of the Báb
63. Shrine of the Báb in Mount Carmel

Glossary

Abjad	Alphabet. A writing system in which only consonants are represented. Also used as a term for the Arabic numeral system, where each consonant has an abjad numerical value. Therefore, words have a numerical value consisting of the sum of the digits for each letter.
Ab	Ab (father) e.g. Abu'l-Qásim (father of Qásim)
'Abd	'Abd (slave or servant) e.g. 'Abdu'l-Bahá (Servant of the Glory)
AH	Anno Hejirae (Latin, "in the year of the Hijira", used in the West). H or Hijra for "after the Hijrah", the date Muḥammad migrated from Mecca to Medina setting the beginning of the Islamic calendar.
'Álim, pl. 'ulamá' (Pers. var.[1] 'ulamá)	Scholar, professional;—pl. learned ones; scholar (of Islamic law), scientist. The 'ulamá' are Muslim scholars recognized as having specialist knowledge of Islamic sacred law and theology.
Áqá	Master, sire.
Azalí	A follower of Mírzá Yaḥyá (Ṣubḥ-i-Azal)
Báb	Door; gate; chapter, section, column. The Báb (*al-Báb*) is the title assumed by Siyyid Mírzá 'Alí Muḥammad.
Bábí	A follower of the Faith of the Báb
Bahá'	Glory (often written as Bahá)
Bahá'í	A follower of the Faith of Bahá'u'lláh
BCE, CE	Common (or current) era is a more general form of AD (Latin, *Anno Domini*, "in the year of the Lord"). BCE ("before the common era") is a more general form of BC (before Christ).
Ḥadíth, pl. aḥádíth	Speech; discussion; narrative; Prophetic tradition, hadith. Narrative relating deeds and utterances of the Prophet Muḥammad and his Companions.
Ḥájí	A person who has completed the pilgrimage to Mecca.
Imám, pl. a'imma (English Imam)	A title of the first twelve linear descendants of Muḥammad. Title also used by religious leaders, especially in Iran. See Mullá entry below.
Jináb	Threshold; a place of refuge, hence, a title of respect, your honour, excellency.
Khán, fem. Khánum	Title of dignitary or a courtesy title, e.g., Muḥammad Khán, Maryam Khánum.
Man Yuẓhiruhu'lláh	"*Him Whom God shall make Manifest*". A title given by the Báb to the promised One to follow Him, a reference to Bahá'u'lláh.
Mírzá	Preceding a name it refers to an educated person, e.g., Mírzá Muḥammad. A title of nobility (a son of a

1 Fem. = feminine; Pers. = Persian; pl. = plural; var. = variation.

	prince) when placed after a name, e.g. Muḥammad Mírzá.
Mujtahid	An original authority in Islamic law. Highest rank of Shi'ite divine. Now called an áyatu'lláh in contemporary Iran.
Mullá	Persian for a school master, doctor, learned man, priest. The title has now degenerated into a derogatory term for a semi-literate, backward, often bigoted village religious leader.
Qá'im	Literally "rising", commonly translated as "He Who shall arise". Name given to the long-awaited Promised One of Islám. See also Ṣáḥibu'z-Zamán.
Ṣáḥib az-Zamán (Pers. Ṣáḥibu'z-Zamán)	"The Lord of the Age". A title of the Qá'im or twelfth Imám, and the Báb. See also Qá'im.
Sayyid (var. Siyyid)	Master; gentleman; mister; sir; chieftain; title of Muḥammad's direct descendants.
Sharí'a	Sharia law or Islamic law that is based on the text of the Qur'án. Muslim traditions (hadiths) are often included. See ḥadíth entry above.
Shaykh	A venerable gentleman; elder; chief; religious leader, e.g., Shaykh Yúsuf.
Shí'a (Pers. var. shí'ih)	The second-largest branch of Islám—the dominant branch in Iran—follows the religious tradition of the twelve Imams (A'imma)
Shí'í (Pers. var. shí'ih), pl. shí'yún	adjective for member, follower. English: shiite, shi'ite.
Súra (Pers. var. súrih)	A row or series. Name given to a chapter of the Qur'án.
Tablet	Name given to an epistle Written by the Báb, Bahá'u'lláh or 'Abdu'l-Bahá.

Titles can be combined in a single name such as in *Ḥájí Mírzá Siyyid Ḥasan Kirmání*, meaning a person who has made the pilgrimage to Mecca, coming from an educated background, a descendant of the Prophet Muḥammad, whose name is Ḥasan, and being born in the city of Kirmán.

Brief chronology of the life of the Báb

Birth of the Báb in Shíráz	20 Oct 1819
Death of Shaykh Aḥmad-i-Aḥsá'í	1826
Death of Siyyid Muḥammad Riḍá, the father of the Báb	1828
The Báb moves to Búshihr to engage in commerce	1835–1836
The Báb resides for about one year in Karbilá	1841–1842
Marriage of the Báb to Khadíjih Bagum in Shíráz	Aug 1842
Death (shortly after he was born) of Aḥmad, son of the Báb	1843
Death of Siyyid Káẓim in Karbilá	31 Dec 1843
Declaration of the Mission of the Báb to Mullá Ḥusayn	22 May 1844
The Báb dispatches the "Letters of the Living" to teach His Faith	July–Aug 1844
Bahá'u'lláh accepts the Cause of the Báb	circa Sep 1844
The Báb and Quddús depart Shíráz for Mecca	late Sep 1844
Declaration of the mission of the Báb in Mecca	Dec 1844
Arrival to Búshihr	15 May 1845
The Báb returned to Shíráz and is arrested by the governor	late June 1845
Vaḥíd, the Sháh's envoy, interviews the Báb and accept His Faith	May 1846
The Báb arrested and given death sentence	Sep 1846
The Báb leaves Shíráz for Iṣfahán with the governor's permission	Sep 1846
Governor of Iṣfahán hosts the Báb at his home for four months	until March 1847
Governor of Iṣfahán passes away	4 March 1847
Departure of the Báb for Tehran to meet the Sháh	March 1847
The Báb reaches the village of Kulayn, 40 km SSW of Tehran	29 March 1848
The Sháh redirects the escort of the Báb to Máh-Kú fortress	mid-April 1847
The Báb arrives in Tabríz and is imprisoned 40 days	late May 1847
Imprisonment of the Báb in Máh-Kú fortress	Jul 1847–9 Apr 1848
Mullá Ḥusayn visits the Báb in Máh-Kú fortress	March 1848
Incarceration of the Báb in the Chihríq fortress	early May 1848–June 1850
Conference of Badasht	June–July 1848
Interrogation of the Báb in Tabríz	July 1848
The Báb is returned to Chihríq	Aug 1848
Death of Muḥammad Sháh and accession of Náṣiri'd-Dín Sháh	4 Sep 1848
Beginning of the Shaykh Ṭabarsí upheaval	Oct 1848
Martyrdom of Mullá Ḥusayn	2 Feb 1849
End of the Shaykh Ṭabarsí upheaval and martyrdom of Quddús	16 May 1849
The Seven Martyrs of Tehran	Feb 1850
Zanján upheaval	May 1850–Jan 1851

Dispensation of the Báb

The Báb is sent to Tabríz from <u>Ch</u>ihríq for trial	19 June 1850
Martyrdom of Vaḥíd in Nayríz	29 June 1850
Martyrdom of the Báb in Tabríz	9 July 1850
Passing of <u>Kh</u>adíjih Bagum, wife of the Báb, in <u>Sh</u>íráz	15 Sep 1882
Passing of Fáṭimih Begum, mother of the Báb, in Iraq	circa 1882

Foreword

The Faith founded by the Báb in the middle of the 19th century is considered by many as the most important religious and social movement of recent Iranian history. While His mission lasted but a few years, and most of those years were spent in a remote and isolated prison, yet the Báb was able to write works comprising thousands of pages, and through them, His message reached people in all parts of Iran. Many from diverse backgrounds, old and young, men and women, clerics and laymen, peasants and scholars, joined the ranks of His believers.

The Báb announced the dawn of a new Revelation and the imminent spiritual rebirth of mankind. He initially alluded to messianic expectations prevalent specifically among Shí'a Muslims, but soon drew attention to the imminent appearance of a Messenger of God, bearing a new revelation for the people, just as Moses had aforetime, as well as Christ, Muḥammad and the other Prophet Founders. According to the testimony of the Báb, this prophetic figure, *He Whom God shall make manifest*, was at the core of His message. However, He also addressed the most pressing social needs of the people of His time and prepared the way towards reform, progress, and prosperity by calling for a critical re-evaluation of tradition and of prevailing religious beliefs and practices.

The teachings of the Báb aroused the opposition of certain powerful Muslim clerics, who viewed the new Message as a threat to their political, religious, and financial privileges. The number of believers increased swiftly, and the means traditionally employed by rival clerics to oust each other, proved insufficient to stop the growth of the new Faith. Eventually, a number of Muslim clerics managed to convince the sháh and the prime minister that the Bábís presented a danger to their authority. The Bábís became subject to violent attacks, and although they bravely fought back in some places, eventually they were massacred. Less than a decade after the Báb had first intimated His claim to the first believers, the new movement appeared to have been all but destroyed. It was Bahá'u'lláh who gathered the remaining Bábís in Baghdád and infused a new spirit into the community, before He, in 1863, put forth His claim to be the new Divine Manifestation foretold by the Báb.

The dramatic circumstances surrounding the rise and decline of the Bábí Faith, but also its far-reaching influence and its potential for fundamental change in society, motivated Western observers to investigate what they considered a truly revolutionary movement. However, early accounts by diplomats, journalists and historians are generally inaccurate and suffer from limited access to reliable sources. The Writings of the Báb were, after all, not easy to obtain, and even then, their study often proved difficult to the uninitiated reader. Some writers thus preferred to project their own religious or political agendas onto "Babism" as they called it.

The Bahá'í community has sustained awareness of the Báb and His teachings over the past one and a half centuries. To them, the Báb is the forerunner to Bahá'u'lláh, the founder of their Faith. However, the Báb is also considered a Manifestation of God, since He initiated a new divine revelation. Although the Riḍván proclamation of Bahá'u'lláh in 1863 in Baghdád can be considered the beginning of the Bahá'í Faith, yet the Badí' calendar begins in 1844 with the proclamation of the Báb, and dates related to Him are also celebrated as Holy Days in the Badí' calendar.

The history of the Báb and His followers is considered by Bahá'ís as an integral part of their own Faith's earliest history and of their religious identity. Shoghi Effendi[1] therefore edited and translated large portions of the handwritten account of Nabíl Zarandí about the mission of the Báb as a narrative "of the early days of the Bahá'í revelation". He also encouraged Bahá'ís to study *The Dawn-Breakers* and the history of the Báb and the Bábís as a source of inspiration.

In light of such frequent emphasis and given the importance of the Báb for Bahá'ís, it is no wonder that many believers do not limit their interest and fascination to historical accounts, but wish to gain a deeper understanding of what the Báb taught and wrote. Although His Writings are superseded by the voluminous and weighty Writings of Bahá'u'lláh, yet a deeper appreciation of the true nature of the mission of the Báb can be gained by studying His Writings. For Bahá'ís this can best be achieved by approaching them from the perspective of their own Faith, that is in light of the explanations and elucidations of Bahá'u'lláh, and also of 'Abdu'l-Bahá[2] and Shoghi Effendi—a fact duly considered by the author of the present book.

Most of the Writings of the Báb are now kept in archives around the world, the largest collection of which is held at the Bahá'í World Center in Haifa. Only a tiny portion of His vast oeuvre has so far been made available in translation, and even the original Persian and Arabic works remain accessible only in manuscript form. Their publication and systematic study remain a major task for future generations. The depth and richness of the Writings of the Báb and the significance of His revolutionary message cannot yet be properly estimated as we still know very little about His teachings. One fascinating aspect is that within only a few years, He revealed a whole new religion, with distinct teachings on creation, cosmology, epistemology, ethics, laws and ordinances as well as devotional practices. And yet, from a Bahá'í perspective, most of these were never meant to be put into practice, but rather intended as a symbolic reminder of the imminent advent of the Promised One He had foreseen for the immediate future.

Boris Handal's *The Dispensation of the Báb* offers for the first time a systematic overview of some of the major teachings of the Báb as well as His laws and ordinances. It has been prepared in a manner not only to be appreciated by academics and those familiar with the original languages, but also by those with

1 Shoghi Effendi (1897–1957), Guardian of the Cause of God in the Bahá'í Faith.

2 'Abdu'l-Bahá (1844–1921), successor of Bahá'u'lláh and Centre of His Covenant.

a more general and personal interest. His book contains a compilation of many available English translations of the Writings of the Báb, and in addition summarizes the findings of many relevant studies on His teachings published over recent decades. It thus provides its readers with information that they would otherwise have to glean from a wide array of sometimes scattered sources. In addition to facilitating a personal study of the divine words of the Báb and thereby increasing one's knowledge, many passages will also prove a source of spiritual inspiration for believers.

Boris Handal has produced a handbook that no doubt has been a desideratum to all those who held a particular fascination for the Báb and a general interest in His Writings, but did not see a practical way as how to approach them. Finally, this gap is closed.

Dr Armin Eschraghi
Frankfurt, Germany
January 2022

Preface

I decided to write this book about the Revelation of the Báb because I found in His teachings a wonderful treasure of spiritual and mystical gems.

Siyyid 'Alí Muḥammad, titled the Báb (*the Gate*, in Arabic), was born in Shíráz, Iran, on 20 October 1819. The title *Siyyid* denotes a descendant from Muḥammad, the Prophet of Islam. In 1844, at the age of 24, He revealed His divine mission to humanity as a new Messenger of God. As a result the Báb was forced to leave His home town and was later exiled, tortured and imprisoned at various remote locations. His life was ended tragically at the age of 30 by a firing squad on 9 July 1850 in the city of Tabríz at the combined instigation of government and religious powers.

I first came across the name of the Báb fifty years ago when, as a teenager, I was investigating the teachings of Bahá'u'lláh (1817–1892), the Founder of the Bahá'í Faith. The quest of identity as an adolescence generated a strong desire to investigate alternative philosophical and mystical movements challenging conventional truths. I became formally a Bahá'í when I was seventeen years old.

From the outset, I was captivated by the idea that the role of the Báb was to announce the coming of Bahá'u'lláh. It had happened as in the Gospels when John the Baptist was foretelling the advent of Jesus: "Repent, for the kingdom of heaven is near" (Matthew 3:2). I easily connected to the story as John the Baptist was a vivid figure known to me since my days of Christian religious education both at the school and at the parish. I also read in the Bahá'í books that, "... *the appearance of the Báb was the early light of the true morn, whereas the manifestation of the Blessed Beauty, Bahá'u'lláh, was the shining forth of the sun.*"[1] The Báb and Bahá'u'lláh were referred to as the Twin Manifestations of God and as the two latest Divine Messengers to address humanity.

The sepulchres of the Báb and Bahá'u'lláh are in the Holy Land, in Palestine (present-day Israel). I always had a special affection for that part of the world as my paternal grandparents had both come from Bethlehem, Jesus' birthplace, and my eldest aunt was born in Jerusalem. The family's lineage included Christian clans from many centuries ago who settled in the Holy Land. The Handals were the descendants from three German brothers—hence the Teutonic surname—who came to Palestine fighting for a European crusade in the twelfth century. After Saladin's victory, they decided to stay in the Holy Land and married local women.[2] There were other Christian Arab families assimilating European surnames because of intermarriages with crusaders. Typical from these mixed-race family names are *Franji* meaning Franks, *Sawaya* for Savoy, *Chanbour* from Chambord, *Rok* from Roque, *Bernar* from Bernard, *Lousinnian* from Lusignan,

---

1 'Abdu'l-Bahá, *The Promulgation of Universal Peace*, pp. 138–139.

2 See Boris Handal, "Finding the Lamp", pp. 135–140; & Handal & Handal, Historia de la Familia Handal. Unpublished manuscript. 1983.

while the *Douaihi* surname comes from de Douai. Interestingly, to close the full circle, my recent DNA ethnicity test showed a 7% of my make-up comprised Ashkenazi Jewish blood. From my mother's side I inherited the Scottish freckles and the Spanish religiosity, while my innate sense of spirituality was impacted by influences from both East and West.

I have visited my ancestral town several times, including Jesus' manger and His sepulchre in Jerusalem. More recently, I travelled to Jordan, the land of John the Baptist. While looking at the vast wildernesses where John the Baptist used to wander, preach and baptize—the immense Dead Sea and the arid shores of the Jordan River—I particularly reflected on his mission announcing the Messiah and how he was martyred for that cause.

I have also been blessed to visit the sepulchre of the Báb in the city of Haifa. There, one wonders about the spiritual magic of that Holy Land celebrated as "the nest of all the Prophets of God"[1] with all justice. His remains had been re-entombed in 1909 at a spot previously designated by Bahá'u'lláh. The location of His remains in Persia was kept secret for fifty years due to the relentless persecution of the Bábís (His followers). From Iran to Palestine, the remains had been discreetly transported within a box in a litter carried by mules[2] and later by sea, thus blessing Iraq , Syria and Lebanon on a nearly 3,000 km route.[3]

Interestingly, I learned on my journey of truth that my grandmother had been a long-term resident of Haifa where the Báb is buried. While visiting that thriving city I was thrilled to ascend the steep northern slopes of Mount Carmel to pay my respects to the blessed remains of the Báb.

According to a still remembered old Christian tradition, Jesus had also traversed Mount Carmel, the "Vineyard of the Lord", two thousand years ago.[4] Like Him, many other Biblical personages made their residence in that hallowed highland including Abraham, Isaac, Joseph, David, Solomon, Moses, Isaiah, Elijah and Zechariah.[5]

Millions of people have visited the Shrine of the Báb since it was erected. This graceful edifice stands supreme, overlooking not only the city of Haifa but all the surrounding Biblical geography. Its superb dome has been compared in beauty to St. Peter's Basilica in Rome[6] reflecting its splendour on the immensity of the great Mediterranean Sea. The institution of such an august edifice is referred to by Isaiah (2:2–4) in the following exalted terms:

---

1 Shoghi Effendi, *God Passes By,* p. 183.

2 A ta<u>kh</u>tarawán (Pers. Ta<u>kh</u>t-i-Rawán) or a mule-borne litter with poles, a mode of overland transportation.

3 See Day, *Journey to a Mountain;* & Lady Blomfield, *The Chosen Highway*, p. 31.

4 Carmel (Karmel in Hebrew means "fresh (planted)" or "vineyard (planted)" (of God). See Tillyer, *Union with God*, p. 6; & Cheyne & Black, *Encyclopaedia Biblica*, p. 705.

5 Javidukht Khadem, *Zikrullah Khadem*, pp. 279–80.

6 Ruiz-Domènec, et al, *The Báb o la Puerta a un Mundo Mejor.* 2019.

> And it shall come to pass in the last days, that the mountain of the Lord's house shall be established in the top of the mountains, and shall be exalted above the hills; and all nations shall flow unto it. And many people shall go and say, Come ye, and let us go up to the mountain of the Lord, to the house of the God of Jacob; and he will teach us of his ways, and we will walk in his paths ....

Walking those magical and sacred places, I reflected on the fact that Prophets of God such as Jesus and Bahá'u'lláh have been announced—like kings being publicly trumpeted by heralds. Heralding a new Messenger of God seems to be part of the mysterious process of God's revelations to His human creation. The advent of each Messenger of God is such a uniquely distinctive, historical event that it inspires oracles, dreams and visions, is foretold in ancient prophecies, and is even accompanied by astronomical events such as the guiding "star" in the story of the Wise Men and their journey to Bethlehem (Matthew 2:1–2).

The Báb represents the return of Elijah and John the Baptist (Malachi 4:5; Matthew 16:13–16),[1] and the appearance of the Promised One of Islam, namely, the Qá'im ("He Who shall arise" or "He Who ariseth"). In nineteenth century Iran, such a prophetic figure was earnestly expected by all. Consequently, the news that the "Qá'im has appeared"[2] spread like wildfire all over the country, carried on foot and on horseback along the roads and streets, and through the bazaars in towns and villages, till it penetrated the religious seminaries and homes of the nation. Thousands became followers of the Báb throughout the country; and, nowadays, the Bahá'í community represents the largest non-Muslim religious minority group in Iran. The premise of the ecclesiastical system was that they ruled on behalf of the expected Qá'im. The Báb was therefore challenging their absolutist theocracy by associating Himself with the Qá'im.

More than merely producing a new religious canon, the Báb brought a fresh world-view of the divine, the human and the social. Through His vast written revelation the Báb majestically proclaimed the fulfilment of the prophetic Great Day of God promised in all the religious scriptures of the past. The eternal truths enshrined in His teachings appeal uniquely to the human soul.

As part of all things being made new, the Báb delivered a distinct divine philosophy, drastically changing religious and ritual laws as well as legislating on individual and social matters, thus overturning the life of the nation. In the words of the Universal House of Justice:

> ... the Báb came to purge and purify, to uproot the withered and spent customs of a wayward age, and to wash away the obscuring dust from the eyes of those blinded by illusion.[3]

1 Sears, *Thief in the Night*, p. 92; & Shoghi Effendi, *God Passes By*, p. 58.

2 Ḥaydar 'Alí Uskú'í, *Haji Mirza*, p. 102.

3 Letter October 2019 of the Universal House of Justice addressed "To all who have come to honour the Herald of a new Dawn".

The teachings of the Báb attracted fiery opposition from the establishment, leading to His torture, isolation and imprisonment, and eventual execution. His martyrdom was preceded by the death of thousands of Bábís, a feature unique in the history of all religions where the Prophet usually dies before the sacrifice of the followers; and yet His Faith survived against all odds, and became known and esteemed around the world.

At a time when the persecution of the believers in Iran was at its peak following the Islamic revolution, I vividly remember the event held at midday, 9 July 1981 commemorating the 131st anniversary of the Martyrdom of the Báb, with public dignitaries attending. In the land of the Incas and at an altitude of 4,000 metres, Radio Bahá'í of Peru was airing its first public broadcast with the all-subduing words of the Báb: *"I am the Countenance of God Whose splendour can never be obscured, the Light of God Whose radiance can never fade."*[1] The believers were weeping; overwhelmed by the thought of how the Faith of the Báb had triumphed so visibly over ignorance and prejudice, and this in a place 14,000 kilometres away from its cradle.[2]

This book, relying as it does on over 600 passages from the Writings of the Báb, presents a panoramic view of His teachings that highlight His position as an independent Messenger of God, and announce the imminent advent of Bahá'u'lláh. Within these pages, is an account of a Personage to Whom the well-known British Orientalist, Professor Edward Granville Browne (1862–1926), referred to as "that Jesus of the age".[3]

Extrapolating from the words of Professor Browne, the eminent English clergyman and Biblical scholar Dr Thomas Kelly Cheyne (1841–1915) concludes:

> Such a prophet was the Bāb; we call him 'prophet' for want of a better name .... His combination of mildness and power is so rare that we have to place him in a line with super-normal men. But he was also a great mystic and an eminent theosophic speculator. We learn that, at great points in his career, after he had been in an ecstasy, such radiance of might and majesty streamed from his countenance that none could bear to look upon the effulgence of his glory and beauty.[4]

The revelation of the Báb is like an endless and mysterious ocean. The Báb calls it a *"wondrous surging"*[5] and *"concealed"*[6] *"ocean of divine Truth"*.[7] You can always taste a drop and form an opinion, either from the surface or from its

1 The Báb, *Selections*, p. 12.
2 Boris Handal, *The Khamsis*, p. 219.
3 E. G. Browne, *New History*, p. 303.
4 Thomas Cheyne, *The Reconciliation of Races and Religions*, pp. 8–9.
5 The Báb, *Selections*, p. 158.
6 The Báb, *Selections*, pp. 10–39.
6 The Báb, *Selections*, p. 158.
6 The Báb, *Selections*, p. 154.
7 The Báb, *Selections*, p. 125.

nethermost depths depending on your effort to plunge into it or not. What you encounter—its chemical composition, fauna and flora, and even its temperature—will depend not only on the endless and secretive nature of an ocean but also on your own inner condition and idiosyncrasies. From some unknown realm, the Word of God is ready to mirror its light and warmth to your soul if only you are spiritually prepared to receive it.

Being a mathematician, I can call each of the millions of themes contained in the Writings of the Báb a "fractal"—one of those exquisite geometrical figures that are never-ending and infinitely complex. If you zoom into a fractal, it will look self-similar without being self-same; and some, when inspected at increasing resolution, will reveal more niceties. The process of creating fractals is fascinating because, deep inside their unlimited iterations, they become at each stage down more visually appealing, colourful, dynamic and seamlessly like a reflection of the universe. Such a personal journey is unique and beyond duplication. The learning then multiplies; or rather, it grows exponentially, at each stage immersing you in increasingly mystical depths and scope, leading to new vistas.

I invite the reader to be part of the journey, to discover the truths enshrined in the treasury of the teachings of the Báb and their relationship with the Bahá'í Faith, and to meet Him through His beautiful and inspiring Writings as outlined in this book. Each of the twenty-one chapters is self-contained, meaning they can be read separately in any sequence.

As in the Gospels, there is so much energy, complexity, magic and mysticism in the words of the Báb that they resonate perfectly in our current times as much as they did nearly 200 years ago. In these divine utterances there is a mysterious power able to transform souls and societies regardless of space and time.

Though separated from our own time by two centuries," the Universal House of Justice wrote in 2018, "the society in which the Báb appeared resembles the present-day world for the sense of oppression and for the longing of so many to find answers to slake the soul's thirst to know.[1]

The Báb lives on in His realms above, preparing hearts and minds to recognize Bahá'u'lláh, and capturing our love and veneration. As the poet beautifully put it:

And therefore mine eyes will admire Thee forever,
And therefore mine ears will listen to Thee in the silence of my soul,
And therefore my heart will guard Thee in the desert of my spirit,
And therefore my thoughts hold to Thee during every day,
And as long as I live, Thy memory and Thy praise will live in me forever![2]

Boris Handal

---

1 Message of the Universal House of Justice dated 30 April 2018. See http://universalhouseofjustice.bahai.org/ridvan-messages/20180421_001d

2 From the poem *The Beloved Prophet-Martyr of Shíráz* by Washington Araújo (personal correspondence with the author).

Bahá'í Romanization of Persian and Arabic terms

Readers are advised that, as much as possible, the author has used the transcription standard adopted by Shoghi Effendi in 1923 for Bahá'í literature in the Persian and Arabic languages. This system was adapted from the standards set by the Tenth International Congress of Orientalists held in Geneva in 1894.

Due to the lack of a uniform transcription system for Arabic and Persian before Shoghi Effendi's ministry, the writing of Bahá'í terms was inconsistent. When drawing on early texts, the integrity of the original source has most often been maintained, although at times the correct transcription has been used to assist with the flow of the narrative. Hence, the spelling of some terms in this book remains as in the original sources. For example, the word *Bahá'í* is sometimes spelt as *Bahai* or *Baha'i* in early publications or the term *Bábí* martyr is written as *Babi*. In several instances the term *Báb* is transcribed as *Bab* and such rendering has not been amended particularly in the titles of books and published articles.

The unpublished titles or parts of Holy Books such as Kitáb-i-Aqdas, Qayyúmu'l-Asmá', Persian Bayán, Qur'án, the Old and New Testament etc., have been not been italicized. The translation of some expressions, such as "*Him Whom God shall make Manifest*" referring to Bahá'u'lláh, have been italicized.

Introduction

The middle of the nineteenth century witnessed the emergence of a religious movement of inestimable importance for the destiny of humanity. Its origin was in the obscure kingdom of Persia in southwestern Asia—now modern Iran—during the despotic rule of the Qajar dynasty (1789–1925). Their kings used pompous names such as Sháhán-Sháh, the "King of Kings" and Ẓillu'lláh, the "Shadow of God (on earth)".

This religious movement was born on a spring evening on 22 May 1844 in the city of Shíráz, "the mother of all cities".[1] It immediately evoked the distrust of the civil and religious authorities, convulsing the entire Persian population. It then spread throughout the Ottoman Empire and beyond to what are now Pakistan, India and Russia.

The Person at the centre of this religious movement was an awe-inspiring young merchant Who declared that the source of His words and vision was God Himself. The Báb proclaimed Himself to be an independent Prophet comparable to Abraham, Moses, Jesus and Muḥammad. The Báb's given name was Siyyid Mírzá 'Alí-Muḥammad, and He was a direct descendant of Prophet Muḥammad through both His father and His mother. His chosen title, *The Báb,* means *The Gate.* He was also referred to as the *Remembrance of God* and the *Primal Point.* During the six years of the valiant ministry of the Báb, He came to occupy a central place in the hearts of thousands who responded to His call: *"I am the Báb, the Gate of God ...."*[2]

Announced by all Messengers

The purpose of this religious movement was to announce the glad-tidings of the advent of the kingdom of God promised by Jesus Christ and by all the Prophets of the past, the time of the "Wonderful Counsellor", the "Strong God", the "Eternal Father", the "Prince of Peace"; when "the greatness of His government" would not have an end and He "will reign on David's throne and over his kingdom, establishing and upholding it with justice and righteousness ..." (Isaiah 9:6–7), the "day which will not be followed by night" (Zechariah 14:7).

The Báb announced that the time had come when the prophecies of the past were to be fulfilled and "They will neither harm nor destroy on all my holy mountain, for the earth will be filled with the knowledge of the Lord as the waters cover the sea" (Isaiah 11:9). His claim was that this was the era when God "will judge between many peoples and will settle disputes for strong nations far and wide" whereas "they will beat their swords into ploughshares" (Micah 4:3), when "all nations and tongues" (Isaiah 66:18) will be gathered together in "one flock and one shepherd" (John 10:16). The Qur'án also spoke about the day in which

---

1 Amanat, "The Persian Bayan and the Shaping of the Babi Renewal", p. 347.

2 Nabíl-i-A'ẓam, *The Dawn-Breakers,* p. 63.

the Lord shall come and when humanity will meet Him (78:2; 39:68–69; 83:4–6; 89:21–22).

Millennial prophecies about the land of Elam, part of old Persia that included Shíráz, intrigued several Biblical scholars. A "great Prince" of Persia, said Daniel, "which standeth for the children of thy people" (Daniel 12:1) will appear. Jeremiah added, "I will set my throne in Elam [Persia], and will destroy from thence the King and the princes, saith the Lord" (Jeremiah 49:38). "I cannot give venture on giving any reason why Elam, or Assyria," Horatius Bonar affirmed, "should be so especially blessed on the Latter Days."[1]

When the West looks East

In the nineteenth century, several leading historians from the West followed and documented the unfolding divine drama. "*Many persons from all parts of the world,*" 'Abdu'l-Bahá wrote, "*set out for Persia, and began to seek with their whole hearts.*"[2] Nicolas I, Czar of Russia, commissioned a report on the Bábí movement to identify any political implications for his kingdom. Bábí manuscripts were acquired by the Institute of Oriental Languages within the Russian Foreign Office, the French Bibliothèque Nationale and the British Museum and British Library.[3] In 1871 the poet Matthew Arnold wrote an essay titled *A Persian Passion Play* in which he declared that "most people in England have a least heard the name."[4]

"Never," Shoghi Effendi said, "in the religious history of mankind has a Prophet of God been so highly honoured within a century of His Mission, by almost His own generation, and with so much love and world-wide concurrence."[5] According to the Universal House of Justice, the influence of the Báb:

> ... spread with extraordinary rapidity, reaching beyond the limits of Persia. Observers were astonished alike by the fast-swelling numbers of His followers and by their deeds of unsurpassed bravery and devotion. Accounts of the Báb's life—the swift arc it traced and the tragic drama that ended it—induced curious souls to travel to Persia and investigate further, and inspired a range of artistic tributes to His Person.[6]

Amongst those scholars was the French historian, novelist and diplomat, A. L. M. Nicolas; the diplomat, Joseph Arthur, Comte de Gobineau; the renowned Orientalist, Professor Edward Granville Browne of Cambridge University; the French Orientalist and Semitic scholar Ernest Renan; and the distinguished

---

1 William Sears, *Thief in the Night*, p. 121.

2 E. G. Browne, *A Traveller's Narrative*, p. 29.

3 Hasan Balyuzi, *Edward Granville Browne and the Bahá'í Faith*.

4 Matthew Arnold, "A Persian Passion Play", p. 668.

5 Ugo Giachery, *Shoghi Effendi*, p. 59.

6 Message from the Universal House of Justice on the occasion of the Bicentenary of the Birth of the Báb, October 2019.

historian, traveller and polyglot, Arminius Vámbéry. Many of them resided for periods of time in Persia, and had first hand access to the history they recorded.

The Comte de Gobineau (1816–1882) reported:

> Withdrawn within himself, always absorbed in pious practices, of extreme simplicity of manner, of a fascinating gentleness, those gifts further heightened by his great youth and his marvellous charm, he drew about himself several persons who were deeply edified. People then began to speak of his science and of the penetrating eloquence of his discourses ....[1]

Edward Granville Browne (1862–1926) remarked:

> His sorrowful and persecuted life, his purity of conduct and youth; his courage and uncomplaining patience under misfortune; his complete self-negation; the dim ideal of a better state of things which can be discerned through the obscure mystic utterances of the Bayán;[2] but most of all, his tragic death, all serve to enlist our sympathies on behalf of the young Prophet of Shíráz. The irresistible charm which won him such devotion during his life still lived on, and still continues to influence the minds of the Persian people.[3]

Ernest Renan (1823–1892) wrote of the Báb:

> A gentle and unpretentious man, a sort of modest and pious Spinoza, has found himself almost against his own will raised to the rank of miracle worker, of incarnation of the divine; and has become the leader of a numerous, ardent and fanatical sect, which has very nearly brought about a revolution comparable to that of Islam. Thousands of martyrs have run to him with joy before death. A day unequalled perhaps in the history of the world was that of the day of the great butchery which was made of the *babis* of Teheran.[4]

Other tributes from the twentieth century included that of Sir Francis Younghusband (1863–1942), British Army officer, explorer and spiritual writer who remarked:

> The story of the Báb ... was the story of spiritual heroism unsurpassed ... his life must be one of those events in the last hundred years which is really worthy of study ....[5]

Joseph Estlin Carpenter (1844–1927), a pioneer in the study of comparative religions, wrote:

---

1 Emily Périgord, *Translation of French Foot-Notes of the Dawn-Breakers*. p. 10.

2 The Persian Bayán is one of the main scriptural texts of the Báb.

3 Nabíl-i-A'ẓam, *The Dawn-Breakers*, p. 516.

4 Ernest Renan, *The Apostles*, p. 201.

5 Francis Younghusband, *The Gleam*, pp. 183–184.

> From that subtle [Persian] race issues the most remarkable movement which modern Muhammadanism has produced .... It, too, claims to be a universal teaching; it has already its noble army of martyrs and its holy books; has Persia, in the midst of her miseries, given birth to a religion which will go round the world?[1]

Lord Curzon, Viceroy of India and British Foreign Secretary (1850–1925):

> ... tales of magnificent heroism illumine the bloodstained pages of Bábí history .... Of no small account, then, must be the tenets of a creed that can awaken in its followers so rare and beautiful a spirit of self-sacrifice.[2]

Theatrical plays were produced in Europe such as *God's Heroes* by Laura Clifford Barney, which was published in Paris in 1910. In Russia, the 1903 drama, *Báb,* by the poetess Isabella Grinevskaya was played in St. Petersburg and subsequently translated into French and German.[3] In 1925 the French writer Jules Bois recalled the impact of the story of the Báb on European literary circles:

> All Europe was stirred to pity and indignation [over the martyrdom of the Bāb] .... Among the littérateurs of my generation, in the Paris of 1890 the martyrdom of the Bāb was still as fresh a topic as had been the first news of his death. We wrote poems about him. Sarah Bernhardt entreated Catulle Mendès for a play on the theme of this historic tragedy.[4]

It was *The Times*, the most widely read Western newspaper, that produced the first reference accessed by the Christian world about the advent of the Báb. In its regular edition of 1 November 1845, an article was published under the title "Persia"[5] describing the latest movements of the Báb and the suffering of the Bábís.

The Promised One has come

Three themes in the teachings of the Báb kindled the fury of the conservative Muslim clerics. The first of these was that, besides calling Himself the "Gate of God", He also proclaimed to be the long-awaited "Qá'im"[6] who was the Promised One of Islam, a sacred and prophetic personage who was referred to in the Islamic literature as *Ṣáḥibu'z-Zamán*, meaning the "Lord of the Age".[7] In July 1848, despite being a state prisoner, the Báb had imposingly proclaimed to the Crown Prince of Persia—the future Náṣiri'd-Dín Sháh—and the high 'ulamá' of his court:

---

1 Joseph Estlin Carpenter, *Comparative Religion*, p. 74.

2 George Curzon, *Persia and the Persian Question*, p. 501.

3 The pen name of Beyle Friedberg (1864–1944). See Shoghi Effendi, *God Passes By*, p. 56.

4 Jules Bois, "The New Religions of America"; quoted in *God Passes By*, p. 56.

5 Moojan Momen, *The Bábí and Bahá'í Religions, 1844–1944*, p. 69.

6 The word *Qá'im* comes from the expression Qá'im-i-Al-i-Muḥammad (He Who shall arise from the Family of Muḥammad). The Qá'im has been a promised and expected Divine Messenger in Islam for over 1,000 years.

7 Nabíl-i-A'ẓam, *The Dawn-Breakers*, p. 289.

I am, I am, the promised One! I am the One whose name you have for a thousand years invoked, at whose mention you have risen, whose advent you have longed to witness, and the hour of whose Revelation you have prayed God to hasten. Verily I say, it is incumbent upon the peoples of both the East and the West to obey My word and to pledge allegiance to My person.[1]

In the same way that the Muslims were anticipating the appearance of the "Lord of the Age", a prophetic personage was likewise awaited in the Judeo-Christian world. While the Jewish people were awaiting for Elijah (Malachi 4:5) to precede the Messiah, the Christian expectation was the return of John the Baptist to herald the second advent of the Christ (Matthew 16:13–16).[2]

The year 1844 was seen as a momentous time in nineteenth century Christianity. For the "adventist" churches, particularly for the Millerites,, 1844 marked the "cleansing of the sanctuary" related to the "abomination of desolation" prophesied by Daniel at the end of 2,300 days (years) (Daniel 8:13–14; Matthew 24:30).[3] Furthermore, in 1844 Jews were allowed to return to their homeland, thus marking the fulfillment of the time of the gentiles (Luke 21:24–27).[4] The year 1844 was also an important historical milestone in technological terms with the invention of the telegraph, soon to be followed by the sewing machine, glass-plate photography, and the typewriter amongst other innovations.

A new religion—the Bábí Faith

The second insurmountable challenge to the Muslim clergy was that the Báb inaugurated a new independent religion and broke away from Islam. He abrogated several ordinances from the Qur'án and its associated traditions as well as ordinances from the Bible. The Báb replaced them with new ordinances pertaining to marriage, divorce, prayer, tithes, fasting, inheritance, and many other personal observances.

Suddenly, a new spiritual revolution began to erupt that challenged fundamental religious beliefs. For example, spiritual and general physical cleanliness were commended above mere liturgical or ritual purity with an emphasis on the supreme purification made possible by the Word of God.[5] On

---

1 Nabíl-i-A'ẓam, *The Dawn-Breakers*, p. 315. The Promised One of Islam was expected 1,000 years after the death of the last Imám of Shí'í Islam, a prophecy to be fulfilled in CE 1844 (AH 1260). See Stephen Lambden, "From a Primal Point to an Archetypical Book", p. 154.

2 Shoghi Effendi, *God Passes By*, p. 58.

3 The Millerites were the followers of the teachings of William Miller, who in 1831 publicly declared his belief that the Second Advent of Jesus Christ would occur about the year 1843–1844. See Sears, *Thief in the Night*, pp. 75, 6, & 27.

4 'Abdu'l-Bahá, *Some Answered Questions*, pp. 40–41.

5 Other purifiers were fire, wind and earth (Persian Bayán 5:14.)

the one hand, the teachings of the Báb strongly emphasized clean water[1] to attain not only physical but also spiritual purity. On the other hand, according to the Báb, whoever entered His religion automatically became pure, and this included his or her belongings.[2]

Christian nations were approved in terms of hygiene—in defiance of the country's religious law that framed Westerners as *impure*. Christians were also praised for their industries, commerce, arts and postal services, and people were encouraged to approach them, especially if they were "merchants and engage in useful professions".[3]

The Persian Bayán mentions Jesus over 40 times and he is characterized by his meekness, suffering and patience. In various sections the Persian Bayán[4] reprimands Christians for not having recognized Muḥammad from Jesus' prophecies about the coming of Aḥmad (that is, the "Most Praised", one of Muḥammad's names) and blames the Christian clergy for misleading the faithful. Muḥammad revealed in Qur'án 61:6 that Jesus had referred to "a Messenger to come after me, whose name shall be Aḥmad". Several authors[5] agree that this prophecy relates to Christ's statements about the coming of the Paraclete (John 14:16, 14:25; 15:26, 16:7; 1 John 2:1), a Greek term which has been translated as the Comforter, Advocate or Helper. Rudolf Bultmann (1884–1976), the theologian of the demythologization of Christianity, affirmed that Jesus was referring to a third person, another Son of Man, Who would be Himself.[6] 'Abdu'l-Bahá wrote: "*His Holiness Moses made a covenant concerning the Promised One, i.e. His Holiness Christ, and announced the good news of His Manifestation to the world. His Holiness Christ made a covenant concerning the Paraclete and gave the tidings of His coming. His Holiness the Prophet Muḥammad made a covenant concerning His Holiness the Báb ....*"[7] Shoghi Effendi also indicates that the Paraclete reference alludes to Bahá'u'lláh.[8] Bahá'u'lláh, in commenting about Jesus' statement "I go away and come again unto you",[9] specifically refers this as a prophecy about Muḥammad while simultaneously inferring the concept of the oneness of all Manifestations of God.

Muḥammad was also announced in several passages of the Old Testament, including references to the *Saint of Mount Paran* (Habbakuk 3:3) and the

---

1 The Báb, Persian Bayán 6:2.

2 The Báb, Persian Bayán 5:14; Arabic Bayán 5:7

3 Amanat, "The Persian Bayan and the Shaping of the Babi Renewal", p. 345.

4 The Báb, Persian Bayán 4:15, 6:13 & 8:9.

5 See 'Abdullah Yúsuf 'Alí. *The Meaning of the Holy Qur'án*; Luis Marques, *Cartas a un Buen Católico*; Julio Cortés, *El Corán*; & George Townshend, *Christ and Bahá'u'lláh*.

6 Rudolf Bultmann, *The Gospel of John*.

7 'Abdu'l-Bahá in *Bahá'í World Faith*, p. 358.

8 Shoghi Effendi, *God Passes By*, p. 95.

9 Bahá'u'lláh, *Kitáb-i-Íqán*, pp. 20–21.

statement of Moses in Deuteronomy (18:15–18) that God "will raise up for you a prophet like me from among you, from your brothers".[1]

The Báb declared the religious and political establishment obsolete, oppressive and outworn. According to Ruiz-Domènec and Arjomandi, the Báb

> "… launched a mass movement that dared to denounce and oppose one of the main drivers of the old way of exercising sovereignty: clericalism, traditionalism and ideological religion."[2]

The Báb unapologetically replaced almost every brick of the 'old edifice' and built a new one in its stead. The 'ulamá' and secular powers found the revolutionary theology of the Báb disturbing and heretical. They experienced it as a challenge to their temporal authority and they were determined to destroy it. However, despite severe persecutions and ordeals, the divinely ordained teachings of the Báb survived. While the old order was in a disintegration or auto-destruction mode, a process of integration was occurring simultaneously. During His short Ministry the Báb provided ordinances for new systems and structures, which would soon be replaced by another Messenger Who would follow Him.

The Báb appeared in a patriarchal and misogynistic society where women were kept hidden from public view. Fresh and revolutionary provisions in the Persian Bayán[3] prescribing that Bábí "*men and women, are allowed to look* [at each other], *speak and sit together*"[4] were enough for women like Ṭáhirih,[5] to publicly discard the Islamic face veil (*niqáb*), thereby undermining deep-seated gender-related beliefs and generating a great religious outcry.[6] The Báb never disapproved her actions.[7] Veiling of women's faces was never a teaching of the Qur'án but was a cultural tradition. It is not presently mandated in any Muslim country although it has been enforced by certain sectarian communities such as the Ṭálibán and ISIS. All forms of veiling were formally and controversially abolished in Iran in 1936 by Reza Shah (Riḍá Sh̲áh); but the enforced dress code of the ḥijáb was re-established by the Islamic Iranian Republic in 1979.

Equally in contravention of conventional Islamic beliefs, the Báb commanded, according to Armin Eschraghi, that "women should not be forced to hide their hair when saying their obligatory prayer."[8] Ṭáhirih, a poet, theologian and a philosopher, is also famous for advocating for women rights, and renowned as

---

1 *Brothers*, in the Biblical context, refers to the Arabs who were the descendants of Ismael.

2 Ruiz-Domènec & Arjomandi, *The Báb o la Puerta a un Mundo Mejor*, p. 41.

3 The Báb, Arabic Bayán 8:9; & Persian Bayán 8:10.

4 The Báb in Armin Eschraghi, "Undermining the Foundations of Orthodoxy", p. 232.

5 Janet Ruhe-Schoen, *Rejoice in My Gladness.*

6 Nabíl-i-A'ẓam, *The Dawn-Breakers,* p. 293.

7 Moojan Momen, "The Social Basis of the Babi Upheavals in Iran", p. 303.

8 Armin Eschraghi, "Undermining the Foundations of Orthodoxy", p. 244.

the most distinguished woman in the Faith of the Báb.[1] For her proselytism and zeal, she was executed in August 1852. Her last words were "You can kill me as soon as you like, but you will never stop the emancipation of women."[2]

It is noteworthy that on 6 November 1850, *El Barcelonés,* a Spanish newspaper, while reporting the execution of the Báb to a European audience, highlighted the gender-egalitarian dimension of His teachings:

> Despatches from Tehran report that the head of the Bábí religion, together with twelve of his followers, has been executed by firing squad in Tabríz. One of the religion's principal dogmas is the proclamation of women's fundamental rights, and the number of converts it is daily acquiring from among the ranks of the fairer sex is rather considerable ....[3]

The Báb discarded the Islamic (lunar) calendar that determined the timing of important rituals like fasting, fundamental religious commemorations, and the pilgrimage to Mecca. By inaugurating a new calendar, all time-related religious practices of the past were abrogated. The calendar of the Báb is based on solar cycles and is entirely new in its names and structure. This new calendar is called *Badí',* meaning *"wondrously new".*

As part of His overhaul of the archaic religious establishment, for His new religious dispensation, the Báb withdrew from the clergy their ministerial prerogative to formally interpret sacred texts and advance religious jurisprudence. Congregational prayers were also barred, thus, effectively bringing the institution of the priesthood to an end. The Báb also challenged the established order by changing units of weight and measurements, taxes and other transactional standards.[4] Furthermore, He exhorted rich people to share their wealth with the poor and discouraged mendicancy.[5]

In creating a new liturgical, ritual and ceremonial system for His Faith, the Báb removed the religious concept of spiritual impurity or uncleanliness associated with objects and animals in the Old and New Testaments and the Qur'án. All things from the past were plunged into a sea of purity and made clean again.[6] *"He created all things anew ..."*[7] the Báb wrote.

For the Báb, the act of abrogation constituted more than annulling and replacing the regulations of Judaism, Christianity or Islam. He advanced the theology of religious abrogation by introducing the concept of perfecting and consummating the previous religious dispensation. His proposition was in line

---

1 Shoghi Effendi, *God Passes By,* p. 347.
2 Hatcher & Hemmat, *The Poetry of Ṭáhirih,* p. 14.
3 Amín Egea, "Chronicles of a Birth", p. 61.
4 The Báb, Arabic Bayán 5:19.
5 The Báb, Arabic Bayán 8:17.
6 The Báb, Arabic Bayán 10:5.
7 The Báb in Eschraghi, "Undermining the Foundations of Orthodoxy", p. 226.

with the words of Jesus, "Do not think that I have come to abolish the Law of the Prophets; I have not come to abolish them but to fulfill them" (Matthew 5:17–18). In other words, the supreme spiritual law of Moses (e.g., the Ten Commandments) was never cancelled by Jesus, except for Pentateuchal ordinances and regulations, such as the offering of lambs as religious sacrifice (Ephesians 2:15). Jesus redefined how Saturday was to be observed as the day of rest, modified dietary injunctions and rituals, and made many more amendments such as precluding acts of revenge, groundless divorce[1], oaths and swearing. These changes bewildered the Jewish priesthood.

Further, the Báb introduced the concept of *consummation* of one religion into the succeeding one, as a form of being naturally subsumed. The *Merriam-Webster Dictionary* defines "consummation" as the process "to become perfected".[2] Hence, God's progressive revelation takes on a new meaning in the words of the Báb: *"Say, the testimony of God hath been fulfilled in the Bayán, and through its revelation the grace of God hath attained its highest consummation for all mankind."*[3]

Although the Báb abrogated the laws of Islám, He never criticised Muḥammad or the Qur'án. The focus of His mission was the inauguration of a new Dispensation—whose immediate cradle was Islám itself—and on providing a new interpretation of Islám. In the Bayán is written: *"The fruit of the religion of Islám is faith in the Manifestation* [of the Báb] ..."[4] and *"This Religion is indeed, in the sight of God, the essence of the Faith of Muḥammad"*.[5] In one of His many testimonies about the Holy Book of Islám, the Báb wrote: *"Verily, each letter of the Qur'án is invested with as many manifest meanings as the number of the atoms of all things that are embraced by the knowledge of God."*[6] The Báb alluded to Muḥammad as the *"Friend"*,[7] *"Apostle of God"*,[8] the *"Seal of the Prophets"*,[9] *"Messenger"*,[10] *"Prophet of God"*,[11] the *"Repository of His good-pleasure"*,[12] among many other exalted designations.

---

1 For Jesus, the only basis for divorce was adultery (Matthew 5:31-32).
2 *Merriam-Webster Dictionary* (online). Available from: www.merriam-webster.com/dictionary/consummating
3 The Báb, *Selections*, p. 137.
4 Emily McBride Périgord, *Translation of French Foot-Notes*, p. 30.
5 The Báb, *Selections*, p. 137.
6 The Báb in Nader Saiedi, *Gate of the Heart*, p. 56.
7 The Báb in Nader Saiedi, *Gate of the Heart*, p. 93.
8 The Báb, *Selections*, p. 30.
9 The Báb, *Selections*, p. 71.
10 The Báb, *Selections*, p. 137.
11 The Báb, *Selections*, p. 117.
12 The Báb, *Selections*, p. 137.

Symbolism in previous prophecies

A third major set of changes made by the Báb is the interpretation of prophecies and teachings from previous Holy Books as being primarily symbolic rather than literal, thus challenging the interpretations common at the time. He explained that **resurrection** refers not to physical bodies rising from physical death but to the revival of spiritual qualities and capacities. **Heaven**, He explained meant acceptance of God and His Messengers, while **hell** represented the rejection of Truth. Further, the **devil**, according to the Báb, should not be understood as an evil independent entity but rather as the egotistical self of a human being manifest as defiance and rebellion.[1] The Quranic **Bridge** (*Ṣiráṭ*) to Paradise was a metaphor for the Manifestation of God and His religion.[2] In general, for the Báb, many conventional religious notions were relative rather than absolute.

The **return** or **second coming** meant the revival of spiritual attributes and qualities of the previous Messenger rather than a physical recurrence of a particular Personality.[3] In the new theology, **purgatory** was understood as the period between the death of a Messenger and the appearance of the next One,[4] the night between two consecutive religions.

Controversially, the new Faith claimed that Muḥammad was not the last Messenger as was understood by the term **Seal of the Prophets**, but rather one more link in the chain of divine progressive revelation to humanity that will continue till "*the end that hath no end.*"[5] By **Seal**, the Báb explained, was meant the sealing of the cycle of prophecy, which was followed by the opening of the cycle of fulfillment.[6] Many of these spiritual allegories were further elaborated by Bahá'u'lláh in the Kitáb-i-Íqán (Book of Certitude) written in 1861–1862.[7]

The Báb taught of the existence of an eternal spiritual world, a celestial kingdom, a cosmogonic interworld[8] that is linked in causation to the terrestrial plane. The whole creation, He stated, was a reflection of this heavenly domain, this realm of divine mysteries and heavenly figures, with spiritual influence on earthly destinies, referred to in the Bahá'í Faith as the "Concourse on High". In regard to that interaction between those material and immaterial planes, Bahá'u'lláh wrote that "*... whatever is on the heavens or on the earth has its counterpart in that world.*"[9]

---

1 The Báb, Persian Bayán 2:7; 8:4.
2 The Báb, Persian Bayán 2:12.
3 The Báb, Persian Bayán 1:1; 2:2; 8:9.
4 The Báb, Persian Bayán 2:8.
5 Shoghi Effendi, *The World Order of Bahá'u'lláh*, p. 116.
6 Bahá'u'lláh, *Gleanings*, p. 60.
7 The *Kitáb-i-Íqán* (Book of Certitude).
8 Stephen Lambden, *Some Aspects of Isrá'íliyyát*, p. 167. Available from www.academia.edu/download/64024691/lambden02.pdf
9 Moojan Momen, "Relativism", p. 192.

A call to progress

A call was made to the Qajar rulers to learn from the West in order to develop the country. This was an anathema to a corrupt and prejudiced religious establishment perpetuating obscurantism and spreading spiritual lethargy. "The Báb's religious philosophy or philosophy of history," wrote Heshmat Moayyad, "was not retrospectively oriented or retrogressive; it was, rather, future-oriented and progressive."[1]

The revolutionary teachings of the Báb encountered fiery opposition from both the religious establishment and the government. In a country with no separation between state and religion, political and religious leaders joined forces to unleash unprecedented terror and violence. The accusation of heresy made by the clergy was upheld by the civil authorities throughout Iran from the Sháh (Muḥammad Sháh Qájár) to the provincial and local governors.

A mostly ignorant population fell prey to the rhetoric of prejudice and hate, and followed their religious masters in harassing the new believers in public. In turn, the believers of the new movement faced and accepted death rather than denying the faith they had happily embraced, as did the first Christian martyrs in ancient Rome. The Báb Himself was caught in this vortex of bloodshed, and was eventually executed by a firing squad in the barracks square in Tabríz in July 1850. Ironically, the plaza was known at the time as the Square of the *Ṣáḥibu'z-Zamán* ["the Lord of the Age"], a title of the Báb Himself.[2] Meanwhile, the Báb valiantly faced all assaults on His person for six consecutive years—a period of time that moved with increasing intensity to its climax. *"He was afraid of no one;"* Bahá'u'lláh wrote, *"He was regardless of consequences"*[3] and 'Abdu'l-Bahá remarked, *"The Báb did not run away."*[4] French Historian A. L. M. Nicolas wrote:

> Christians believe that if Jesus Christ had wished to come down from the cross he could have done so easily; he died of his own free will because it was written that he should and in order that the prophecies might be fulfilled. The same is true of the Báb, so the Bábís say, who, in this way, gave a clear sanction to his teachings. He likewise died voluntarily because his death was to be the salvation of humanity.[5]

The martyrdom of the Báb was preceded and followed by waves of organized persecutions engulfing thousands of Bábís to whose lives He testifies and accords honour:

> *How numerous the souls raised to life who were exposed to dire humiliation in Thy Path for exalting Thy Word and for glorifying Thy divine Unity! How profuse the blood that hath been shed for the sake of Thy Faith to vindicate*

1 Heshmat Moayyad, "The historical relationship", pp. 71.

2 Peter Berger, *From Sect to Church.*

3 Bahá'u'lláh, *The Kitáb-i-Íqán*, p. 230.

4 'Abdu'l-Bahá, *'Abdu'l-Bahá in London*, p. 118.

5 Périgord, *Translation of French Foot-Notes*, p. 60. (*Dawn-Breakers*, p. 515). Tr. of A. L. M. Nicolas, *Siyyèd Ali-Mohammed, dit le Bâb*, p. 376.

the authenticity of Thy divine Mission and to celebrate Thy praise! How vast the possessions that were wrongfully seized in the Path of Thy love in order to affirm the loftiness of Thy sanctity and to extol Thy glorious Name! How many the feet that have trodden upon the dust in order to magnify Thy holy Word and to extol Thy glory! How innumerable the voices that were raised in lamentation, the hearts that were struck with terror, the grievous woes that none other than Thee can reckon, and the adversities and afflictions that remain inscrutable to anyone except Thyself; all this to establish, O my God, the loftiness of Thy sanctity and to demonstrate the transcendent character of Thy glory.[1]

Claims of the Báb

In addition to the disruptive effect of the Báb's religious innovations, His claims about Himself further enflamed public discourse and enquiry concerning His divinity and aspirations for mankind. In superb and eloquent terms, the Báb revealed His pre-existent, exalted station in answer to the summons of Divine Providence. The magnificence of those statements remind us of Jesus' lofty self-references claiming to be the Son of God (John 3:16), "the way and the truth and the life" (John 14:6), and that "All that belongs to the Father is mine", and "... before Abraham was, I am." (John 8:58)

The superlative titles adopted by the Báb such as the "*Most Mighty Remembrance*",[2] the "*Great Announcement*",[3] the "*Supreme Testimony of God*",[4] the "*First while also being the Last*", the "*Hidden and the Manifest*"[5] amongst others, inspired His followers while incurring the ire of the conservative religious establishment. There were similarly angry reactions to the many other titles that the Báb used, such as: the "*Gate of the Remnant of God*",[6] the "*Báb* [Gate] *of Truth*", the "*Inscribed Mystery*", the "*Exalted Mystery of God*",[7] the "*Essence of all good*",[8] the "*resplendent Light of God*",[9] the "*glorious Remnant of the Light of God*",[10] the "*Lamp which the Finger of God hath lit within its niche and caused to shine with deathless splendor*",[11] and the "*true mystic Fane of God*".[12] In the words of the Báb,

---

1 The Báb, *Selections,* pp. 188–189.
2 The Báb in Nader Saiedi, *Gate of the Heart,* p. 95.
3 The Báb, *Selections,* p. 72.
4 The Báb, *Selections,* p. 12.
5 The Báb in Nader Saiedi, *Gate of the Heart,* p. 100.
6 The Báb, *Selections,* p. 55.
7 The Báb in Nader Saiedi, *Gate of the Heart,* p. 134.
8 The Báb, *Selections,* p. 15.
9 The Báb, *Selections,* p. 61.
10 The Báb, *Selections,* p. 71.
11 The Báb, *Selections,* p. 74.
12 The Báb, *Selections,* p. 15.

"Whoso recognizeth Me, assurance and all good are in store for him, and whoso faileth to recognize Me, infernal fire and all evil await him ...."[1]

"The angels and the spirits, arrayed rank upon rank," the Báb declared, *"descend, by the leave of God, upon this Gate and circle around this Focal Point in a far-stretching line"*; and that He is a *"pillar of glorification."*[2] In more allegorical terms, the Báb named Himself the *"mystic Bird warbling in the loftiest heights of heaven"*,[3] the *"Youth of the East and the West"*,[4] the *"Sacred Tree"*,[5] the *"Maid of Heaven begotten by the Spirit of Bahá"*, and as one *"Whom the Almighty hath graciously chosen for His Own Self."*[6] In another passage, the Báb reminded us of the divine authority conferred upon Him in this new era:

> *Whosoever hath recognized Me, hath known all that is true and right, and hath attained all that is good and seemly; and whosoever hath failed to recognize Me, hath turned away from all that is true and right and hath succumbed to everything evil and unseemly.*[7]

Furthermore, the following two quotes give us all a further glimpse of the supranatural nature He claimed to embody:

> *I am the Primal Point from which have been generated all created things.*[8]

> *The substance wherewith God hath created Me is not the clay out of which others have been formed. He hath conferred upon Me that which the worldly-wise can never comprehend, nor the faithful discover ....*[9]

The Bábí-Bahá'í Faith

The influence of the Faith of the Báb continues to grow, not only by virtue of its divine power, but also because of its doctrinal transmigration into the Revelation of Bahá'u'lláh. Bahá'u'lláh, a Persian nobleman, arose to champion the Cause of the Báb around September 1844,[10] and eventually became the leader of the Bábí community while the Báb was imprisoned in Máh-Kú and Chihríq, rallying the believers together in events such as the Conference of Badasht (June-July 1848) where the new laws of the Báb were proclaimed.

As Dr Moshe Sharon, Professor Emeritus of Islamic and Middle Eastern Studies at the Hebrew University of Jerusalem states, the Báb:

---

1 The Báb, *Selections*, p. 12.
2 The Báb, *Selections*, p. 50.
3 The Báb, *Selections*, p. 67.
4 The Báb in Nader Saiedi, *Gate of the Heart*, p. 158.
5 The Báb, *Selections*, p, 56.
6 The Báb, *Selections*, p. 50.
7 The Báb, *Selections*, p. 11.
8 The Báb, *Selections*, p. 12.
9 The Báb, *Selections*, p. 11.
10 Nabíl-i-A'ẓam, *The Dawn-Breakers*, pp. 105–7.

> ... created a coherent system inaugurating a new Prophetic cycle, abrogating the Islamic dispensation, and pointing to a very clear future continuation of His Dispensation, identifying the subsequent Manifestation [Bahá'u'lláh] and indicating its time.[1]

Not only do both theophanies share the same history but also the same theological foundation. The twin and epic births of those two dispensations in the middle of the nineteenth century together formed a Global Faith.[2] In Shoghi Effendi's words, the "Dispensation [of the Báb] **in a sense** will last as long as Bahá'u'lláh's lasts."[3] However, in a chronological sense, the Dispensation of the Báb lasted 19 years, and ended with the public Declaration of Bahá'u'lláh in CE 1863.

"There are no fundamental differences between the doctrinal systems of the Bab and Baha-u'llah [sic]" wrote the eminent Austrian-born American sociologist Peter Berger. "The Bahá'í doctrine of God and revelation is identical with that of the Bayán."[4]

Shoghi Effendi referred to the Báb and Bahá'u'lláh as the "twin Luminaries of the Bahá'í Revelation".[5] And Bahá'u'lláh alludes to Himself and the Báb as these two divine stars in the following terms:

> *This Point* [the Báb] *is the focal centre of the circle of Names and marketh the culmination of the manifestations of Letters in the world of creation. Through it have appeared indications of the impenetrable Mystery, the adorned Symbol, He Who standeth revealed in the Most Great Name—a Name which is recorded in the luminous Tablet and is inscribed in the holy, the blessed, the snow-white Scroll. ... Then the eternal Light of God shed its radiance, flared up in the midmost heart of the firmament of testimony and produced two Luminaries* [The Báb and Bahá'u'lláh].[6]

The unique circumstance where two Messengers of God were physically present at the same time raises the question regarding the "status" of the Supreme Manifestation prior to His declaration during the lifetime of the Báb. Although Bahá'u'lláh could be called a "follower" and a "disciple" of the Báb during that time, a better mind-set is promoted if Bahá'u'lláh is acknowledged as a "supporter" and a "promoter" of the Bábí Faith.[7]

Survey of the teachings of the Báb

The book, written mostly for a Western audience, reviews the teachings, exhortations and laws enunciated by the Báb, and presents His legacy to

---

1 Moshe Sharon, *Notes and Observations*, p. 19.

2 Bahá'u'lláh, *The Kitáb-i-Aqdas*, p. 4.

3 Shoghi Effendi, *Dawn of a New Day*, p. 94. Present author's emphasis.

4 Peter Berger, *From Sect to Church*, p. 49.

5 Shoghi Effendi, *God Passes By*, p. 237.

6 Bahá'u'lláh, *Tablets of Bahá'u'lláh*, pp. 101–102.

7 See Shoghi Effendi, *God Passes By*, pp. 66–7.

humanity as an independent Manifestation of God. Further, the fundamentals of the Revelation of the Báb are examined through His own writings as well as through the elucidations of Bahá'u'lláh, 'Abdu'l-Bahá and Shoghi Effendi. It aims to offer a phenomenological exploration of the revelation of the Báb and His principles in a systematic, didactical and comprehensive way.

A balance has been attempted to convey not only the "Oriental" context but also the Western perspective, irrespective of its background, whether secular or faith-based. Hence, connections have been made to New and Old Testament related themes to acknowledge the Judeo-Christian dimension embedded in the revelation of the Báb.

Little of the literature of the Báb has been translated into English. It is acknowledged that the vastness of the Bábí corpus of scriptures as well as the limited availability of authorized translations make a truly comprehensive review of His Writings impossible at this time.

The present narrative draws abundantly upon the Words of the Báb, encouraging the reader to delve directly into His Writings. The brevity of the commentary is intentional and has the goal of fostering focus on the Words of the Báb. When analysis was deemed necessary, the primary sources drawn on to provide this analysis were the Writings of Bahá'u'lláh, 'Abdu'l-Bahá, Shoghi Effendi and the Universal House of Justice.

While sifting through the available texts, about three hundred themes were identified within the Writings of the Báb, and grouped together into four broad areas. The first area as presented in the present volume pertains to the divine philosophy of the Báb as a fresh theological framework about the nature of God and His creation, and in the context of God's progressive revelation throughout history. It also discusses the nature of the Revelation of the Báb, important events of His life and on the vastness of His written works, particularly, on the Qayyúmu'l-Asmá and the Persian Bayán. In addition, there is an elaboration on the many purposes of the religion of the Báb including its greatness, the universality of His mandate and the aggressive opposition that the new teachings attracted in nineteenth century Persia.

The second part pertains to examples from the Báb's Writings on ethical and mystical concepts, including individual and community exhortations and prohibitions, both social and individual. Moral precepts, spiritual principles and various ordinances are presented and substantiated with numerous passages. There is also a survey of the Writings of the Báb regarding social development and the new Badí' calendar. This second area addresses the importance of nurturing a devotional life as well as the context around popular Bábí prayers and invocations that are still in use in the Bahá'í community. It closes with the tender addresses of the Báb regarding members of His immediate family.

The third part pertains to the continuity between the teachings of the Báb and the teachings of Bahá'u'lláh from a doctrinal and legislative perspective, with emphasis on the Figure of *Him Whom God shall make Manifest.* It explores in detail the conditions in which *He Whom God shall make manifest* (Bahá'u'lláh) would appear after the death of the Báb. This is followed by an exposition about Bábí and Bahá'í laws showing their close association and the continuity from one to the other. Chapter 18 describes how the emergence in the second half of the nineteenth century of the Faith of Bahá'u'lláh fulfilled the prophecies and purpose of the dispensation of the Báb, and carried its spiritual legacy into the future.

The fourth part of this book compiles the main laws of previous religions in the context of the teachings of the Báb. There is a detailed analysis of past religious laws confirmed, modified or abrogated by the Báb and also of Bábí laws abrogated or amended by Bahá'u'lláh.

The Dispensation of the Báb draws on the Writings of the Báb from a variety of sources, but mainly from: *Selections from the Writings of the Báb, Gate of the Heart, Selections from the Writings of E. G. Browne, Translation of French Foot-Notes of the Dawn-Breakers* and quotations from Bahá'u'lláh, 'Abdu'l-Bahá, Shoghi Effendi and the Universal House of Justice. Other reference books accessed and consulted by the author about the Writings of the Báb include A. L. M. Nicolas' French translations of the Persian Bayán,[1] the Arabic Bayán[2] and the Dalá'il-i-Sab'ih ("The Seven Proofs").[3] Many other significant works are listed in the Bibliography for the reader's perusal and further exploration.

With regards to the multitude of meanings that can be drawn from the Writings of the Báb, Bahá'u'lláh has emphasized that "*No understanding can grasp the nature of His* [the Báb's] *Revelation, nor can any knowledge comprehend the full measure of His Faith.*"[4] Yet, the Báb has stated that every human soul can recognize that His revelation has "*proceeded from God*" by virtue of "*spontaneous love for the true Word of God*", and can respond "*in a spirit of utter humility and lowliness—a spirit which is one of the mightiest signs of true love and understanding*".[5] This book therefore is an invitation to every individual to undertake a personal journey of spiritual exploration into the unfathomable insights of the revelation of the Primal Point.

For those who have had the inestimable privilege of identifying themselves with the Bahá'í Faith, my most firm and sincere hope in writing these pages has also been to share my excitement in learning about the Báb and His universal teachings.

---

1 A. L. M. Nicolas, *Le Béyan Persan.*

2 A. L. M. Nicolas, *Le Beyan Arabe.*

3 A. L. M. Nicolas, *Le Livre des Sept Preuves de la Mission du Bab.*

4 Bahá'u'lláh, *The Kitáb-i-Íqán*, p. 274.

5 The Báb, *Selections*, pp. 31 & 120.

Part I
Divine Revelation

1
God and His Creation

The Báb reformulated classical theologies and composed an elaborated system of new religious beliefs. The teachings of the Báb cast a new light on former dogmas by refining them further into an original conceptual framework. He reinterpreted and augmented theological concepts found in the Old and New Testaments, and the Qur'án while adding a new "divine philosophy" pertaining to the conception of God, His nature and essence, and His creation.

The Faith of the Báb subsumed into the Bahá'í Faith, a new theophany that recognized the divinity, majesty, power and mystical beauty of its predecessor. The divine philosophy of the Báb was further developed when Bahá'u'lláh elaborated on the eternal truths enunciated by His Herald. Bahá'u'lláh effected this in the Kitáb-i-'Íqán[1] as well as in other Tablets. The Báb stated that "... *today the Bayán is in the stage of seed; at the beginning of the manifestation of Him Whom God shall make Manifest its ultimate perfection will become apparent.*"[2] Referring to this phenomenon, Douglas Martin wrote that "... the Báb's writings also contain the seeds of new perspectives and concepts which were to animate the worldwide Bahá'í enterprise."[3]

The following are the main themes of this chapter:

- The Essence of God
- The Primal Will
- The Word of God
- The Creation
- The seven stages of Creation

Essence of God

According to the Báb, **God's essence** is an eternal entity as God's "*beginning hath had no beginning other than His Own firstness and His end knoweth no end save His Own lastness.*"[4] Further, according to the Báb, God is He "*Who from time immemorial hath abided and will forever continue to abide within His transcendent eternity, exalted above the reach and ken of all created beings.*"[5]

The Báb adds that "*any praise made by His creation, and any description comprehended by His servants, is the outcome of their limited creation and the*

---

1 Written in Persian and Arabic in Baghdád in 1861/1862. Translated by Shoghi Effendi as *The Kitáb-i-Íqán: The Book of Certitude* in 1931.

2 The Báb, *Selections*, pp. 107–108.

3 Robert Weinberg, *The Primal Point*, p. 105.

4 The Báb, *Selections*, p. 112.

5 The Báb, *Selections*, p. 111.

attributes that their minds may invent within the created realm ..."[1] and "*the soul, while bound by the ephemeral and transitory things of this world, is confined, in its understanding, to limited phenomena only*".[2] "*Such conclusive truth hath been revealed through the gaze of the heart, and not that of intellect.*"

God's independence is proclaimed in absolute terms: "*God is sanctified from His servants and no direct relationship ever existeth between Him and any created thing, while ye have all arisen at His bidding.*"[3] He is "*invested with the independent sovereignty of His exalted Being*"[4] and "*sanctified from every comparison.*"[5]

An essential message in the Writings of the Báb is that the essence of God **is beyond human comprehension** even of the most prominent human intellects:

> *Immeasurably exalted is God above the claim of the philosophers that the cause of the originated beings is the Pre-existence of the Essence, seeking thereby to connect God with the contingent realm, and desiring to demonstrate the presence of the eternal intelligible forms, by virtue of the subtlety of the Indivisible, within His Essence ....*[6]

From the above passage, it is clear that the Báb upholds the **strictest monotheism** and does not accept plurality within the divine essence whether in the form of polytheism or the idea of a **triune god**. In His descriptions of God the Báb affirms that "*He* [God] *hath not begotten anything*"[7] and "*Naught is mentioned besides Him, and no plurality whatsoever can be uttered in the absolute indivisible Unity of His Essence.*"[8] The Báb unequivocally proclaims that God

> *... is the Beginning and the End, the Manifest and the Hidden, the Maker and the Sustainer, the Omnipotent and the All-Knowing, the One Who heareth and perceiveth all things, He Who is invincible in His power and standeth supreme in His Own identity, He Who quickeneth and causeth to die, the All-Powerful, the Inaccessible, the Most Exalted, the Most High.*[9]

That the essence of God **cannot be known through human intellect**, is explained by the Báb with an example from the material world: "*... just as the root principles of religion and its faithful people have progressed beyond the physical realm, the divine signs have also infinitely advanced beyond the limited physical realm.*"[10] In a prayer, the Báb revealed:

---

1 The Báb in Nader Saiedi, *Gate of the Heart*, p. 196. Note: Many quotes from the Báb by Nader Saiedi are provisional translations.
2 The Báb in Nader Saiedi, *Gate of the Heart*, p. 177.
3 The Báb, *Selections*, p. 131.
4 The Báb, *Selections*, 125.
5 The Báb, *Selections*, 125.
6 The Báb in Nader Saiedi, *Gate of the Heart*, p. 190.
7 The Báb in Nader Saiedi, *Gate of the Heart*, p. 96.
8 The Báb in Nader Saiedi, *Gate of the Heart*, p. 190.
9 The Báb, *Selections*, p. 112.
10 The Báb in Nader Saiedi, *Gate of the Heart*, p. 228.

> *Thy majesty is so transcendent that no human imagination can reach it and Thy consummate power is so sublime that the birds of men's hearts and minds can never attain its heights.*[1]

He adds, "... *inasmuch as there can never be any descent for the Essence of God, nor can any mention ever be uttered, other than of Him, at His level.*"[2] Further, He states

> [It is impossible] *to fabricate any name or attribute for the Essence of God, and unto none is given any proof for, or path to, His recognition. The proof of His Essence hath always been, and will ever be, His Essence, and it is impossible for the contingent to be considered His proof.*[3]

"*No creature can ever comprehend Thee as beseemeth the reality of Thy holy Being,*" says the Báb, "*and no servant can ever worship Thee as is worthy of Thine unknowable Essence.*"[4] The Báb affirms that, in the same way that God's Essence is utterly independent, so God's knowledge is also absolute:

> *Inasmuch as it is evident that His life is His Essence, since His life doth not rely on the existence of any living thing besides Him, then the same is true with regard to His knowledge. He, glorified be He, hath been omniscient from and throughout His immemorial eternity, without the existence of any object of knowledge.*[5]

The Primal Will

The Báb introduces the concept of Primal Creation or the Primal Will as the **cause that all entities**, spiritual and material, come into being:

> Verily, the Source of the originated is the Primal Creation, which God hath created for Itself, by Itself; no other mention can ever be made besides It.[6]

In a way, the Primal Will can be considered as an evolutionary conceptualization of the **Holy Spirit**: "In the beginning God created the heaven and the earth. And the earth was without form, and void; and darkness was upon the face of the deep. And the Spirit of God moved upon the face of the waters." (Genesis 1:1–2) The Essence of God Himself, which exists on a higher plane, the Báb states, is not the cause of the creation. The Báb affirmed in this regard:

> *For that Essential Pre-existence which is not the cause of any thing, and beside Whom nothing is present, and at Whose rank none can ever be*

---

1. The Báb, *Selections*, p. 194.
2. The Báb in Nader Saiedi, *Gate of the Heart*, pp. 195.
3. The Báb in Nader Saiedi, *Gate of the Heart*, pp. 231.
4. The Báb, *Selections*, pp. 200–201.
5. The Báb in Nader Saiedi, *Gate of the Heart*, p. 195.
6. The Báb in Nader Saiedi, *Gate of the Heart*, p. 196.

mentioned, is solely the Ancient Pre-existence of the Eternal Essence, which hath ever existed by virtue of His own Existence.[1]

Assuming that the creation comes directly from God is incorrect because "*He is verily independent of the whole of creation.*"[2] "*Thy might is potent over all things and all created things exist by Thy Will*"[3] the Báb further affirms in a prayer.

The Primal Will, or simply the Will, **derives from God's essence**: "*He hath created all beings by His Will,*" the Báb wrote, "*and created the Will by Itself. Verily that Will is the First Point mentioned at the level of the contingent world.*"[4] And further: "*He hath fashioned the Will from nothingness, through Itself, and ordained It to be the Cause of all that is other than It, with no descent of anything from His Essence unto the Will*"[5] since "*Everything thou beholdest hath been called into being through the operation of His Will.*"[6]

The Báb therefore rejects "*the views of those who have considered the Essence to be the Cause of all causes ... For verily, that Cause is His Handiwork, and that Handiwork is not preceded by any cause.*"[7] The Primal Will is the agent originating creation, both spiritual and material:

> *The Primal Will, once it is manifested in this world at the behest of God, speaketh of all things, and by virtue of its speaking thereof, all things are brought into existence.*[8]

Therefore, the Essence of God, the Primal Will and the creation are separate entities:

> *Then behold naught in the heavens, the earth, and that which lieth between them, save as the effects thereof. They all, verily, are fashioned by the Will and have proceeded from It, while It is verily created by Itself and abideth beneath Its Own Essence. It hath proceeded from God, Its Lord, and unto God, Its Fashioner, It shall return ....*[9]

"*Everything thou beholdest,*" says the Báb, "*hath been called into being through the operation of His Will.*"[10] In expanding on the transcendence of the Primal Will above the universe, the Báb elaborates:

> *[T]hou must bear witness that the Will is in one sense all things and, in another, devoid of them all; in one respect It is before all things and, in*

---

1 The Báb in Nader Saiedi, *Gate of the Heart*, p. 190.
2 The Báb, *Selections*, p. 49.
3 The Báb, *Selections*, p. 198.
4 The Báb in Nader Saiedi, *Gate of the Heart*, p. 196.
5 The Báb in Nader Saiedi, *Gate of the Heart*, p. 192.
6 The Báb, *Selections*, p. 125.
7 The Báb in Nader Saiedi, *Gate of the Heart*, p. 192.
8 The Báb in Nader Saiedi, *Gate of the Heart*, p. 195.
9 The Báb in Nader Saiedi, *Gate of the Heart*, p. 174.
10 The Báb, *Selections*, p. 125.

another, devoid of them all; in one gaze It is above all things and, in another, beneath them all. For, verily, all those different directions have been created by the Will and generated through the modes of Its revelation. Therefore, It is more manifest to things than even their own reality, inasmuch as the first is a creature, created by It, the last is a creature created by It, the seen is a creature fashioned by It, and the hidden is a creature fashioned by It.[1]

The Word of God

The Word of God is considered also as an expression of the Primal Will. According to the Báb, "*The verses of God are like unto a living, invigorating water, which is sent down out of the heaven of His Primal Will upon the earth of your nearness to God*"[2] which can be used to purify our spiritual soil. Further, the Báb attests in a prayer: "*In truth I have created Thee through Thyself, then at My Own behest I have fashioned all things through the creative power of Thy Word.*"[3]

The Báb explains that the Word of God has a creative effect on the universe:

> *No power besides God can achieve this, inasmuch as that which is uttered by God out of the Tree of Truth would instantly create, by itself, the inmost reality of the said thing ... for the Word of God is the utter Truth, and whatever is mentioned by it acquireth reality at once, that it may provide further evidence of this truth, which is His utter Truth .... Unless one fixeth his gaze upon the inmost reality of all things ... he will not arrive at the true realization of 'Verily, the Word of God is the truth,' since it is through the very utterance of the Word that the entity acquireth truth in its inmost reality.*[4]

The Báb likens the divine verses to "*living waters*"[5] and to "*seeds of godly attributes*"[6] that have been sown in the soil of people's hearts. Justice is mentioned as another example of the creative power of the Word of God:

> *For instance, the commonly used word 'justice'* ('adl)*: when uttered by God, glorified be His mention, this word becometh the source of justice as destined within the realm of the Will. Thus when a word issueth forth from the Concourse on High, it assumeth its ultimate and supreme meaning* (the Will). *... Were all to gather together to produce even a semblance of that 'Justice,' they would assuredly fail to do so... The same is true with regard to the word 'Justice' as spoken by the Apostle of God, for verily its spirit is derived from His Spirit, while its literal pronunciation is associated with His body ....*[7]

---

1 The Báb in Nader Saiedi, *Gate of the Heart*, p. 174.
2 The Báb in Nader Saiedi, *Gate of the Heart*, p. 81.
3 The Báb, *Selections*, p. 159.
4 The Báb in Nader Saiedi, *Gate of the Heart*, p. 291.
5 The Báb, *Selections*, p. 58.
6 The Báb in Nader Saiedi, *Gate of the Heart*, p. 79.
7 The Báb in Nader Saiedi, *Gate of the Heart*, p. 64.

In addition, the Word of God is also identified with the Prophet Himself. In the Qayyúmu'l-Asmá' the Báb calls Himself *"the Supreme Word of God!"*[1] and in the Epistle to Muḥammad Sháh, He declared Himself to be *"one of the sustaining pillars of the Primal Word of God."*[2]

Referring to Himself, the Báb wrote:

> *This is a Word that hath verily glorified, exalted, magnified, sanctified, and praised His Lord in the daytime and in the night season. Gaze not upon this Word except as thou beholdest the sun in the heaven, and perceive not him who believeth in Him save as thou lookest at the mirror ....*
>
> *This is the Utterance of the Power of God, that appeareth through the Most Great Word, this Youth, Whom the faithful call in truth by the name 'Alí .... We have verily revealed this Book unto the Most Great Word and ordained Him, in truth, to be the Midmost Point in the realm of justice.*[3]

Creation

In the words of the Báb, the creation of God *"hath had no beginning and can have no end, otherwise it would necessitate the cessation of His celestial grace."*[4] Further, He states that the whole universe hath been fashioned with perfection:

> *Know thou first of the truth, that verily God, glorified be He, hath not created anything save He hath made it with utmost perfection according to His power. Had it been otherwise, His artifact would not have been perfect and thus would not have been worthy of attribution by God to Himself .... Nay rather, God hath created all beings as it behoveth His glory.*[5]

The Báb affirms that God creation came out from a state of non-existence:

> *Praise be unto Thee! The way in which Thou hast called into being Thy creation out of non-existence preventeth all created things from recognizing Thee, and the manner in which Thou hast fashioned the creatures, with the limitations imposed upon them, proclaimeth their utter nothingness before the revelations of Thine attributes.*[6]

God's creation is a reflection of Him in all things, bearing testimony to His attributes because He has *"deposited within the realities of all created things the emblem of His recognition."*[7] He further explains that:

> *... God hath created in the truth-sign of any thing that is called a thing, the signs of all beings, that it would not be difficult for anyone to recognize the*

1 The Báb, *Selections*, p. 55.
2 The Báb, *Selections*, p. 11.
3 The Báb in Nader Saiedi, *Gate of the Heart*, p. 266.
4 The Báb, *Selections*, p. 125.
5 The Báb in Saiedi, "Phenomenology of Occultation and Prayer", p. 208.
6 The Báb, *Selections*, p. 197.
7 The Báb, *Selections*, p. 112.

manifestations of the tokens of His grace, and the effulgences of His modes of justice, so that all beings may witness the revelation of His sovereignty in the creation of all things, manifestly and truly, in such wise that none may see anything but that he would behold Him before seeing that object.[1]

The independence of God is made clear in the following statement of the Báb: *"The purpose of God in creating man is but for him to know Him. Indeed God hath knowledge of all things and is self-sufficient above the need of all mankind."*[2] Along with other elements of the universe, **the purpose of man's life is to reveal His signs**. The Báb writes:

Every created entity in itself reflecteth the Greater World... Verily God hath fashioned all things in the form of His Divine Unity in such wise that when a servant is purified from all protestation and doubt and instead reflecteth the splendours of the divine revelation unto him and through him, in utmost equity, he will be naught but the sign of the Divine Self, that "verily there is none other God but Him, the Beloved, the Compassionate."[3]

Further, God has made known Himself to human beings so "*that they may recognize their Creator and that, out of the grace of the Pre-existent, the contingent beings may attain their supreme End.*"[4] Knowledge of God is gained in part through knowledge of the aspects of human beings conceptualized as "soul", "self" or "heart".[5]

The soul, as a spiritual creation reflecting God Himself, is described in the following way:

It is the Sign of God shown by Him in the world ... that it may be revealed unto them that verily He is the Truth. Behold with the eye of thy heart, for, verily, the truth of thy being is the Divinity of thy Lord, revealed unto thee and through thee. Thou art He Himself, and He is thou thyself, except that indeed thou art that thou art, and He is that He is .... Verily, God, magnified be He, ceaselessly sheddeth His effulgence, gazeth upon thee through thee, and embraceth thee through thee. This station is thine uttermost paradise and ultimate Goal.[6]

Seven stages of creation

A staged concept of creation had originally been postulated in Greek philosophy, and was further expounded in Neoplatonism. The Neoplatonic cosmology also found its way into Sufism, Jewish philosophy and Buddhism. According to a hadith, Ja'far aṣ-Ṣádiq, the sixth Imam of Shi'i Islam, enumerated

---

1 The Báb in Nader Saiedi, *Gate of the Heart*, p. 60.

2 The Báb, *Selections*, p. 62.

3 The Báb in Nader Saiedi, *Gate of the Heart*, p. 58.

4 The Báb in Nader Saiedi, *Gate of the Heart*, p. 251.

5 The Báb, *Selections*, p. 80.

6 The Báb in Nader Saiedi, *Gate of the Heart*, p. 251.

seven stages of Creation referred to as the Arc of Descent. This ontological view was explicated by Ibn 'Arabí, to describe the cyclical process from unity to material diversity, (the Arc of Descent), and its reverse—i.e., from diversity to the spiritual perfection of unity in the Presence of God—referred to as the Arc of Ascent. This was further elaborated by Shaykh Aḥmad-i-Aḥsá'í.[1]

According to the Báb, all beings and things experience seven stages of creation, from origin to end. The stages are: *Will, Purpose* or *Determination, Predestination or Destiny, Fate* or *Decree, Execution* or *Permission,* Term or *Fixed time* and the *Book.* These stages of creation were reconceptualized by the Báb in various works in relation to other dimensions such as progressive revelation. Bahá'u'lláh also used a seven-stage framework to explain the process of creation to denote the formation of any entity either physical or spiritual.[2]

'Abdu'l-Bahá explained the meaning of arcs of descent and ascent.

> *The Theosophists believe that man will return time and again on the arc of ascent until he reaches the Supreme Centre, where matter becomes as a spotless mirror, the light of the spirit shines forth in the plenitude of its power, and essential perfection is attained. However, those who have thoroughly investigated the questions of divinity know of a certainty that the material worlds terminate at the end of the arc of descent; that the station of man lies at the end of the arc of descent and the beginning of the arc of ascent, which is opposite the Supreme Centre; and that from the beginning to the end of the arc of ascent the degrees of progress are of a spiritual nature. The arc of descent is called that of "bringing forth" and the arc of ascent that of "creating anew". The arc of descent ends in material realities and the arc of ascent in spiritual realities. The point of the compass in describing a circle does not reverse its motion, for this would be contrary to the natural movement and the divine order and would disrupt the regularity of the circle.*[3]

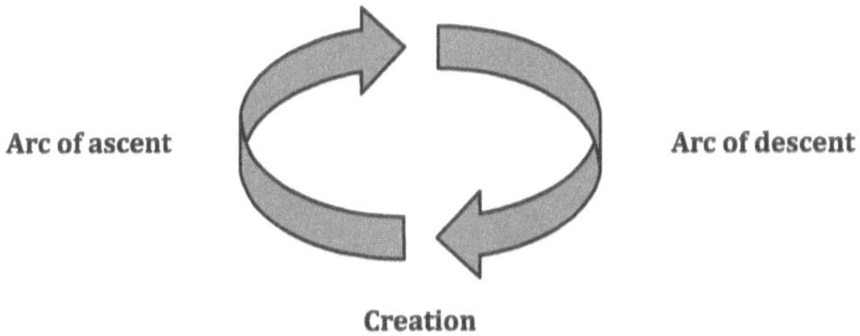

The arc of ascent would be better represented as the movement through the mineral, vegetable and animal kingdoms, to the human realms and the spirit of

---

1 Nader Saiedi, *Logos and Civilization*, pp. 53–60.

2 See Moojan Momen, "The God of Bahá'u'lláh"; and Keven Brown, *Selections from the Bahá'í Writings and from Shaykh Ahmad.*

3 'Abdu'l-Bahá, *Some Answered Questions*, p. 330.

faith realms. Always moving towards divinity. The arc of descent is the opposite movement starting from the divine, going through consummation and realization until extinction and assimilation is reached. The arc of ascent can also be construed as our personal and developmental journey to God while simultaneously moving away from the defects of the material world.[1]

In the **arc of descent, Will** is the active force of creation. This is the stage where things (material or immaterial entities) are brought to mind like a sign of existence before the appearance of means. At that first stage of Will, only the essence of things are considered. This is the stage of free choice coming into being before the creation of things themselves because a willingness that something occurs needs to exist. **Purpose** or **Determination** is the stage when the agent receives an entitlement or resolution to exist and to become part of the realm of "thingness". Things (or entities) exist because there was a rational volition to exist. The Báb said that **Will** is like the father and **Purpose** is the mother.[2]

Predestination is the third stage where Will and Purpose interact as active and recipient entities so that contingency can be realized in the form of "length and breadth, stability and change, fixed time, and the like."[3] At this stage all potentialities and limitations are called into being. It is the stage of creation designing "*the necessary and indispensable relationships which exist between the realities of things,*" according to 'Abdu'l-Bahá.

Predestination and **fate** represent the active and the passive components respectively of a creative dyad. **Fate** is the consummation of **predestination.** "*These relationships constitute predestination, and the manifestation thereof in the plane of existence is fate.*" 'Abdu'l-Bahá explained that "[*w*]*ill is that active force which controlleth these relationships and these incidents.*"[4] If **Predestination** is about "measuring the materials of a bed for length, breadth, and shape", then **fate** "corresponds to [actually] composing them into a bed", according to Shaykh Aḥmad.[5] 'Abdu'l-Bahá uses the example that "... *God hath created a relation between the sun and the terrestrial globe that the rays of the sun should shine and the soil should yield.*"[6]

At the stages of **predestination** and **fate,** elements of choice and free will can be factored in. However, as Nader Saiedi notes, "... the Báb makes clear, the relation of divine causation and knowledge to human action cannot be comprehended within the categories of human reason."[7] In general, the Báb does not encourage a dichotomy approach between determinism and free will but a

---

1 John Hatcher, *The Purpose of Physical Reality*, p. 98.

2 Kevin Brown, *Creation.*

3 Shaykh Aḥmad Aḥsá'í, cited by Farshid Kazemi, "Mysteries of Alast".

4 'Abdu'l-Bahá, *Selections from the Writings of 'Abdu'l-Bahá*, p. 185.

5 Robin Mihrshahi, A Wondrous New Day.

6 'Abdu'l-Bahá, *Selections*, p. 198.

7 Nader Saiedi, *Gate of the Heart*, p. 213.

middle path with many pluralities occurring at the **Predestination** and **Fate** stages:

> *It is in the station of Destiny that pluralities appear, lights are distinguished from shadows, and essences are differentiated from attributes. It is by virtue of this station that the wicked becometh wicked on account of his free choice, and the just becometh just, through the grace of God, on account of his free choice. Thus Destiny is "the womb of the pure realm of contingency" and "the most great depth." ... Verily, the reason for the manifestation of these distinctions in the station of Destiny is the very manifestation of freedom inasmuch as, verily, naught cometh into being in the world save through its own free choice. Though it is created free even in the station of the Will, its freedom is not reckoned by anyone except the Subtile, the All-Perceiving. The same is true with regard to the second station, for the aspect of the acceptance of good and evil is the third station, which cannot appear except after the union of the previous two stations* [Will and Determination].[1]

The **Predestination** and **fate** dyad is followed by the execution stage where the material realization of the nothingness occurs. The **Term** stage represents the life cycle of the "thingness" and the **book** stage constitutes its final consummation within God's creation. After the ensuing **execution** stage, nothing can be changed except through divine intercession as Bahá'u'lláh explains:

> *Know thou, O fruit of My Tree, that the decrees of the Sovereign Ordainer, as related to fate and predestination, are of two kinds. Both are to be obeyed and accepted. The one is irrevocable, the other is, as termed by men, impending. To the former all must unreservedly submit, inasmuch as it is fixed and settled. God, however, is able to alter or repeal it. As the harm that must result from such a change will be greater than if the decree had remained unaltered, all, therefore, should willingly acquiesce in what God hath willed and confidently abide by the same.*[2]

This **arc of descent** can also apply to the realm of personal matters such as prayers as the Hand of the Cause Abu'l-Qasim Faizi explains:

> The Báb says that there are seven stages. Every existence, every living thing, or non-living thing, must go through these seven stages, from its birth to its death. I want to explain this because of the problem of prayers. [S]uppose you are sitting here, in your room and you think about your life, your requirements, and whatever you need for your life, and so on. Suppose suddenly you think that you need a table. He says as long as you are sitting here, it is in the stage of desire. Only you desire to have a table. But the moment you decide and you get up to do something about it, the desire is changed into will. Now the third thing is matter. You need some material for it. You go and choose the best planks of wood that are available, and you are free to do so throughout the world .... After that you

---

1 The Báb in Nader Saiedi, *Gate of the Heart*, p. 214.

2 Bahá'u'lláh, *Gleanings from the Writings of Bahá'u'lláh*, p. 133.

> need someone to make it for you. You need a carpenter. Again, you are free to choose anyone you like throughout the world. Would you like to have the best carpenters of Denmark who are very famous for their furniture? All right, go to Denmark and have it done. And when you take your material to the carpenter and tell him you want a table, he asks, "What kind of table?" You say that you want a desk. How large do you want it? Here also you are free to give him the measurements. All right, you give him the measurements. You give him everything. From here on your freedom is stopped. Why? Because when you go home, the planks of wood you gave to the carpenter have been cut according to your measurements. But now you say you wanted a desk really five by nine, and you told him three by four. When you go back, he says that he has already cut the wood. Now, the Báb says, here is where your prayers will not have any effect. It's cut and you cannot change it. You cannot take it back to its original form. Up to that point you must attract the attention of God. You must devotedly pray to God that each step you take will be guided by Him, until such time as you give your final decision. When the final decision is made, then no matter how much you pray, it's impossible to change it. You see how much is in these seven steps. Five steps are in our own hands. Then there is the sixth step, which is completion, and the seventh one is death. For everything there is a time to die. Therefore, whatever we want to do, please think it over, pray for the guidance of God, for the material, for the proper men to do it, anything we want, and then God will kindly out of His own bounty, our of His own favor, guide us. But after we have made our decision, determination, and decided upon something, then there is no use of praying.[1]

The teachings of the Báb and His elucidations about God and His creation—namely, the essence of God, the Primal Will, the Word of God and how the world of beings and things come into existence—bring completely new insights to clearly explain those eternal spiritual concepts that sustain God's revelation to humanity.

Although paralleling the theology of the Abrahamic religions, which constitute more than half of the faith adherents in the world, the preceding analysis reveals how much the teachings of the Báb have augmented and transformed what had already been revealed. The divine philosophy of the Báb emphasized the oneness of God, and that humanity came to exist from the same God and through the Primal Will.

According to sociologist Mangol Bayat, the Báb "aimed at revealing a new religion and not just reforming Shia Islam ...."[2] As such, Babiism brought a distinct theophany, proposing that, even within the dogma of the eternal unity of

---

1 Abu'l-Qasim Faizi. *Talk given by Hand of the Cause of God*, p. 16.

2 Bayat Mangol. *Mysticism and dissent*, p. 88.

God, "there is constant renewal—new conditions, new creation, new order, while divergences and contradictions are merely illusory."[1]

Reflecting on the distinctive nature and claims of this new revelation, the Báb calls His Faith *"a new Cause"*, *"the Wondrous Cause"* (*al-Amr al-Badí'*), the "*Wondrous Truth*" (*al-Ḥaqq al-Badí'*), the *"pure religion"* (*al-dín al-<u>kh</u>áliṣ*) and a "*new* [Prophetic] *creation*" (*<u>kh</u>alq al-badí'*).[2]

1 idem, p. 102.
2 Amanat, "The Persian Bayan and the Shaping of the Babi Renewal", p. 337.

Image Section 1

Figure 2 - The shop which was used by the Báb during His days in Bú<u>sh</u>ihr

Figure 3: Site of the Kázirán gate, entrance to the city to <u>Sh</u>íráz

Figure 4: The market-street of Vakil, Shíráz

Figure 5: Masjid-i-Vakíl where the Báb addressed the congregation, Shíráz—Entrance door

Figure 6: View of the Masjid-i-Vakíl, Shíráz—Section of the interior

Figure 7: View of the pulpit in the Masjid-i-Vakíl, Shíráz from where the Báb addressed the congregation

Figure 8: Room (left hand side) where the Báb was born

Figure 9: View of the House of the Báb where He declared His Missions—Entrance

Figure 10: The Báb's sitting room

Figure 11: The room used by the mother of the Báb—Fáṭimih Begum

Figure 12: Bedchamber of the Báb

Figure 13: View of the upper room of the House of the Báb in Shíráz where He declared His Mission

Figure 14: View of the upper room of the House of the Báb in Shíráz where He declared His Mission

Figure 15: View of the upper room of the House of the Báb in Shíráz where He declared His Mission

Figure 16: Orange tree planted by the Báb in the courtyard of His House

2
God and His Manifestations

In His writings, the Báb clarified the relationship between religions, stating that all are part of a single and eternal process progressively revealing God's will to humanity. He explained that the Messengers of God are the mouthpieces of the Creator and the channel through which the penetrating effect of the Word of God can be transmitted to humanity.

In addition, the Báb explained through His written revelation the reason for the rejection of the Prophets throughout ages, and elaborated upon classical theological concepts associated with the Resurrection, the Day of God and other themes outlined in the Scriptures of the past.

The main interrelated themes discussed in this chapter are:

- The Primal Will and the Manifestations of God
- The various stations of the Manifestations of God
- Recognizing the Manifestations of God
- God reveals Himself progressively to humanity through His Manifestations—known as the principle of progressive revelation
- The great Day of God and the Resurrection
- Reaching towards the presence of God

The Primal Will and the Manifestations of God

The Báb stated that God's essence is beyond human comprehension. Hence, throughout history the Messengers of God have been the channel through which the grace and guidance of God are imparted. Addressing the Báb, God states:

> *O Spirit of God! Call Thou to mind the bounty which I bestowed upon Thee when I conversed with Thee in the midmost heart of My Sanctuary and aided Thee through the potency of the Holy Spirit that Thou mightest, as the peerless Mouthpiece of God, proclaim unto men the commandments of God which lie enshrined within the divine Spirit.*[1]

The Báb states that each Messenger of God constitutes the Primal Will Itself:

> *... the One Who is manifest in all the Messengers that have ever been sent or will ever be sent, is the same Will.*[2]

In a beautiful paragraph, the Báb explains the effect of the Primal Will on humanity through the *intervention of each Messenger of God:*

> *If, however, thou art sailing upon the sea of creation, know thou that the First Remembrance* [The Báb], *which is the Primal Will of God, may be likened unto the sun. God hath created Him through the potency of His might, and*

---

1 The Báb, *Selections*, pp. 63–64.

2 The Báb in Nader Saiedi, *Gate of the Heart*, p. 245.

He hath, from the beginning that hath no beginning, caused Him to be manifested in every Dispensation through the compelling power of His behest, and God will, to the end that knoweth no end, continue to manifest Him according to the good-pleasure of His invincible Purpose.

And know thou that He [The Báb] *indeed resembleth the sun. Were the risings of the sun to continue till the end that hath no end, yet there hath not been nor ever will be more than one sun; and were its settings to endure forevermore, still there hath not been nor ever will be more than one sun. It is this Primal Will which appeareth resplendent in every Prophet and speaketh forth in every revealed Book. It knoweth no beginning, inasmuch as the First deriveth its firstness from It; and knoweth no end, for the Last oweth its lastness unto It.*

In the time of the First Manifestation the Primal Will appeared in Adam; in the day of Noah It became known in Noah; in the day of Abraham in Him; and so in the day of Moses; the day of Jesus; the day of Muḥammad, the Apostle of God; the day of the "Point of the Bayán"; the day of Him Whom God shall make Manifest; and the day of the One Who will appear after Him Whom God shall make Manifest [Bahá'u'lláh]. *Hence the inner meaning of the words uttered by the Apostle of God, "I am all the Prophets," inasmuch as what shineth resplendent in each one of Them hath been and will ever remain the one and the same sun.*[1]

The Messengers can be considered equal in rank. In the same passage, the Báb emphasizes the need **to recognize the Primal Will in each Prophet in order to recognize God**:

All that hath ever dawned and set is verily the same sun. In like manner, the One Who is manifest in all the Messengers that have ever been sent or will ever be sent, is the same Will. Give heed then unto the recognition of that Will in all Its Revelations. This is thy recognition of thy Lord, and thy certitude in thy Fashioner. There is no beginning and no end for that divine Creation, for He traverseth from the beginning that hath no beginning to the end that hath no end.[2]

The process whereby the Primal Will engages with humanity is referred to as the "Revelation of God". In the following passage the Báb likens the Primal Will to the Tree of Existence in the context of the divine revelation:

The revelation of the Divine Reality hath everlastingly been identical with its concealment and its concealment identical with its revelation. That which is intended by "Revelation of God" is the Tree of divine Truth that betokeneth none but Him, and it is this divine Tree that hath raised and will raise up Messengers, and hath revealed and will ever reveal Scriptures.

1 The Báb, *Selections*, pp. 125–126.
2 The Báb in Nader Saiedi, *Gate of the Heart*, p. 245.

> *From eternity unto eternity this Tree of divine Truth hath served and will ever serve as the throne of the revelation and concealment of God among His creatures, and in every age is made manifest through whomsoever He pleaseth.*[1]

More importantly, the Báb teaches us that the only way to recognize God is through the acceptance of the Manifestations of God:

> *Therefore wert thou to look at all the Revelations from the first, which was that of Adam, to infinity, thou wouldst not see anything endued with reality except through God, and wouldst fail to recognize the Manifestation of Divinity except through the Exalted Tree of His Revelation, which is naught but the Primal Will. This is the decree, for naught else is possible in this contingent world.*[2]

It is clear therefore from the teachings of the Báb that the Words of God pronounced by the Manifestation "*... are the Word of the Will Himself, which is naught but the Word of God.*"[3] In Biblical terms, "In the beginning was the Word, and the Word was with God, and the Word was God."[4] That the **Words pronounced by the Manifestation can be attributed to God**, is explained by the Báb:

> *Those who have been, or will ever be, in the presence of This Tree recognize that these words proceed from His pure primordial nature, and that speaking in such a mode is easier and closer to Him than speaking in the mode of prayers, sermons, rational arguments, or the Persian modes. For this is the language of His Inmost Reality which referreth unto naught but God alone. It is for that reason that the divine verses are called the Words of God and praised as the divine Logos.*[5]

The two stations of the Manifestations of God

One of the central teachings of the Báb is, generally speaking, that the **Manifestations of God** have a dual nature. The first is the **human** and the second is that of the **divine**.

In His human station, the Manifestation of God can be seen as **another human being in the physical plane**. Talking about Himself, the Báb said: "*Indeed I am a man like unto you. However, God bestoweth upon Me whatever favors He willeth and He pleaseth, and that which your Lord hath decreed in the Mother Book is unbounded.*"[6] In the Bible, Jesus said to a man: "Why do you call me good? ... No

---

1 The Báb, *Selections*, p. 112.

2 The Báb in Nader Saiedi, *Gate of the Heart*, p. 183.

3 The Báb in Nader Saiedi, *Gate of the Heart*, p. 48.

4 John 1:1.

5 The Báb in Nader Saiedi, *Gate of the Heart*, p. 48.

6 The Báb, *Selections*, p. 73.

one is good—except God alone."[1] Likewise, in the Qur'án, Muḥammad was commanded to say: "I truly fear—if I were to disobey my Lord—the torment of a tremendous Day."[2]

The other aspect of this dual nature is that of the *"vicegerency of God"*[3] where the Manifestations of God *"proclaim unto men the commandments of God which lie enshrined within the divine Spirit."*[4] 'Abdu'l-Bahá refers to this dimension as that of the *"... divine manifestation and heavenly splendour."*[5]

Within this realm, the Manifestation may speak as the voice of divinity itself. It is here that the Báb describes the relationship between God and the Manifestation as **becoming** one:

> *The Primal Will, once it is manifested in this world at the behest of God, speaketh of all things, and by virtue of its speaking thereof, all things are brought into existence. When He revealeth, 'I am verily the Mirror of God,' a mirror is created in which naught is seen save the Countenance of God.*[6]

This plane is, *"the unseen station, where naught is seen in the Will save God"*,[7] and *"the station of His unknown and unknowable Essence, the Manifestation of His Divinity."*[8] In the Qayyúmu'l-Asmá', the Báb wrote: *"The Lord hath, in truth, inspired Me: Verily, verily, I am God, He besides Whom there is none other God, and I am indeed the Ancient of Days ...."*[9] The above does not mean that the Manifestation of God **is** God, rather that God at that moment is revealing Himself through His Manifestation. In this connection Jesus said: "I am in the Father and the Father in me."[10] In the Qur'án, for example, Muḥammad revealed the following words that God spoke to Moses indicative of that exalted station: "Verily I am God; there is no god but I; therefore serve Me, and perform the prayer of My remembrance."[11] Likewise, Jesus said: "No one comes to the Father except through Me."[12]

In this regard, Bahá'u'lláh also affirms that:

> *Were any of the all-embracing Manifestations of God to declare: "I am God," He, verily, speaketh the truth, and no doubt attacheth thereto. For it hath*

---

1 Mark 10:18.
2 Qur'án 10:15.
3 The Báb, *Selections*, p. 66.
4 The Báb, *Selections*, p. 64.
5 'Abdu'l-Bahá, *Some Answered Questions*, p, 172.
6 The Báb in Nader Saiedi, *Gate of the Heart*, p. 175.
7 The Báb in Nader Saiedi, *Gate of the Heart*, p. 184.
8 The Báb in Nader Saiedi, *Gate of the Heart*, p. 46.
9 The Báb, Selections, p. 58.
10 John 14:11.
11 Qur'án 20:14.
12 John 14:6.

been repeatedly demonstrated that through their Revelation, their attributes and names, the Revelation of God, His names and His attributes, are made manifest in the world. Thus, He hath revealed: "Those shafts were God's, not Thine." And also He saith: "In truth, they who plighted fealty unto Thee, really plighted that fealty unto God."[1]

Another facet of this divine station is when the Manifestation does not assume the dimension of One identical with the Godhead (i.e. that of "*essential unity*") but rather of a particular Divine Messenger—in this case the Báb—Whom God has summonsed to reveal, instruct, exhort, and admonish humanity on His behalf. For example:

> *I have called Thee into being, have nurtured Thee, protected Thee, loved Thee, raised Thee up and have graciously chosen Thee to be the manifestation of Mine Own Self, that Thou mayest recite My verses as ordained by Me, and may summon whomsoever I have created unto My Religion which is none other than this glorious and exalted Path.*[2]

The Báb also states human and divine stations are **connected**:

> *Thus, all His revealed divine verses stream forth on behalf of God .... All else beyond this supreme Sign present within Him is His creation ....*
>
> *And within the inmost reality of all things there hath been, and will forever continue to be, a sign from God through which the unity of the Lord is celebrated. This sign, however, is a reflection of His Will present within it, through which naught is seen but God. However, within the Will, that supreme Sign is the Will Itself, the Supreme Mirror of God, which hath never referred, nor will it ever refer, to aught but God. ... He is the possessor of two signs, that of God and that of creation, and through the latter he worshippeth God and boweth in adoration before Him. In like manner, all things adore their Beloved through the sign of Creation, though it hath never reached, nor will it ever reach, beyond its own sign from God, which is present within it and pointeth unto Him.*[3]

As noted in the preceding section, all the Manifestations are of the same degree because They are "*the same sun*".[4] The Manifestations **share a mystical identity** since They are all **Manifestations of the Primal Will** and at the same time form a pre-existent unity with the Primal Will. For example, Jesus said, "Truly, truly, I say to you, before Abraham was, I am." (John 8:58) He also prayed "... Father, glorify me in your own presence with the glory that I had with you before the world existed." (John 17:5) According to the Báb, "*Every Manifestation*

---

1 Bahá'u'lláh, *Gleanings*, p. 54.

2 The Báb, *Selections*, p. 158.

3 The Báb in Nader Saiedi, *Gate of the Heart*, p. 46.

4 The Báb in Nader Saiedi, *Gate of the Heart*, p. 245.

is but a revelation of Thine Own Self with each of Whom we have truly appeared and we bow down in adoration before Thee."[1]

Recognizing the Manifestations of God

The Báb explains that while we cannot recognize the Essence of God, we can recognize His Manifestations as a means by which knowledge of God is gained. *"True knowledge, therefore,"* says the Báb, *"is the knowledge of God, and this is none other than the recognition of His Manifestation in each Dispensation."*[2]

The Báb refers to the Manifestations of God as the "Suns of Truth"—**through Whom we gain knowledge of God**:

> *Inasmuch as the recognition of the Eternal and Unseen Essence hath been impossible ..., He, therefore, hath enjoined all, from the beginning that hath no beginning to the end that hath no end, to recognize the Sun of Truth, Who is the Mirror of His Essence and the Primal Will, Who is the Throne of His Manifestation. He hath accepted the recognition of that Sun of Truth as the recognition of His own Reality ....*[3]

Hence, **all human attributes originate from God** and not from ourselves:

> *If in the Day of His manifestation a king were to make mention of his own sovereignty, this would be like unto a mirror challenging the sun, saying: "The light is in me." It would be likewise, if a man of learning in His Day were to claim to be an exponent of knowledge, or if he who is possessed of riches were to display his affluence, or if a man wielding power were to assert his own authority, or if one invested with grandeur were to show forth his glory. Nay, such men would become the object of the derision of their peers, and how would they be judged by Him Who is the Sun of Truth!*[4]

Moreover, the **Manifestations of God are necessary to educate people** *"otherwise the religion of God is too mighty and glorious for anyone to comprehend through aught but itself; rather by it all else is understood"*.[5] The Báb stated in this regard:

> *Yet, inasmuch as the acknowledgement of such an exalted Cause is difficult for most people, He hath brought these mighty stations to the level of the body of words, in such wise that none hath the power to produce the like thereof, so that the divine testimony would be as conclusive to all beings as the Day-Star shining in the zenith of heaven.*[6]

---

1 The Báb, *Selections*, p. 4.
2 The Báb, *Selections*, p. 89.
3 The Báb in Nader Saiedi, *Gate of the Heart*, p. 184.
4 The Báb, *Selections*, p. 100.
5 The Báb, *Selections*, p. 109.
6 The Báb in Nader Saiedi, *Gate of the Heart*, p. 228.

The process of conversion, that is, recognizing a Manifestation of God, is a unique one **through which the human soul becomes a mirror** illumined by the Sun of Truth. *"How beloved it hath been,"* says the Báb, *"and continueth to be, before God that in each Revelation pure mirrors will reflect the Tree of Truth."*[1]

He also affirms:

> *They that truly believe in God and in His signs, and who in every Dispensation faithfully obey that which hath been revealed in the Book—such are indeed the ones whom God hath created from the fruits of the Paradise of His good-pleasure, and who are of the blissful.*[2]

Believing is an act of love because "[*T*]*he recognition of Him Who is the Bearer of divine Truth is none other than the recognition of God, and loving Him is none other than loving God.*" *"Take heed then that perchance ye may,"* the Báb further says, *"through the grace of God and His signs, be enabled to redeem your souls."*[3]

Believing is also an act of affirmation to which all can universally attain:

> *The One true God may be compared unto the sun and the believer unto a mirror. No sooner is the mirror placed before the sun than it reflects its light. The unbeliever may be likened unto a stone. No matter how long it is exposed to the sunshine, it cannot reflect the sun. Thus the former layeth down his life as a sacrifice, while the latter doeth against God what he committeth. Indeed, if God willeth, He is potent to turn the stone into a mirror, but the person himself remaineth reconciled to his state. Had he wished to become a crystal, God would have made him to assume crystal form. For on that Day whatever cause prompteth the believer to believe in Him, the same will also be available to the unbeliever.*[4]

There is indeed **no excuse to reject the Manifestation of God** because people are given *"the choice either to believe in God their Lord, and put their whole trust in Him, or to shut themselves out from Him and refuse to believe with certitude in His signs."*[5] According to the Báb, the one who denies *"suffereth himself to be wrapt in veils."*[6]

Among the **most powerful veils is arrogance**:

> *Since all men have issued forth from the shadow of the signs of His Divinity and Lordship, they always tend to take a path, lofty and high. And because they are bereft of a discerning eye to recognize their Beloved, they fall short of their duty to manifest meekness and humility towards Him. Nevertheless,*

1 The Báb in Nader Saiedi, *Gate of the Heart*, p. 393.
2 The Báb, *Selections*, p. 147.
3 The Báb, *Selections*, p. 147.
4 The Báb, *Selections*, p. 103.
5 The Báb, *Selections*, p. 147.
6 The Báb, *Selections*, p. 103.

> *from the beginning of their lives till the end thereof, in conformity with the laws established in the previous religion, they worship God, piously adore Him, bow themselves before His divine Reality and show submissiveness toward His exalted Essence. At the hour of His manifestation, however, they all turn their gaze toward their own selves and are thus shut out from Him, inasmuch as they fancifully regard Him as one like unto themselves.*[1]

And for those who decide to enter **the sea of negation**, the Báb has these words:

> *But they who turn away from God and His signs in each Dispensation, those are the ones who sail upon the sea of negation. God hath, through the potency of His behest, ordained for Himself the task of ensuring the ascendancy of the sea of affirmation and of bringing to naught the sea of negation through the power of His might. He is in truth potent over all things. Verily it is incumbent upon you to recognize your Lord at the time of His manifestation, that haply ye may not enter into negation, and that, ere a prophet is raised by God, ye may find yourselves securely established upon the sea of affirmation. For if a prophet cometh to you from God and ye fail to walk in His Way, God will, thereupon, transform your light into fire. Take heed then that perchance ye may, through the grace of God and His signs, be enabled to redeem your souls.*[2]

That some people believe, and some do not, is a **combination of predisposition and choice** as the Báb explains:

> *If man knew how God created His creation, no one would ever blame another. This means that God has created mankind* (<u>kh</u>alq) *according to the creatures' already existing propensities for acceptance or rejection [of the truth]. The cause of rejection is the same as the cause of acceptance, namely choice* (i<u>kh</u>tiyár). *God has given to each what he deserves according to his already existing propensity* (bi-má huwa 'alayhi). *This divine knowledge is the knowledge of potentialities.*[3]

> *Consider how at the time of the appearance of every Revelation, those who open their hearts to the Author of that Revelation recognize the Truth, while the hearts of those who fail to apprehend the Truth are straitened by reason of their shutting themselves out from Him. However, openness of heart is bestowed by God upon both parties alike. God desireth not to straiten the heart of anyone, be it even an ant, how much less the heart of a superior creature, except when he suffereth himself to be wrapt in veils, for God is the Creator of all things.*[4]

---

1 The Báb, *Selections*, p. 92.
2 The Báb, *Selections*, p. 145.
3 The Báb in Todd Lawson, "Interpretation as Revelation", p. 252.
4 The Báb, *Selections*, p. 133.

The progressive revelation of God to humanity

The Báb confirms that **God has always guided humanity** by the progressive revelation of Himself through His Manifestations or Messengers:

> *God hath raised up Prophets and revealed Books as numerous as the creatures of the world, and will continue to do so to everlasting.*[1]

> *Thy Lord hath never raised up a prophet in the past who failed to summon the people to His Lord, and today is truly similar to the times of old, were ye to ponder over the verses revealed by God.*[2]

> *There should be no doubt that, before this Adam, there have been infinite worlds and endless Adams in God's creation, to a degree that none besides God can, or ever will, reckon.*[3]

Further, the Báb indicates that the sending of the prophets **is like a chain linking all religions** progressively:

> *The Lord of the universe hath never raised up a prophet nor hath He sent down a Book unless He hath established His covenant with all men, calling for their acceptance of the next Revelation and of the next Book; inasmuch as the outpourings of His bounty are ceaseless and without limit.*[4]

The Báb explains the concept of progressive revelation as the rising and setting of the sun:

> *No matter how innumerable its risings, there is but one sun, and upon it depends the life of all things. It is clear and evident that the object of all preceding Dispensations hath been to pave the way for the advent of Muḥammad, the Apostle of God. These, including the Muḥammadan Dispensation, have had, in their turn, as their objective the Revelation proclaimed by the Qá'im. The purpose underlying this Revelation, as well as those that preceded it, has, in like manner, been to announce the advent of the Faith of Him Whom God will make manifest, And this Faith—the Faith of Him Whom God will make manifest* [Bahá'u'lláh]—*in its turn, together with all the Revelations gone before it, have as their object the Manifestation destined to succeed it. And the latter, no less than all the Revelations preceding it, prepare the way for the Revelation which is yet to follow.*[5]

The succession of religions **does not signify that the previous one is inferior** to the one that follows. The Báb uses the analogy of an **embryo** to demonstrate the relationship between the divine Revelations:

---

1 The Báb, *Selections*, p. 125.
2 The Báb, *Selections*, p. 161.
3 The Báb in Nader Saiedi, *Gate of the Heart*, p. 196.
4 The Báb, *Selections*, p. 87.
5 The Báb, *Selections*, pp. 105–106.

> *This doth not mean, however, that one ought not to yield praise unto former Revelations. On no account is this acceptable, inasmuch as it behooveth man, upon reaching the age of nineteen, to render thanksgiving for the day of his conception as an embryo. For had the embryo not existed, how could he have reached his present state? Likewise had the religion taught by Adam not existed, this Faith would not have attained its present stage. Thus consider thou the development of God's Faith until the end that hath no end.*[1]

Further, the Báb says that in each dispensation, the new revelation constitutes the renewal of the previous one: *"Indeed no religion shall We ever inaugurate unless it be renewed in the days to come. This is a promise We solemnly have made."*[2] Hence, the Báb claims that if Muslims had been observing the Qur'án they would have accepted Him without reservation but were instead like the pious Christians who failed to accept Muḥammad as the next Manifestation:

> *In these days how few are those who abide by the standard laid down in the Qur'án. Nay, nowhere are they to be found, except such as God hath willed. Should there be, however, such a person, his righteous deeds would prove of no avail unto him, if he hath failed to follow the standard revealed in the Bayán; even as the pious deeds of the Christian monks profited them not, inasmuch as at the time of the manifestation of the Apostle of God* [Muḥammad]*—may the blessings of God rest upon Him—they contented themselves with the standard set forth in the Gospel.*[3]

All prophets were rejected by most of the people among whom They appeared, and so was the Báb. According to Shoghi Effendi "the Báb says that every religion of the past was fit to become universal."[4] In particular, the Báb refers to the case of Christianity where most believers failed to recognize Muḥammad who appeared 600 years after Jesus Christ.

> *Ponder upon the people unto whom the Gospel was given. Their religious leaders were considered as the true Guides of the Gospel, yet when they shut themselves out from Muḥammad, the Apostle of God, they turned into guides of error, notwithstanding that all their lives they had faithfully observed the precepts of their religion in order to attain unto Paradise; then when God made Paradise known unto them, they would not enter therein.*[5]

The **nature of this rejection** is also elaborated by the Báb:

> *It is recorded in a tradition that of the entire concourse of the Christians no more than seventy people embraced the Faith of the Apostle of God. The blame falleth upon their doctors, for if these had believed, they would have been followed by the mass of their countrymen. Behold, then, that which*

---

1 The Báb, *Selections*, p. 89.
2 The Báb, *Selections*, p. 159.
3 The Báb, *Selections*, p. 102.
4 Shoghi Effendi in *The Compilation of Compilations*, Vol. II, p. 4.
5 The Báb, *Selections*, p. 143.

> *hath come to pass! The learned men of Christendom are held to be learned by virtue of their safeguarding the teaching of Christ, and yet consider how they themselves have been the cause of men's failure to accept the Faith and attain unto salvation!*[1]

That the **religious leadership acted as a hindrance** to acceptance of the Messengers of God is further attested by the Báb: *"At the time of every revelation the people of that revelation were veiled by the learned* ('ulamá') *of that revelation."*[2] He further states:

> *Had they been content with their own veiled condition and had they not dealt unjustly with anyone and not issued commands contrary to what has been revealed in the Book of God, they would have had cast themselves into hellfire. But now, their own punishment as well as that of whoever imagines them to be the ulama of Islam—nay, rather [the punishment] of whoever failed or will fail to believe in the Revelation of God, will be upon them.*[3]

The great Day of God and the Resurrection

The appearance of the Báb marks the **beginning of the cycle of fulfilment** and the **end of the Adamic cycle**, which was the cycle of prophecy. *"Verily I say, this is the Day spoken of by God in His Book ...,"* said the Báb.[4] *"When God sent forth His Prophet Muḥammad, on that day the termination of the prophetic cycle was foreordained in the knowledge of God."*[5]

The cycle of fulfilment preordained in all previous dispensations was acclaimed as the "Day of God" or the "Days of God":

> *O My servants! This is God's appointed Day which the merciful Lord hath promised you in His Book; wherefore, in very truth, glorify ye abundantly the name of God while treading the Path of the Most Great Remembrance* [the Báb] ....[6]

Along with the concept of the Day of God comes that of the "Day of Resurrection". The Holy Books include many references to this concept. In the Book of Daniel, it is written, "And many of them that sleep in the dust of the earth shall awake, some to everlasting life, and some to shame and everlasting contempt" (Daniel 12:2). In the New Testament it is written: "For the trumpet will sound, the dead will be raised imperishable, and we will be changed" (1 Corinthians 15:52). In the Qur'án (4:87) Muḥammad says "He will surely assemble you all together on the Day of Resurrection, about which there is no doubt."

1 The Báb, *Selections*, pp. 123–124.
2 The Báb in Eschraghi, "Undermining the Foundations of Orthodoxy", p. 234.
3 The Báb in Eschraghi, "Undermining the Foundations of Orthodoxy", p. 234.
4 The Báb in Nabíl-i-A'ẓam, *The Dawn-Breakers,* p. 92.
5 The Báb, *Selections*, p. 161.
6 The Báb, *Selections*, p. 72.

The above prophecies are generally misinterpreted and wrongly understood to mean the literal rising of the dead from their graves. The Day of Resurrection actually refers to the resurrection of the previous Manifestation of God in the appearance of the subsequent Manifestation of God. For the Báb, **the resurrection is not a resurrection of the physical body but of the spiritual Being**—that same "Word" that "was made flesh" in Jesus "and dwelt amongst us"[1] and was subsequently incarnated in Muḥammad. This leads to another question: if the Day of Resurrection occurs when the next Manifestation of God brings a new Revelation, how long does it last? The answer to this is clearly stated by the Báb:

> ... *what is meant by the Day of Resurrection is this, that from the time of the appearance of Him Who is the Tree of divine Reality, at whatever period and under whatever name, until the moment of His disappearance, is the Day of Resurrection.*[2]

The Báb further explains:

> *For example, from the inception of the mission of Jesus ... till the day of His ascension was the Resurrection of Moses .... And from the inception of the Revelation of the Apostle of God—may the blessings of God be upon Him—till the day of His ascension was the Resurrection of Jesus—peace be upon Him—wherein the Tree of Divine Reality appeared in the person of Muḥammad .... And from the moment when the Tree of the Bayán appeared until it disappeareth is the Resurrection of the Apostle of God, as is divinely foretold in the Qur'án.*[3]

The Day of Resurrection is sometimes used synonymously with the term 'Day of Judgement'; and so it is, because all the people of the world are judged whenever the new Manifestation of God appears and declares His Mission. According to the Persian Bayán (2:9), when the Manifestation of God appears, the spiritual lives of all the inhabitants of earth come to an end. Those who accept Him are spiritually resuscitated. Those who reject Him remain in their spiritual graves.

As well as there being a Day of Judgement for all mankind, every individual soul faces a day of judgement at the end of its physical life, when each of us must answer to God as to how we responded to the Manifestation for that Era. In the Persian Bayán (2:10) it is stated that the bodies of people once allegorically dead become their own graves. In the resurrection to occur with the appearance of the Manifestation of God, each spirit will be asked about its faith (2:10). If a believer, its grave shall become a garden of paradise; otherwise, he or she will belong in hell. The Báb wrote:

> ... *the soul of no believer shall be taken but his grave shall become as a garden of the Gardens of Paradise, wherein God hath created that which he*

---

1 John 1:14, KJB.
2 The Báb, *Selections*, pp. 107–107.
3 The Báb in Nader Saiedi, *Gate of the Heart*, p. 107.

> *loves ready for him. So also there is none who shall disbelieve in the Bayán but shall suffer what the pen dares not write. Happy that person whose soul shall be taken after that he hath believed in Him whom God shall manifest and his words, for he is a believer in the Bayán and all that is in the Bayán.*[1]

Thus the Báb teaches that at the end of their physical lives, those who recognize the Manifestation will enter paradise whereas those who reject Him will live in Hell.

The Báb also elaborated on another way of understanding spiritual life and death in terms of the death of the ego:

"True death," the Báb says, *"is realized when a person dieth to himself at the time of His Revelation in such wise that he seeketh naught except Him."*[2] *"True resurrection from the sepulchres"* the Báb further affirms, *"means to be quickened in conformity with His Will, through the power of His utterance."*[3]

In conclusion, we can understand that **each time a Manifestation arrives, a Day of Resurrection occurs**. *"It is for this reason,"* the Báb states, *"that the Day of Resurrection is said to be the greatest of all days, yet it is like unto any other day ...."*[4] *"The Day of Resurrection is a day on which the sun riseth and setteth like unto any other day. How oft hath the Day of Resurrection dawned, and the people of the land where it occurred did not learn of the event."*[5]

Resurrection also has an additional meaning—that of *the consummation of the previous dispensation:*

> *The stage of perfection of everything is reached when its resurrection occurreth. The perfection of the religion of Islám was consummated at the beginning of this Revelation; and from the rise of this Revelation until its setting, the fruits of the Tree of Islám, whatever they are, will become apparent. The Resurrection of the Bayán* [The Báb] *will occur at the time of the appearance of Him Whom God will make manifest.*[6]

Reaching towards the presence of God

Along with this new conceptualization of Resurrection comes the religious concept of "reaching towards the presence of God". The Bible says, "They will be punished with everlasting destruction and shut out from the presence of the Lord and from the glory of his might" (2 Thessalonians 1:9) and the Qur'án reads: "On the day when they will be brought into the presence of their Lord, their greeting to each other will be, 'Peace be with you.'" (33:44) The "presence" here is meant to be understood as a symbolic presence.

---

1 The Báb in Momen, *Selections from the Writings of E. G. Browne*, p. 326.
2 The Báb, *Selections*, p. 157.
3 The Báb, *Selections*, p. 158.
4 The Báb, *Selections*, p. 79.
5 The Báb, *Selections*, p. 78.
6 The Báb, *Selections*, p. 107.

The Báb explains that reaching the presence of God refers to attaining the presence of a Manifestation of God during His earthly life:

> *There is no paradise more wondrous for any soul than to be exposed to God's Manifestation in His Day, to hear His verses and believe in them, to attain His presence, which is naught but the presence of God, to sail upon the sea of the heavenly kingdom of His good-pleasure, and to partake of the choice fruits of the paradise of His divine Oneness.*[1]

> *For on that Day all men will be brought before God and will attain His Presence; which meaneth appearance before Him Who is the Tree of divine Reality and attainment unto His presence; inasmuch as it is not possible to appear before the Most Holy Essence of God, nor is it conceivable to seek reunion with Him. That which is feasible in the matter of appearance before Him and of meeting Him is attainment unto the Primal Tree.*[2]

In explaining the meaning of "heaven" and "hell" the Báb affirmed that "*no Paradise is more sublime for My creatures than to stand before My face and to believe in My holy Words, while no fire hath been or will be fiercer for them than to be veiled from the Manifestation of My exalted Self and to disbelieve in My Words.*"[3]

The converted were lovingly encouraged to attain the presence of the Báb during their lifetime:

> *And hadst thou attained the presence of thy Lord in this land, and been of them that truly believe that the Face of God is beheld in the person of the Primal Point, it would have been far more advantageous than prostrating thyself in adoration from the beginning that hath no beginning until the present time ....*[4]

Through God's progressive revelation we know that Khrishna, Zoroaster, Buddha, Abraham, Moses, Christ, Muḥammad, the Báb and Bahá'u'lláh were all Manifestations of God—forming something like a divine chain of divine Messengers. In the words of Bahá'u'lláh, "*Everyone of them is the Way to God that connecteth this world with the realm above.*"[5]

The theology of the Báb also contains many motifs from the Old and New Testament and the Qur'án, including references to the second coming, resurrection, atonement, heaven, hell and purgatory—all of which are re-interpreted—while providing new insights.

In brief, the divine philosophy of the Báb constitutes the most advanced theological framework witnessed by humanity up until the middle of the nineteenth century when the Revelation of Bahá'u'lláh supervened.

---

1 The Báb, *Selections*, p. 77.
2 The Báb, *Selections*, p. 108.
3 The Báb, *Selections*, p. 87.
4 The Báb, *Selections*, p. 36.
5 Bahá'u'lláh, *Gleanings*, p. 50.

3
Divine annunciations

The coming of the Prophets of God has always been announced in the sacred texts of the religions of the world and documented in history. This was particularly the case between John the Baptist and Jesus, and between the Báb and Bahá'u'lláh, in the Christian and Bábí-Bahá'í religions. This chapter will narrate those two annunciatory accounts as well as the story of the Magi of Bethlehem and the story of Salmán, which are situated in the context of the Zoroastrian Faith.

Mission of the Báb

Part of the mission of the Báb as the "Gate" was to announce the imminent appearance of another Divine Figure in the person of Bahá'u'lláh.

"*Now what He intended by the term Báb* [Gate] *was this,*" 'Abdu'l-Bahá explained, "*that He was the channel of grace from some great Person still behind the veil of glory, Who was the possessor of countless and boundless perfections, by Whose will He moved, and to the bond of Whose love He clung ....*"[1] Shoghi Effendi further elaborated that the "twofold mission" of the Báb was to be "the Bearer of a wholly independent Revelation and the Herald of One still greater than His own."[2]

In various Writings, the Báb reaffirmed His role as the Forerunner of Bahá'u'lláh. According to the Báb:

> *I, verily, have not fallen short of My duty to admonish that people, and to devise means whereby they may turn towards God, their Lord, and believe in God, their Creator. ... I truly have nurtured all things for this purpose. How, then, can anyone be veiled from Him?*[3]

The Báb and Bahá'u'lláh are two Messengers of God inextricably linked to each other both historically and doctrinally. They are designated as the "Twin Manifestations of God". The Báb wrote regarding the appearance of Bahá'u'lláh:

> *I behold His appearance even as the sun in the midmost heaven, and the disappearance of all even as that of the stars of the night by day.*[4]
>
> *I Myself am but the first servant to believe in Him, and in His signs, and partake of the sweet savours of His words from the first-fruits of the Paradise of His knowledge. Yea, By His glory! He is the Truth. There is none other God but Him. All have arisen at His bidding.*[5]

---

1 'Abdu'l-Bahá, *A Traveller's Narrative*, p. 4.
2 Shoghi Effendi, *God Passes By*, p. 27.
3 The Báb, *Selections*, p. 156.
4 Bahá'u'lláh, *Epistle to the Son of the Wolf*, p. 173.
5 Bahá'u'lláh, *Epistle to the Son of the Wolf*, p. 141.

Salmán the Persian

At the time of Muḥammad, Zoroastrians were awaiting another prophet. One of those believers was Rúz-bih Khushnúdán (later known as Salmán the Persian) who is mentioned twice in the Kitáb-i-Íqán. According to Marzieh Gail: "There was a man named Salmán the Persian and he had spent many years of his life traveling in search of a Prophet. He was born in a Persian village and as a boy had tended the sacred fire [in a Zoroastrian temple]."[1]

Salmán travelled to Damascus and became a Christian. For years he was searching for a new prophet. He served under four wise men who were announcing the coming of another Messenger of God. The last wise man once told him: "O Rúz-bih! when thou hast taken up my body and buried it, go to Ḥijáz for there the Day-star of Muḥammad will arise. Happy art thou, for thou shalt behold His face!"[2] According to Marzieh Gail:

> In those days it was not safe to travel, because if you were caught they sold you into slavery. When Salmán was going toward Arabia they caught him, and sold him to a Jew of Medina. Salmán worked in the palm groves; it was his job to take care of the camel that turned the wheel which brought water up from the sub-soil for distribution into irrigation trenches. One day Salmán was up at the top of a palm tree, and he heard his master speaking down below. His master was saying that a man had arisen in Mecca who was calling himself a Prophet. Salmán began to tremble all over; he became so agitated that he almost fell on his master's head. He slid down the tree, and his owner struck him, saying, "What is it to you?"[3]

Finally, Salmán became the first Persian soul to recognize Muḥammad as the new Messenger of God and became His dedicated courier.

The Magi of Bethlehem

The priests of the Zoroastrian religion are called Magi (Magus in the singular), and are known to have been experts in astronomy. The Magi are mentioned in the Gospel of Matthew as persons who came from the Orient (Persia) looking for the Promised Messenger of God and following the star of Bethlehem (Matthew 2:1–2). They are also alluded to as believers in the Qur'án (22:17) along with Christians and Jews.

Bahá'u'lláh narrates the story of the Zoroastrian Magus in *The Kitáb-i-Íqán*:

> *In like manner, when the hour of the Revelation of Jesus drew nigh, a few of the Magi, aware that the star of Jesus had appeared in heaven, sought and followed it, till they came unto the city which was the seat of the Kingdom of Herod. The sway of his sovereignty in those days embraced the whole of that land.*

---

1 Marzieh Gail, *Six Lessons on Islám*, p. 5.

2 Bahá'u'lláh, *The Kitáb-i-Íqán*, p. 65.

3 Marzieh Gail, *Six Lessons on Islám*, p. 5.

These Magi said: "Where is He that is born King of the Jews? for we have seen His star in the east and are come to worship Him!" When they had searched, they found out that in Bethlehem, in the land of Judea, the Child had been born. This was the sign that was manifested in the visible heaven. As to the sign in the invisible heaven—the heaven of divine knowledge and understanding—it was Yaḥyá [John the Baptist], *son of Zachariah, who gave unto the people the tidings of the Manifestation of Jesus. Even as He hath revealed: "God announceth Yaḥyá* [John the Baptist], *to thee, who shall bear witness unto the Word from God, and a great one and chaste." By the term "Word" is meant Jesus, Whose coming Yaḥyá* [John the Baptist], *foretold. Moreover, in the heavenly Scriptures it is written: "John the Baptist was preaching in the wilderness of Judea, and saying, Repent ye: for the Kingdom of heaven is at hand."*[1]

The Báb and John the Baptist

The Báb came to announce the coming of Bahá'u'lláh. This is similar in some ways to the role of John the Baptist in relation to Jesus. Although John the Baptist is not to be considered as an independent Manifestation of God, Bahá'u'lláh identified Him in the Kitáb-i-Badí' as a prophet and a messenger.[2] Notwithstanding that John the Baptist does not share the same prophetic rank as the Báb, the comparison is meaningful. John the Baptist said: "He is the one who comes after me, the straps of whose sandals I am not worthy to untie" (John 1:27). The Báb similarly said of Bahá'u'lláh, "*Were He to appear this very moment, I would be the first to adore Him, and the first to bow down before Him*."[3]

About John, Jesus said: "Truly I tell you, among those born of women there has not risen anyone greater than John the Baptist" and Bahá'u'lláh said that the rank of the Báb "*excelleth that of all the Prophets and His Revelation transcendeth the comprehension and understanding of all their chosen ones*."[4]

John the Baptist had left a number of commandments, and taught his disciples to be baptized (Luke 3:3), to repent (Luke 3:8), to pray (Luke 11:1), to be just (Luke 3:13), not to commit violence (Luke 3:14) and to be fair (Luke 3:14). The Báb, by comparison, left a collection of precepts and ordinances contained in a vast number of revealed works.

Tragically, both the Báb and John the Baptist were martyred in their thirties. Both were executed by temporal powers leaving enthusiastic disciples waiting for the imminent coming of the Promised One. John was martyred by the order of Herod Antipas—the Tetrarch and ruler of Galilee—while the Báb suffered a similar fate by the order of the Amír Kabír (Khán-i-Faráhání Taqí), the chief minister to the Sháh of Iran. Like the Báb and Bahá'u'lláh, John and Jesus were

---

1 Bahá'u'lláh, *The Kitáb-i-Íqán*, pp. 63–64.

2 Research Department Memorandum to the Universal House of Justice, 25 August 1989. https://bahai-library.com/uhj_john_baptist_interpretation

3 Bahá'u'lláh, *Epistle to the Son of the Wolf*, p. 171.

4 Shoghi Effendi, *The World Order of Bahá'u'lláh*, pp. 125–12.

contemporary—Jesus being baptised by John (Matthew 11:11). Jesus died after John and, similarly, Bahá'u'lláh survived the Báb. The respective practices and mission of John the Baptist and Jesus, though related, were different. Likewise there were differences in the practices and Mission of the Báb and Bahá'u'lláh.

The parallels between John the Baptist and the Báb are remarkable.[1] Shoghi Effendi commented that the Báb was "the 'Return of John the Baptist' expected by the Christians."[2] Indeed, Bahá'u'lláh had stated:

> *By God! The relationship between the Revelation of the Primal Point (the Báb) and this most wondrous, this most glorious Revelation is identical to that of the Revelation of John, son of Zechariah (John the Baptist,) and the Spirit of God (Jesus) .... Furthermore, just as John the Baptist came invested with laws and ordinances, and just as the advent of Jesus Christ occurred during His time, the Primal Point* [Báb]—*may My life be a sacrifice unto Him—declared thus, after making a universal covenant and heralding the Revelation to come: "Verily, the end is nigh, and ye are fast asleep."*[3]

And in the *Tablet to the Pope*, Bahá'u'lláh draws attention to the parallels between the preaching, in their annunciatory roles, of John the Baptist and the Báb:

> *O followers of the Son! We have once again sent John unto you, and He, verily, hath cried out in the wilderness of the Bayán: O peoples of the world! Cleanse your eyes! The Day whereon ye can behold the Promised One and attain unto Him hath drawn nigh! O followers of the Gospel! Prepare the way! The Day of the advent of the Glorious Lord is at hand! Make ready to enter the Kingdom. Thus hath it been ordained by God, He Who causeth the dawn to break.*[4]

The Báb and Jesus

Even more striking are the correlations between the lives of Jesus and the Báb. This is not a coincidence but a providential association as highlighted by Shoghi Effendi, who, in speaking of the life of the Báb, states, "... we cannot fail to discern a remarkable similarity to the distinguishing features of the career of Jesus Christ."[5]

Although the Báb was a Siyyid (i.e., a descendant of the Prophet Muḥammad through Fáṭima) and Jesus was of the priestly line of Levites through Mary, neither belonged to an aristocratic or scholarly class. Jesus was a carpenter and the Báb was a merchant.

---

1 See Jack McLean, *John the Baptist*; & Christopher Buck, "The Identity of the Ṣábi'ún", pp. 172–186.
2 Shoghi Effendi, *God Passes By*, p. 58.
3 Bahá'u'lláh, *Kitáb-i-Badí'*, p. 79.
4 Bahá'u'lláh, *The Summons of the Lord of Hosts*, p. 63.
5 Shoghi Effendi, *God Passes By*, p. 56.

Both the Báb and Jesus were born with innate knowledge, already evidenced in Their childhood to a degree that astonished the erudite.[1] Here we will digress for a moment to remind the reader that Bahá'u'lláh, too, was born with innate knowledge, the signs of which were also visible in His childhood. There is another interesting parallel, this time between Jesus and Bahá'u'lláh, in Their recognition of Their respective heralds. Jesus was among the first to be baptised by John the Baptist, and referred to him as "a burning and a shining light" (John 5:35). Likewise, on receiving a scroll penned by the Báb, announcing His Revelation, Bahá'u'lláh "... instantly acclaimed its truth, and arose to champion its cause."[2] Thereafter, Bahá'u'lláh, the Supreme Manifestation of God for this Age, "appeared in the guise of, and continued to labor as, one of the foremost disciples of the Báb."[3]

Both the Báb and Jesus were known for Their forbearance, meekness and mildness. Both performed miracles although reluctantly—Jesus saying, "Only an evil, adulterous generation would demand a miraculous sign" (Matthew 12:38–40). Some of His disciples believed after seeing a miracle (Luke 7:11), but others such as the fishermen—namely, the two pairs of brothers: Peter and Andrew, and James and John—followed Him solely based on His Word (Matthew 4:18–22; see also Mark 2:14). Likewise, the Báb warned that *"He who recounteth any miracle, other than the verses, is veiled from any truth,"*[4] stating further than:

> *Were any man to be adorned with all spiritual virtues in utmost contentment in all the worlds, and yet assert in this Day that his heart is not utterly satisfied with the revelation of verses in the absence of witnessing miracles, then all his acquiescence would be brought to naught in the Book of God, and no other mode of resignation would be of any profit to him.*[5]

Nonetheless, according to the chronicles, the Báb was involved in some supranatural events. He miraculously healed people[6] near to death,[7] cured a married couple of infertility,[8] appeared simultaneously in two places,[9] tamed nature,[10] read people's minds,[11] was recognized in visions,[12] augmented food for

---

1 Nabíl-i-A'ẓam, *The Dawn-Breakers*, p. 75.
2 Shoghi Effendi, *God Passes By*, p. 67.
3 Shoghi Effendi, God Passes By, p. 128.
4 The Báb in Nader Saiedi, *Gate of the Heart*, p. 370.
5 The Báb in Nader Saiedi, *Gate of the Heart*, p. 307.
6 Nabíl-i-A'ẓam, *The Dawn-Breakers*, pp. 236.
7 Nabíl-i-A'ẓam, *The Dawn-Breakers*, pp. 196–197.
8 Nabíl-i-A'ẓam, *The Dawn-Breakers*, pp. 208–209.
9 Nabíl-i-A'ẓam, *The Dawn-Breakers*, pp. 246–247.
10 Nabíl-i-A'ẓam, *The Dawn-Breakers*, p. 309.
11 Nabíl-i-A'ẓam, *The Dawn-Breakers*, pp. 174–175.
12 Nabíl-i-A'ẓam, *The Dawn-Breakers*, pp. 303–304, 246–247, & 305.

sharing,[1] experienced a form of transfiguration[2] and foresaw future events[3] even as a child.[4] The Báb also triumphed over death as John Esslemont wrote:

> On the 9 July 1850, the Báb Himself, Who was then in His thirty-first year, fell a victim to the fanatical fury of His persecutors. With a devoted young follower named 'Aqá Muḥammad 'Alí [Mírzá Muḥammad-'Alí-i-Zunúzí], who had passionately begged to be allowed to share His martyrdom, He was led to the scaffold in the old barrack square of Tabríz. About two hours before noon the two were suspended by ropes under their armpits in such a way that the head of Muḥammad 'Alí [Mírzá Muḥammad-'Alí-i-Zunúzí] rested against the breast of his beloved Master. A regiment of Armenian soldiers was drawn up and received the order to fire. Promptly the volleys rang out, but when the smoke cleared, it was found that the Báb and His companion were still alive. The bullets had but severed the ropes by which they were suspended, so that they dropped to the ground unhurt. The Báb proceeded to a room nearby, where He was found talking to one of His friends. About noon they were again suspended. The Armenians, who considered the result of their volleys a miracle, were unwilling to fire again, so another regiment of soldiers had been brought on the scene, who fired when ordered. This time the volleys took effect.[5]

"The purity of their own lives," adds William Sears about the Báb and Jesus, "shamed the people among whom they taught."[6] They both condemned the *status quo* and openly challenged the religious establishment attracting opposition and persecution.

The advent of Jesus and the Báb was also foretold by oriental sages. John the Baptist foretold the coming of Jesus. In the case of the Báb, Shaykh Aḥmad-i-Aḥsá'í (1753–1826) and Siyyid Káẓim (1793–1843) foretold His advent. Shaykh Aḥmad-i-Aḥsá'í had stated that "Ere long shall ye behold the countenance of your Lord resplendent as the moon in its full glory...", and "One of the most mighty signs that shall signalise the advent of the promised Hour is this: 'A woman shall give birth to One who shall be her Lord.'"[7] Siyyid Káẓim, his successor, went even further assuring that the Promise One was already alive, living among the population and would soon manifest Himself. In the West, the Adventist William Miller (1782–1849) had predicted 1844 as the year of the Second Coming of Jesus Christ.[8]

---

1 Mírzá Ḥabíbu'lláh Afnán, *The Genesis of the Bábí-Bahá'í Faiths*, p. 36.
2 Mírzá Ḥabíbu'lláh Afnán, *The Genesis of the Bábí-Bahá'í Faiths*, p. 21.
3 Nabíl-i-A'ẓam, *The Dawn-Breakers*, p. 213.
4 Mírzá Ḥabíbu'lláh Afnán, *The Genesis of the Bábí-Bahá'í Faiths*, p. 6.
5 John Esslemont, *Bahá'u'lláh and the New Era*, pp. 17–18.
6 William Sears, *Thief in the Night*, p. 87.
7 Nabíl-i-A'ẓam, *The Dawn-Breakers*, p. 12.
8 Carolyn Sparey Fox, *Seeking a State of Heaven*, p. 12.

The Báb and Jesus were both young at the beginning of their ministries. The Báb began His ministry at the age of twenty-four years while Jesus was in His thirtieth year. Both ministries were of short duration: six years for the Báb and three for Jesus. Jesus had twelve main disciples while the Báb appointed the eighteen "Letters of the Living,"[1] and many from among both groups were martyred. The first apostle of Jesus, Peter, was called the "rock" while the first disciple of the Báb, Mullá Ḥusayn, was called "the gate of the Gate". Mary Magdalene and Ṭáhirih became the prominent women within their respective religious dispensations, encouraging their fellow believers to arise and promulgate the teachings.

While the Báb exhorted His disciples to "*Scatter throughout the length and breadth of this land, and, with steadfast feet and sanctified hearts prepare the way for His* [Bahá'u'lláh] coming",[2] Jesus summoned His disciples to "Go into all the world and proclaim the gospel to the whole creation" (Mark 6:15). The Báb wrote "*... I give you to drink , by the leave of God, the sovereign Truth, of the crystal-pure waters of His Revelation which are gushing out from the incorruptible Fountain situated upon the Holy Mount*",[3] while Jesus said, "Indeed, the water I give them will become in them a spring of water welling up to eternal life" (John 4:14). Likewise, the Báb and Jesus said, respectively, "*I am the Gate of God ...*"[4] and "I am the Gate ..." (John 10:9).

Both Prophets were publicly martyred on charges of heresy after farcical trials where they were pressed by religious and secular authorities to renounce their faith in exchange for freedom. During their interrogations similar questions were asked. The Báb was asked, "what do you teach and what do you intend?"[5] and Jesus was asked, "Are you the king of the Jews?" (Matthew 27:11). The Báb[6] and Jesus (Matthew 20:17–19) both prophesied their own martyrdoms.

While Jesus was trialled under orders of Pontius Pilate, the Roman governor of the province of Judaea, the Báb was prosecuted at the instigation of the prime minister, in both cases the verdict being supported by a synod of divines. Similarly, They suffered interrogation for an extended period, and were publicly paraded under the gaze of hostile crowds. Both Messengers passed from this world just prior to a holy day commemoration, Jesus during the Passover Day of Preparation, on the eve of the Sabbath; and the Báb just before Ramaḍán (the Islamic fasting month). Comparably, both were raised off the ground during their execution: Jesus was painfully nailed to a cross, and the Báb was suspended with ropes hanging from a nail. In both cases, the martyrdoms were treated as a public

1 The "Letters of the Living" were the first 18 believers in the Báb. See *Dawn-Breakers,* pp. 80–82.

2 The Báb in Nabíl-i-A'ẓam, *The Dawn-Breakers,* p. 47.

3 The Báb, *Selections,* p. 50.

4 The Báb, *Selections,* p. 50.

5 Ḥuseyn Hamadání, *The Táríkh-i-Jadíd,* p. 294.

6 The Báb, *Selections,* p. 59.

spectacle. The remains of the Báb were paraded through the streets as a further degradation.

At noon, a three-hour period of darkness accompanied the agony of Jesus as He hung dying on the cross. Likewise, the Báb died at noon at which time a deep darkness descended on the land. Prior to Their deaths both pronounced similar statements. Jesus exclaimed: "Forgive them, Father, for they know not what they do" (Luke 23:34) and the Báb declared:

> *Had you believed in Me, O wayward generation, every one of you would have followed the example of this youth,*[1] *who stood in rank above most of you, and willingly would have sacrificed himself in My path. The day will come when you will have recognised Me; that day I shall have ceased to be with you.*[2]

> At the time of Jesus' last breath "surrounded darkness came over the whole land until three, because the sun's light failed" (Luke 23:44) while at the ... very moment the shots were fired [at the Báb], a gale of exceptional severity arose and swept over the whole city. A whirlwind of dust of incredible density obscured the light of the sun and blinded the eyes of the people. The entire city remained enveloped in that darkness from noon till night."[3]

While the body of Jesus was placed in a sealed tomb, the sacred remains of the Báb were flung into the city moat, and, in both cases the remains were guarded. When Their disappearance was discovered, the guards made wild claims to excuse their apparent dereliction of duty. In point of fact, the followers of the Báb had secretly recovered His remains, and they were kept safe for six decades until they could finally be laid to rest. Jesus and the Báb and were both buried in the Holy Land on Mount Zion and on Mount Carmel respectively—that is, lineally, within a hundred kilometres of each other.

This chapter reviewed the relationship between John the Baptist and Jesus, and how this was echoed in the relationship between the Báb and Bahá'u'lláh. John the Baptist had been the forerunner of Jesus, as likewise the Báb was the herald of Bahá'u'lláh. We also reflected upon the great congruence in the lives of Jesus and the Báb, and how both had sacrificed their lifeblood in the name of God and His religion. Although two millennia separate the Báb and Bahá'u'lláh from John the Baptist and Jesus, the lives of these four heavenly personages parallel each other in so many aspects and circumstances that we cannot but wonder upon the degree to which the imprint of God was designed in advance. Thus, Providence displays a divine and eternal pattern of operation, unique and mysterious, yet coherent and filled with striking resemblances.

---

1 Reference to Anís ("Close Companion"), the youth (Mírzá Muḥammad-'Alí-i-Zunúzí) who had entreated the Báb that he be executed together with Him.

2 The Báb in Nabíl-i-A'ẓam, *The Dawn-Breakers,* p. 514.

3 Nabíl-i-A'ẓam, *The Dawn-Breakers,* p. 514.

4
The Báb as a Manifestation of God

The Revelation of the Báb was a significant event in the religious history of Persia and of humankind because of His teachings and His own history. A. L. M. Nicolas, the aforementioned Iranian-based French diplomat, once wrote on the power and reach of the teachings of the Báb especially in reference to Dalá'il-i-Sab'ih, *The Seven Proofs*:

> My reflections on the strange book [*The Seven Proofs* by the Báb] that I had translated, filled me with a kind of intoxication and I became, little by little, profoundly and uniquely a Bábí. The more I immersed myself in these reflections, the more I admired the greatness of the genius of him who, born in Shíráz, had dreamt of uplifting the Muslim world ....[1]

An addition, Nicolas (1864–1937), wrote that the life of the Báb, "... is one of the most magnificent examples of courage which it has been the privilege of mankind to behold, and it is also an admirable proof of the love which our hero felt for his fellow countrymen.[2] The Orientalist Arminius Vámbéry (1832–1913) stated that the Báb "has expressed doctrines worthy of the greatest thinkers".[3] The Comte de Gobineau (1816—1882) wrote that the expositions of the Báb opened to people "unlimited horizons, varied, colored, mysterious, with shadows broken here and there by patches of blinding light which transported those imaginative people of Persia into a state of ecstasy.[4]

Within a broader discussion on the nature of the Revelation of the Báb, this chapter examines some events associated with His life and with the substance of His Writings.

The following are the main themes of this chapter:

- The Báb as a Person
- First intimations of the station of the Báb
- The nature of the Revelation of the Báb
- The spiritual substance of the Báb in mystical terms

The Báb as a Person

What do we know about the Person of the Báb from contemporary observers?

The Báb once commented on His life before His declaration in May 1844: *"Likewise behold the Point of the Bayán. His behavior prior to the declaration of*

---

1 A. L. M. Nicolas in Momen, *The Bábí and Bahá'í Religions 1844–1944*, p. 37.

2 Emily McBride Périgord, *Translation of French Foot-Notes*, pp. 60–61.

3 William Sears, *Thief in the Night*, p. 97.

4 Emily McBride Périgord, *Translation of French Foot-Notes*, p. 10.

His mission is clearly evident unto those who knew Him."[1] All the testimonies below show how deeply the Báb touched people's personal lives.

Siyyid Mírzá 'Alí Muḥammad (the Báb) was born on 20 October 1819. 'Abdu'l-Bahá in "A Traveller's Narrative" affirms that the Báb's father passed away a few years after His birth.[2] The Child was then raised by His maternal uncle, Ḥájí Mírzá Siyyid 'Alí. From a tender age, the Báb showed signs of extraordinary capacity and virtue.[3] He was sent for instruction to the school of Shaykh 'Ábid who later related an incident showing the natural aptitude of the Báb:

> "I asked the Báb to recite the opening words of the Qur'án: 'Bismi'lláhi'r-Raḥmáni'r-Raḥím." He hesitated, pleading that unless He were told what these words signified, He would in no wise attempt to pronounce them. I pretended not to know their meaning. "I know what these words signify," observed my pupil; "by your leave, I will explain them." He spoke with such knowledge and fluency that I was struck with amazement. He expounded the meaning of "Alláh," of "Raḥmán," and "Raḥím," in terms such as I had neither read nor heard. The sweetness of His utterance still lingers in my memory. I felt impelled to take Him back to His uncle and to deliver into his hands the Trust he had committed to my care. I determined to tell him how unworthy I felt to teach so remarkable a child. I found His uncle alone in his office. "I have brought Him back to you," I said, "and commit Him to your vigilant protection. He is not to be treated as a mere child, for in Him I can already discern evidences of that mysterious power which the Revelation of the Ṣáḥibu'z-Zamán[4] alone can reveal. It is incumbent upon you to surround Him with your most loving care. Keep Him in your house, for He, verily, stands in no need of teachers such as I."[5]

After He reached the age of fifteen years, the Báb engaged in business in the city of Búshihr under His uncle's tutelage and, later, independently. Several witnesses reported encountering the Báb in His youth in Búshihr. They commented upon His "good nature, his equanimity, his dignified bearing, his piety, his virtue, his work ethic, his generosity, his contentment, and his insight"[6] as well as "His downcast eyes, his extreme courtesy, and the serene expression of his face ...."[7] He was also described as "... a handsome man with a thin beard, dressed in clean clothes, wearing a green shawl and a black turban."[8]

---

1 The Báb, *Selections,* p. 96.

2 'Abdu'l-Bahá, *A Traveller's Narrative,* p. 4.

3 Stephen Lambden, "An Episode in the Childhood of Sayyid Alí Muḥammad".

4 *Ṣáḥibu'z-Zamán* ("Lord of the Age"), the *Promised One* of Islam.

5 Nabíl-i-A'ẓam, *The Dawn-Breakers,* p. 75.

6 Fereydun Vahman, "The Báb", p. 11.

7 Fereydun Vahman, "The Báb", p. 17.

8 Abbas Amanat, *Resurrection and Renewal,* p. 133.

At one point, the Báb left His trade to travel to the Islamic shrines in Iraq for spiritual contemplation and to dedicate Himself to the study of religious texts. An eyewitness who met the Báb at the holy shrines in Karbilá, where He spent one year engaged in pilgrimage and pious reflection, observed:

> On a certain day, I entered the Shrine of the Imám Ḥusayn, intending to make pilgrimage there, when I beheld a youth in a kind of spiritual trance. He was immersed in a silent state of sanctification, and tears were streaming down his face. Without willing it, I began to go towards him—but as I did not wish to disturb him, I instead seated myself in a corner to wait until he had concluded his pilgrimage. The more attention I paid to him, the more fascinated I grew with his expressions of modesty and shame. I witnessed from him such things as I cannot possibly describe .... So courteous was his demeanor, so cheerful his face as he spoke these words that I could not help but be totally captivated by him.[1]

An account from those times describes the Báb as follows:

> Even before departure from the holy land [the 'Atábat], where devotion attracts Muslims from all over Iran, everybody talked about him as an extraordinary young man. People thought of him as possessing a mystical consciousness. When it came to his peculiarity and his incomprehensible utterances, they attributed them to his profound wisdom. It was especially through the Shírází pilgrims, the ordinary people who returned from Karbilá, that his fame spread in his homeland.[2]

Mullá Ḥusayn, the first Bábí, remembered his first encounter during which the Báb "overwhelmed [him] with expressions of affection and loving-kindness." Mullá Ḥusayn was "profoundly impressed by the gentle yet compelling manner in which that strange Youth spoke to [him]", and was enthralled by "His gait, the charm of His voice, the dignity of His bearing."[3] Mullá Ḥusayn recalled the occasion of this meeting at the House of the Báb:

> Overwhelmed with His acts of extreme kindness, I arose to depart. "The time for evening prayer is approaching," I ventured to observe. "I have promised my friends to join them at that hour in the Masjid-i-Ílkhání." With extreme courtesy and calm He replied: "You must surely have made the hour of your return conditional upon the will and pleasure of God. It seems that His will has decreed otherwise. You need have no fear of having broken your pledge." His dignity and self-assurance silenced me.[4]

---

1 Fereydun Vahman, "The Báb", p. 19.

2 Abbas Amanat, *Resurrection and Renewal*, p. 148. al-'Atabát al-'Álíyát ("the Supreme Shrines"; *'atabát* is "steps" or "thresholds") refers to the Shí'a holy shrines in the Iraqi cities of Karbalá', Najaf, Káẓimayn and Sámarrá. The term is also used for the Shrines of the Báb and Bahá'u'lláh.

3 Nabíl-i-A'ẓam, *The Dawn-Breakers*, pp. 69–70.

4 Nabíl-i-A'ẓam, *The Dawn-Breakers*, pp. 55–56.

In a beautiful supplication to God, the Báb offers the following lines describing **His tumultuous life** after the Declaration of His Mission in May 1844. As is known, the life of the Báb ended with His martyrdom in 1850 in the city of Tabríz when He was still thirty years old.

> ... *at the age of twenty-five I proceeded to thy sacred House* [Mecca],[1] *and by the time I returned to the place where I was born, a year had elapsed. There I tarried patiently in the path of Thy love and beheld the evidences of Thy manifold bounties and of Thy loving-kindness until Thou didst ordain for Me to set out in Thy direction and to migrate to Thy presence. Thus I departed therefrom by Thy leave, spending six months in the land of Ṣád* [Iṣfahán][2] *and seven months in the First Mountain* [Máh-Kú],[3] *where Thou didst rain down upon Me that which beseemeth the glory of Thy heavenly blessings and befitteth the sublimity of Thy gracious gifts and favors. Now, in My thirtieth year, Thou beholdest Me, O My God, in this Grievous Mountain* [Chihríq][4] *where I have dwelt for one whole year.*[5]

Another Bábí, Ḥájí Naṣír, also related his experiences of the Báb:

> When His Holiness the Most Great Remembrance [the Báb] was being conveyed to Ádharbayján, I left Qazvin after Him in order to attain His blessed presence. At every station I reached, the governmental soldiers had taken that Wronged One to the next station. Therefore, I increased the pace of my search and eagerly reached my goal. I gave some gratuity to the soldiers who allowed me to enter the room where His Holiness was staying.
>
> I greeted Him and expressed my respect. He granted me permission to sit. I sat. He was drinking tea, and because of the consideration of wisdom and the soldiers' attitude, He was cautious and did not utter a word. I was lost in the wonder of His beauty and His majestic splendor.
>
> I was gazing at His half-finished cup of tea and entertained the wish to have the bounty of drinking from that cup. At that instant, He motioned me to drink from the same cup. He also gestured to me to return to Qazvin. Therefore, with a heart filled with sadness and a mind agitated by the deeds of the wrong-doers, I returned to Qazvin.[6]

Dr William Cormick was an Irish doctor attached to the prince court who was called to attend the Báb in the prison of Tabríz in 1848. This is his narration:

> You ask me for some particulars of my interview with the founder of the sect known as Bábís.

---

1 October 1844–July 1845.
2 September 1846–April 1847.
3 July 1847–10 April 1848.
4 April 1848–June 1850.
5 The Báb, *Selections*, pp. 180–181.
6 Ahang Rabbani, *Witness to Shaykh Ṭabarsí.*

> Nothing of any importance transpired in this interview, as the Báb was aware of my having been sent with two other Persian doctors to see whether he was of sane mind or merely a madman, to decide the question whether to put him to death or not. With this knowledge he was loth to answer any questions put to him. To all enquiries he merely regarded us with a mild look, chanting in a low melodious voice some hymns, I suppose. Two other Sayyids,[1] his intimate friends, were also present, who subsequently were put to death with him, besides a couple of government officials. He only once deigned to answer me, on my saying that I was not a Musulmán[2] and was willing to know something about his religion, as I might perhaps be inclined to adopt it. He regarded me very intently on my saying this, and replied that he had no doubt of all Europeans coming over to his religion. Our report to the Sháh at that time was of a nature to spare his life. He was put to death some time after by the order of the Amír-i-Niẓám Mírzá Taqí Khán. On our report he merely got the bastinado, in which operation a farrásh, whether intentionally or not, struck him across the face with the stick destined for his feet, which produced a great wound and swelling of the face. On being asked whether a Persian surgeon should be brought to treat him, he expressed a desire that I should be sent for, and I accordingly treated him for a few days, but in the interviews consequent on this I could never get him to have a confidential chat with me, as some Government people were always present, he being a prisoner.
>
> He was very thankful for my attentions to him. He was a very mild and delicate-looking man, rather small in stature and very fair for a Persian, with a melodious soft voice, which struck me much. Being a Sayyid, he was dressed in the habits of that sect, as were also his two companions. In fact his whole look and deportment went far to dispose one in his favour. Of his doctrine I heard nothing from his own lips, although the idea was that there existed in his religion a certain approach to Christianity. He was seen by some Armenian carpenters, who were sent to make some repairs in his prison, reading the Bible, and he took no pains to conceal it, but on the contrary told them of it. Most assuredly the Musulmán fanaticism does not exist in his religion, as applied to Christians, nor is there that restraint of females that now exists.[3]

A leading religious dignitary related the following account of his meeting with the Báb during His sojourn (September 1846–March 1847) in the city of Iṣfahán:

> I attained the presence of that Great One at the house of the Imám Jum'ih and there beheld a youth who[se] face was most luminous. I presented Him with twelve questions; He answered most of them clearly and eloquently of the others He remained silent. The power and majesty with

---

1 *Sayyids* (or *siyyids*) are descendants of the Prophet Muḥammad.

2 *Musulmán* is a Persian form of *Muslim*.

3 E. G. Browne, *Materials for the Study of the Bábí Religion*, pp. 260–262.

> which He spoke confounded me; I am convinced He is the promised Qá'im and I am fed up and disgusted with all the accusations and sneers with which His followers are afflicted.[1]

Aḥmad, the recipient of the celebrated **Tablet of Aḥmad** from Bahá'u'lláh, narrated:

> His beautiful face and His powerful Words and presence sufficed all things. But when they served tea and a cup was offered to the Báb, He immediately took it, called the servant of the same Mullá and very graciously gave it to him.[2]

The Báb also wrote: *"This is a youth of fair-complexion, black-eyed, with fine eyebrows, beautiful arms and shoulders whose dignity is like that of the prophets of the old."*[3]

In brief, all the above reports, either from native Persians or from foreigners, whether believers or not, depict the mild and dignified person of the Báb.

First intimations of the station of the Báb

In some of His writings, the Báb affirms that **the first intimations of His divine station** took place before adulthood:

> *Verily God hath inspired Thee with divine verses and wisdom while still a child and hath graciously deigned to bestow His favor upon the peoples of the world through the influence of Thy Most Great Name, for indeed men have not the least knowledge of the Book.*[4]

> *Verily, God hath taught Thee the Book and the Wisdom* (*Ḥikmah*) *in Thy childhood, and shown favor unto the people of the earth by virtue of Thy Most Great Name.*[5]

In another of His Writings, He maps out **the timeline of His life**.

> *Thou art aware, O My God, that since the day Thou didst call Me into being out of the water of Thy love till I reached fifteen years of age I lived in the land which witnessed My birth* [Shíráz]. *Then Thou didst enable Me to go to the seaport* [Búshihr] *where for five years I was engaged in trading with the goodly gifts of Thy realm and was occupied in that with which Thou hast favored Me through the wondrous essence of Thy loving-kindness. I proceeded therefrom to the Holy Land* [Karbilá] *where I sojourned for one year. Then I returned to the place of My birth. There I experienced the revelation of Thy sublime bestowals and the evidences of Thy boundless*

---

1 Cited in Houri Faláhi-Skuce, *A Radiant Gem*, p.172.

2 Naysan and Zohre Faizi, *Penned by A. Q. Faizi*, p. 52.

3 Mohammadhosseini, "The Commentary on the Sura of Joseph", p. 9.

4 The Báb, *Selections*, p. 64.

5 The Báb in Nader Saiedi, *Gate of the Heart*, p. 144.

> *grace. I yield Thee praise for all Thy goodly gifts and I render Thee thanksgiving for all Thy bounties.*[1]

In 1843 a significant event occurred in the life of the Báb—He received His **first divine epiphany**:

> *God beareth Me witness, I was not a man of learning, for I was trained as a merchant. In the year sixty* [CE 1843–1844] *God graciously infused my soul with the conclusive evidences and weighty knowledge which characterize Him Who is the Testimony of God—may peace be upon Him—until finally in that year I proclaimed God's hidden Cause and unveiled its well-guarded Pillar, in such wise that no one could refute it.*[2]

Such an auspicious event could be compared to Jesus Christ's prophetic anointment through a dove addressing Him at His baptism by John: "This is my beloved Son, with whom I am well pleased" (Matthew 3:17). The utterances of the Angel Gabriel to Muḥammad, then illiterate, while in a cave at Mount Hira, are also reminiscent of such prophetic events: "Read! in the name of your Lord who created man from a clinging substance" (Qur'án 96:1–5). Similarly, Bahá'u'lláh received the first intimation of His divine mission while enchained in the Síyáh-Chál ("black pit") of Tehran, when beheld a celestial Maiden announcing to Him: "*Verily, We shall render Thee victorious by Thyself and by Thy pen ....*"[3]

According to the Báb:

> *The spirit of prayer which animates My soul is the direct consequence of a dream which I had in the year before the declaration of My Mission. In My vision I saw the head of the Imám Ḥusayn* [Muḥammad's martyred grandson] ... *which was hanging upon a tree. Drops of blood dripped profusely from His lacerated throat. With feelings of unsurpassed delight, I approached that tree and, stretching forth My hands, gathered a few drops of that sacred blood, and drank them devoutly. When I awoke, I felt that the Spirit of God had permeated and taken possession of My soul. My heart was thrilled with the joy of His Divine presence, and the mysteries of His Revelation were unfolded before My eyes in all their glory.*[4]

As to the *date of the first intimation* of His prophetic mission, the Báb remarked:

> *In truth, the first day that the spirit descended in the heart of this servant was the fifteenth of the month of Rabí'u'l-Avval* [4 April 1844].[5]

On another occasion the Báb wrote on the same theme:

---

1 The Báb, *Selections*, pp. 180–181.
2 The Báb, *Selections*, p. 12.
3 The Báb in Shoghi Effendi. *God Passes By*, p. 101.
4 The Báb in Nabíl-i-A'ẓam, *The Dawn-Breakers*, p. 253.
5 Fereydun Vahman, "The Báb", p. 23.

> *Remember! The emanation of all these verses and prayers and all these unlearned sciences is because of a dream which I once had of the holy head of the Lord of Martyrs, upon him be peace, detached from his holy body, together with the heads of other companions. I drank seven handfuls of his holy blood with greatest joy, and it is now the blessing of that blood which illumined my heart with such verses and prayers.*[1]

The nature of the Revelation of the Báb

In His Epistle to Muḥammad Sháh, the Báb sheds light on the nature of His revelation:

> *Naught is seen in Me in the station of My heart save God alone, which is the manifestation of Lordship from God, My Lord and My Fashioner.Naught is witnessed in the station of My spirit, the indivisible substantive Intellect ... but Muḥammad, the Apostle of God .... That which thou observeth in the station of My soul is naught but all the thirteen Sacred Manifestations ..., nor canst thou perceive in the station of My body aught but the station of the dust for the realization of the three stations of fire, air, and water ....*[2]

The Revelation of the Báb can be understood in the light of the **two divine stations** conferred on each Manifestation to which we referred earlier. The first station of "*essential unity*" is the position where God speaks directly through the Manifestation since the Manifestation perfectly reflects the attributes of God, and the second station, that of "*distinction*",[3] is where each Manifestation is associated with a specific revelation. The Báb Himself declares in the Bayán:

> *He is the possessor of two signs, that of God and that of creation, and through the latter he worshippeth God and boweth in adoration before Him. In like manner, all things adore their Beloved through the sign of Creation, though it hath never reached, nor will it ever reach, beyond its own sign from God, which is present within it and pointeth unto Him.*[4]

As with the first position, we found that in various instances the Writings of the Báb portray the Voice of God in the first person:

> *He, verily, is the One Who, under all conditions, proclaimeth: 'I, in very truth, am God!'*[5]
>
> *I am He that liveth in the Abhá Realm of Glory.*[6]

---

1 The Báb in Abbas Amanat, *Resurrection and Renewal*, p. 131.
2 The Báb in Nader Saiedi, *Gate of the Heart*, p. 103.
3 Bahá'u'lláh, *The Kitáb-i-Íqán*, p. 176.
4 The Báb in Nader Saiedi, *Gate of the Heart*, p. 46.
5 The Báb, Persian Bayán; cited in *Epistle to the Son of the Wolf*, pp. 142–143.
6 The Báb in Nader Saiedi, *Gate of the Heart*, p. 351.

> *Verily, I am God and there is none other God but Me, the Lord of all things. Verily, all else other than Me is My creation. Therefore, O My creation, adore Me alone!*[1]

The Báb affirms that **He was the Voice of God** speaking to Moses on Mount Sinai, because the Primal Will is sempiternal ("eternal and unchanging; everlasting") and exists in each Manifestation.[2] The Báb as the "*Focal Point of God's Primal Will*"[3] was the spirit that talked to Moses from a fire or burning bush on Mount Sinai[4] (Exodus 3:2–22): "I am the God of thy father, the God of Abraham, the God of Isaac, and the God of Jacob." (Exodus 3:6) In several paragraphs[5] the Báb refers to His presence in this supernatural transfiguration scene as the "*Flame of that supernal Light that glowed upon Sinai in the gladsome Spot and lay concealed in the midst of the Burning Bush.*"[6]

> *O ye that circle the throne of glory! Hearken unto My Call which is raised from the midst of the Burning Bush, "Verily I am God and there is none other God but Me. Hence worship Me, and for the sake of Him Who is the Most Great Remembrance [The Báb], offer ye prayers, purged from the insinuations of the people, for verily your Lord, the One true God, is none other than the Sovereign Truth."*[7]

> *Indeed We conversed with Moses by the leave of God from the midst of the Burning Bush in the Sinai and revealed an infinitesimal glimmer of Thy Light upon the Mystic Mount and its dwellers, whereupon the Mount shook to its foundations and was crushed into dust ....*[8]

The Báb also defines His essence as *transcending eternity:*

> *He is the First, yet not defined as such, and He is the Last, but not described as such. He is the Seen, and not praised as such, and He is Hidden, and not recognized as such.*[9]

Moreover, given the principle of essential unity among the Manifestations of God in the light of the Primal Will, the Báb declares:

> *Verily I have attained the Day of the First Manifestation and by the bidding of the Lord and as a token of His grace, I shall attain the Day of the Latter*

---

1 The Báb in Nader Saiedi, *Gate of the Heart*, p. 42.
2 See Stephen Lambden, "The Sinaitic Mysteries", pp. 65–184.
3 The Báb, *Selections*, p. 105.
4 See Stephen Lambden, "The Sinaitic Mysteries", pp. 65–184.
5 See Stephen Lambden, "The Sinaitic Mysteries", pp. 65–184.
6 The Báb, *Selections*, p. 74.
7 The Báb, *Selections*, p. 69.
8 The Báb, *Selections*, p. 72.
9 The Báb in Nader Saiedi, *Gate of the Heart*, p. 270.

Manifestation. There is no God but Him and at the appointed hour everyone shall bow down unto Him in adoration.[1]

Regarding the station of Divine Revelation, the Báb describes how God fashioned Him to occupy such an exalted position of Prophethood. Speaking in God's voice He said:

> *I have fashioned all created things for Thy sake, and I have, by virtue of My Will, set Thee sovereign Ruler over all mankind. Moreover, I have decreed that whoso embraceth My religion shall believe in My unity, and I have linked this belief with remembrance of Thee, and after Thee the remembrance of such as Thou hast, by My leave, caused to be the "Letters of the Living",*[2] *and of whatever hath been revealed from My religion in the Bayán. This, indeed, is what will enable the sincere among My servants to gain admittance into the celestial Paradise.*
>
> *Verily, the sun is but a token from My presence so that the true believers among My servants may discern in its rising the dawning of every Dispensation.*
>
> *In truth I have created Thee through Thyself, then at My Own behest I have fashioned all things through the creative power of Thy Word. We are All-Powerful. I have appointed Thee to be the Beginning and the End, the Seen and the Hidden. Verily We are the All-Knowing.*
>
> *No one hath been or will ever be invested with prophethood other than Thee, nor hath any sacred Book been or will be revealed unto anyone except Thee. Such is the decree ordained by Him Who is the All-Encompassing, the Best-Beloved.*[3]

The Báb also proclaims Himself as **God's Representative on earth** invested with supreme authority:

> *Point to Thy truthful breast through the power of truth and exclaim: I swear by the One true God, herein lieth the vicegerency of God; I am indeed the One Who is regarded as the Best Reward and I am indeed He Who is the Most Excellent Abode.*[4]

---

1 The Báb, *Selections*, p. 10.

2 The "Letters of the Living" were the first 18 believers in the Báb. See *Dawn-Breakers*, pp. 80–82. In the Persian Bayán, they are referred to as: *"All of these formed the name of the Living One, for these are the names that are the nearest to God; the others are guided by their clear and significant actions, for God began the creation of the Bayán through them, and it is to them that the creation of the Bayán will again return. They are the lights which in the past have eternally prostrated themselves and will prostrate themselves eternally in the future, before the celestial throne."* (Périgord, *Translation of French Foot-Notes*, pp. 14–15).

3 The Báb, *Selections*, pp. 158–159.

4 The Báb, *Selections*, p. 66.

Are ye in doubt concerning the Báb? Verily He is the One Who holdeth, by Our leave, the kingdoms of earth and heaven in His grasp, and the Lord is in truth fully aware of what ye are doing ....[1]

Author Mangol Bayat stated that the Báb declared that all created beings and things belong exclusively to God, for God is the Creator, and thereby the sole owner of heaven and earth. Since God, the Báb argued, created all and everything for the sake of the Prophet, who is the Manifestation of God, and whose existence sustains the universe, the Manifestation is thereby the "master of all things". As a divine being, the One who manifests the Will of God ranks higher than all reigning monarchs, all 'ulamá', and above all the wealthy and the mighty.[2]

At the same time, the Báb expresses as a human being His feelings of **utter nothingness** in relation to God's designs for Him:

Verily, that which We sprinkled upon thee out of the ocean of Names and Attributes is due to the sweet melodies of This Bird, Who hath first soared in the air of the Supreme Cloud of Subtlety and then warbled in the inner depths of these allusions; thereby it shone forth and was manifest, circled around and revolved, rose up and stood upright ... sighed and bemoaned, cried and wept, then fell with anguish upon the earth, trembling like unto a fish out of water, proclaiming the words of His Lord, as permitted by God: O My God! I plead My grief solely unto Thee. Ennoble My Cause, and fulfill that which Thou hast promised Me ....[3]

The **weight of the mantle of revelation** upon His shoulders is a theme that very often appears in the Writings of the Báb:

God had, in truth, proposed Our Mission unto the heavens and the earth and the mountains, but they refused to bear it and were afraid thereof. However, Man, this 'Alí, Who is none other but the Great Remembrance of God, undertook to bear it.[4]

The spiritual substance of the Báb in mystical terms

The Báb expresses the mystical nature of His own being with these words addressed to Himself in which He adopts a numinal feminine figure associated with the Holy Spirit:

O Qurratu'l-'Ayn![5] *Let the Maid of Heaven, the inmate of the Exalted Paradise, drape Herself in a coarse vesture and put on a veil of the most beautiful silk. Then let Her step out of Her mansion, appearing by Herself, upon the earth, in the beauty of the black-eyed damsel. Let Her listen to the sweet praise out of Thy holy breaths upon the Seat of the Throne and in the celestial spheres, that haply those intoxicated and bewildered amongst the*

1 The Báb, *Selections*, p. 73.
2 Mangol Bayat, *Mysticism and dissent*, p. 104.
3 The Báb in Nader Saiedi, *Gate of the Heart*, p. 80.
4 The Báb, *Selections*, p. 70.
5 *Qurratu'l-'Ayn* ("Solace of the Eyes") is one of the titles of the Báb.

dwellers on earth may be awakened by Thy Cause, to an extent less than a single hair from the back of Her head, as ordained by God. God verily knoweth all things ....

O People of the earth! By the righteousness of the One true God, I am the Maid of Heaven begotten by the Spirit of Bahá, abiding within the Mansion hewn out of a mass of ruby, tender and vibrant; and in this mighty Paradise naught have I ever witnessed save that which proclaimeth the Remembrance of God by extolling the virtues of this Arabian Youth. Verily there is none other God but your Lord, the All-Merciful. Magnify ye, then, His station, for behold, He is poised in the midmost heart of the All-Highest Paradise as the embodiment of the [glorification] (tasbíl) *of God in the Tabernacle wherein* [exaltation of His unity] (tahlíl) *is intoned ....*

O Qurratu'l-'Ayn! Permit Her to divest Herself of Her coarse robe, put on the garment She donneth in Her reserved Chamber. For verily the dwellers of heaven have wailed out of their yearning for Her hair, arrayed (malfúl) *beneath Her veil. God is verily merciful unto His believing servants.*

Return, O Thou Immortal Maid of Heaven, unto the holy Sanctuary within Thy Mansion. Thou wouldst receive Thy reward solely from Me, written down, verily, by Mine own hand in this Book through a single letter of My Command that hath been inscribed around the Fire.[1]

In the Revelation of the Báb we found a marvellous case of divine emanation with fresh teachings. We also reviewed the effect that the Báb had, before and during His ministry, upon those who met Him and recognized Him as a unique Personage with a distinctive light. Despite being held captive during most of His prophetic life, the Primal Point attracted the attention of the whole country and beyond within a relatively brief period of time.

People were attracted to the tolerance and universality of His teachings, and to the elevated character of His ethical code and exhortations, which revealed both His full humanity and His divinity. With a discourse focused on higher and elevated concepts, couched in a most eloquent style, the Writings of the Báb awoke and captivated a nation submerged in lethargy and obscurity.

1 The Báb in Nader Saiedi, *Gate of the Heart*, pp. 153–154.

5
Verses of the Báb

The Revelation of the Báb offered the gift of salvation to all humanity: His verses *"are a light unto those who believe in them and a fire of afflictive torment for those who turn away and reject them."*[1] He refers to His writings as *"the new or wondrous verses"* (*al-áyát al-badí'a*).[2]

The verses of the Báb were revealed in a beautiful and melodious chant characterized by some witnesses as the "gentle intonation of His voice", "the soft and gentle murmur of His voice", and the "magic of His voice".[3]

The following themes are covered in this chapter:

- Verses, signs and miracles
- The abundance of His Revelation
- The Writings of the Báb

Verses, signs and miracles

Undoubtedly, as the bearer of such a weighty undertaking, the Báb had been granted **a knowledge that only came from God**. Bahá'u'lláh states:

> *God, verily, hath deigned to bestow upon the Point of the Bayán a hidden and preserved Knowledge, the like of which God hath not sent down prior to this Revelation. More precious is it than any other knowledge in the estimation of God—glorified be He! He, verily, hath made it His testimony, even as He hath made the verses to be His testimony.*[4]

The Báb was also **granted full authority to disseminate His teachings**:

> *Verily God hath granted leave to His Remembrance to say whatsoever He willeth in whatever manner He pleaseth. Indeed whatsoever He chooseth is none other than what is chosen by Us. The Lord, in truth, witnesseth all things.*[5]

Regarding the Báb, **His divine verses are the most powerful proof** of His revelation and He condemns the request for miracles.[6] According to Mírzá Abu'l-Faḍl the terms **divine verse, sign** and **miracle** can be simultaneously rendered by the same Arabic word *áyah* or *áyat* (plural, *áyát*).[7] Hence, a divine verse can

---

1 The Báb, *Selections*, p. 163.
2 Mohammadhosseini, "The Commentary on the Sura of Joseph", p. 15.
3 Nabíl-i-A'ẓam, *The Dawn-Breakers*, p. 61, 175, 202.
4 Bahá'u'lláh, *Epistle to the Son of the Wolf*, p. 175.
5 The Báb, *Selections*, p. 72.
6 See the Báb, Selections, pp. 119–120.
7 Mírzá Abu'l-Faḍl, *Miracles and Metaphors*, pp. 99–198.

also be interpreted as a miracle or sign of God. For example, in His Will and Testament, 'Abdu'l-Bahá designated Shoghi Effendi as the "*sign of God* [*Áyatu'lláh*], *the Chosen Branch,* [and] *the Guardian of the Cause of God.*"[1]

In Islam, the claim to be a revealer of divine verses could be made only by the Prophet. "Muslims were very sensitive to any claim to be capable of revealing divine verses," wrote Ruhu'llah Mehrabkhani:

> No one could claim that verses (*núzúl-i-áyát*) had been revealed to him subsequent to the mission of the Prophet of Islám. They believe that áyát (verses) came only to the Prophet Muḥammad through the Angel Gabriel. The Prophet did not himself reveal verses but received them from God via Gabriel often having to wait months or even years before receiving them .... The Muslim notion of Divine Revelation is such that the áyát are considered to be the proof of the prophethood of Muḥammad.[2]

Moses prophesied: "I will raise up for them a prophet like you from among their brothers. And I will put my words in his mouth, and he shall speak to them all that I commend him" (Deut. 18:18–22). Jesus stated, "For he whom God has sent utters the words of God, for he gives the Spirit without measure" (John 3:34).

In this regard, the Báb wrote:

> *Verily We made the revelation of verses to be a testimony for Our message unto you. Can ye produce a single letter to match these verses? Bring forth, then, your proofs, if ye be of those who can discern the one true God. I solemnly affirm before God, should all men and spirits combine to compose the like of one chapter of this Book, they would surely fail, even though they were to assist one another.*[3]

> *Whoever seeks to prove the truth of the Point of the Bayán* [i.e. the Báb] *through anything but divine verses has veiled himself from the greatest proof and the noblest path ...*[4]

Moreover, the words of the Báb must be **obeyed without hesitation**:

> *Behold the one who calleth thee unto God. Should he* [the Báb] *possess an incontrovertible testimony from his Lord in such manner that none is able to produce the like thereof, his cause would then be proven to be true and there would be no doubt about it. Obey then his words and ask not why or wherefore .... Shouldst thou acknowledge his testimony thou wouldst have no place to flee to save to obey him, even if he calleth night day, poison sugar, false true, and knowledge ignorance.*[5]

---

1 'Abdu'l-Bahá, *The Will and Testament of 'Abdu'l-Bahá*, p. 11.

2 Ruhu'llah Mehrabkhani, "Some Notes on Fundamental Principles", pp. 22–43, esp. 29–35.

3 The Báb, *Selections*, p. 43.

4 Armin Eschraghi, "Undermining the Foundations of Orthodoxy", p. 228.

5 The Báb in Nader Saiedi, "Phenomenology of Occultation and Prayer", p. 212.

Consequently, the Báb abolished the formal Islamic emphasis on oral traditions known as *hadiths*. Islamic jurisprudence is formulated partly on the Qur'án and partly on the Sunna, i.e., the sayings and actions attributed to Muḥammad and His first descendants (the Imams) as narrated in the hadiths. The Báb asserts:

> *In the Qur'án nothing other than this proof has been revealed. Had they all understood this, it would have been easier for them, rather than to profess faith in God through matters they narrate themselves and for which there is no proof in the book of God (Persian Bayán, 6:8).*[1]

Verses revealed by the Manifestations of God are of such mystic calibre that they cannot be compared with texts written by ordinary human beings:

> *The evidence set forth by God can never be compared with the evidences produced by anyone of the peoples and kindreds of the earth; and beyond a shadow of doubt no evidence is set forth by God save through the One Who is appointed as His supreme Testimony. Moreover, the proof of revealed verses doth, alone and of itself, conclusively demonstrate the utter impotence of all created things on earth, for this is a proof which hath proceeded from God and shall endure until the Day of Resurrection.*[2]

Thus, the Báb dismisses any possibility of any individual or group writing comparable verses to His own revelation:

> *Say, O peoples of the earth! Were ye to assemble together in order to produce the like of a single letter of my works, ye would never be able to do so, and verily God is cognizant of all things ....*[3]

> *Were all the people that dwell on earth to assemble together, they would be unable to produce a single verse like unto the ones which God hath caused to stream forth from the tongue of the Point of the Bayán.*[4]

God has ordained the Writings of the Báb to be "*His matchless testimony for all created things*",[5] and "*if any living creature were to pause to meditate he would undoubtedly realize that these verses are not the work of man, but are solely to be ascribed unto God.*"[6]

The teachings of the Prophets are the most conclusive evidence of their truth. In the Bible, the disciples of Jesus tell Him: "Now we can see that you know all things and that you do not even need to have anyone ask you questions. This makes us believe that you came from God" (John 16:30). In the Bayán, the Báb

---

1 Armin Eschraghi, "Undermining the Foundations of Orthodoxy", p. 228.
2 The Báb, *Selections*, p. 109.
3 The Báb, *Selections*, p. 58.
4 The Báb, *Selections*, pp. 104–105.
5 The Báb, *Selections*, p. 104.
6 The Báb, *Selections*, p. 105.

cites the Qur'án to prove that the teachings of a Prophet, rather than miracles, are themselves a proof of His divine mission:

> *Concerning the sufficiency of the Book as a proof, God hath revealed: 'Is it not enough for them that We have sent down unto Thee the Book to be recited to them? In this verily is a mercy and a warning to those who believe.'* [Qur'án 29:50] *When God hath testified that the Book is a sufficient testimony, as is affirmed in the text, how can one dispute this truth by saying that the Book in itself is not a conclusive proof?*[1]

Further, referring to the period of 1,270 years between Muḥammad and the Báb when no divine revelation took place, it is written in the *Persian* Bayán:

> *Had human beings been able to accomplish this deed surely someone would have brought forth at least one verse during the period of twelve hundred and seventy years which hath elapsed since the revelation of the Qur'án until that of the Bayán. However, all men have proved themselves impotent and have utterly failed to do so, although they endeavored, with their vehement might, to quench the flame of the Word of God.*[2]

According to the Báb, not only were those who claimed the capacity to produce similar verses "*powerless to bring forth proofs similar*"[3] to that which God had revealed through His Manifestations, but "*God hath wiped out all those who have opposed Them from the beginning that hath no beginning until the present day and hath conclusively demonstrated the Truth through the power of Truth.*"[4] Divinely revealed verses are divine by nature and therefore **acquired human knowledge cannot match them**:

> *Indeed, were all the inhabitants of heaven and earth and whatever existeth between them to assemble together, they would utterly fail and be powerless to produce such a book, even though We made them masters of eloquence and learning on earth.*[5]

The abundance of His Revelation

When, on 22 May 1844, the Báb declared His mission for the first time to a religious student named Mullá Ḥusayn,[6] He was still 24 years old according to His own assertion.[7] His father died when the Báb was very young and He was raised by His oldest maternal uncle. As a child and young adult, the Báb developed an expertise in calligraphy, which was a highly valued art for His cultural milieu at the time. He also attended classes in Islamic religious themes and Arabic

1 The Báb, *Selections*, p. 82.
2 The Báb, *Selections*, p. 105.
3 The Báb, *Selections*, p. 131.
4 The Báb, *Selections*, p. 132.
5 The Báb, *Selections*, p. 35.
6 Nabíl-i-A'ẓam, *The Dawn-Breakers*, pp. 47–97.
7 See the Báb, *Selections*, p. 109.

language. Like many of the children of that generation and social stratum, the education provided was elementary. In His words:

> *I swear on my own soul that I did not read a word of the conventional sciences, and in the past there were no books of sciences with me whose words I have memorized, and there is no reason for this divine gift but God's generosity and his benevolence. Today if someone asks me of various scholarly matters cited in books, I swear to God that I do not know the answer, and I do not even know the grammar and syntax, and I am proud of it, since God in the Day of Resurrection will prove to all that I was assisted by his generosity.*[1]

Despite being "*devoid of those sciences wherein all are learned*",[2] the Báb claims that He

> *... reciteth verses after such fashion without thought or hesitation, writes a thousand verses of prayer in the course of five hours without pause of the pen, and produceth commentaries and learned treatises on such lofty themes as the true understanding of God and of the oneness of His Being, in a manner which doctors and philosophers confess surpasseth their power of understanding, then there is no doubt that all that hath been manifested is divinely inspired.*[3]

The **youthfulness** of the Báb was a constant cause of criticism from His enemies. In His words, they believed "*How strange then that this twenty-five-year-old untutored one should be singled out to reveal His verses in so astounding a manner.*"[4]

'Abdu'l-Bahá says,

> *Among the Shí'ih* [Shí'yún] *it is universally acknowledged that He never studied in any school, nor acquired learning from any teacher. To this the people of Shíráz, each and all, bear witness. Nevertheless, He suddenly appeared before the people, endowed with consummate knowledge, and though but a merchant, confounded all the divines of Persia.*[5]

According to what was revealed to Muḥammad, no one could produce a book comparable to the Qur'án itself (Qur'án 11:13, 2:23), hence the Báb was accused of heresy. Yet, even the most complex Islamic theological questions submitted to the Báb received a brilliant elucidation, and this without Him having received any formal religious instruction, and **out of pure inspiration.**[6] When the Sháh of Iran commissioned Siyyid Yaḥyá Dárabí, entitled Vaḥíd, "the most learned, the most

1 The Báb in Abbas Amanat, "The Shaping of the Babi Community", p. 117.
2 The Báb, *Selections*, p. 109.
3 The Báb, *Selections*, p. 109.
4 The Báb, *Selections*, p. 118.
5 'Abdu'l-Bahá, *Some Answered Questions*, p. 30.
6 Asadu'lláh Fáḍil, "The Life of the Báb".

eloquent, and the most influential of his subjects" to personally meet the Báb in order to investigate the validity of His divine claims, this high-ranking officer converted to the new Faith with no further hesitation at the third interview.[1]

Claiming the *abundance of His verses* as proof of His revelation, the Báb turned to the divines of those times who were arrogant because of their knowledge. *"Notwithstanding their life-long diligent study,"* He wrote, *"what pains do these divines take when writing a single line in Arabic! Yet after such efforts the result is but words which are unworthy of mention."*[2]

The Báb described the **rapidity with which He revealed verses** as *"a most glorious sign within the realm of miracles ... a daunting and highly perplexing matter, recognized by all as being impossible to attain by anyone save the One Whom God willeth."*[3] Further, the Báb remarks, *"the supreme honour is not in the mere composition of the outward appearance of the words, but in traversing the kingdom of Names and Attributes in less than the twinkling of an eye."*[4]

In describing how the Writings of the Báb were revealed, Mírzá Abu'l-Faḍl wrote, "Most of them He wrote in their presence, without pause or reflection, not even writing a rough copy first, as is customary with men of learning and literature .... They flowed from Him without any reflection."[5] The flow of revelation could have been even greater but for the limitations of the amanuensis:

> *He reciteth verses at a speed consonant with the capacity of His amanuensis to set them down. Thus, it may well be considered that if from the inception of this Revelation until now He had been left unhindered, how vast then would have been the volume of writings disseminated from His pen.*[6]

Rumours circulated among the populace that the Báb "could handle his pen with amazing speed—to such a degree that when he would take hold of a corner of the paper he would cover it so rapidly with script that when he got to the end of the page the first part of it was not yet dry."[7] It is interesting to know that the Báb "was so affected by the intensity of revelation that for many days He did not partake of any food; His only means of subsistence was a little tea."[8]

In one passage the Báb **claimed to be able to reveal the equivalent of the Qur'án in five days and nights**. In another passage He claimed He could achieve this in two days and two nights. By comparison, the Qur'án comprising 6,346 verses was revealed over a period of twenty-three years while the *New*

---

1 Nabíl-i-A'ẓam, *The Dawn-Breakers*, p. 171.
2 The Báb, *Selections*, p. 109.
3 The Báb in Nader Saiedi, *Gate of the Heart*, p. 75.
4 The Báb in Nader Saiedi, *Gate of the Heart*, p. 75.
5 Mírzá Abu'l-Faḍl, *Bahá'í Proofs*, pp. 30–42.
6 The Báb, *Selections*, p. 82.
7 Ustád Muḥammad-'Alíy-i-Salmání. *My Memories of Bahá'u'lláh*, p. 4.
8 Ma'ani & Ewing, *Laws of the Kitáb-i-Aqdas*, p. 60.

Testament, which consists of nearly 8,000 verses, was compiled from the works of nine authors. The Báb states that He completed a book of prayers within six hours and was able to write a thousand verses of prayer within the space of five hours without halting His pen. The Báb claims that when He is able to produce

> *... commentaries and learned treatises on such lofty themes as the true understanding of God and of the oneness of His Being, in a manner which doctors and philosophers confess surpasseth their power of understanding, then there is no doubt that all that hath been manifested is divinely inspired.*[1]

In the Bayán (1847–1848) it is written that ... *"He hath, up to the present, revealed no less than five hundred thousand verses on different subjects ..."*[2] and that "*... no less than a hundred thousand verses similar to these have already been disseminated among the people, not to mention His epistles, His prayers or His learned and philosophical treatises.*"[3] Many of His writings were lost or went into private hands. Some others were stolen as Nabíl the historian related:

> One day, when the Báb had dismounted close to a well in order to offer His morning prayer, a roving Bedouin suddenly appeared on the horizon, drew near to Him, and, snatching the saddlebag that had been lying on the ground beside Him, and which contained His writings and papers, vanished into the unknown desert. His Ethiopian servant set out to pursue him, but was prevented by his Master, who, as He was praying, motioned to him with His hand to give up his pursuit. "Had I allowed you," the Báb later on affectionately assured him, "you would surely have overtaken and punished him. But this was not to be. The papers and writings which that bag contained are destined to reach, through the instrumentality of this Arab, such places as we could never have succeeded in attaining. Grieve not, therefore, at his action, for this was decreed by God, the Ordainer, the Almighty."[4]

The Writings of the Báb

Although much of His Writings have been lost over time, it is estimated that the extant Writings of the Báb total **5 million words**. Much of this has not been translated into English.[5] Five million words would typically fill 20,000 printed pages—equivalent to more than six Bibles. The Appendix lists the best-known works of the Báb.

In 2013 the Universal House of Justice stated that "... over 2,000 unique works [of the Báb] have been identified. Most of these Writings have been collected; however, 74 are known to have been revealed, but the texts are not available.

1 The Báb, *Selections*, p. 109.
2 The Báb, *Selections*, p. 97.
3 The Báb, *Selections*, pp. 81–82.
4 Nabíl-i-A'ẓam, *The Dawn-Breakers*, p. 132.
5 Steven Phelps, *A Partial Inventory*, p. 2.

Nearly 1,600 of the collected works have been authenticated."[1] According to Stephen Phelps, "Over 90% of the works of the Báb, well over half of the works of Bahá'u'lláh, and one third of the works of 'Abdu'l-Bahá are in Arabic; the remainder are in Persian or a mixture of the two."[2]

"The books of the Báb have not as yet been printed in the original," Shoghi Effendi's secretary wrote on his behalf in 1941. "Except for the *Bayán*, the *Seven Proofs* [Dalá'il-i-Sab'ih], and *Commentary on the Surih of Joseph* [Qayyúmu'l-Asmá'], we cannot be sure of the authenticity of most of His other works as the text has been corrupted by the unfaithful."[3] Added to this is the difficulty in translating the Writings of the Báb due to the complexity of His written language in both Persian and Arabic, the vocabulary and the context of the verses, innovative and challenging grammatical forms, as well as the many abstruse and cryptic expressions therein. "The style of the Báb's writings is new," two Arabic scholars wrote, "and can't be compared with the standards of style of the people in the past."[4] In general, the collection, cataloguing, authentication and translation of the Writings of the Báb is one of the main lines of the action being pursued at the Centre for the Study of the Texts, at the Bahá'í World Centre.

The Revelation of the Báb is unique in the annals of religious history as regards His prolific written production. Here is a Prophet Who wrote most of His time, perhaps due to his long periods of captivity in Shíráz, Iṣfahán, Máh-Kú, and Chihríq. Quantitatively speaking, as outlined above, the number of verses revealed by the Báb far exceed the sum total of what has been attributed to Moses, Jesus and Muḥammad. As printing houses were still developing in Iran in the first half of the nineteenth century, and those establishments were more concerned with the publication of Islamic texts, the only dissemination possible for the Writings of the Báb was through hand-copying of manuscripts from believer to believer—and this could only be done clandestinely. Nevertheless, through His Writings, the Báb reached the masses of Iran in the shortest period possible, even during His imprisonment in the mountains. At one time, the Báb required the support of more than one amanuensis to record His inexhaustible flow of revelation and constantly feed the stream of divine literature.

Time was too short to prepare the people for the advent of *Him Whom God shall make Manifest.* Although much of the Báb's revelation was couched in a highly complex and unique style of Arabic, to reach out to the masses, the Báb also wrote in Persian, the indigenous language of Iran. This was in contrast to the conventional practice amongst the Muslim elite, whose texts were published only in Arabic and only for the use of their educated peers. The Báb redefined religious

---

1 *The Universal House of Justice.* Letter 6 June 2013 to an individual believer. Last retrieved 30 September 2021 https://Bahái-library.com/uhj_numbers_sacred_writings.

2 Steven Phelps, *A Partial Inventory of the Works*, p. 2.

3 Shoghi Effendi, *Messages of Shoghi Effendi to the Indian Subcontinent*, p. 210.

4 Behmardi & McCants, "A Stylistic Analysis of the Báb's Writings", p. 114.

literature by using visual information to represent complex theological concepts through pentagrams (*Hayakils*) and circular tables (*dawa'irs*).[1] Further, the writing style of the Báb reached the human heart, and it can be characterized as conversational and "shaped in the form of a discourse with the amanuensis", with the "frequent use of the intimate second person singular [thou]."[2] The Báb also maintained an active correspondence with a range of enquirers about the new Faith. In all of the above mentioned, we can recognize the objective of the Báb to democratise religious literature and make it accessible to the broader population despite the onslaughts of persecution.

The literature of the Báb is notable for its eloquence, an attribute that the Báb Himself highlights in relation to His written revelation:[3] *"Verily the ordinances of God concerning all things were formerly set forth in eloquent Arabic."*[4] The Báb wrote in various styles. According to the Persian Bayán (6:1), His writings can be classified into five categories. The first four types of compositions were written in Arabic in the form of (a) divine verses; (b) prayers, supplications and devotions; (c) interpretations and commentaries; and (d) scientific treatises, rational discourses and scriptural divisions.[5] The fifth mode comprises His texts and writings in the Persian language, which in turn can be categorized according to the four mentioned modes referred to above.[6]

The written Revelation of the Báb constituted the **standard of belief** for all mankind during the Dispensation of the Báb, which started on 23 May 1844 with His Declaration to Mullá Ḥusayn, and ended with the public declaration of Bahá'u'lláh at Riḍván in 1863.

According to the Báb, the written Book of a Manifestation of God is the "Silent Book" (Kitáb-i-Ṣámit) while, during His earthly life, the Manifestation of God is the "Speaking Book" (Kitáb-i-Náṭiq) or "Living Book".[7] The Báb describes His Writings thus:

> *This is the divinely-inscribed Book. This is the outspread Tablet. Say, this indeed is the Frequented Fane, the sweet-scented Leaf, the Tree of divine Revelation, the surging Ocean, the Utterance which lay concealed, the Light above every light. ... Indeed every light is generated by God through the power of His behest. He of a truth is the Light in the kingdom of heaven and earth and whatever is between them. Through the radiance of His light God*

1 Denis MacEoin, *Rituals in Babism and Baha'ism*, p. 22.

2 Amanat, "The Persian Bayan and the Shaping of the Babi Renewal", p. 343.

3 Behmardi & McCants, "A Stylistic Analysis of the Báb's Writings", p. 118.

4 The Báb, *Selections*, p. 24.

5 See Elham Afnan, "A Twofold Mission".

6 See Stephen Lambden, "From a Primal Point to an Archetypical Book".

7 See the Báb, Persian Bayán, 2:3; *Selections from the Writings of E. G. Browne* p. 328; and Bahá'u'lláh *The Kitáb-i-Aqdas*, pp. 67 & 81, and Note 155, p. 231. There will be more on this topic in Chapter 15.

imparteth illumination to your hearts and maketh firm your steps, that perchance ye may yield praise unto Him.

Say, this of a certainty is the Garden of Repose, the loftiest Point of adoration, the Tree beyond which there is no passing, the blessed Lote-Tree, the Most Mighty Sign, the most beauteous Countenance and the most comely Face.[1]

1 The Báb, *Selections*, pp. 154–155.

6
Qayyúmu'l-Asmá and the Persian Bayán

This chapter discusses two of the most important works of the Báb, the Qayyúmu'l-Asmá ("The Self-Subsisting Lord of All Names") and the Persian Bayán.

The revelation of the Qayyúmu'l-Asmá began on the night of the Declaration of the Báb, and the revelation of the Persian Bayán occurred during the exile of the Báb in the Máh-Kú fortress (located in the north western Zagros Mountains). The former was revealed in Arabic whereas the latter was written in Persian. The Qayyúmu'l-Asmá is considered to be the Qur'án of the Bábís[1] while the Persian Bayán is regarded as the Mother Book of the Dispensation of the Báb.[2] The Qayyúmu'l-Asmá was characterized by Bahá'u'lláh as *"the first, the greatest, and mightiest of all books"*[3] while the Persian Bayán was referred to as "Peerless among the doctrinal works [of the Báb] ...."[4]

Qayyúmu'l-Asmá'

The Qayyúmu'l-Asmá is also called the Commentary on the Surah of Joseph. It consists of 111 chapters each of which comprises 42 verses. The book is a re-interpretation by the Báb of the story of Joseph, an important chapter (Súra 12 Yúsuf, 111 verses) of the Qur'án entitled the "Best of the Stories" (from Qur'án 12:3) as well as a narrative from the Bible (Genesis chapters 37–50).

The first of those chapters was revealed on the same night that the Báb declared His mission in May 1844 to Mullá Ḥusayn, the first believer. The Surah of Joseph, also known as *The Self-Subsisting Lord of All Names*, provides a profound explanation of the symbolic mystical meaning of the story of Joseph. Joseph, the son of Jacob, was sold by his brothers as a slave but eventually became Egypt's highest-ranking officer or magistrate. Later the brothers met Joseph while trading in Egypt. When recognized by him, the brothers were forgiven rather than punished, and this was followed by Joseph's reunion with his father, Jacob. 'Abdu'l-Bahá linked the Joseph of the Qayyúmu'l-Asmá to Bahá'u'lláh:

> *Since in His commentary on the Súrih of Joseph, the Báb—may my life be offered up for His sake—hath identified Joseph as the Manifest Beauty, the true Joseph, and hath referred to Him as "our great and omnipotent Master," then whenever thou readest it, thou wilt but weep and grieve for the wrongs suffered by the Blessed Beauty. This commentary is not currently at hand for me to send to thee.*[5]

---

1 Shoghi Effendi, *God Passes By*, p. 23.
2 See Bahá'u'lláh, *The Kitáb-i-Aqdas*, p. 213.
3 Baha'u'lláh in Shoghi Effendi, *God Passes By*, p. 23.
4 Shoghi Effendi, *God Passes By*, p. 24.
5 'Abdu'l-Bahá, *Light of the World*, p. 145.

Mullá Ḥusayn recounted how the Báb revealed the first chapter to him in a private meeting on the night of 23 May 1844:

> He took up His pen, and with incredible rapidity revealed the entire Súrih of Mulk, the first chapter of His commentary on the Súrih of Joseph. The overpowering effect of the manner in which He wrote was heightened by the gentle intonation of His voice which accompanied His writing. Not for one moment did He interrupt the flow of the verses which streamed from His pen. Not once did He pause till the Súrih of Mulk was finished. I sat enraptured by the magic of His voice and the sweeping force of His revelation.[1]

According to the Báb, the Qayyúmu'l-Asmá was completed in forty days. Only a few hand-written copies of the Qayyúmu'l-Asmá have survived for posterity, some of which are kept at the Bahá'í World Centre.[2] Regarding its dissemination, the Báb remarked:

> *The Commentary on the Súrih of Joseph had, in the first year of this Revelation, been widely distributed. Nevertheless, when the people realized that fellow supporters were not forthcoming they hesitated to accept it; while it never occurred to them that the very Qur'án whereunto unnumbered souls bear fealty today, was revealed in the midmost heart of the Arab world, yet to outward seeming for no less than seven years no one acknowledged its truth except the Commander of the Faithful [Imám 'Alí]*[3]*—may the peace of God rest upon him—who, in response to the conclusive proofs advanced by God's supreme Testimony, recognized the Truth and did not fix his eyes on others. Thus on the Day of Resurrection God will ask everyone of his understanding and not of his following in the footsteps of others.*[4]

Shoghi Effendi has described the Qayyúmu'l-Asmá as:

> ... the celebrated commentary on the súrih of Joseph, entitled the *Qayyúmu'l-Asmá*, whose fundamental purpose was to forecast what the true Joseph (Bahá'u'lláh) would, in a succeeding Dispensation, endure at the hands of one who was at once His arch-enemy and blood brother. This work, comprising above nine thousand three hundred verses, and divided into one hundred and eleven chapters, each chapter a commentary on one verse of the above-mentioned súrih, opens with the Báb's clarion-call and dire warnings addressed to the "concourse of kings and of the sons of kings"; forecasts the doom of Muḥammad Sháh; commands his Grand Vizír,[5] Ḥájí Mírzá Áqásí, to abdicate his authority; admonishes the entire Muslim ecclesiastical order; cautions more specifically the members of the

---

1 Nabíl-i-A'ẓam, *The Dawn-Breakers*, p. 61.

2 Todd Lawson, *Gnostic apocalypse and Islam*, pp. 30–31.

3 'Alí was the cousin and son-in-law of Muḥammad, is considered to be the first believer, and he was the first Imám.

4 The Báb, *Selections*, p. 90.

5 Ṣadr-i-A'ẓam or prime minister.

Shí'a community; extols the virtues, and anticipates the coming, of Bahá'u'lláh, the "Remnant of God," the "Most Great Master;" and proclaims, in unequivocal language, the independence and universality of the Bábí Revelation, unveils its import, and affirms the inevitable triumph of its Author. It, moreover, directs the "people of the West" to "issue forth from your cities and aid the Cause of God;" warns the peoples of the earth of the "terrible, the most grievous vengeance of God;" threatens the whole Islamic world with "the Most Great Fire" were they to turn aside from the newly-revealed Law; foreshadows the Author's martyrdom; eulogizes the high station ordained for the people of Bahá, the "Companions of the crimson-colored ruby Ark;" prophesies the fading out and utter obliteration of some of the greatest luminaries in the firmament of the Bábí Dispensation; and even predicts "afflictive torment," in both the "Day of Our Return" and in "the world which is to come," for the usurpers of the Imamate, who "waged war against Ḥusayn (Imám Ḥusayn)[1] in the Land of the Euphrates [Iraq]."[2]

The following are some key extracts from the Writings of the Báb identifying the importance of the Qayyúmu'l-Asmá as *"a shining light for all mankind."*[3] The Qayyúmu'l-Asmá:

- **follows the holy books from all religions**: O concourse of the people of the Book! *Fear ye God and pride not yourselves in your learning. Follow ye the Book which His Remembrance hath revealed in praise of God,* the True One. He Who is the Eternal Truth beareth me *witness,* whoso followeth this Book hath indeed followed all the past Scriptures which have been sent down from heaven by God, the Sovereign Truth. Verily, He is well informed of what ye do ....[4]
- **is the Remembrance of God**: This book is the Remembrance of God that, in truth, is revealed unto the Most Great Word for the entire world.[5]
- **was revealed in a special language**: This Book We have, verily, revealed in the language of Our Remembrance and it is in truth a wondrous language.[6]
- **should be recited frequently**: Recite ye as much as convenient from this Qur'án both at morn and at eventide, and chant the verses of this Book, by the leave of the eternal God, in the sweet accents of this Bird which warbleth its melody in the vault of heaven.[7]

1 Prophet Muḥammad's grandson who was killed in Karbilá in CE 860.
2 Shoghi Effendi, *God Passes By*, p. 23.
3 The Báb, *Selections*, p. 41.
4 The Báb, *Selections*, p. 44.
5 The Báb in Nader Saiedi, *Gate of the Heart*, p. 141.
6 The Báb, *Selections*, p. 45.
7 The Báb, *Selections*, pp. 55–56.

- **should be recited in the month of Ramaḍán:**[1] O Concourse of Light! Hearken unto My Call in this Sacred Month: this verily is "the month of Ramaḍán, in which the Qur'án was revealed."...*Whoso glorifieth the Month of God and His Book, which is revealed in very truth to proclaim My truth and the Mighty Truth, and reciteth during that month a single letter thereof, shall assuredly receive the blessings of the All-Merciful, His angels, and those endued with knowledge amongst His servants.*[2]
- **is the Utterance of the Power of God**: This is the Utterance of the Power of God (Dhikr), that appeareth through the Most Great Word (Kalimah), this Youth, Whom the faithful call in truth by the name 'Alí. ... We have verily revealed this Book unto the Most Great Word and ordained Him, in truth, to be the Midmost Point in the realm of justice.[3]
- **is divinely inspired**: We have, of a truth, sent down this divinely inspired Book unto Our Servant. ... Ask ye then Him Who is Our Remembrance of its interpretation, inasmuch as He, as divinely ordained and through the grace of God, is invested with the knowledge of its verses...[4]

  O concourse of light! By the righteousness of God, We speak not according to selfish desire, nor hath a single letter of this Book been revealed save by the leave of God, the Sovereign Truth. Fear ye God and entertain no doubts regarding His Cause, for verily, the Mystery of this Gate is shrouded in the mystic utterances of His Writ and hath been written beyond the impenetrable veil of concealment by the hand of God, the Lord of the visible and the invisible.[5]
- **is free from error:** O people of the city! Ye have disbelieved your Lord. If ye are truly faithful to Muḥammad, the Apostle of God and the Seal of the Prophets, and if ye follow His Book, the Qur'án, which is free from error, then here is the like of it—this Book, which We have, in truth and by the leave of God, sent down unto Our Servant. If ye fail to believe in Him, then your faith in Muḥammad and His Book which was revealed in the past will indeed be treated as false in the estimation of God. If ye deny Him, the fact of your having denied Muḥammad and His Book will, in very truth and with absolute certainty, become evident unto yourselves.[6]
- **is Proof for East and West:** O peoples of the earth! By the righteousness of God, this Book hath, through the potency of the sovereign Truth, pervaded the earth and the heaven with the mighty Word of God concerning Him Who is the supreme Testimony, the Expected Qá'im, and

---

1 Ramaḍán is the fasting month in the Islamic world.
2 The Báb in Nader Saiedi, *Gate of the Heart*, p. 125.
3 The Báb in Nader Saiedi, *Gate of the Heart*, p. 140.
4 The Báb, *Selections*, pp. 44–45.
5 The Báb, *Selections*, p. 57.
6 The Báb, *Selections*, p. 46.

verily God hath knowledge of all things. This divinely inspired Book hath firmly established His Proof for all those who are in the East and in the West, hence beware lest ye utter aught but the truth regarding God, for I swear by your Lord that this supreme Proof of Mine beareth witness unto all things ....[1]

- **Is God's proof similar to one given to Muḥammad**: This Book which We have sent down is indeed abounding in blessings and beareth witness to the Truth, so that the people may realize that the conclusive Proof of God in favor of His Remembrance is similar to the one wherewith Muḥammad, the Seal of the Prophets, was invested, and verily great is the Cause as ordained in the Mother Book.[2]
- **is the straight Path of God**: O concourse of the faithful! Incline your ears to My Voice, proclaimed by this Remembrance of God. Verily God hath revealed unto Me that the Path of the Remembrance which is set forth by Me is, in very truth, the straight Path of God, and that whoever professeth any religion other than this upright Faith, will, when called to account on the Day of Judgment, discover that as recorded in the Book no benefit hath he reaped out of God's Religion ....[3]
- **Is an honour upon Persia (Iran):** O people of Persia! Are ye not satisfied with this glorious honor which the supreme Remembrance of God hath conferred upon you? Verily ye have been especially favored by God through this mighty Word.[4]

Persian Bayán

The Persian Bayán is another outstanding work by the Báb which has been characterized as the "epitome"[5] of His teachings and as "the most weighty, the most illuminating and comprehensive of all His works."[6] In this book the Báb categorically proclaimed Himself as the *Qá'im* ("He Who will arise"), the Promised One of the Islamic Faith.[7]

It was written between 1847 and 1848 during His imprisonment in the Máh-Kú fortress. Shoghi Effendi, strongly highlighted the significance of the Persian Bayán:

> Peerless among the doctrinal works of the Founder of the Bábí Dispensation; consisting of nine Váḥids (Unities) of nineteen chapters each, except the last Váḥid comprising only ten chapters; not to be confounded with the smaller and less weighty Arabic Bayán, revealed during the same period; fulfilling the Islamic prophecy that "a Youth from

1 The Báb, *Selections*, pp. 59–60.
2 The Báb, *Selections*, pp. 70–71.
3 The Báb, *Selections*, p. 63.
4 The Báb, *Selections*, p. 153.
5 Muḥammad Afnán, "The Báb's Bayán".
6 Nabíl-i-A'ẓam, *The Dawn-Breakers*, pp. 248.
7 The Báb, *Persian* Bayán 1:15.

Baní-Háshim ... will reveal a new Book and promulgate a new Law;" wholly safeguarded from the interpolation and corruption which has been the fate of so many of the Báb's lesser works, this Book, of about eight thousand verses, occupying a pivotal position in Bábí literature, should be regarded primarily as a eulogy of the Promised One rather than a code of laws and ordinances designed to be a permanent guide to future generations.[1]

The word Bayán can be translated from Arabic as "clear proof, indisputable evidence". In *God Passes By*, Shoghi Effendi rendered "Bayán" as "Exposition".[2] Other English terms for the word Bayán are "Revelation", "Explanation",[3] "Utterance"[4] and "Clarification".[5] The term Bayán refers to both the Persian Bayán and the Arabic Bayán.[6] The Arabic Bayán can be considered a condensed version of the Persian Bayán paralleling many of the themes and structure of the latter book. The Persian Bayán was dictated by the Báb as it was being revealed to his secretary Siyyid Ḥusayn and an original is kept at the Bahá'í World Centre.

The Báb stated His Bayán is the "*Word of the Point of Truth*"[7] and "*Our conclusive testimony unto all things.*"[8] The Báb also stated the term Bayán ("Exposition") is one of God's names:

> *... the first Who called Himself by the name Bayán was God, glorified and exalted be He, as He hath revealed, "I verily am God, there is none other God but Me, the One, the Bayán."*[9]

The Bayán is described as containing "*the sum total of all the Scriptures, whether of the past or of the future*"[10] and its teachings are the source of human knowledge:

> *Should myriads of men of learning, versed in logic, in the science of grammar, in law, in jurisprudence and the like, turn away from the Book of God, they would still be pronounced unbelievers.*[11]

The Bayán is the standard measure amongst mankind:

> *The Bayán shall constitute God's unerring balance till the Day of Resurrection which is the Day of Him Whom God will make manifest. Whoso acteth in conformity with that which is revealed therein will abide in*

1 Shoghi Effendi, *God Passes By*, p. 25.
2 Shoghi Effendi, *God Passes By*, p. 25.
3 Amanat, "The Persian Bayan and the Shaping of the Babi Renewal", p. 338.
4 Muḥammad Afnán, "The Báb's Bayán".
5 Behmardi & McCants, "A Stylistic Analysis of the Báb's Writings", p. 116.
6 Mojan Momen, "*Selections from the Writings of E. G. Browne*", p. 317.
7 The Báb in Nader Saiedi, *Gate of the Heart*, p. 240.
8 The Báb in Nader Saiedi, *Gate of the Heart*, p. 284.
9 The Báb in Nader Saiedi, *Gate of the Heart*, p. 263.
10 The Báb, *Selections*, p. 159.
11 The Báb, *Selections*, p. 104.

> *Paradise, under the shadow of His affirmation and reckoned among the most sublime Letters in the presence of God; while whoso deviateth, were it even so much as the tip of a grain of barley, will be consigned to the fire and will be assembled neath the shadow of negation. This truth hath likewise been laid bare in the Qur'án where in numerous instances God hath set down that whoever should pass judgment contrary to the bounds fixed by Him, would be deemed an infidel ....*[1]

Bahá'u'lláh refers to the *Kitáb-i-Aqdas*, the **Mother Book of the Bahá'í Dispensation,** as the "*unerring Balance*":

> *Say: O leaders of religion! Weigh not the Book of God with such standards and sciences as are current amongst you, for the Book itself is the unerring Balance established amongst men. In this most perfect Balance whatsoever the peoples and kindreds of the earth possess must be weighed, while the measure of its weight should be tested according to its own standard, did ye but know it.*[2]

The Báb states "*... shouldst thou hearken unto the verses of the Bayán and acknowledge its truth, only then would the revealed verses of God profit thee.*"[3] The depth of the Bayán is fathomless:

> *For should all the oceans in the heavens and on the earth turn into ink, all the beings into pens, and all the souls into those who inscribe, they would be incapable of interpreting even a single letter of the Bayán, inasmuch as God hath destined neither a beginning nor an end for any letter thereof.*[4]

The Báb instructs His followers to read the Bayán in the context of His earlier and later writings:

> *Say! Gain ye certitude in that which God hath revealed in the Bayán, for understanding the Bayán is dependent on understanding the totality of its revelation from beginning to end. For that which was revealed first is based upon the Qur'ánic laws; only later were the true measures of the Dispensation of the Bayán manifested. Neither be ye shrouded from the later writings by the earlier writings, nor fix your eyes merely on the later writings and ignore the earlier ones. ... Yet, the later the revelation of the writings, the more manifest is the divine intention therein.*[5]

The Báb affirms the uniqueness of the verses of the Bayán as God's "*matchless testimony for all created things.*"[6] He further remarks that, "*Were all the people that dwell on earth to assemble together, they would be unable to produce a single*

---

1 The Báb, *Selections*, p. 102.
2 Bahá'u'lláh, *The Kitáb-i-Aqdas*, para. 99, p. 56.
3 The Báb, *Selections*, pp. 80–81.
4 The Báb in Nader Saiedi, *Gate of the Heart*, p. 290.
5 The Báb in Nader Saiedi, *Gate of the Heart*, p. 290.
6 The Báb, *Selections*, p. 104.

verse like unto the ones which God hath caused to stream forth from the tongue of the Point of the Bayán."[1]

The Báb also states that the verses of the Bayán offer a divine proof equivalent to a miracle:

> *On this, that he who adduceth any proof other than the Book of God and the verses of the Bayán, other than the powerlessness of all to produce their like, is veiled from any proof. He who recounteth any miracle, other than the verses, is veiled from any truth. He who claimeth to reveal divine verses should not be opposed by anyone.*[2]

Bahá'u'lláh explained the authority the Báb had to change the laws from previous dispensations:

> *God hath in that Book* [the Bayán], *and by His behest, decreed as lawful whatsoever He hath pleased to decree, and hath, through the power of His sovereign might, forbidden whatsoever He elected to forbid.*[3]

According to Shoghi Effendi, the Bayán "at once abrogated the laws and ceremonials enjoined by the Qur'án regarding prayer, fasting, marriage, divorce and inheritance."[4] As a new Revelation of God, these laws replaced and abrogated those of the previous dispensations particularly on religious observances. In the Persian Bayán 3:16, the Báb wrote:

> *It is not permissible to engage in religious acts save those ordained in the Writings of the Point of the Bayán, for in this Dispensation the writings of the Letters of the Living all proceed directly from the Sun of Truth Himself.*[5]

The Persian and Arabic Bayán were translated into French by A. L. M. Nicolas at the beginning of the twentieth century.[6] A selection of passages from the Persian Bayán was published by the Universal House of Justice in a compilation entitled *Selection from the Writings of the Báb* in 1976.[7] 'Abdu'l-Bahá instructed that the publication of the *Kitáb-i-Aqdas* must precede the publications of the Bayán so that people of the world do not think that Bahá'ís follow the latter.[8] The Bayán, as with many of the Writings of the Báb, is a difficult text to translate, requiring expertise across various disciplines, because some of its passages are

1 The Báb, *Selections*, pp. 104–105.

2 The Báb in Nader Saiedi, *Gate of the Heart*, p. 370.

3 Bahá'u'lláh, *Gleanings from the Writings of Bahá'u'lláh*, p. 149.

4 Shoghi Effendi, *God Passes By*, p. 25.

5 Saiedi, Nader. *Modernity in the Writings of the Báb*. Last retrieved 30 September 2021 at https://user-hrqc9mo.cld.bz/Modernity-in-the-Writings-of-the-Báb/1 (page 4)

6 A. L. M. Nicolas, *Le Beyan Arabe*, and *Le Béyan Persan*.

7 The Báb, *Selections*.

8 Ishráq Khávári, *Má'ida-yi Ásmání*, vol 2, p. 16–7; & Denis MacEoin, *The Sources for Early Bábí Doctrine and History*.

highly symbolic and abstruse, with multiple meanings, and were written in a language structure, religious and cultural background, prevalent in the first half of the nineteenth century.[1]

The Bayán and Him Whom God shall make manifest

He/Him Whom God shall make Manifest (from the Arabic من يظهره الله, *Man Yuẓhiruhu'lláh*), mentioned repeatedly in the Writings of the Báb is a reference to Bahá'u'lláh. Chapters 15 & 16 of the present book are devoted to *Him Whom God shall make Manifest* revealing the absolute servitude of the Báb to Him:

> *Cause this Tree then to be made into a magnificent Scroll to be offered to the presence of Him Whom Thou wilt make manifest on the Day of Judgement, that He may graciously allow the entire company of the followers of the Bayán to be restored to life and that He may, through His bounty, inaugurate a new creation.*[2]

> *Abandon me not to myself, O my Lord, nor deprive me of recognizing Him Who is the Manifestation of Thine Own Self, nor account me with such as have turned away from Thy holy presence ....*[3]

The central theme of the Bayán is *He Whom God shall make manifest.* Writing about the Bayán, Bahá'u'lláh said: *"God is My witness that the Bayán was sent down for no other purpose than to celebrate My praise, did ye but know. In it the pure in heart will find only the fragrance of My love, only My Name that overshadoweth all that seeth and is seen."*[4]

Shoghi Effendi referred to the Bayán as "that monumental repository of the laws and precepts of the new Dispensation ...."[5] He also stated the Bayán is "the treasury enshrining most of the Báb's references and tributes to, as well as His warnings regarding, '*Him Whom God will make manifest*'".

The Báb mentions *Him Whom God shall make Manifest* more than seventy times in the Bayán.[6] The words of the Báb Himself testify to this central theme, "Nothing has the Bayán in view, save *Him Whom God shall make Manifest.*"[7] The Báb also stated:

> *It is only for the glorification of His Name [Him Whom God will make manifest] and the exaltation of His Cause that We have enunciated certain laws at Our behest, or forbidden the acts to which We are averse, so that at*

---

1 Behmardi & McCants, "A Stylistic Analysis of the Báb's Writings", p. 114.

2 The Báb, *Selections,* p. 172.

3 The Báb, *Selections,* p. 216.

4 Bahá'u'lláh, *The Kitáb-i-Aqdas*, para. 179, pp. 84–85.

5 Shoghi Effendi, *God Passes By,* pp 24–25.

6 Moshe Sharon, *Notes and Observations*, p. 4.

7 Hasan Balyuzi, *Edward Granville Browne and the Bahá'í Faith*, p. 84.

> *the hour of His manifestation ye may attain through Him the good-pleasure of God and abstain from the things that are abhorrent unto Him.*[1]

The Bayán prescribes that "*At the time of the manifestation of Him Whom God shall make Manifest everyone should be well trained in the teachings of the Bayán ....*[2]

Regarding *Him Whom God shall make Manifest* the Báb wrote that the "*Bayán is, from beginning to end, the repository of all of His attributes, and the treasury of both His fire and His light*";[3] and that "[*t*]*he Bayán and whosoever is therein revolve round the saying of 'Him Whom God will make manifest'.*"[4] Also, the Báb said that "*every letter revealed in the Bayán is solely intended to evoke submission unto Him Whom God shall make Manifest, for it is He Who hath revealed the Bayán prior to His Own manifestation*"[5] and that "*the Bayán and such as bear allegiance to it are but a present from me unto Thee* [*Him Whom God shall make Manifest*]".[6] The Báb also wrote that Bahá'u'lláh would be the only person who would fully understand the Bayán: "*none shall encompass that which God hath revealed in the Bayán except Him Whom God shall make Manifest ....*"[7] He further declares:

> *For all that hath been exalted in the Bayán is but as a ring upon My hand, and I Myself am, verily, but a ring upon the hand of Him Whom God will make manifest—glorified be His mention! He turneth it as He pleaseth, for whatsoever He pleaseth, and through whatsoever He pleaseth.*[8]
>
> *I have written down in My mention of Him these gem-like words: "No allusion of Mine can allude unto Him, neither anything mentioned in the Bayán.*[9]

Further, the Báb states that the laws of the Bayán would end with the appearance of Bahá'u'lláh: "*The Bayán shall constitute God's unerring balance till the Day of Resurrection which is the Day of Him Whom God will make manifest*",[10] and "*none save Him hath ever elevated/abrogated, or will ever elevate/abrogate, this Book.*"[11] Hence, the Bayán guided the period between the Báb and Bahá'u'lláh:

---

1 The Báb, *Selections*, p. 149.
2 The Báb, *Selections*, p. 85.
3 The Báb, *Selections*, p. 101.
4 The Báb in Shoghi Effendi, *The World Order of Bahá'u'lláh*, p. 100.
5 The Báb, *Selections*, p. 104.
6 The Báb, *Selections*, p. 7.
7 The Báb in Nader Saiedi, *Gate of the Heart*, p. 65.
8 The Báb, *Selections*, p. 168.
9 The Báb in Shoghi Effendi. *God Passes By*, p. 30.
10 The Báb, *Selections*, p. 102.
11 The Báb in Nader Saiedi, *Gate of the Heart*, p. 276.

> *And from the time of the setting of the Sun* [of the Báb] *until the Rising of the Sun of Him Whom God will make manifest, there will be no more binding Writings, and the Letters of the Living*[1] *and all the believers in God and in the Bayán will be under their* [the Writings of the Point of the Bayán] *shadow.*[2]

For the Báb, obeying the precepts of the Bayán is acting in accordance with the will of *Him Whom God shall make Manifest*:

> *Whoso acteth in conformity with that which is revealed therein will abide in Paradise, under the shadow of His affirmation and reckoned among the most sublime Letters in the presence of God; while whoso deviateth, were it even so much as the tip of a grain of barley, will be consigned to the fire and will be assembled neath the shadow of negation.*[3]

> *For in the Day of the Revelation of Him Whom God will make manifest, the Bayán will fix Its eyes upon Its believers while saying unto them: 'Is there any spirit related to Me who would step forth in this Day to acknowledge Him Whom God will make manifest, and thus be faithful to the covenant of his Lord that is established in Me?' It would rejoice if its faithful believers recognize its Revealer, and would be saddened if its faithful believers cause its Revealer any grief.*[4]

The Báb makes clear that the purpose of the Bayán is to train the Bábís "*so that none of the followers may outwardly cling to the Bayán and thus forfeit their allegiance unto Him. If anyone does so, the verdict of 'disbeliever in God' shall be passed upon him.*"[5] Therefore the Bayán contains many warnings to be vigilant so that no veils exist to hinder the recognition of the Manifestation to come:

> *O congregation of the Bayán, and all who are therein! Recognize ye the limits imposed upon you, for such a One as the Point of the Bayán Himself hath believed in Him Whom God will make manifest, before all things were created. Therein, verily, do I glory before all who are in the kingdom of heaven and earth. Suffer not yourselves to be shut out as by a veil from God after He hath revealed Himself.*[6]

The Báb encouraged the printing of the Bayán to enable everyone to know and remember *Him Whom God shall make Manifest* so that there would be no excuses for failing to recognize Him.[7]

---

1 The "Letters of the Living" were the first 18 believers in the Báb. See *Dawn-Breakers*, pp. 80–82.

2 The Báb in Nader Saiedi, *Gate of the Heart*, p. 347.

3 The Báb, *Selections*, p. 102.

4 The Báb in Nader Saiedi, *Gate of the Heart*, pp. 276–277.

5 The Báb, *Selections*, p. 85.

6 The Báb, *Selections*, p. 168.

7 The Báb, Persian Bayán 8:7.

Structure of the Bayán

Both the Persian Bayán and the Arabic Bayán were initially designed to include nineteen vahids (unities) of nineteen chapters each, called *gates* (*abwáb*), i.e. a total of 361 sections in each book. However, both the Persian and Arabic Bayán are unfinished. The Persian Bayán has only eight complete vahids (unities) and the ninth váḥid has only ten gates (*abwáb*). The Arabic Bayán has only eleven vuḥdán (pl. of váḥid, "unity").

That the two Bayáns were left incomplete about two years before the martyrdom of the Báb may have been intentional.[1] "The incompleteness of the Bayán," Nader Saiedi wrote, "eloquently attests that the dispensation of the Bayán was not like other typical religions with a long time span in which the details of its laws and commandments were to be institutionalized."[2] For some believers this interruption was a clear indication of the imminence of *Him Whom God shall make Manifest* as God never left a Revelation unfinished.[3]

According to Shoghi Effendi, "The Báb specified that the 'Bayán' is not complete and that '*He Whom God would manifest*' (Bahá'u'lláh) would complete it, though not in its actual form, but only spiritually in the form of another book. The 'Íqán [Kitáb-i-'Íqán][4] is believed to be its continuation."[5] The Kitáb-i-Íqán ("The Book of Certitude") was revealed by Bahá'u'lláh in Baghdád in 1861–1862, the year before the public declaration of His mission.[6]

The Writings of the Báb while incarcerated in Máh-Kú

Muḥammad Sháh, imagined that the oblivion, loneliness and humiliation of incarceration would quench the divine heart of the Báb. However, the flame burning in Shíráz was destined to shed its light from a mountain fortress in Máh-Kú. The light of the Faith of the Báb burned with the greatest intensity in that desolate region.

The confinement of the Báb in the Máh-Kú fortress lasted for nine months but proved to be one of the most prolific periods of His revelation. The outpouring of writings emanating from His pen was accompanied by intensification in the ardour of His adherents. This was manifest in events such as the Badasht Conference where old structures and laws were abolished, and new laws were proclaimed.[7]

The Dalá'il-i-Sab'ih ("The Seven Proofs")—"the most important of the polemical works of the Báb"[8]—was revealed during His confinement on the Máh-

---

1 Muḥammad Afnán, "The Báb's Bayán".

2 Nader Saiedi, *Logos and Civilization*, p. 127.

3 Hasan Balyuzi, *Eminent Bahá'ís*, p. 132.

4 Kitáb-i-Íqán written in Baghdád by Bahá'u'lláh in 1861/1862.

5 Shoghi Effendi, *Dawn of a New Day*, p. 78.

6 Shoghi Effendi, *God Passes By*, p. 138.

7 Nabíl-i-A'ẓam, *The Dawn-Breakers*, pp. 288–301.

8 Shoghi Effendi, *God Passes By*, p. 26.

Kú fortress. Here, too, was revealed the Tablet to Muḥammad Sháh, which is distinguished for the emphatic terms with which the sovereign was addressed and rebuked for having decreed the imprisonment of the Báb in Máh-Kú. In this Tablet, the monarch is made aware of the ephemeral nature of his power and is condemned for his pernicious use of that power. He is also informed of the wretched circumstances that the Messenger of God has endured as a result.

The town of Máh-Kú is dominated to the south and north by the peaks of the north western end of the Zagros mountain range. The Máh-Kú fortress is a little north of the town and it sits at the base of a high, overhanging cliff. Hence, it is impossible for the inhabitants of the fortress to observe a full moon. For this reason people say that Máh-Kú means "where is the moon?" The Báb called it "Jabal-i-Básiṭ" (meaning "Open Mountain"). Máh-Kú and Básiṭ share the same abjad value of 72. Of Máh-Kú the Báb wrote in the Bayán: *"He dwells in a mountain of which the inhabitants could not even pronounce the name 'Jannat' (Paradise) which is an Arabic word; how then could they understand its meaning? Imagine then what can happen in the matter of the essential truths!"*[1]

The castle fortress where the Báb was imprisoned was in a deplorable condition. According to architect/historian Dr Andreh Marouti, the fortress is about 500 years old. "The surviving ruins indicates the greatness of the building during its heyday," he also wrote. "These include high walls, various corridors, nested inner fences, carved stone terraces, and watchtowers made of carved stone materials."[2] The castle contained, many square rooms, together with several courtyards and platforms. Under the main floor there were vaults intended for storage. The doorway to the cell of the Báb had no door, nor was He provided with a lamp for light at night. Yet, this notwithstanding, the Báb referred to it as "the greatest of the gardens of Paradise" where the "Tree of Truth"[3] was planted.

From the fortress there was a path that led down to the village. The ruins of the fortress can still be seen at the base of the mountain cliff, a few hundred meters from the valley where the village of Máh-Kú was located.[4] Temperatures can reach as low as −23°C and it has been written by Nabíl the historian that "The water which the Báb used for His ablutions was of such icy coldness that its drops glistened as they froze upon His face."[5] The temperature range is such that in summer the temperature can soar to 37°C with heavy rainfall in spring.[6]

1 The Báb in Emily McBride Périgord, *Translation of French Foot-Notes*, p. 30.

2 Andreh Marouti, "Infrastructure for Trade Routes", p. 251.

3 Emily McBride Périgord, *Translation of French Foot-Notes*, p. 31.

4 The village has since spread up the hill towards the fortress and been absorbed into the large city of Mákú, which has spread along the mountain gorge of the Zangmár River. The city centre is 4 km to the west.

5 Nabíl-i-A'ẓam, *The Dawn-Breakers*, pp. 252.

6 *Wikipedia.* Maku, Iran. Last retrieved on 15 May 2022 from https://en.wikipedia.org/wiki/Maku,_Iran

The Báb reveals His grief and suffering living forsaken in the harsh mountains of Máh-Kú. "*For assuredly*," the Báb wrote, "*whatsoever God hath decreed for Me shall come to pass and naught else save that which God hath ordained for us shall ever touch us.*"[1]

> *In this mountain I have remained alone, and have come to such a pass that none of those gone before Me have suffered what I have suffered, nor any transgressor endured what I have endured!*[2]
>
> *How veiled are ye, O My creatures, ... who, without any right, have consigned Him unto a mountain [Máh-Kú], not one of whose inhabitants is worthy of mention.... With Him, which is with Me, there is no one except him who is one of the Letters of the Living of My Book. In His presence, which is My Presence, there is not at night even a lighted lamp! And yet, in places [of worship] which in varying degrees reach out unto Him, unnumbered lamps are shining! All that is on earth hath been created for Him, and all partake with delight of His benefits, and yet they are so veiled from Him as to refuse Him even a lamp!*[3]
>
> *How can I praise Thee, O Lord, for the evidences of Thy mighty splendor and for Thy wondrous sweet savors which Thou hast imparted to Me in this fortress, in such measure that nothing in the heavens or on the earth can compare with them? Thou hast watched over Me in the heart of this mountain where I am compassed by mountains on all sides. One hangeth above Me, others stand on My right and My left and yet another riseth in front of Me. Glory be unto Thee, no God is there but Thee. How often have I seen rocks from the mountain hurtling down upon Me, and Thou didst protect Me therefrom and preserved Me within the stronghold of Thy divine Unity.*[4]

The Persian Bayán was revealed upon the mountain of Máh-Kú (July 1847–10 April 1848). The Báb dictated the entire Persian Bayán to his amanuensis, one of the Letters of the Living, Siyyid Ḥusayn Yazdí. Some scholars[5] believe that while the majority of the Writing occurred in Máh-Kú, it was finished in His subsequent imprisonment in Chihríq (April 1848–June 1850).

The Writings of the Báb while incarcerated in Chihríq

Máh-Kú and Chihríq are both located in the mountains of Ádharbayján in the northwest of Persia.

The fortress of Chihríq is less than 1 km to the west of the village of Chihríq-i-Ulya and 19 km southeast of the Ottoman (now Turkey) border and was inhabited by Christian Armenians until twenty years before the Báb arrived. The adjacent

---

1 The Báb, *Selections*, p. 15.
2 The Báb, *Selections*, p. 16.
3 The Báb, *Selections*, p. 87.
4 The Báb, *Selections*, p. 183.
5 Nader Saiedi, *Gate of the Heart*, pp. 260–261.

village included an Armenian Church and cemetery. The fortress was built in pre-Islamic times, abandoned, and then used by Iranian forces fighting Russian invaders in 1911. It was later used during the Simko Shikak tribal Kurdish revolt (1918 to 1922) against the Qájárs and is now known as "Shimko Castle". According to Andreh Marouti the fortress was over 80 m high, "and its area was more than 12,000 m^2. It had twelve main towers and four towers inside the mansion of Yahya Khan Chehriqi [the fortress guardian]."[1]

The Báb spent two years (April 1848–June 1850) in Chihríq and named it the Grievous Mountain. Chihríq and the word "Shadíd" ("grievous") have the same abjad value of 318. A number of important works were revealed there, such as the Kitáb-i-Asmá' ("Book of Divine Names") and the Kitáb-i-Panj Sha'n ("The Book of Five Modes or Grades"). The latter was one of the last of His books in which He categorically identifies *Him Whom shall make manifest* with Bahá'u'lláh: *"Do ye know Bahá'u'lláh or not? For He is the glory of Him Whom shall make manifest."*[2]

In July 1850, M. Mochenin, a Russian travelling agent passed by Chihríq and reported seeing the Báb with the following words: "I saw the Bala-Khanih [upper house] from the heights of which the Báb taught his doctrine. The multitude of hearers was so great that the court was not large enough to hold them all; most of them stayed in the streets and listened with religious rapture to the verses of the new Qur'án."[3] In 1944, Shoghi Effendi announced that part of the village of Chihríq-i-Ulya ("Upper" Chihríq) had been purchased[4] and in 1954 he announced that advanced negotiations were in progress to acquire the castle itself.[5]

Ádharbayján, literally the "Land of Fire guardians" in old Persian, refers to the Zoroastrians who are famous for their constancy in tending the sacred fire in their temples. Their Prophet Zarathustra (Zoroaster) is among a company of other now unknown prophets in the Qur'án in which His followers are referred to as "those who dwelt at Rass". According to 'Abdu'l-Bahá, this signifies the Araxes River in Qafqaz, (the Caucasus). The region is also mentioned in Islamic traditions as "Kuh-i-Qaf' (Mount Qaf).[6]

The fact that Ádharbayján is implied in Islamic traditions as a place of prophecy is corroborated by the Báb:

> *What must needs befall us in Ádhirbayján is inevitable and without parallel. When this happeneth, rest ye in your homes and remain patient as we have*

1 Marouti, "Infrastructure for Trade Routes", p. 252.

2 The Báb in Adib Taherzadeh, *The Covenant of Bahá'u'lláh*, p. 44.

3 Moojan Momen, *The Bábí and Bahá'í Religions*, p. 75.

4 *Bahá'í News*, No. 169, July 1944, p. 2. Last retrieved 15 September 2022 at https://bahai.works/index.php?title=File:Baha%27i_News_169.pdf&page=2

5 *Bahá'í News*, No. 58, November 1954. Last retrieved 30 June 2022 at https://bahai.works/File:Canadian_Bahai_News_58.pdf

6 Qur'án, 25:40 & 50:12. See 'Abdu'l-Bahá, Additional Tablets, Extracts and Talks, p. 19.

remained patient. As soon as the Mover moveth make ye haste to attain unto Him, even though ye have to crawl over the snow.[1]

The Revelation of the Báb was vast. The Qayyúmu'l-Asmá' was a central book for the Bábís because it contained a broad and substantial exposition of the teachings of the Báb at an earlier stage of His mission. For this reason the Qayyúmu'l-Asmá' was considered as the Qur'án of the followers of the Báb.

The Persian Bayán was the main repository of the doctrines of the Báb, and is referred to by Shoghi Effendi as the Mother Book of the Bábí Dispensation. No previous revelation had ever had such a strong focus on the next Messenger of God. In the Persian Bayán and several other books, the Báb penned innumerable passages pertaining to the advent of *Him Whom God shall make Manifest,* "His Beloved".[2] The majority of the Writings of the Báb attest to His devotion to Bahá'u'lláh, for Whom the Báb sacrificed His life in 1850.

1 The Báb, *Selections*, pp. 16–17.

2 Shoghi Effendi, *The World Order of Bahá'u'lláh*, pp. 125–126.

7
The Faith of the Báb

The Faith of the blessed Báb was stupendous and brilliant in its magnificence. Its grandeur is best depicted by the remarks pronounced by Bahá'u'lláh, 'Abdul-Bahá and Shoghi Effendi, situating the Bábí Faith at the pinnacle and end of the six-thousand year prophetic cycle commenced by Adam.

Eminent scholars across three centuries have written extensively of the significance of the Bábí Faith for humanity. Prophetic references from past Holy Books also indicate the potency of His dispensation.

The purpose and significance of the Bábí Faith is considered in this chapter in the light of the twofold mission of the Báb as an independent Messenger of God, bringing a new Revelation to mankind; and, simultaneously, as the Harbinger of the coming of Bahá'u'lláh. Having been divinely entrusted with these two commissions within a short six-year ministry meant that the Báb lived a life of extreme intensity, and revealed His teachings with an astonishing degree of rapidity and abundance. "We behold," wrote Shoghi Effendi, "as we survey the episodes of this first act of a sublime drama, the figure of its Master Hero, the Báb, arise meteor-like above the horizon of Shíráz, traverse the sombre sky of Persia from south to north, decline with tragic swiftness, and perish in a blaze of glory."[1]

The following are the main themes of this chapter:

- The purpose of the Faith of the Báb
- The act of conversion
- The greatness of the Revelation of the Báb according to:

- Bahá'u'lláh
- 'Abdu'l-Bahá
- Shoghi Effendi

The purpose of the Faith of the Báb

In the *Qayyúmu'l-Asmá* the Báb calls His Faith "*a new Cause*", "*the Wondrous Cause*" (*al-Amr al-Badí'*), the "*Wondrous Truth*" (*al-Ḥaqq al-Badí'*), the "*pure religion*" (*al-dín al-khális*)[2] and "*a new* [Prophetic] *creation*" (*khalq-i-badí'*).[3]

Primarily, the Báb declared that He had revealed Himself for the advent of Bahá'u'lláh:

---

1 Shoghi Effendi, *God Passes By*, p. 3.

2 Stephen Lambden, "From a Primal Point to an Archetypical Book", p. 152.

3 Amanat, "The Persian Bayan and the Shaping of the Babi Renewal", p. 337.

> *I have revealed Myself for His Manifestation, and have caused My Book, the Bayán, to descend upon you for no other purpose except to establish the truth of His Cause.*[1]

The Báb also says that the purpose of His Faith is to "*purge and purify you from uncleanliness in anticipation of the Day of the One true God*"[2] and His "*verses, clear and conclusive, are a token of the mercy of thy Lord and a source of guidance for all mankind.*"[3] The Báb was chosen by God "*to warn the people, to guide the believers aright and to elucidate the secrets of the Book*"[4] and had "*appeared in the midmost heart of Islám.*"[5]

In unequivocal terms, the Báb declares to Muḥammad Sháh the purpose of His advent:

> *I swear by God, the Peerless, the Incomparable, the True One: for no other reason hath He—the supreme Testimony of God—invested Me with clear signs and tokens than that all men may be enabled to submit to His Cause.*
>
> *... All the keys of heaven God hath chosen to place on My right hand, and all the keys of hell on My left ....*[6]

About His Faith He further declares:

> *Verily this is the true Faith of God, and sufficient witness are God and such as are endowed with the knowledge of the Book. This is indeed the eternal Truth which God, the Ancient of Days, hath revealed unto His omnipotent Word—He Who hath been raised up from the midst of the Burning Bush. This is the Mystery which hath been hidden from all that are in heaven and on earth, and in this wondrous Revelation it hath, in very truth, been set forth in the Mother Book by the hand of God, the Exalted ....*[7]
>
> *Verily We have taken a covenant from every created thing upon its coming into being concerning the Remembrance of God, and there shall be none to avert the binding command of God for the purification of mankind, as ordained in the Book which is written by the hand of the Báb.*[8]

The Báb did not fully declare His mission at the beginning because of the limited understanding of the people at that time. He said, "*... I did not wish My identity to be known by men, and gave instructions that My name should be concealed, because I was fully aware of the incapacity of this people ....*"[9] In

1 Bahá'u'lláh, *Gleanings*, p. 147.
2 The Báb, *Selections*, p. 62.
3 The Báb, *Selections*, p. 163.
4 The Báb, *Selections*, p. 67.
5 The Báb, *Selections*, p. 108.
6 The Báb, *Selections*, p. 12.
7 The Báb, *Selections*, p. 41.
8 The Báb, *Selections*, p. 65.
9 The Báb, *Selections*, p. 121.

declaring His station to the Letters of the Living[1] in May 1844 He guided them to refrain from informing others of His identity. That same year He went on pilgrimage to Mecca to make a public declaration of His station in the very heart of the Islamic world. However, the Báb had intimated about His station in previous Writings and given an indication of being the *Qá'im* to a few believers such as 'Azím.[2]

All the Prophets of God initially concealed Their stations. For example, in the early days, Christ "commanded his disciples not to tell anyone that He was the Christ." (Matthew, 16:20) He was only publicly announced and greeted with "Hosanna! Blessed is he who comes in the name of the Lord" (Mark 11:9) when He entered Jerusalem. Bahá'u'lláh, likewise, only manifested His mission in Baghdád between 21 April and 2 May 1863, after concealing the Divine Message from the eyes of men for nearly ten years.

When the mission of the Báb became publicly known, He began addressing all the people of the earth in passages such as this:

> *Verily, on the First Day We flung open the gates of Paradise unto all the peoples of the world, and exclaimed: "O all ye created things! Strive to gain admittance into Paradise, since ye have, during all your lives, held fast unto virtuous deeds in order to attain unto it." Surely all men yearn to enter therein, but alas, they are unable to do so by reason of that which their hands have wrought.*[3]

The Báb indicates that it is within His power to coerce the whole world to His Cause:

> *Should it be Our wish, it is in Our power to compel, through the agency of but one letter of Our Revelation, the world and all that is therein to recognize, in less than the twinkling of an eye, the truth of Our Cause ....*[4]

Yet, even if men were compelled to accept the Cause of the Báb, it does not mean that they would be united in its vision, except through the mercy of God (see Qur'án 11:120):

> *Had it been Our wish, We would have brought all men into one fold round Our Remembrance, yet they will not cease to differ* [Qur'án 11:120], *unless God accomplish what He willeth through the power of truth.*[5]

Nevertheless, the Báb claimed that His power of conversion had no limits:

---

1 The first eighteen disciples of the Báb. Eventually, the Báb declared Himself a Letter of the Living becoming all together the Váḥid (unit) of the Bayán.

2 Fereydun Vahman, *The Báb: A Sun in a Night not Followed by Dawn*, p. 58.

3 The Báb, *Selections*, p. 145.

4 The Báb, *Selections*, p. 168.

5 The Báb, *Selections*, p. 67.

> *I have committed Myself into the hands of God. My trust is in Him. Such is the power which He has bestowed upon Me that if it be My wish, I can convert these very stones into gems of inestimable value, and can instil into the heart of the most wicked criminal the loftiest conceptions of uprightness and duty.*[1]

The act of conversion

The Báb prayed that, eventually, the whole world would embrace His Faith showing the universal character of His revelation. "*O Lord! Enable all the peoples of the earth to gain admittance into the Paradise of Thy Faith,*" the Báb wrote, "*so that no created being may remain beyond the bounds of Thy good-pleasure.*"[2]

For the Báb, "*... the essence of religion is none other than submission unto this Remembrance.*"[3] He compares the believers with the non-believers: The former are referred to as "*those endowed with the eyes of the spirit*" who "*circle like moths round the Light of Truth until they are consumed*",[4] and will "*receive those musk-scented breaths which I have nursed in the midmost heart of My throne.*"[5] The latter are described as those whose "*hearts are deprived of the power of true insight, and thus they cannot see.*"[6] Yet, all are obliged to recognize Him as the new Manifestation of God:

> *Verily in this Day all that dwell on earth are the servants of God. As to those who truly believe in God and are well assured in the signs revealed by Him, perchance He will graciously forgive them the things their hands have committed, and will grant them admission into the precincts of His mercy. He, in truth, is the Ever-Forgiving, the Compassionate. But the verdict of divine chastisement is pronounced against those who have turned away disdainfully from Me and have repudiated the conclusive proofs and the unerring Book with which God hath invested Me, and on the Day of Severing they shall find no protector or helper.*[7]

The relationship between the believer and the Manifestation of God is like that of a mirror reflecting the sun. "*Gaze not upon this Word,*" says the Báb, "*except as thou beholdest the sun in the heaven, and perceive not him who believeth in Him save as thou lookest at the mirror ....*"[8] Elaborating on this analogy He says:

> *How beloved it hath been, and continueth to be, before God that in each Revelation pure mirrors will reflect the Tree of Truth. But the mirrors are not illumined by themselves, independent of the Primal Will, for had they been radiant by themselves, they would have been speaking before the Day*

---

1 Nabíl-i-A'ẓam, *The Dawn-Breakers*, pp. 213–214.
2 The Báb, *Selections*, p. 191.
3 The Báb in Nader Saiedi, *Gate of the Heart*, p. 142.
4 The Báb, *Selections*, p. 79.
5 The Báb, *Selections*, p. 57.
6 The Báb, *Selections*, p. 79.
7 The Báb, *Selections*, pp. 19–20.
8 The Báb in Nader Saiedi, *Gate of the Heart*, p. 266.

> *of Revelation. ... All the mirrors abide by His bidding, return unto Him, utter His glory, and seek shelter beneath His shadow.*[1]

According to the Bayán, all human beings have been created *níkú*[2] (meaning "good", "beautiful", or "righteous and virtuous"). This challenges the tradition of original sin. The Báb teaches that God's creation is perfect,[3] the soul being a sign of Himself[4] and the human heart being His home and reflecting His attributes:[5]

> *He hath ordained that His home be the heart of His servant; by it the reality of existence shall be recognized, and the Fashioner of men be praised, and the bounty of existence pour forth through His ever-flowing Pen.*[6]

The following four sections reflect on the greatness of the Revelation of the Báb and give us glimpses of its glory.

Bahá'u'lláh on the greatness of the Faith of the Báb

Bahá'u'lláh refers to the Báb as the "*Essence of Essences*",[7] the "*immortal Youth*",[8] the "*Sea of Seas*",[9] the "*Point round Whom the realities of the Prophets and Messengers revolve*", for which "*the soul of every Divine Messenger hath thirsted*", through Whom "*God hath proved the hearts of the entire company of His Messengers and Prophets*"[10] and "*through Whom the point of creation hath been made to revolve in both the visible and invisible worlds.*"[11]

"*We, verily, believe in Him*" affirms Bahá'u'lláh, "*Who, in the person of the Báb, hath been sent down by the Will of the one true God, the King of Kings, the All-Praised.*"[12] Moreover, in the Kitáb-i-Íqán, Bahá'u'lláh refers to the Báb in the following way:

> *... all names and attributes revolve round His Essence and circle about the threshold of His sanctuary. For He it is Who traineth all names, revealeth all attributes, conferreth life upon all beings, proclaimeth the divine verses, and arrayeth the heavenly signs. Nay, shouldst thou gaze with thine inner eye, thou wouldst find that all save Him fade into utter nothingness and are as a thing forgotten in His holy presence.*[13]

---

1 The Báb in Nader Saiedi, *Gate of the Heart*, p. 393.
2 Mohammadhossein, *The Báb as a Primary Source of Bahá'u'lláh's Teachings.*
3 Nader Saiedi, *Gate of the Heart*, p. 316.
4 Nader Saiedi, "Phenomenology of Occultation and Prayer", p. 207.
5 Nader Saiedi, *Gate of the Heart*, p. 43.
6 The Báb in Nader Saiedi, *Gate of the Heart*, p. 43.
7 Shoghi Effendi. *God Passes By*, p. 57.
8 Bahá'u'lláh in *Immortal Youth*, p. 24; *Days of Remembrance*, no. 27.
9 Shoghi Effendi, *God Passes By*, p. 57.
10 Shoghi Effendi, *God Passes By*, p. 3.
11 Bahá'u'lláh, *Prayers and Meditations*, p. 300.
12 Bahá'u'lláh, *Gleanings*, p. 73.
13 Bahá'u'lláh, *Gems of Divine Mysteries*, pp. 65–66.

Explaining the scope of the Revelation of the Báb, Bahá'u'lláh refers to an Islamic prophecy: "*Knowledge is twenty and seven letters. All that the Prophets have revealed are two letters thereof. No man thus far hath known more than these two letters. But when the Qá'im shall arise, He will cause the remaining twenty and five letters to be made manifest.*"[1] Similarly, in referring to the Báb, Bahá'u'lláh stated that "*The purpose in creating the world and making it to flourish was His Manifestation.*"[2] Bahá'u'lláh writes:

> *Behold how great and lofty is His station! His rank excelleth that of all the Prophets and His Revelation transcendeth the comprehension and understanding of all their chosen ones.*[3]

Bahá'u'lláh demonstrates His deep love for the Báb and reminds us of Him in a prayer for fasting:

> *Magnify Thou, O Lord my God, Him Who is the Primal Point, the Divine Mystery, the Unseen Essence, the Dayspring of Divinity, and the Manifestation of Thy Lordship, through Whom all the knowledge of the past and all the knowledge of the future were made plain, through Whom the pearls of Thy hidden wisdom were uncovered, and the mystery of Thy treasured name disclosed, Whom Thou hast appointed as the Announcer of the One through Whose name the letter B and the letter E have been joined and united, through Whom Thy majesty, Thy sovereignty and Thy might were made known, through Whom Thy words have been sent down, and Thy laws set forth with clearness, and Thy signs spread abroad, and Thy Word established, through Whom the hearts of Thy chosen ones were laid bare, and all that were in the heavens and all that were on the earth were gathered together, Whom Thou hast called 'Alí-Muḥammad in the kingdom of Thy names, and the Spirit of Spirits in the Tablets of Thine irrevocable decree, Whom Thou hast invested with Thine own title, unto Whose name all other names have, at Thy bidding and through the power of Thy might, been made to return, and in Whom Thou hast caused all Thine attributes and titles to attain their final consummation. To Him also belong such names as lay hid within Thy stainless tabernacles, in Thine invisible world and Thy sanctified cities.*[4]

We conclude with "the most memorable and touching" tribute from the pen of Bahá'u'lláh to "His Beloved",[5] the Báb:

> *Amidst them all, We stand life in hand wholly resigned to His Will, that perchance through God's loving kindness and grace, this revealed and*

---

1 Bahá'u'lláh, *The Kitáb-i-Íqán*, pp. 243–244.

2 Javidukht Khadem, *Zikrullah Khadem*, p. 254.

3 Bahá'u'lláh, *The Kitáb-i-Íqán*, p. 244.

4 *Bahá'í Prayers*, pp. 258–259.

5 Shoghi Effendi, *The World Order of Bahá'u'lláh*, p. 125.

manifest Letter may lay down His life as a sacrifice in the path of the Primal Point, the most exalted Word.[1]

'Abdu'l-Bahá on the greatness of the Faith of the Báb

'Abdu'l-Bahá referred to the Báb as the "*Morn of Truth, the splendor of Whose light shineth throughout all regions*", and as the "*Harbinger of the Most Great Light*".[2] In His Will and Testament, 'Abdu'l-Bahá testified to "*the foundation of the belief of the people of Bahá*" that "*His holiness the exalted One (the Báb) is the Manifestation of the unity and oneness of God and the Forerunner of the Ancient Beauty.*"[3]

'Abdu'l-Bahá explains that among the first pronouncements of the Báb was His being the Promised One, and that later His mission focused on proclaiming the coming of Bahá'u'lláh:

> *It was then supposed that He claimed to be the medium of grace from His Highness the Lord of the Age (upon Him be peace);*[4] *but afterwards it became known and evident that His meaning was the Gatehood [Bábíyyat] of another city and the mediumship of the graces of another Person Whose qualities and attributes were contained in His books and treatises.*[5]

Importantly, 'Abdu'l-Bahá stated that the Bahá'í Faith is based on belief in both the Báb and Bahá'u'lláh:

> *This is the foundation of the belief of the people of Bahá (may my life be offered up for them): "His Holiness, the Exalted One (the Báb), is the Manifestation of the Unity and Oneness of God and the Forerunner of the Ancient Beauty. His Holiness the Abhá Beauty (may my life be a sacrifice for His steadfast friends) is the Supreme Manifestation of God and the Dayspring of His Most Divine Essence. All others are servants unto Him and do His bidding."*[6]

In a tribute to the Báb, 'Abdu'l-Bahá wrote:

> *As for the Báb ... it was at a young age, that is, in the twenty-fifth year of His blessed life, that He arose to proclaim His Cause. Among the Shí'yún it is universally acknowledged that He never studied in any school, nor acquired learning from any teacher. To this the people of Shíráz, each and all, bear witness. Nevertheless, He suddenly appeared before the people, endowed with consummate knowledge, and though but a merchant, confounded all*

---

1 Bahá'u'lláh, *Kitáb-i-Íqán*, p. 252.

2 'Abdu'l-Bahá in Shoghi Effendi, *The World Order of Bahá'u'lláh*, p. 127.

3 'Abdu'l-Bahá, *Will and Testament*, p. 19.

4 It was a Shí'a belief that the *Sahibu'z-Zaman* ("The Lord of the Age") disappeared in the year CE 844 (AH 260) and that during his occultation he communicated with the faithful through four gates (e.g, babs). The *Sahibu'z-Zaman* was to return 1,000 years later in CE 1844 (AH 1260)

5 'Abdu'l-Bahá, *A Traveller's Narrative*, p. 6.

6 'Abdu'l-Bahá, *The Will and Testament of 'Abdu'l-Bahá*, p. 19.

the divines of Persia. Alone, He undertook a task that can scarcely be conceived, for the Persians are known throughout the world for their religious fanaticism. This illustrious Being arose with such power as to shake the foundations of the religious laws, customs, manners, morals, and habits of Persia, and instituted a new law, faith, and religion. Though the eminent men of the State, the majority of the people, and the leaders of religion arose one and all to destroy and annihilate Him, He single-handedly withstood them and set all of Persia in motion. How numerous the divines, the leaders, and the inhabitants of that land who with perfect joy and gladness offered up their lives in His path and hastened to the field of martyrdom!

The government, the nation, the clergy, and prominent leaders sought to extinguish His light, but to no avail. At last His moon rose, His star shone forth, His foundation was secured, and His horizon was flooded with light. He trained a large multitude through divine education and exerted a marvellous influence upon the thoughts, customs, morals, and manners of the Persians. He proclaimed the glad-tidings of the manifestation of the Sun of Bahá to all His followers and readied them for faith and certitude.[1]

Shoghi Effendi on the greatness of the Faith of the Báb

Shoghi Effendi lists in *God Passes By* some of the references from Scriptures of the past that pertain to the Báb:

From the Qur'án

> ... the first of the two "*Messengers*," Whose appearance had been prophesied in the Qur'án, had been sent down. The first "*Trumpet-Blast*", destined to smite the earth with extermination, announced in the latter Book [the Qur'án], had finally been sounded. "*The Inevitable*," "*The Catastrophe*," "*The Resurrection*," "*The Earthquake of the Last Hour*," foretold by that same Book, had all come to pass. The "*clear tokens*" had been "*sent down*", and the "*Spirit*" had "breathed", and the "*souls*" had "*waked up*", and the "*heaven*" had been "*cleft*", and the "*angels*" had "*ranged in order*", and the "*stars*" had been "*blotted out*", and the "*earth*" had "*cast forth her burden*", and "*Paradise*" had been "*brought near*", and "*hell*" had been "*made to blaze*", and the "*Book*" had been "*set*", and the "*Bridge*" had been "*laid out*", and the "*Balance*" had been "*set up*", and the "*mountains scattered in dust*." ... The "*day whose length shall be a thousand years*," foretold by the Apostle of God in His Book, had terminated.[2]

From the Old Testament

> The "*cleansing of the Sanctuary*," prophesied by Daniel and confirmed by Jesus Christ in His reference to "*the abomination of desolation*," had been accomplished.[3]

---

1 'Abdu'l-Bahá in *Immortal Youth*, pp. 33–34; & *Days of Remembrance*, no. 26.

2 Shoghi Effendi, *God Passes By*, p. 58.

3 Shoghi Effendi, *God Passes By*, p. 58.

From the New Testament

> The "*Second Woe*," spoken of in the Apocalypse of St. John the Divine, had, at long last, [had] appeared .... The "*forty and two months*," during which the "*Holy City*," as predicted by St. John the Divine, would be trodden under foot, had elapsed. The "*time of the end*" had been ushered in, and the first of the "*two Witnesses*" into Whom, "*after three days and a half the Spirit of Life from God*" would enter, had arisen and had "*ascended up to heaven in a cloud.*" The "*Man Child*," mentioned in the Book of Revelation, destined to "*rule all nations with a rod of iron*," had released, through His coming, the creative energies which, reinforced by the effusions of a swiftly succeeding and infinitely mightier Revelation, were to instill into the entire human race the capacity to achieve its organic unification, attain maturity and thereby reach the final stage in its age-long evolution.[1]

Significantly, the ministry of the Báb was short—only six years. 'Abdu'l-Bahá confirmed all the above prophetic events were fulfilled during this time:

> *The Exalted One—may my life be offered up for Him—hath said that on the day of His Revelation all these events came to pass swifter than the twinkling of an eye, and that "fifty thousand years"*[2] *were traversed in a single hour.*[3]

This chapter reviewed the grandeur of the Faith of the Báb as characterized by Bahá'u'lláh, 'Abdu'l-Bahá and Shoghi Effendi. The prophetic references about the advent of the Báb clearly highlight His revelation as the most formidable spiritual and historical phenomenon prior to the coming of Bahá'u'lláh. Here is a Faith that transformed humanity's past and present. Given His dual mission as an independent Manifestation of God and the forerunner of a new one, the Báb's re-interpreted the teachings and laws of previous religions and, at the same time, foretold the new world order of *Him Whom God shall make Manifest.*

---

1 Shoghi Effendi, *God Passes By*, p. 58.

2 Qur'án 4:78.

3 'Abdu'l-Bahá, *Light of the World*, p. 152.

8
The universal declaration of the Báb

The universal declaration of the Báb was delivered through a broad range of epistles. The recipients of these epistles included: Muḥammad Sháh and his prime minister; the kings and their sons; the Concourse of Shí'í Muslims and divines; the people of the world; the Sharíf of Mecca;[1] Sulṭán 'Abdu'l-Majíd of the Ottoman Empire; Najíb Páshá, the Valí of Baghdád; and the people of the Qur'án.[2] There were also addresses to the "people of the Book".

In the Qur'án, this term was generally understood to refer to the Jews, the Christians, the Sabaeans, and the Zoroastrians. Nowadays, the tendency amongst Muslims is to include the believers of all revealed religions including Hindus and Buddhists. However, Bahá'u'lláh clarifies that, in some verses of the Qur'án, "*people of the Book*" specifically alludes to "*the divines of that age*" who misinterpret or hide the truth (see Qur'án 3:70–71) and who have "*repelled their fellow-men from the straight path of God*" (see Qur'án 3:99).[3]

The epistles of the Báb declared to all sections of humanity that the promised Day of God had dawned and that He, as a Manifestation of God, was the supreme spiritual authority for it:

> *Say: He [the Báb], verily, is the most perfect Balance established amongst the nations, through Whom the measures of all things are made manifest by Him Who is the All-Knowing, the All-Wise.*[4]

To further understand the sheer volume and might of the universal proclamation of the Báb, Bahá'u'lláh stated that the Báb "*hath specifically revealed an Epistle unto the divines of every city, wherein He hath fully set forth the character of the denial and repudiation of each of them.*"[5] According to Professor E. G. Browne, the author of the *Nuqṭatu'l-Káf*, the Báb instructed a believer to send copies of His messages announcing that He was the Qá'im to "all the lands of Islam" and accordingly copies were sent to "all corners of the earth".[6]

Muḥammad Sháh

The Báb states that He acted as a Manifestation of God when addressing His Tablets to Muḥammad Sháh: "*By My life! But for the obligation to acknowledge*

---

1 Muḥammad ibn 'Abd al-Mu'ín ibn 'Awn was the Sharíf of Mecca when the Báb was in Mecca.

2 Shoghi Effendi, *God Passes By*, p. 24.

3 Bahá'u'lláh, *The Kitáb-i-Íqán*, p. 16.

4 Bahá'u'lláh, *Days of Remembrance*, para. 28.4.

5 Bahá'u'lláh, *The Kitáb-i-Íqán*, p. 229.

6 Denis MacEoin, *The Sources for Early Bábí Doctrine and History*, p. 16.

the Cause of Him Who is the Testimony of God ... I would not have announced this unto thee."[1]

Three themes are found in the several epistles of the Báb sent to Muḥammad S͟háh. The first is His summons to the king to accept and propagate the new Faith along with several warnings concerning the monarch's negative attitude towards the Faith. Secondly, the Báb details His sufferings and expresses His longing for martyrdom. Thirdly, the monarch is asked to convene a meeting with the divines to ascertain the truth of His Cause.

Within the first theme the Báb informs the S͟háh about His sublime station, reminding him that He represents the standard of belief:

> *Whosoever hath recognized Me hath known all that is true and right and hath attained all that is good and seemly, and whosoever hath failed to recognize Me hath turned away from all that is true and right and hath succumbed to everything evil and unseemly.*[2]
>
> *I swear by the truth of God! Wert thou to know that which I know, thou wouldst forgo the sovereignty of this world and of the next, that thou mightest attain My good-pleasure, through thine obedience unto the True One ....*[3]

In one of the epistles of the Báb, the king is summoned to assist the Faith of God:

> *O King of Islám! Aid thou, with the truth, after having aided the Book, Him Who is Our Most Great Remembrance, for God hath, in very truth, destined for thee, and for such as circle round thee, on the Day of Judgment, a responsible position in His Path.*[4]

The Báb also requests the S͟háh "*to subdue, with the truth and by His leave, the countries, for in this world thou hast been mercifully invested with sovereignty ....*"[5] Moreover, the Báb gives him the task of sharing His Message with the Sulṭán of the Ottoman Empire and with the other kings of the region:

> We indeed sent down a Book ... unto thee [Muhammad S͟háh] to the end that thou command that there be written the like of what We sent down therein in golden ink (*al-midád al-d͟hahab*) in a noble, *nask͟h* script (*k͟hatt, nask͟h karím*). Then shall thou dispatch this book [Epistle] of thy Lord unto the Ottoman Sovereign (*malik al-rúm*) [i.e. Sulṭán 'Abd al-Majíd] then unto all the [other] kings (*mulúk*).[6]

---

1 The Báb, *Selections*, p. 12.
2 The Báb, *Selections*, p. 11.
3 The Báb, *Selections*, p. 16.
4 The Báb, *Selections*, pp. 41–42.
5 The Báb, *Selections*, p. 42.
6 The Báb in Sholeh Quinn, "Muhammad Shah Qajar", p. 167.

The monarch is promised that in the next world he would "*dwell, nigh unto the Seat of Holiness, with the inmates of the Paradise of His good-pleasure ...*"[1] if he abides by the decrees of the Báb. He is also told of the consequences of accepting or rejecting the Cause of the Báb:

> *I swear by God, O Sháh! If thou showest enmity unto Him Who is His Remembrance, God will, on the Day of Resurrection, condemn thee, before the kings, unto hellfire, and thou shalt not, in very truth, find on that Day any helper except God, the Exalted.*[2]
>
> *Were ye to return, however, ye would be granted whatever ye desire of earthly possessions and of the ineffable delights of the life to come, and ye would inherit such glorious might and majesty as your minds can scarce conceive in this mortal life. But if ye fail to return then upon ye shall be your transgressions.*[3]

The Sháh's rejection of the message of the Báb means that even his good deeds were unacceptable:

> *Ever since the Cause of thy Lord hath appeared none of thy deeds hath been acceptable, and thou hast been lost in palpable error while all thou couldst see appeared to thee as deeds performed for the sake of thy Lord. In truth thy day is nigh at hand and thou shalt be questioned concerning all this, and assuredly God is not heedless of the deeds of the wicked.*[4]

Muḥammad Sháh is also blamed for the persecution of the believers and for the rejection of the Báb by the majority of the people of Iran. "*Had it not been for thee,*" the Báb observes, "*thy supporters would not have disdainfully rejected Me, though they have gone more widely astray than the foolish.*"[5] In addition, the king is accused of hypocrisy and reminded that the Báb Himself is a descendant of the Prophet Muḥammad.

> *Why dost thou burden thy soul with that which is far more abject than the deeds of Pharaoh, and still callest thyself one of the faithful? How dost thou peruse the verses of the Qur'án, while thou art of the unjust? Never would the Jews, nor the Christians nor any such people as have rejected the truth consent to inflict wrongs upon the son of their Prophet's daughter. Woe betide thee, for the day of chastisement is approaching. Dost thou not dread the wrath of thy Lord, the Almighty, the Lord of the heavens, the Lord of all worlds? Indeed these manifest verses are conclusive testimony for those who seek true guidance.*[6]

---

1 The Báb, *Selections*, p. 42.
2 The Báb, *Selections*, pp. 41–21.
3 The Báb, *Selections*, p. 27.
4 The Báb, *Selections*, p. 25.
5 The Báb, *Selections*, p. 25.
6 The Báb, *Selections*, p. 26.

The Báb also makes the Sháh aware of the responsibility he bears for the persecution and martyrdom of the Bábís throughout Iran:

> *Were the veil to be removed from thine eye thou wouldst crawl unto Me on thy breast, even through the snow, from fear of the chastisement of God which is swift and near at hand. By the righteousness of Him Who hath created thee, wert thou to be acquainted with that which hath transpired during thy reign, thou wouldst wish not to have issued from thy father's loins, but rather to have passed into oblivion. However, that which God, thy Lord, had ordained hath presently come to pass, and woe betide the oppressors in this day.*[1]

Regarding sovereignty, the Báb reminds the Sháh that all dominion belongs to Him, "*inasmuch as sovereignty, as recorded in the Mother Book by the hand of God, is surely invested in Him Who is His Remembrance ...*"[2] and warns: "*Let not thy sovereignty deceive thee, O Sháh, for 'every soul shall taste of death,' and this, in very truth, hath been written down as a decree of God.*"[3]

In a similar vein to the admonition to subdue the ego, the Báb reminds the monarch not to become emboldened by material wealth because the Báb Himself is the "*Inheritor of the earth and all that is therein.*"[4] "*Fear thou God,*" Muḥammad Sháh is advised, "*and pride not thyself on thine earthly possessions, inasmuch as what God doth possess is better for them that tread the path of righteousness.*"[5] Yet, the Sháh need not fear that the Báb plans to dispossess him of his kingship, since the Báb is not motivated by earthly possessions:

> *I have no desire to seize thy property, even to the extent of a grain of mustard, nor do I wish to occupy thy position. If thou followest Me not, then unto thee be the things thou dost possess, and unto Me the land of unfailing security.*[6]

> *Methinks thou dost imagine that I wish to gain some paltry substance from this earthly life. Nay, by the righteousness of My Lord! In the estimation of them that have fixed their eyes upon the merciful Lord, the riches of the world and its trappings are worth as much as the eye of a dead body, nay even less.*[7]

The Báb reprimands the monarch for being the cause of the sufferings of a Manifestation of God:

> *I swear by the Most Great Lord! Wert thou to be told in what place I dwell, the first person to have mercy on Me would be thyself. In the heart of a*

1 The Báb, *Selections*, p. 26.
2 The Báb, *Selections*, p. 42.
3 The Báb, *Selections*, p. 41.
4 The Báb in Shoghi Effendi, *God Passes By*, p. 7.
5 The Báb, *Selections*, p. 19.
6 The Báb, *Selections*, p. 26.
7 The Báb, *Selections*, pp. 20–21.

> *mountain is a fortress [Máh-Kú] ... the inmates of which are confined to two guards and four dogs. Picture, then, My plight ....*[1]
>
> *If thou obeyest Me not, wherefore dost thou look disdainfully upon Me and seek to treat Me with sore injustice? Verily, behold My habitation—a lofty mountain wherein no one dwelleth.*[2]

The Báb also explains that His submission is to God's will, stating "*Unto God do I commit Mine affair and yours, and He verily is the best Judge.*"[3]

> *Whatever reacheth Me is ordained to reach Me; and that which hath come unto Me, to him who giveth will it revert. By the One in Whose hand is My soul, he hath cast no one but himself into prison. For assuredly whatsoever God hath decreed for Me shall come to pass and naught else save that which God hath ordained for us shall ever touch us. Woe betide him from whose hands floweth evil, and blessed the man from whose hands floweth good. Unto no one do I take My plaint save to God; for He is the best of judges. Every state of adversity or bliss is from Him alone, and He is the All-Powerful, the Almighty.*[4]
>
> *Ye cannot alter the things which the Almighty hath prescribed unto Me. Naught shall touch Me besides that which God, My Lord, hath preordained for Me. In Him have I placed My whole trust and upon Him do the faithful place their complete reliance.*[5]

The Báb also affirms His longing for martyrdom in the Cause of God: "*I am well pleased to lay down My life in Thy path and erelong to return to Thy presence*";[6] therefore, He has no fear of a death sentence.

> *If thou hast decided to shed My blood, wherefore dost thou delay? Thou art now endowed with power and authority. For Me it will prove an infinite bounty conferred by God, while for thee and for them that would commit such an act it will amount to a chastisement meted out by Him.*[7]
>
> *How great the blessedness that would await Me, wert thou to pass a verdict such as this; and what immense joy would be Mine, shouldst thou agree to do this! This is a bounty which God hath reserved for them that enjoy near access to His court. Give then thy leave and wait no longer. In truth, mighty is thy Lord, the Avenger.*[8]

---

1 The Báb, *Selections*, p. 14.
2 The Báb, *Selections*, p. 26.
3 The Báb, *Selections*, p. 27.
4 The Báb, *Selections*, p. 15.
5 The Báb, *Selections*, p. 27.
6 The Báb, *Selections*, pp. 27–28.
7 The Báb, *Selections*, p. 22.
8 The Báb, *Selections*, p. 22.

> *Shouldst thou find me deserving of death, then by the sanctified Essence of God, know that I long for it more than the babe yearneth for its mother's breast.*[1]

An important theme of the epistle sent to Muḥammad Sháh by the Báb is His condemnation of the royal bureaucracy and in particular the religious authorities located in Tehran. In one of the epistles, the Báb calls for a meeting to demonstrate the truth of His Faith—a request that was denied:

> *If thou art not apprehensive that the truth might be revealed and the works of the ungodly be brought to naught, why summonest thou not the divines of the land, and then summon Me, so that I may confound them forthwith, even as those disbelievers whom I have previously confounded? This is My sure testimony unto thee and unto them, if they speak the truth. Summon thou all of them. Should they then be able to utter words like unto this, thou wouldst know that their cause is worthy of attention. Nay, by the righteousness of My Lord! They are bereft of power, nor are they endued with perception. They professed faith in the past without understanding its significance, then later they repudiated the Truth; for they are devoid of discernment.*[2]

> *If you are not afraid of the triumph of the truth and the abolition of the falsehood, why then are you not summoning the 'ulama* [religious leaders] *of the land and not calling me forth to put them in their place ...? If, however, you intend to shed my blood, then why do you hesitate ...? For me this is blessing and mercy from my God and for you and those who act like you this is toil and suffering from him.*[3]

The Báb informs the monarch of the epistle sent in the first year of His declaration that was intercepted by members of the royal court:

> *In that same year* [year 60] *I dispatched a messenger and a book unto thee, that thou mightest act towards the Cause of Him Who is the Testimony of God as befitteth the station of thy sovereignty. But inasmuch as dark, dreadful and dire calamity had been irrevocably ordained by the Will of God, the book was not submitted to thy presence, through the intervention of such as regard themselves the well-wishers of the government. Up to the present, when nearly four years have passed, they have not duly presented it to Your Majesty. However, now that the fateful hour is drawing nigh, and because it is a matter of faith, not a worldly concern, therefore I have given thee a glimpse of what hath transpired.*[4]

Hence, the Báb blames high level royal court officers and the 'ulamá' for being co-perpetrators in the persecution of the believers:

---

1 The Báb in Fereydun Vahman, "The Báb", p. 51.
2 The Báb, *Selections*, pp. 21–22.
3 Fereydun Vahman, "The Báb", p. 56.
4 The Báb, *Selections*, p. 13.

Woe betide them that wrongfully do injustice to people, and unjustly and deceitfully usurp the property of the believers in violation of His lucid Book; whereas I, Who, in very truth, am the rightful Sovereign of all men, designated by the true, the undeniable Leader, would never infringe on the integrity of the substance of the people, were it to the extent of a grain of mustard, nor would I treat them unjustly. Rather would I consort with them even as one of themselves, and I would be their witness.[1]

Ḥájí Mírzá Áqásí

The Báb specifically condemns the actions of Ḥájí Mírzá Áqásí,[2] Muḥammad Sháh's prime minister or grand vizier, whom Shoghi Effendi referred to as the Anti-Christ of the Bábí Revelation due to his ferocious attacks on the Báb and His followers. For example, he was responsible for the imprisonment of the Báb in the castle of Máh-Kú and, later, in the castle of Chihríq (see chapter 6).

While in Chihríq, the Báb wrote to Muḥammad Sháh about Ḥájí Mírzá Áqásí:

Dost thou imagine him whom thou hast appointed Chancellor in thy kingdom to be the best leader and the best supporter? Nay, I swear by thy Lord. He will bring thee into grievous trouble by reason of that which Satan instilleth in his heart, and verily, he himself is Satan. He comprehendeth not a single letter from the Book of God and is seized with fear by reason of that which his hands have wrought. Fain would he extinguish the light which thy Lord hath kindled, so that the old impiety which is concealed in his inner being may not be revealed. Hadst thou not appointed him as thy Chancellor no one would have paid him the slightest attention. Indeed in the estimation of the people he is naught but manifest darkness.[3]

Ḥájí Mírzá Áqásí had a pernicious influence on the monarch and therefore the Báb directed to him a warning with these condemnatory remarks:

O minister of the King! be fearful of God, for there is no God except He who is the Truth, the Just. Withdraw your soul from the King. Verily, I am the one who has inherited the earth, and whatsoever is upon it by the leave of God the Wise.[4]

O Minister of the Sháh! Fear thou God, besides Whom there is none other God but Him, the Sovereign Truth, the Just, and lay aside thy dominion, for We, by the leave of God, the All-Wise, inherit the earth and all who are upon it, and He shall rightfully be a witness unto thee and unto the Sháh. Were ye to obey the Remembrance of God with absolute sincerity, We guarantee, by the leave of God, that on the Day of Resurrection, a vast dominion shall be yours in His eternal Paradise. Vain indeed is your dominion, for God hath set aside

---

1 The Báb, *Selections*, p. 26.
2 Hasan Balyuzi, *The Báb*, p. 6.
3 The Báb, *Selections*, pp. 25–26.
4 The Báb in Abbas Amanat, *Resurrection and Renewal*, p. 204.

earthly possessions for such as have denied Him; for unto Him Who is your Lord shall be the most excellent abode, He Who is, in truth, the Ancient of Days ....[1]

'Abdu'l-Majid and Najíb Pá<u>sh</u>á

Similar condemnatory remarks were addressed to 'Abdu'l-Majid who reigned as Sulṭán of the Ottoman Empire between 1839 and 1861. The Báb also wrote an Epistle to Najíb Pá<u>sh</u>á, the governor of Ba<u>gh</u>dád.[2] From the Epistle to the Sulṭán, we read:

> *Read the Book of your Lord, O Majid, through the command of your Lord in the preserved Book. Know that God has knowledge of all things in the heavens and on earth, and that you are, on account of the verdict passed on the messenger,*[3] *the lord of great oppression. Fear God, O man, for today no place is there for anyone to flee to except that he believes in the signs of your Lord and is accounted among those who prostrate* [before Him].'[4]
>
> *O man, Thou hast followed Satan regarding the verdict to imprison the messenger of the Remembrance. Fear God after you have read a single wondrous letter from Our Book. Do not repudiate the command of God and send the messenger in accordance with the command We have send down in the Book addressed to you .... You are not aware of the decree of the caliphate. The messenger is a weak servant in those lands. Yet know full well that it is We that sent him .... Know God's decree and send him after [you have read] this Book. ... Follow God's command, O Majid, and not your idle imaginings that lead you astray from the path of God.*[5]

Sovereigns

A number of calls to the kings and their offspring are made in the Qayyúmu'l-Asmá. As Stephen Lambden wrote: "Such statements most clearly illustrate the universalism or globalism of the Báb at the very onset of his mission."[6] For example, in the following passage the kings from East and West are summoned to accept His Faith:

> *Fear ye God, O concourse of kings, lest ye remain afar from Him Who is His Remembrance [the Báb], after the Truth hath come unto you with a Book*

---

1 The Báb, *Selections*, pp. 41–43.

2 The epistles to the Sulṭán and to the Governor of Ba<u>gh</u>dád may not have reached them. See Alkan Necati, *Dissent and Heterodoxy*, p. 52).

3 A reference to Mullá 'Alí-i-Bastámí who was sent by the Báb to teach the Faith to a high Muslim cleric in Iraq. Upon his arrival he was trialled on the charges of heresy and sent to forced labour in Istanbul where he died in 1846. Mullá 'Alí-i-Bastámí was the second Letter of the Living and is considered the first Bábí martyr.

4 The Báb in Alkan Necati, *Dissent and Heterodoxy*, p. 53.

5 The Báb in Alkan Necati, *Dissent and Heterodoxy*, p. 54.

6 Stephen Lambden, "The Messianic Roots", p. 23.

and signs from God, as spoken through the wondrous tongue of Him Who is His Remembrance. Seek ye grace from God, for God hath ordained for you, after ye have believed in Him, a Garden the vastness of which is as the vastness of the whole of Paradise. Therein ye shall find naught save the gifts and favors which the Almighty hath graciously bestowed by virtue of this momentous Cause, as decreed in the Mother Book.[1]

"*O concourse of kings and of the sons of kings!*" the Báb likewise advises in the same book, "*Lay aside, one and all, your dominion which belongeth unto God ....*"[2] In addition, they are given the important mission to take the teachings of the Báb to new lands:

O concourse of kings! Deliver with truth and in all haste the verses sent down by Us to the peoples of Turkey and of India, and beyond them, with power and with truth, to lands in both the East and the West ....[3]

In the Dalá'il-i-Sab'ih ("The Seven Proofs") particular mention is also made of seven influential Islamic monarchs who had not heard about the Faith of the Báb:

Gracious God! Within the domains of Islám there are at present seven powerful sovereigns ruling the world. None of them hath been informed of His [the Báb] *Manifestation, and if informed, none hath believed in Him. Who knoweth, they may leave this world below full of desire, and without having realized that the thing for which they were waiting had come to pass.*[4]

About the character of Christian kings, the Báb commented:

They awaited the coming of the Prophet of God [Muḥammad], *and when He did appear, they failed to recognize Him. Behold how great are the sums which these sovereigns expend without even the slightest thought of appointing an official charged with the task of acquainting them in their own realms with the Manifestation of God! They would thereby have fulfilled the purpose for which they have been created. All their desires have been and are still fixed upon leaving behind them traces of their names.*[5]

Persian religious leaders

The Shí'a[6] clerics are condemned by the Báb:

---

1 The Báb, *Selections*, p. 63.
2 The Báb, *Selections*, p. 41.
3 The Báb, *Selections*, p. 63.
4 The Báb, *Selections*, p. 117.
5 The Báb, *Selections*, p. 117.
6 The predominant branch of Islam in Iran.

O concourse of Shí'ihs! Fear ye God and Our Cause which concerneth Him Who is the Most Great Remembrance of God. For great is its fire, as decreed in the Mother Book.[1]

O concourse of divines! Fear God from this day onwards in the views ye advance, for He Who is Our Remembrance in your midst, and Who cometh from Us, is, in very truth, the Judge and Witness. Turn away from that which ye lay hold of and which the Book of God, the True One, hath not sanctioned, for on the Day of Resurrection ye shall, upon the Bridge, be, in very truth, held answerable for the position ye occupied.[2]

In all His Tablets, God hath verily ordained vain imaginings and conjecture to be a manifest sin ... God verily hath made it unlawful for you to pronounce, in clear defiance of truth, any injunction or to exercise any legal judgment while bereft of the absolute knowledge of this Book.[3]

O Concourse of the Learned! Ye have been forbidden after [the revelation of] *this Book to teach anything other than it. Acquaint the people with the prescriptions (aḥkám) of the Book and turn away from the obsolete (báṭil) writings that are spread amongst you ....*[4]

Religious leaders

The clergy of all religions are reprimanded by the Báb:

O concourse of the people of the Book! Fear ye God and pride not yourselves in your learning ... He Who is the Eternal Truth beareth me witness, whoso followeth this Book hath indeed followed all the past Scriptures which have been sent down from heaven by God, the Sovereign Truth. Verily, He is well informed of what ye do.... Such as are the true followers of Islám would say: "O Lord our God! We have hearkened to the call of Thy Remembrance and obeyed Him. Forgive us our sins. Thou art, verily, the Eternal Truth, and unto Thee, our infallible Retreat, must we all return."[5]

Muslims

To the Muslim world, the Báb identified the Qur'án with His own revelation:

O ye concourse of the believers! Utter not words of denial against Me once the Truth is made manifest, for indeed the mandate of the Báb hath befittingly been proclaimed unto you in the Qur'án aforetime. I swear by your Lord, this Book is verily the same Qur'án which was sent down in the past.[6]

---

1 The Báb , *Selections*, p. 55.
2 The Báb , *Selections*, p. 44.
3 The Báb in Nader Saiedi, *Gate of the Heart*, p. 137.
4 The Báb in Eschraghi, "Undermining the Foundations of Orthodoxy", p. 237.
5 The Báb, *Selections*, p. 44.
6 The Báb, *Selections*, p. 67.

People of the West

The Báb summoned, in the Qayyúmu'l-Asmá', the people of the West to aid His Cause:

> *Issue forth from your cities, O peoples of the West and aid God ere the Day when the Lord of mercy shall come down unto you in the shadow of the clouds with the angels circling around Him, exalting His praise and seeking forgiveness for such as have truly believed in Our signs. Verily His decree hath been issued, and the command of God, as given in the Mother Book, hath indeed been revealed ....*[1]

Mankind

The Báb addresses specific passages, mostly in the Qayyúmu'l-Asmá, to the inhabitants of the Earth. For instance, the Báb identifies Himself with the Sovereign Truth of God:

> *O people of the Kingdom! ... I swear by your true Lord, by Him Who is the Lord of the heavens and of the earth, that the divine Promise concerning His Remembrance is naught but the sovereign truth and, as decreed in the Mother Book, it shall come to pass ....*[2]

> *O peoples of the earth! Verily the true God calleth saying: He Who is the Remembrance is indeed the sovereign Truth from God, and naught remaineth beyond truth but error, and naught is there beyond error save fire, irrevocably ordained ....*[3]

The Báb declares Himself a Proof for both the East and the West:

> *O peoples of the earth! ... This divinely inspired Book hath firmly established His Proof for all those who are in the East and in the West, hence beware lest ye utter aught but the truth regarding God, for I swear by your Lord that this supreme Proof of Mine beareth witness unto all things ....*[4]

Similarly, the Báb makes a call to mankind to accept His revelation:

> *O people of the earth! Whoso obeyeth the Remembrance of God and His Book hath in truth obeyed God and His chosen ones and he will, in the life to come, be reckoned in the presence of God among the inmates of the Paradise of His good-pleasure.*[5]

---

1 The Báb, *Selections,* p. 56.
2 The Báb, *Selections,* p. 58.
3 The Báb, *Selections,* p. 66.
4 The Báb, *Selections,* p. 60.
5 The Báb, *Selections,* p. 43.

> *O peoples of the earth! Cleave ye tenaciously to the Cord of the All-Highest God, which is but this Arabian Youth, Our Remembrance—He Who standeth concealed at the point of ice amidst the ocean of fire.*[1]

> *O people of the Throne! Incline your ears unto My voice, calling unto you from this Yellow Leaf, burgeoning from the Green Branch that hath risen from out of the Snow-White Tree, and brought forth, by the leave of God, within the depths of the Seventh Sea, around the Point of Fire, that: Verily, I am God, there is none other God but Me.*[2]

The Báb exhorts the people of the world to embrace His Cause and not to follow the promptings of the previous generations:

> *O peoples of the earth! I swear by your Lord! Ye shall act as former generations have acted. Warn ye, then, yourselves of the terrible, the most grievous vengeance of God. For God is, verily, potent over all things.*[3]

> *Say, O peoples of the world! Do ye dispute with Me about God by virtue of the names which ye and your fathers have adopted for Him at the promptings of the Evil One? God hath indeed sent down this Book unto Me with truth that ye may be enabled to recognize the true names of God, inasmuch as ye have strayed in error far from the Truth.*[4]

Likewise, the Báb promises that God will forgive all sins except that of disbelief:

> *O children of men! If ye believe in the one True God, follow Me, this Most Great Remembrance of God sent forth by your Lord, that He may graciously forgive you your sins. Verily He is forgiving and compassionate toward the concourse of the faithful.*[5]

> *O peoples of the earth! Bear ye allegiance unto this resplendent light wherewith God hath graciously invested Me through the power of infallible Truth, and walk not in the footsteps of the Evil One, inasmuch as he prompteth you to disbelieve in God, your Lord, and verily God will not forgive disbelief in Himself, though He will forgive other sins to whomsoever He pleaseth. Indeed His knowledge embraceth all things ....*[6]

The Báb assures all people that any act done in the service of the Cause of God will always be remembered:

---

1 The Báb, *Selections*, p. 54.

2 The "Yellow Leaf", "Green Branch" and the "Snow-White Tree" are allegories referring to Moses' prophetic station and His divine Call (Exodus 3:1 ff, 4:6–7). See also the Báb in Nader Saiedi, *Gate of the Heart*, p. 137.

3 The Báb, *Selections*, p. 72.

4 The Báb, *Selections*, p. 65.

5 The Báb, *Selections*, p. 45.

6 The Báb, *Selections*, p. 48.

O peoples of the world! Whatsoever ye have offered up in the way of the One True God, ye shall indeed find preserved by God, the Preserver, intact at God's Holy Gate ....[1]

The Báb's epistles, written as an independent Manifestation of God, are addressed to the most powerful monarchs and dignitaries of both East and West at that time as well as to the peoples of the world. The Writings of the Báb reveal His spiritual sovereignty, the universal scope of His Cause, and His vision for humanity.

The epistles of the Báb were phrased in an imposing and commanding language. In particular, the message to Muḥammad S͟háh contained a strong call summoning him to obey the Voice of God to humanity, which was none other than the Word of the Báb. The passages of this powerful summons, which were revealed in the Qayyúmu'l-Asmá', were of such majesty and severity that when, on one occasion, a copy of this document fell into the hands of a governor,[2] the latter immediately and publicly denounced the Báb for treating his sovereign so irreverently.

1 The Báb, *Selections*, p. 48.

2 Nabíl-i-A'ẓam, *The Dawn-Breakers*, p. 146.

9
Opposition to the Faith of the Báb

On the basis of the principle of God's progressive revelation, the Báb challenged the idea of prophetic finality that is embedded in most religious systems. Having misinterpreted the prophecies in their sacred scriptures of a future "Messiah", a "Second Coming" or a returning "Avatar"; all believers—be they Hindus, Jews, Buddhists, Zoroastrians, Christians or Muslims—believe that their respective religions will be restored to their former glory, rather than superseded.

The declaration of the Báb as a new Manifestation of God infuriated many Muslims who considered Muḥammad as the final Prophet. The Báb, therefore, attracted fierce hostility, particularly from the Muslim 'ulamá'. During the six years of His ministry, the Báb and His followers were subjected to much suffering and tribulation. Many of the Writings of the Báb reflect His grief but also His resolve to pursue His mission to its ultimate victory:

> *O Qurratu'l-'Ayn!*[1] *Persevere steadfastly as Thou art bidden and let not the faithless amongst men nor their utterances grieve Thee, since Thy Lord shall, by the righteousness of God, the Most Great, pass judgment upon them on the Day of Resurrection, and surely God witnesseth all things.*[2]

> *Though the ocean of woe rageth on every side, and the bolts of fate follow in quick succession, and the darkness of griefs and afflictions invade soul and body, yet is my heart brightened by the remembrance of Thy countenance and my soul is as a rose-garden from the perfume of Thy nature.*[3]

This chapter discusses the nature of the opposition encountered by the Faith of the Báb. The following themes are covered in this chapter:

- Persecution of the believers
- Excuses for rejecting the Báb
- Persecution of the Báb by Muslims
- Principle of finality in Islam
- Divine assistance promised to the believers during persecutions

Persecution of believers

Shoghi Effendi wrote that the persecutions of the Báb, endured with "calm and heroic fortitude",[4] were more intense than those sustained by Jesus Christ, because while Jesus was attacked by the rabbinic establishment, the Báb was

---

1 *Qurratu'l-'*Ayn ("Solace of the Eyes") is one of the titles of the Báb.
2 The Báb, *Selections*, p. 71.
3 The Báb in Browne, *A Traveller's Narrative*, p. 18.
4 Shoghi Effendi, *Bahá'í Administration*, p. 196.

besieged by the combined forces of the religious authorities and the government "which, from the moment of His declaration to the hour of His death, persisted, unitedly and by every means at their disposal, in conspiring against the upholders ["of a much hated creed"[1]] and in vilifying the tenets of His Revelation."[2]

In relation to these distresses, the Báb affirms, *"... behold what calumnies are uttered, so unseemly that the pen is stricken with shame at the mention of them."*[3] *"How profuse the blood,"* the Báb addresses God, *"that hath been shed for the sake of Thy Faith to vindicate the authenticity of Thy divine Mission and to celebrate Thy praise! How vast the possessions that were wrongfully seized in the Path of Thy love in order to affirm the loftiness of Thy sanctity and to extol Thy glorious Name!"*[4]

"Great is the blessedness of those", observes the Báb referring to the thousands of martyrs in His ministry, *"whose blood Thou hast chosen wherewith to water the Tree of Thine affirmation, and thus to exalt Thy holy and immutable Word."*[5] Referring to the wisdom behind those tragedies, He writes:

> *These decrees were ordained by Thee so that all created things might bear witness that they have been brought into being for the sake of naught else but Thee. Thou hast withheld from them the things that bring tranquillity to their hearts, that they might know of a certainty that whatever is associated with Thy holy Being is far superior to and exalted above aught else that would satisfy them; inasmuch as Thine indomitable power pervadeth all things, and nothing can ever frustrate it. Indeed Thou hast caused these momentous happenings to come to pass that those who are endued with perception may readily recognize that they were ordained by Thee to demonstrate the loftiness of Thy divine Unity and to affirm the exaltation of Thy sanctity.*[6]

Many of the Bábí martyrs came from a modest background. Once the Báb said: *"Through the poor and lowly of this land, by the blood which these shall have shed in His path, will the omnipotent Sovereign ensure the preservation and consolidate the foundation of His Cause."*[7] The meaning of "the abased will be exalted" (Matthew 23:12) and "the last will be first" (Matthew 20:16) was epitomized in the person of the "*sifter of wheat*", who embraced the Cause of the Báb in Iṣfahán. By all accounts, he was a simple man who eventually gave his life in the path of the Báb as portrayed in the Persian Bayán:

> *Iṣfáhán, that outstanding city, is distinguished by the religious fervour of its shí'ah inhabitants, by the learning of its divines, and by the keen expectation,*

1 Shoghi Effendi, *God Passes By*, p. 36.
2 Shoghi Effendi, *God Passes By*, p. 57.
3 The Báb, *Selections*, p. 97.
4 The Báb, *Selections*, p. 188.
5 The Báb, *Selections*, p. 190.
6 The Báb, *Selections*, p. 189.
7 The Báb in Nabíl-i-A'ẓam, *The Dawn-Breakers*, p. 213.

shared by high and low alike, of the imminent coming of the Ṣáḥibu'z-Zamán.[1] *In every quarter of that city, religious institutions have been established. And yet, when the Messenger of God had been made manifest, they who claimed to be the repositories of learning and the expounders of the mysteries of the Faith of God rejected His Message. Of all the inhabitants of that seat of learning, only one person, a sifter of wheat, was found to recognise the Truth, and was invested with the robe of Divine virtue!*[2]

Excuses for rejecting the Báb

Some of the reasons advanced for rejecting the Báb pertain to His physical characteristics while others reflect various misconceptions about spiritual reality, all of which are "veils" impeding people from recognizing the Truth. The word "veil" occurs in the Writings of the Báb in such sentences as "*Were I to remove the veil, all would recognize Me as their Best Beloved*"[3] or "*Erelong the veil shall be lifted from your eyes at the appointed time.*"[4]

Some of those who rejected the Báb challenged His claim on the basis of **His age**, "*How can He speak of God while in truth His age is no more than twenty-five?*"[5] Others criticised His unconventional use of Arabic grammar. To the latter He responded:

> *The Qur'án itself does in no wise accord with the rules and conventions current amongst men. The Word of God can never be subject to the limitations of His creatures. Nay, the rules and canons which men have adopted have been deduced from the text of the Word of God and are based upon it. These men have, in the very texts of that holy Book, discovered no less than three hundred instances of grammatical error, such as the one you now criticise. Inasmuch as it was the Word of God, they had no other alternative except to resign themselves to His will.*[6]

Some "veils" noted by the Báb are readily recognized. For example, the **presumption of knowledge** can lead to rejection:

> *How often the most insignificant of men have acknowledged the truth, while the most learned have remained wrapt in veils. Thus in every Dispensation a number of souls enter the fire by reason of their following in the footsteps of others.*[7]

---

1 *Ṣáḥibu'z-Zamán* ("Lord of the Age") is one of prophetic titles of the Báb.
2 The Báb in Nabíl-i-A'ẓam, *The Dawn-Breakers*, p. 99.
3 The Báb, *Selections*, p. 15.
4 The Báb, *Selections*, p. 46.
5 The Báb, *Selections*, p. 47.
6 The Báb in Nabíl-i-A'ẓam, *The Dawn-Breakers*, pp. 318–319.
7 The Báb, *Selections*, pp. 90–91.

Let not names shut you out as by a veil from Him Who is their Lord, is the Báb's advice, even the name of Prophet, for such a name is but a creation of His utterance.[1]

Further, the Báb admonishes those who consider themselves as pious:

Some of the people of the city have declared: 'We are the helpers of God,' but when this Remembrance came suddenly upon them, they turned aside from helping Us.[2]

Blind adherence to religious rituals was yet another barrier in recognizing the Báb:

Likewise consider the manifestation of the Point of the Bayán. There are people who every night until morning busy themselves with the worship of God, and even at present when the Daystar of Truth is nearing its zenith in the heaven of its Revelation, they have not yet left their prayer rugs. If anyone of them ever heard the wondrous verses of God recited unto him, he would exclaim: "Why dost thou keep me back from offering my prayers?[3]

Twelve hundred and seventy years have elapsed since the declaration of Muḥammad, and each year unnumbered people have circumambulated the House of God [Mecca]. *In the concluding year of this period He Who is Himself the Founder of the House* [The Báb] *went on pilgrimage. Great God! There was a vast concourse of pilgrims from every sect. Yet not one recognized Him, though He recognized every one of them—souls tightly held in the grasp of His former commandment.*[4]

The Báb also observes that **religious leaders** were instrumental in the rejection of Him by the masses. Addressing 'Abdu'ṣ-Ṣáḥib, a high-level priest, the Báb remarked:

Thou hast set thyself up as one of the learned in the Faith of Islám, that thou mightest save the believers, yet thou didst cause thy followers to descend into the fire, for when the verses of God were sent forth thou didst deprive thyself therefrom and yet reckoned thyself to be of the righteous ....[5]

To this same divine, the Báb issued a reproach for **his failure to use his leadership** to lead his followers to the new Revelation:

Therefore unto thee shall be assigned the fire which was meant for those who turned away from God in that land, inasmuch as thou art their leader; would that thou might be of them who heed. Hadst thou faithfully obeyed the Decree of God, all the inhabitants of thy land would have followed thee, and

1 The Báb in *Epistle to the Son of the Wolf*, p. 172.
2 The Báb, *Selections*, p. 45.
3 The Báb, *Selections*, p. 80.
4 The Báb, *Selections*, pp. 89–90.
5 The Báb, *Selections*, p. 32.

> *would have themselves entered into the celestial Paradise, content with the good-pleasure of God forevermore.*[1]

Arrogance, selfish desires, ignorance and disdain contributed to the spiritual blindness of many:

> *Ye may contend: "How doth He speak on our behalf?" Have ye not perused the unseemly words ye uttered in the past, as reflected in the text of My Book, and still ye feel not ashamed?*[2]
>
> *Say, how dare ye flagrantly deny the verses sent down from the heaven of justice, yet ye read the Books of God revealed in the past? How do ye repudiate the meeting with your Lord which was appointed with you aforetime, and fail in this Day to heed His warning? Indeed, by adhering to forms and by following the promptings of your selfish desires, ye have deprived yourselves of the good-pleasure of your Lord ...,*[3]
>
> *Today, however, when only belief in this Faith truly profiteth you, ye have debarred yourselves therefrom by reason of the things which are disadvantageous unto you and will inflict harm upon you ....*[4]

Rejection was also defended on the pretext of a perceived lack of proof. People asked, *"How can we recognize Him when we have heard naught but words which fall short of irrefutable proofs?"*[5] Some people even requested that He alter the verses of God:

> *When the verses of this Book are recited to the infidels they say: "Give us a book like the Qur'án and make changes in the verses." Say: "God hath not given Me that I should change them at My pleasure." I follow only what is revealed unto Me.*[6]

Some individuals refused to accept the Báb because of the **small size of the Bábí community** in its first years: *"Nevertheless, when the people realized that fellow supporters were not forthcoming, they hesitated to accept it* [the Qayyúmu'l-Asmá'].[7] Some disregarded His teachings despite the public acceptance by some prominent citizens:

> *Were all the peoples of the world to testify unto a thing and were He to testify unto another, His testimony will be regarded as God's testimony, while aught else but Him hath been and will ever be as naught; for it is through His might that a thing assumeth existence. Consider the extent of the adherence of these people to matters of faith. When dealing with their own affairs they*

---

1 The Báb, *Selections*, p. 32.
2 The Báb, *Selections*, pp. 87–88.
3 The Báb, *Selections*, p. 162.
4 The Báb, *Selections*, p. 88.
5 The Báb, *Selections*, p. 33.
6 The Báb, *Selections*, p. 66.
7 The Báb, *Selections*, p. 90.

> *are well content with the testimony of two just witnesses, and yet despite the testimony of so many righteous men they hesitate to believe in Him Who is the Bearer of the divine Truth.*[1]

The Báb reproaches those who argue that **they could not understand** the Bayán. They ask, "*We are unable to comprehend the eloquence of the verses in the Bayán, how can we regard it as a testimony?*"[2] In turn, the Báb poses a question, "*What is there in the Bayán which keepeth thee back from recognizing these verses as being sent forth by God, the Inaccessible, the Most Exalted, the All-Glorious?*"[3]

Persecution of the Báb by Muslims

The Báb wrote that persecution of Him by the Islamic clergy was based on ignorance:

> *As to those who have debarred themselves from the Revelation of God, they have indeed failed to understand the significance of a single letter of the Qur'án, nor have they obtained the slightest notion of the Faith of Islám, otherwise they would not have turned away from God ... thinking that they are doing righteous work for the sake of God.*[4]

Belief in the concept of finality in Islam

The followers of most of the previous belief systems claim the finality of their religions. A controversial interpretation of a verse from the Qur'án is used by Muslim theologians to say that, after Muḥammad, there will be no more Messengers of God: "Muḥammad is not the father of any of your men, but the Messenger of God and the seal of the Prophets" (33:40). Apart from being a reference to finality, the word *Seal* can also mean the official validation of a document. This meaning can be relevant in understanding the above verse of the *Qur'án*, as the validation of the previous Prophets and their revelations.[5] Crucial to understanding this verse is the definition of the word Prophet. Seal of the Prophets signifies the end of the prophetic cycle initiated by Adam and the beginning of the cycle of fulfilment initiated by the Báb and Bahá'u'lláh. The Báb and Bahá'u'lláh, then, are not Prophets but Manifestations of the fulfilment of all previous prophecies.[6] 'Abdu'l-Bahá explained:

> *The Supreme Báb was the promised one of the Koran, with regard to the question of the Seal of the Prophets. Mohammed was known as the Seal of the Prophets. (The Mohammedans think this title means that no prophet will appear after Mohammed.) This belief is not only limited to the Moslems. The*

---

1 The Báb, *Selections*, p. 121.

2 The Báb, *Selections*, p. 120.

3 The Báb, *Selections*, p. 31.

4 The Báb, *Selections*, p. 140.

5 For a more detailed analysis of these topics, see chapter 21 of Ayers & Woźniak, *Studying the Holy Qur'án*, vol. 6.

6 See Vahid Rafati, "The Development of Shaykhí Thought in Shí'i Islam", p. 106.

Jews believed that Moses was the Seal of the Prophets, that he sealed the prophethood of Laws. The Christians believe that after Christ, no prophet with Laws will come, but that Christ himself will descend from heaven.[1]

If the word **Seal** is taken to mean the Final or Last, then, according to Bahá'í teachings, all the Prophets are simultaneously the First and the Last,[2] the Alpha being the Omega of which John the Apostle spoke.[3] It is in this context that the Báb addresses a high ranking Muslim divine:

> *Thy vision is obscured by the belief that divine revelation ended with the coming of Muḥammad, and unto this We have borne witness in Our first epistle. Indeed, He Who hath revealed verses unto Muḥammad, the Apostle of God, hath likewise revealed verses unto 'Alí-Muḥammad* [The Báb].[4]

In light of the reality that all Prophets are the expression of the Primal Will, therefore all are the First and the Last at the same time. Bahá'u'lláh explains this principle in the Kitáb-i-Íqán:

> *Notwithstanding the obviousness of this theme, in the eyes of those that have quaffed the wine of knowledge and certitude, yet how many are those who, through failure to understand its meaning, have allowed the term "Seal of the Prophets" to obscure their understanding, and deprive them of the grace of all His manifold bounties! Hath not Muḥammad, Himself, declared: "I am all the Prophets?" Hath He not said as We have already mentioned: "I am Adam, Noah, Moses, and Jesus?" Why should Muḥammad, that immortal Beauty, Who hath said: "I am the first Adam" be incapable of saying also: "I am the last Adam"? For even as He regarded Himself to be the "First of the Prophets"—that is Adam—in like manner, the "Seal of the Prophets" is also applicable unto that Divine Beauty. It is admittedly obvious that being the "First of the Prophets," He likewise is their "Seal."*[5]

Divine assistance promised during persecutions

In numerous passages, the Báb prayed for the **ultimate success** of the Cause of God in these or similar terms:

> *O Lord! Assist those who have renounced all else but Thee, and grant them a mighty victory. Send down upon them, O Lord, the concourse of the angels in heaven and earth and all that is between, to aid Thy servants, to succor and strengthen them, to enable them to achieve success, to sustain them, to invest them with glory, to confer upon them honor and exaltation, to enrich them and to make them triumphant with a wondrous triumph.*
>
> *Thou art their Lord, the Lord of the heavens and the earth, the Lord of all the worlds. Strengthen this Faith, O Lord, through the power of these servants*

1 'Abdu'l-Bahá in *Star of the West*, IX:10, 8 September 1918, p. 111.
2 Bahá'u'lláh, *The Kitáb-i-Íqán*, p. 161.
3 Revelations 1:8.
4 The Báb, *Selections*, p. 31.
5 Bahá'u'lláh, *The Kitáb-i-Íqán*, p. 161.

and cause them to prevail over all the peoples of the world; for they, of a truth, are Thy servants who have detached themselves from aught else but Thee, and Thou verily art the protector of true believers.

Grant Thou, O Lord, that their hearts may, through allegiance to this, Thine inviolable Faith, grow stronger than anything else in the heavens and on earth and in whatsoever is between them; and strengthen, O Lord, their hands with the tokens of Thy wondrous power that they may manifest Thy power before the gaze of all mankind.[1]

Likewise, there are wonderful passages in His Writings where the Báb assuredly confirms the **final triumph of the Cause of God**:

Say, God hath undisputed triumph over every victorious one. There is no one in heaven or earth or in whatever lieth between them who can frustrate the transcendent supremacy of His triumph.[2]

In the Name of God, the Victor of the most victorious, proclaim: 'God will help all those who arise to serve Him! No one is able to deprive Him of His Majesty, His Dominion, His Sovereignty for in the heaven and the earth and in all the realms of God He is the Victorious and the Conqueror.'[3]

The day of victory is not far away:

Erelong God will bestow upon Thee rulership over all men, inasmuch as His rule transcendeth the whole of creation.[4]

The Day is approaching when God will render the hosts of Truth victorious, and He will purge the whole earth in such wise that within the compass of His knowledge not a single soul shall remain unless he truly believeth in God, worshippeth none other God but Him, boweth down by day and by night in His adoration, and is reckoned among such as are well assured.[5]

To those believers who sought the crown of martyrdom, the Báb wrote:

O My servants! Seek ye earnestly this highest reward, as I have indeed created for the Remembrance of God gardens which remain inscrutable to anyone save Myself, and naught therein hath been made lawful unto anyone except those whose lives have been sacrificed in His Path. Hence beseech ye God, the Most Exalted, that He may grant you this meritorious reward, and He is in truth the Most High, the Most Great.[6]

Finally, there are the words of the Báb addressed to the multitude gathered to witness His martyrdom in the main square of Tabríz on 9 July 1850:

---

1 The Báb, *Selections*, pp. 192–193.
2 The Báb, *Selections*, p. 164.
3 The Báb in *Star of the West*, 10:1, 21 March 1919, p. 6.
4 The Báb, *Selections*, p. 55.
5 The Báb, *Selections*, pp. 153–154.
6 The Báb, *Selections*, p. 67.

> *"Had you believed in Me, O wayward generation, every one of you would have followed the example of this youth* [Anís],[1] *who stood in rank above most of you, and willingly would have sacrificed himself in My path. The day will come when you will have recognised Me; that day I shall have ceased to be with you."*[2]

The Báb made clear His belief that His Faith would eventually be accepted all over the world (Persian Bayán, 5:4). In this regard, Shoghi Effendi affirmed:

> In the 'Bayán' the Báb says that every religion of the past was fit to become universal. The only reason why they failed to attain that mark was the incompetence of their followers. He then proceeds to give a definite promise that this would not be the fate of the revelation of 'Him Whom God would make manifest', that it will become universal and include all the people of the world. This shows that we will ultimately succeed.[3]

Alas, just as light necessarily projects shadows in the physical world and victory follows crisis, triumph was followed by persecutions. During that process, more than four thousand Bábís[4] preferred to perish rather than renounce their beliefs—a sorrowful aftermath that, nevertheless, substantiated the spiritual force of the teachings of the Báb. Indeed, the Faith of the Báb continued to be victorious and to establish its ascendancy worldwide through the Bahá'í Faith. *"With every fresh tribulation,"* Bahá'u'lláh wrote, explaining the principle of crisis and victory, *"He manifested a fuller measure of Thy Cause, and exalted more highly Thy word."*[5]

The Báb shone like a sun on a nation, which Shoghi Effendi described as "the most decadent race in the civilized world, grossly ignorant, savage, cruel, steeped in prejudice, servile in their submission to an almost deified hierarchy"[6] amidst whom the Báb faced—defenceless but gallantly—the Shí'a priesthood, which was "Fiercely fanatic, unspeakably corrupt, enjoying unlimited ascendancy over the masses, jealous of their position, and irreconcilably opposed to all liberal ideas," an "arch-enemy who repudiated His claim, challenged His authority, persecuted His Cause, succeeded in almost quenching His light."[7] The imprisonment, exile, torture and martyrdom willingly suffered by the Báb are a testimony to His immense love and sacrifice for humanity, and further proof of the divinity of His revelation.

---

1 Anís was the youth who was executed with the Báb in July 1850.

2 The Báb in Nabíl-i-A'ẓam, *The Dawn-Breakers*, p. 114.

3 From a letter dated 20 February 1932 written on behalf of Shoghi Effendi to an individual believer, cited in Helen Hornby, *Lights of Guidance*, p. 469.

4 Browne, *A Traveller's Narrative*, p. 28.

5 Bahá'u'lláh, *Prayers and Meditations*, p. 37.

6 Shoghi Effendi, *God Passes By*, p. 4.

7 Shoghi Effendi, *God Passes By*, p. 4.

Part II:
The heavenly treasury of the Báb

10
Virtues, spiritual and mystical principles

The teachings of the Bábí Faith were characterized by its strong sense of ethics and moral empowerment. Evidence of this is its own version of the **golden rule**, *"Gaze upon others with the same eyes with which ye gaze upon your own selves ...."*[1]

The **golden rule** is a principle running through all religions. Bahá'u'lláh said, *"Choose thou for thy neighbour that which thou choosest for thyself."*[2] Muḥammad stated, "None of you [truly] believes until he wishes for his brother what he wishes for himself",[3] while Jesus exhorted "As ye would that men should do to you, do ye also to them likewise." (Luke 6:31) Likewise, the Old Testament exhorts, "Love your neighbour as yourself: I am the Lord" (Leviticus 19:18). Similar statements are present in Buddhism, Hinduism and Zoroastrianism.[4]

This chapter presents selected passages from the Writings of the Báb pertaining to personal attributes, spiritual principles and mystical themes. These passages reveal the beauty of His teachings about the nobility of the human being—a believer should be like a candle or an oil lamp[5] that consumes itself to provide light and warmth to others. The Báb wishes that all believers become fountains of God's light.[6]

Personal ethics

Being and doing

> *As for thine own self, it is thy duty to be pleased in thine inner heart with thine outward action or expression. The reverse is also thy duty. Should thine inner heart desire to pray at night, and thine outward action fail to manifest its wish, then thou wouldst not be numbered amongst those who are content with their inner heart. Likewise, wert thou to desire for thine outer expression one of the delightful favours of this earthly life, and thine*

---

1 The Báb in Nader Saiedi, *Gate of the Heart*, p. 323.

2 *Tablets of Bahá'u'lláh*, p. 64.

3 *an-Nawawí's Forty Hadiths*, No. 13.

4 Buddhism advocates, "Do not do unto others whatever is injurious to yourself" (*Shayast-na-Shayast* 13.29); Hinduism encourages, "One should never do that to another which one regards as injurious to one's own self" (*Brihaspati, Mahabharata* 13.113.8); and Zoroastrianism recommends, "That nature only is good when it shall not do unto another whatever is not good for its own self." (*Dadistan-i-Dinik* 94:5)

5 The Báb, *Persian* Bayán 8:6.

6 The Báb, *Selections*, p. 180.

inner heart deny such a desire, thou wouldst not be recorded in the Book of God amongst those who willingly resign themselves unto His Decree.[1]

Calmness

Let nothing cause thee to be sore shaken, neither let the things which have been destined to take place in this Cause disturb thee.[2]

Cleanliness

God loveth those who are pure. Naught in the Bayán and in the sight of God is more loved than purity and immaculate cleanliness .... He indeed desireth that under all conditions, all may be adorned with such purity, both inwardly and outwardly, that no repugnance may be caused even to themselves, how much less unto others.[3]

Consideration

Be thou for God and for His creatures even as God hath been for God Himself and for His creatures.[4]

Contentment

Be thou contented, in utter acquiescence and at all times, with the Decree of thy Lord, first in thy soul, and then in thine outward manifestation. Thou wouldst attain the utmost state of contentment with the good pleasure of God when thou art pleased with misery even as thou wouldst be with glory, with poverty as with wealth, with exertion as with tranquility, and with sorrow as with joy, in the states of thy soul and the outward condition that God hath destined for thee.

Thus the state of contentment is also incumbent upon thee in thy relations with people.[5]

Bestow upon me my portion, O Lord, as Thou pleasest, and cause me to be satisfied with whatsoever Thou hast ordained for me.[6]

Discernment

Nay, by God, be thou neither a divine without discernment nor a follower without discernment, for both of these shall perish on the Day of Resurrection. Rather it behooveth thee to be a discerning divine, or to walk with insight in the way of God by obeying a true leader of religion. In every nation thou beholdest unnumbered spiritual leaders who are bereft of true discernment, and among every people thou dost encounter myriads of

---

1 The Báb in Nader Saiedi, *Gate of the Heart*, p. 307.
2 The Báb, *Selections*, p. 160.
3 The Báb, *Selections*, p. 80.
4 The Báb in Nader Saiedi, *Gate of the Heart*, p. 302.
5 The Báb in Nader Saiedi, *Gate of the Heart*, p. 306.
6 The Báb, *Selections*, p. 193.

adherents who are devoid of the same characteristic. Ponder for a while in thy heart, have pity on thyself and turn not aside thine attention from proofs and evidences. However, seek not proofs and evidences after thine idle fancy; but rather base thy proofs upon what God hath appointed.[1]

Faith

Whatever one gaineth in the life to come is but the fruit of this faith. Indeed any man whose eye gazeth upon His Words with true faith well deserveth Paradise; and one whose conscience beareth witness unto His Words with true faith shall abide in Paradise and attain the presence of God; and one whose tongue giveth utterance to His Words with true faith shall have his abode in Paradise, wherein he will be seized with ecstasy in praise and glorification of God, the Ever-Abiding, Whose revelations of glory never end and the reviving breaths of Whose holiness never fail.[2]

And in the eyes of God and of the Possessors of knowledge, there is nothing more glorious than to have faith, which is the most precious of all things, and all bounties are under its shadows.[3]

Fear of God

For verily thou wouldst attain the summit of excellence in divine knowledge when thou yearnest for naught but God, and fearest naught but thy transgression. Shouldst thou act according to this lofty path, thou verily wouldst abide in security.[4]

Fear thou God, thy Lord, and make mention of His Name in the daytime and at eventide. Follow not the promptings of the faithless, lest thou be reckoned among the exponents of idle fancies. Faithfully obey the Primal Point Who is the Lord Himself, and be of the righteous.[5]

Firmness

It is a further evidence of the greatness of this Cause that even Aẓím[6] *should have felt so exceedingly troubled and shaken by its power and the immensity of its claim .... Rest assured, the grace of the Almighty shall enable you to fortify the faint in heart and to make firm the step of the waverer. So great shall be your faith that should the enemy mutilate and tear your body to pieces, in the hope of lessening by one jot or tittle the ardour of your love, he would fail to attain his object. You will, no doubt, in the days to come, meet*

1 The Báb, *Selections*, p. 124.
2 The Báb, *Selections*, p. 99.
3 The Báb in Nader Saiedi, *Logos and Civilization*, p. 295.
4 The Báb in Nader Saiedi, *Gate of the Heart*, p. 308.
5 The Báb, *Selections*, p. 160.
6 Name of an early believer.

face to face Him who is the Lord of all the worlds, and will partake of the joy of His presence.[1]

Forgiveness

... were all the people to wrong thee, thou wouldst forgive them and, indeed, do good unto them, even as God, glorified be He, provideth, through His grace, for those who have ungratefully repudiated Him.[2]

Good character

Wert thou even to conceive in thine heart, regarding any matter, other than that which He hath ordained unto all men in the Book, thou wouldst fail to reach, in the realm of good character and virtue, the lofty station of the people who are faithful to the covenant.[3]

Happiness

God desireth not to see, in the Dispensation of the Bayán, any soul deprived of joy and radiance ....[4]

Harmony

In the Bayán God hath forbidden everyone to pronounce judgment against any soul, lest he may pass sentence upon God, his Lord, while regarding himself to be of the righteous, inasmuch as no one knoweth how the Cause of God will begin or end.[5]

Humility

... know thou that neither being a man of learning nor being a follower is in itself a source of glory. If thou art a man of learning, thy knowledge becometh an honor, and if thou art a follower, thine adherence unto leadership becometh an honor, only when these conform to the good-pleasure of God.[6]

Joy and radiance

God desireth not to see, in the Dispensation of the Bayán, any soul deprived of joy and radiance. He indeed desireth that under all conditions, all may be adorned with such purity, both inwardly and outwardly, that no repugnance may be caused even to themselves, how much less unto others.[7]

---

1 The Báb in Nabíl-i-A'ẓam, *The Dawn-Breakers*, p. 313.
2 The Báb in Nader Saiedi, "The Worldview of the Báb", p. 96.
3 The Báb in Nader Saiedi, *Gate of the Heart*, p. 306.
4 The Báb, *Selections*, p. 80.
5 The Báb, *Selections*, p. 144.
6 The Báb, *Selections*, p. 124.
7 The Báb, *Selections*, p. 80.

Kindness

Be lovingly watchful of one another and thus improve your affairs. Should ye find amongst you one who is afflicted with grief, remove his sorrow by any means in your power, and should ye find one stricken with poverty, enrich him to the extent of your ability. If ye find in your midst one who is abased, exalt him to the extent ye can, and if ye find one who is veiled by ignorance, educate him to the degree of your capacity. Should ye find amongst yourselves one who is single, help him to marry, in accordance with the divine law, to the limits of your ability, and should ye find one who is in distress, bring him tranquility by any means in your power ....[1]

Kindness to animals

Should, at a stopping place, any hardship or pain be inflicted upon an animal, the latter would beseech God to torment its owner. It is always necessary to consider the limits of the capacity of animals, in such wise that after the entrance of its owner into the Bayán, it would not be forced to carry a load unless it is less than the limits of its capacity, otherwise, the profit he may gain thereby would be of no benefit to him.[2]

Moderation

Nothing is dearer to God than moderation.[3]

Obedience

Before those who bear witness to the unity of God, there is no paradise more exalted than the very act of observing the ordinances of God.[4]

... Should a hundred thousand souls gather to circumambulate the House [the Ka'ba] *and leave their homes for the day when permission for circumambulating is given, and should on that very day the Tree of Truth appear and command: 'Don't circumambulate!'—should they all immediately abide, they have reached* [true] *circumambulating. However, should they fail, all their deeds will become naught* (*Persian* Bayán 8:2).[5]

Patience

Let not the deeds of those who reject the Truth shut you out as by a veil. Such people have warrant over your bodies only, and God hath not reposed in them power over your spirits, your souls and your hearts. Fear ye God that haply it may be well with you. All things have been created for your sakes,

---

1 The Báb in Nader Saiedi, *Gate of the Heart*, p. 323.

2 The Báb in Nader Saiedi, *Gate of the Heart*, p. 325. In the Bayán the Báb advises not to ride cows or use them for transportation. See Ma'ani & Ewing, *Laws of the Kitáb-i-Aqdas*, p. 180.

3 The Báb in Moojan Momen, *Selections from the Writings*, p. 326.

4 The Báb in Nader Saiedi, *Gate of the Heart*, p. 312.

5 The Báb in Armin Eschraghi, "Undermining the Foundations", p. 227.

and for the sake of naught else hath your creation been ordained. Fear ye God and take heed lest forms and apparels debar you from recognizing Him. Render ye thanksgiving unto God that perchance He may deal mercifully with you.[1]

Perfection

No created thing shall ever attain its paradise unless it appeareth in its highest degree of perfection.[2]

For, in this religion no other command is as rigorously enjoined as the duty of refinement, and it is forbidden that one bring any object into being in a state of imperfection when one hath the power to manifest it in full perfection.

For example, should one build an edifice and fail to elevate it to the utmost state of perfection possible for it, there would be no moment in the life of that edifice when angels would not beseech God to torment him; nay, rather, all the atoms of that edifice would do the same. For each thing, within its own station, yearneth to attain unto the utmost height of excellence in its own level. Thus, should a man who is capable not realize and respond to the yearning of his capability, he will be held accountable therefore ....[3]

Personal speech

Withhold thy tongue from uttering that which might grieve thee and beseech God for mercy.[4]

Piety

Whenever the faithful hear the verses of this Book being recited, their eyes will overflow with tears and their hearts will be deeply touched by Him Who is the Most Great Remembrance for the love they cherish for God, the All-Praised. He is God, the All-Knowing, the Eternal. They are indeed the inmates of the all-highest Paradise wherein they will abide forever. Verily they will see naught therein save that which hath proceeded from God, nothing that will lie beyond the compass of their understanding. There they will meet the believers in Paradise, who will address them with the words "Peace, Peace" lingering on their lips ....[5]

Purity

Purge your hearts of worldly desires, and let angelic virtues be your adorning. Strive that by your deeds you may bear witness to the truth of these words of God .... The days when idle worship was deemed sufficient are

1 The Báb, *Selections*, pp. 161–162.

2 The Báb in Nader Saiedi, *Gate of the Heart*, p. 315.

3 The Báb in Nader Saiedi, *Gate of the Heart*, pp. 317.

4 The Báb, *Selections*, p. 162.

5 The Báb, *Selections*, pp. 62–63.

ended. The time is come when naught but the purest motive, supported by deeds of stainless purity, can ascend to the throne of the Most High and be acceptable unto Him.[1]

Nothing is more beloved before God than to keep water in a state of the utmost purity, to such an extent that if a believer should become aware that the glass of water he holdeth in his hand hath passed through any impure parts of the earth, he would be grieved.[2]

Refinement

Whosoever is adorned with the virtues of God, glorified and exalted be He, must make use of perfumes, and inhale sweet-smelling substances such as clove or other creations of God, the Exalted, the Mighty. Verily God shall sustain such a soul in the station of truth through His name, the Ever-Living.[3]

Righteousness

Strive earnestly for the sake of God and walk in the path of righteousness. Shouldst thou encounter the unbelievers, place thy whole trust in God, thy Lord, saying, Sufficient is God unto me in the kingdoms of both this world and the next. The Day is approaching when God shall bring the faithful together. In truth no God is there other than Him... May the peace of God be with those who have been guided aright through the power of divine guidance.[4]

Servitude

Behold thou that, verily, all things are contained within the treasuries of God. Verily, God, glorified be lie, shall never accept from anyone a gift that existeth in the treasuries of His dominion. Present then unto God that which hath never existed in the treasuries of His majesty, which is naught but powerlessness and its modes. God verily accepteth the deeds of all things through such a gift.[5]

Steadfastness

O people of the Kingdom! By the righteousness of the true God, if ye remain steadfast upon this line which standeth upright between the two lines,[6] *ye shall, in very truth, quaff the living waters from the Fountain of this wondrous Revelation as proffered by the hand of His Remembrance ....*

---

1 The Báb in Nabíl-i-A'ẓam, *The Dawn-Breakers*, p. 93.
2 The Báb in Nader Saiedi, *Gate of the Heart*, pp. 315–316.
3 The Báb in Nader Saiedi, *Gate of the Heart*, p. 79.
4 The Báb, *Selections*, p. 160.
5 The Báb in Nader Saiedi, *Gate of the Heart*, p. 304.
6 A reference to the shape of the Arabic letters for the word *Báb* (باب).

Trust in God

O Lord! Unto Thee I repair for refuge and toward all Thy signs I set my heart. O Lord! Whether traveling or at home, and in my occupation or in my work, I place my whole trust in Thee. Grant me then Thy sufficing help so as to make me independent of all things, O Thou Who art unsurpassed in Thy mercy! Bestow upon me my portion, O Lord, as Thou pleases, and cause me to be satisfied with whatsoever Thou hast ordained for me. Thine is the absolute authority to command.[1]

Worship

Fire and paradise both bow down and prostrate themselves before God. That which is worthy of His Essence is to worship Him for His sake, without fear of fire, or hope of paradise.

Although when true worship is offered, the worshipper is delivered from the fire, and entereth the paradise of God's good-pleasure, yet such should not be the motive of his act. However, God's favor and grace ever flow in accordance with the exigencies of His inscrutable wisdom.[2]

Spiritual principles and mystical themes

About God

Hallowed be the Lord in Whose hand is the source of dominion. He createth whatsoever He willeth by His Word of command 'Be', and it is. His hath been the power of authority heretofore and it shall remain His hereafter. He maketh victorious whomsoever He pleaseth, through the potency of His behest. He is in truth the Powerful, the Almighty. Unto Him pertaineth all glory and majesty in the kingdoms of Revelation and Creation and whatever lieth between them. Verily He is the Potent, the All-Glorious. From everlasting He hath been the Source of indomitable strength and shall remain so unto everlasting. He is indeed the Lord of might and power. All the kingdoms of heaven and earth and whatever is between them are God's, and His power is supreme over all things. All the treasures of earth and heaven and everything between them are His, and His protection extendeth over all things. He is the Creator of the heavens and the earth and whatever lieth between them and He truly is a witness over all things. He is the Lord of Reckoning for all that dwell in the heavens and on earth and whatever lieth between them, and truly God is swift to reckon. He setteth the measure assigned to all who are in the heavens and the earth and whatever is between them. Verily He is the Supreme Protector. He holdeth in His grasp the keys of heaven and earth and of everything between them. At His Own pleasure doth He bestow gifts, through the power of His command. Indeed His grace encompasseth all and He is the All-Knowing.[3]

---

1 The Báb, *Selections*, p. 193.

2 The Báb, *Selections*, pp. 77–78.

3 The Báb, *Selections*, p. 171.

Acceptance of deeds depend on God

Thy purpose in performing thy deeds is that God may graciously accept them; and divine acceptance can in no wise be achieved except through the acceptance of Him Who is the Exponent of His Revelation ... any act which is accepted by the Point of the Bayán is accepted by God, inasmuch as the contingent world hath no other access unto the presence of the Ancient of Days. Whatever is sent down cometh through the Exponent of His Revelation, and whatever ascendeth, ascendeth unto the Exponent of His Revelation.[1]

Believers' station

Verily the faithful is far more exalted than can be described and he is far more glorious than to have to beg and ask, and it is not worthy of his station to be debased and humiliated.[2]

Blessing on homes of the believers

O my God! Let the outpourings of Thy bounty and blessings descend upon homes whose inmates have embraced Thy Faith, as a token of Thy grace and as a mark of loving-kindness from Thy presence.[3]

Exalted art Thou, O Lord God. Let Thy heavenly blessings descend upon homes whose inmates have believed in Thee. Verily, unsurpassed art Thou in sending down divine blessings.[4]

Debts of faith

The fruit of this ordinance is this, that the divine words of glorification, celebration of praise, sanctification, exaltation of unity, and magnification, and all the other parts of religion are tokens that are bestowed as a bounty from the Supreme Truth unto His created beings. Therefore, upon His revelation, it is incumbent upon all to return this bounteous loan unto Him, from the lofty word of the declaration of Divine Unity to the last token of limitation. Were one to repay at once, upon the revelation, his debt, nothing would be reduced from his possessions; rather, he would be acknowledged in both the world and within himself.[5]

Deeds are to be done for the sake of God

The substance of this gate is that no behaviour turneth into a real action unless it is performed for the sake of God. It is for this reason that it is enjoined upon all those who perform any act [whether testifying to Divine Unity or performing a mundane action such as eating food] to utter these

1 The Báb, *Selections*, p. 81.
2 The Báb in Saiedi, "Phenomenology of Occultation and Prayer", p. 204.
3 The Báb, *Selections*, p. 200.
4 The Báb, *Selections*, p. 211.
5 The Báb in Nader Saiedi, *Gate of the Heart*, p. 274.

words at the time of their action: "Verily, I do this for God, the Lord of the heavens and earth, the Lord of all that is seen and unseen, the Lord of creation." Should he recite them in his heart, his action would be rewarded as a result.[1]

Thy purpose in performing thy deeds is that God may graciously accept them; and divine acceptance can in no wise be achieved except through the acceptance of Him Who is the Exponent of His Revelation.[2]

Destiny and free choice

And the truth of this mystery is that none can behold the manifestation of the Action of God, as it befitteth Him, save through the very manifestation of the free choice of the things themselves. ... Verily, at the time of action, the human being is the agent, who acteth by virtue of the Destiny-ordaining Action of the All-Knowing, the All-Informed. ... Indeed, that free choice is bound to the existence of each thing, and naught is called into existence except through its free choice. Verily, at the primordial moment of choice, when God said unto the thing, 'Am I not your Lord?' it would not have replied, 'Yea,' had it been deprived of freedom of choice.[3]

Earthly dominions and earthly riches

This mortal life is like unto the carcass of a dog, around which none would gather, nor would any partake thereof, except those who gainsay the life hereafter. Verily it is incumbent upon thee to become a true believer in God, the All-Possessing, the Almighty, and to turn away from the one who guideth thee into the torment of hellfire.[4]

Essence of knowledge

The essence of all knowledge is the knowledge of good character and traits. Man must act in conformity with them, that by virtue of such knowledge of ethics he shall neither witness any grief in his soul, nor inflict sorrow upon any other soul. All the reasons for ordaining righteousness, abstinence, and other attributes return to this principle.[5]

Essence of knowledge and faith

This is the essence of all knowledge and faith, could anyone but behold, gather the fruit of his existence, and attain utter death before each Revelation, even as all are now dead before the command of His previous Revelation.[6]

---

1 The Báb in Nader Saiedi, *Gate of the Heart*, p. 65.
2 The Báb, *Selections*, p. 81.
3 The Báb in Nader Saiedi, *Gate of the Heart*, p. 214.
4 The Báb, *Selections*, p. 19.
5 The Báb in Nader Saiedi, *Gate of the Heart*, p. 314.
6 The Báb in Nader Saiedi, *Gate of the Heart*, p. 310.

Firmness in the Covenant

Make me steadfast in Thy Cause and grant that I may be reckoned among those who have not violated Thy Covenant nor followed the gods of their own idle fancy.[1]

Fruit of science is recognition

How vast the number of people who are well versed in every science, yet it is their adherence to the holy Word of God which will determine their faith, inasmuch as the fruit of every science is none other than the knowledge of divine precepts and submission unto His good-pleasure.[2]

God is the Most Generous

For granting of gifts doth not cause Thee loss, nor doth the bestowing of favours diminish Thy wealth.[3]

God made His creation perfect

Say! We verily have perfected Our handiwork in the creation of the heavens, earth, whatever lieth between them, and in all things; will ye not then behold?[4]

Heart of the true believer

The heart of the true believer is the throne of God.[5]

Beseech thou God to open, through His grace, the gate of the heart unto thee, inasmuch as, without the light of that sanctuary, man is unable to conceive of contrary attributes within one and the same thing.[6]

Independent investigation of truth

How often a person, having inclined his ears to the holy verses, would bow down in humility and would embrace the Truth, while his leader would not do so. Thus every individual must bear his own responsibility, rather than someone else bearing it for him.[7]

Therefore, it is forbidden in the Bayán for anyone to accept any religion save through evidence and proof, and testimony, and certitude.[8]

---

1 The Báb, *Selections*, p. 215.
2 The Báb, *Selections*, p. 88.
3 The Báb, *Selections*, p. 186.
4 The Báb in Nader Saiedi, *Gate of the Heart*, p. 316.
5 The Báb in Nabíl-i-A'ẓam, *The Dawn-Breakers*, p. 224.
6 The Báb in Nader Saiedi, *Gate of the Heart*, p. 177.
7 The Báb, *Selections*, p. 90.
8 The Báb in Nader Saiedi, *Gate of the Heart*, p. 329.

Inner being

> *Verily the mystery of truth that is mentioned in the sacred traditions, whose knowledge distinguishes the truly learned, is an originated and created sign. God hath shed upon it, and through it, the splendours of his revelation and hath ordained it to be a sign of his own self, that all that is possible to exist out of the grace of God may vibrate, by its aid, towards his recognition and attain, by its aid, unto his truth. It is an originated sign ... the sign of thy truth, the truth of thy being ....*[1]

Life after death

> *Fie upon the world and its people and upon those who take delight in earthly riches, while oblivious of the life to come.*[2]

> *This mortal life is sure to perish; its pleasures are bound to fade away and erelong ye shall return unto God, distressed with pangs of remorse, for presently ye shall be roused from your slumber, and ye shall soon find yourselves in the presence of God and will be asked of your doings.*[3]

> *Say, this earthly life shall come to an end, and everyone shall expire and return unto my Lord God Who will reward with the choicest gifts the deeds of those who endure with patience.*[4]

Love of God

> *The substance of this gate is that no behaviour turneth into a real action unless it is performed for the sake of God. It is for this reason that it is enjoined upon all those who perform any act to utter these words at the time of their action: "Verily, I do this for God, the Lord of the heavens and earth, the Lord of all that is seen and unseen, the Lord of creation." Should he recite them in his heart, his action would be rewarded as a result.*[5]

Man is a reflection of God's attributes

> *Verily hath God created within thyself the similitude of all that He hath fashioned in creation, that thou mayest not be veiled from any effulgence. Verily God hath generated within thy being the entirety of His manifestations.*[6]

Man's highest station

> *Man's highest station, however, is attained through faith in God in every Dispensation and by acceptance of what hath been revealed by Him, and not*

---

1 The Báb in Nader Saiedi, "Phenomenology of Occultation", p. 207.
2 The Báb, *Selections*, p. 22.
3 The Báb, *Selections*, p. 162.
4 The Báb, *Selections*, p. 161.
5 The Báb in Nader Saiedi, *Gate of the Heart*, pp. 312-313.
6 The Báb in Nader Saiedi, *Gate of the Heart*, p. 43.

through learning; inasmuch as in every nation there are learned men who are versed in divers sciences. Nor is it attainable through wealth; for it is similarly evident that among the various classes in every nation there are those possessed of riches. Likewise are other transitory things.[1]

Martyrs

Great is the blessedness of those whose blood Thou hast chosen wherewith to water the Tree of Thine affirmation, and thus to exalt Thy holy and immutable Word.[2]

Miracles

Whoever seeks to prove the truth of the Point of the Bayán [i.e. the Báb] *through anything but divine verses has veiled himself from the greatest proof and the noblest path. ... In the Qur'án nothing other than this proof has been revealed. Had they all understood this, it would have been easier for them, rather than to profess faith in God through matters* [miracles] *they narrate themselves and for which there is no proof in the book of God.*[3]

Paradise and hell

And know thou of a certainty that by Paradise is meant recognition of and submission unto Him Whom God will make manifest, and by the fire the company of such souls as would fail to submit unto Him or to be resigned to His good-pleasure.[4]

Poetry

Treasures lie hidden beneath the throne of God; the key to those treasures is the tongue of poets.[5]

Potentialities of the new Day of God

The newly born Babe of that Day excels the wisest and most venerable men of this time, and the lowliest and most unlearned of that period shall surpass in understanding the most erudite and accomplished divines of this age ....[6]

The year-old germ that holdeth within itself the potentialities of the Revelation that is to come is endowed with a potency superior to the combined forces of the whole of the Bayán.[7]

Know thou, verily, that God revealed the Qur'án even as He hath created all things. Therefore, in this day, should a tiny ant desire to unravel all its verses,

---

1 The Báb, *Selections*, p. 89.
2 The Báb, *Selections*, p. 190.
3 The Báb in Armin Eschraghi, "Undermining the Foundations", p. 228.
4 The Báb, *Selections*, pp. 82–83.
5 The Báb in Nabíl-i-A'ẓam, *The Dawn-Breakers*, pp. 258–259.
6 The Báb in Nabíl-i-A'ẓam, *The Dawn-Breakers*, p. 94.
7 Bahá'u'lláh, *Epistle to the Son of the Wolf*, p. 151.

and its abstruse meanings, and its stations, through the black of its own eye, it shall be capable of achieving that, inasmuch as the mystery of Lordship and the effulgence of the Eternal vibrate within the very atoms of all created things.[1]

Prayer for the believers

Send down upon them that which will bring comfort to their minds, will rejoice their inner beings, will impart assurance to their hearts and tranquillity to their bodies and will enable their souls to ascend to the presence of God, the Most Exalted, and to attain the supreme Paradise and such retreats of glory as Thou hast destined for men of true knowledge and virtue.[2]

Reward and punishment

Thou hast implored to receive an answer concerning the concepts of true reward, the reality of punishment, and the light of rapture. ... For verily, before God and before those who behold paradise in this earthly life, every moment is the very Day of Resurrection. Shouldst thou purify thy vision, and cleanse thy sight, thou wouldst assuredly witness that verily the Balance hath been appointed within thine own soul; paradise hath been brought nigh unto thee on thy right hand; hell hath been made to blaze on thy left; the Maidens with large and lustrous eyes, abiding in their lofty chambers of heaven, have been established upon their thrones; and the essence of the infidels hath been tormented in their terrible stations ....

Wert thou to desire in thy heart the performance of a good deed, God would assuredly reward thee within thy soul. Then, in the life to come, the result of that which God hath immediately conferred upon thee will be revealed unto thee. For God, verily, is the Omniscient, the Omnipotent, and the Swift in Reckoning.[3]

Riches should not be a barrier

How great the number of people who deck themselves with robes of silk all their lives, while clad in the garb of fire, inasmuch as they have divested themselves of the raiment of divine guidance and righteousness; and how numerous are those who wear clothes made of cotton or coarse wool throughout their lives, and yet by reason of their being endowed with the vesture of divine guidance and righteousness, are truly attired with the raiment of Paradise and take delight in the good-pleasure of God. Indeed it would be better in the sight of God were ye to combine the two, adorning yourselves with the raiment of divine guidance and righteousness and

---

1 The Báb in Nader Saiedi, *Gate of the Heart*, p. 59.

2 The Báb, *Selections*, p. 179.

3 The Báb in Nader Saiedi, *Gate of the Heart*, p. 302.

wearing exquisite silk, if ye can afford to do so. If not, at least act ye not unrighteously, but rather observe piety and virtue ....[1]

Servitude

Verily, the most sublime station of reward, and the most exalted position of divine summons, is naught but the state of the servant's turning toward his Lord with utter devotion. For verily God will ever shed upon thee and through thee the splendours of His revelation ....[2]

Spiritual wealth

Glory be unto Thee, O Lord! Although Thou mayest cause a person to be destitute of all earthly possessions, and from the beginning of his life until his ascension unto Thee he may be reduced to poverty through the operation of Thy decree, yet wert Thou to have brought him forth from the Tree of Thy love, such a bounty would indeed be far better for him than all the things Thou hast created in heaven and earth and whatsoever lieth between them; inasmuch as he will inherit the heavenly home, through the revelation of Thy favors, and will partake of the goodly gifts Thou hast provided therein; for the things which are with Thee are inexhaustible. This indeed is Thy blessing which according to the good-pleasure of Thy Will Thou dost bestow on those who tread the path of Thy love.[3]

Spiritual blindness and deafness

Praise be to Thee, O Lord, my Best Beloved! Make me steadfast in Thy Cause and grant that I may be reckoned among those who have not violated Thy Covenant nor followed the gods of their own idle fancy.[4]

Submission to the Will of God

For verily a servant can never advance or ascend to the truth except through witnessing divine alteration in all its modes and conditions. Therefore, should he be the doer of all good deeds, he would still be fearful of his Lord, that He might change them into misdeeds, whenever He desireth and however He pleaseth.[5]

Tests from God

Indeed shouldst Thou desire to confer blessing upon a servant Thou wouldst blot out from the realm of his heart every mention or disposition except Thine Own mention; and shouldst Thou ordain evil for a servant by reason of that which his hands have unjustly wrought before Thy face, Thou wouldst

1 The Báb, *Selections*, p. 149.

2 The Báb in Nader Saiedi, *Gate of the Heart*, p. 248.

3 The Báb, *Selections*, p. 189.

4 The Báb, *Selections*, p. 215.

5 The Báb in Nader Saiedi, *Gate of the Heart*, p. 209.

test him with the benefits of this world and of the next that he might become preoccupied therewith and forget Thy remembrance.[1]

True immortality

How numerous the souls raised to life who were exposed to dire humiliation in Thy Path for exalting Thy Word and for glorifying Thy divine Unity! How profuse the blood that hath been shed for the sake of Thy Faith to vindicate the authenticity of Thy divine Mission and to celebrate Thy praise! How vast the possessions that were wrongfully seized in the Path of Thy love in order to affirm the loftiness of Thy sanctity and to extol Thy glorious Name![2]

Understanding of the Word of God depends on one's spiritual capacity

The Primal Will, once it is manifested in this world at the behest of God, speaketh of all things, and by virtue of its speaking thereof, all things are brought into existence. When He revealeth, 'I am verily the Mirror of God,' a mirror is created in which naught is seen save the Countenance of God. Therefore he [a person] would gaze upon the Bayán, and would always refer to these words, inasmuch as his inmost reality is verily created by this verse. He, therefore, would consider those who fail to believe in those words to be of a lower spiritual station. And he is correct at his own level of existence.

Likewise, when He revealeth, 'I am verily the first to bow down before God,' there would be one whose inmost reality is created in the image of those words. Thus, he would adduce proofs from the Bayán in that manner and gazeth upon him who is above him as he doeth, on account of his inability to comprehend the higher station. For verily his inmost reality is generated beneath the station of the higher one.[3]

The passages from the Writings of the Báb reviewed in this chapter cover an expansive range of themes that demonstrate the level of nobility expected of humanity in this new era. At the same time, we are assured that these refinements in our attitudes and behaviour are achievable with the grace of God. Furthermore, the divine Words revealed by the Báb elevate our understanding of the mysteries of the spiritual realm to hitherto unknown heights.

---

1 The Báb, *Selections,* p. 151.

2 The Báb, *Selections,* p. 188.

3 The Báb in Nader Saiedi, *Gate of the Heart,* p. 175.

Image Section 2

Figure 17: View of the Masjid-i-Jum'ih in Iṣfahán where the Báb prayed

Figure 18: View of the Masjid-i-Jum'ih in Iṣfahán and the pulpit in front of which the Báb prayed

Figure 19: Castle of Máh-Kú, 1930's

Figure 20: Ruins of the Fortress of Máh-Kú

Figure 21: Ruins of Máh-Kú, 1930's

Figure 22: Castle of Máh-Kú, 1930's

Figure 23: The Castle of Máh-Kú

Figure 24: Castle of Máh-Kú

Figure 25: Corner marked X showing where the Báb was bastinadoed in Tabríz

Figure 26: The Fortress of Chihríq

Figure 27: The Barrack-square in Tabríz where the Báb was martyred in 1850

Figure 28: The Tabríz Barrack Square

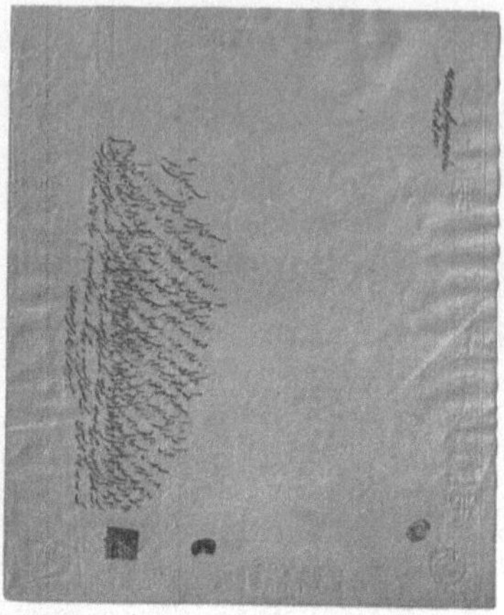

FACSIMILE OF THE BÁB'S TABLET ADDRESSED TO "HIM WHO WILL BE MADE MANIFEST" (BAHÁ'U'LLÁH)

Figure 29: Facsimile of the Báb's Tablet to "Him Who will be Made Manifest (Bahá'u'lláh)

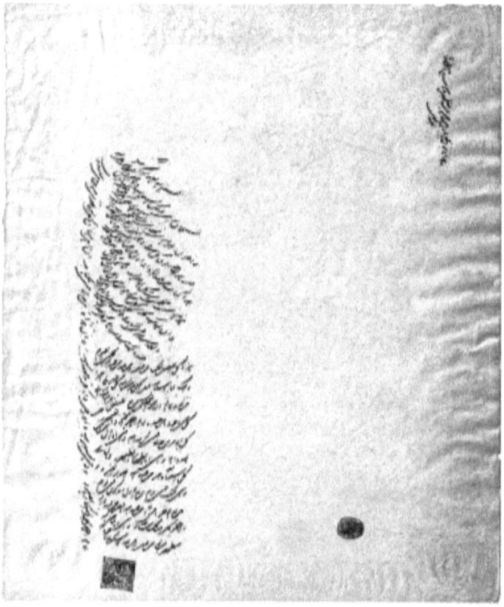

Figure 30: The Báb's Tablet to the First Letter of the Living

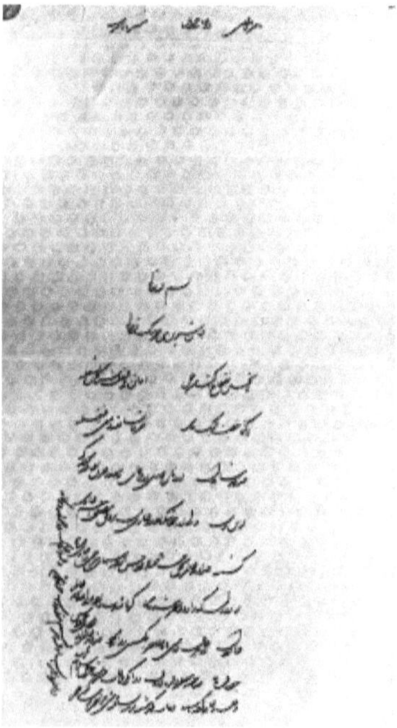

Figure 31: The Báb's letter to His wife, Khadíjih Bagum

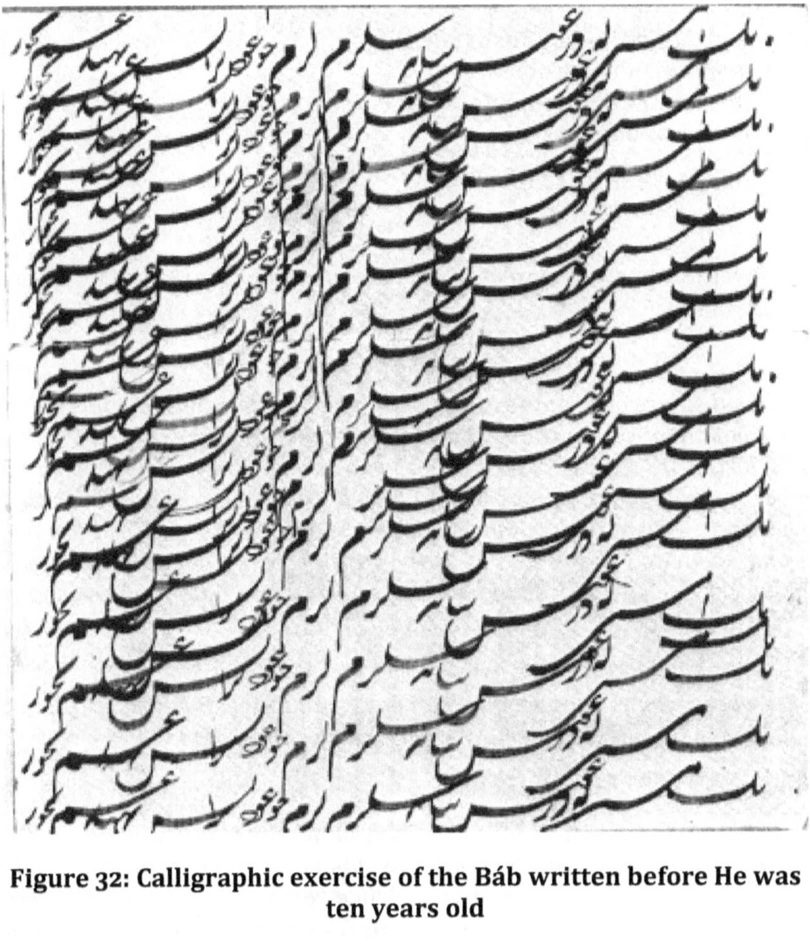

Figure 32: Calligraphic exercise of the Báb written before He was ten years old

11
Individual and community exhortations

In the Bábí Faith, personal transformation was vital to achieve social transformation and, therefore, there are ethical provisions not only for the individual, but also for the community and for the interaction between them.

This chapter presents a compendium of important exhortations and prohibitions from the Writings of the Báb on the following:

- Exhortations in relation to oneself
- Other individual ordinances
- Exhortations in relation to others
- Some prohibitions

Exhortations in relation to oneself

Prayer

> *The most acceptable prayer is the one offered with the utmost spirituality and radiance.*[1]

Fasting

> *The substance of this gate is that before fasting thou must comprehend God's purpose thereof, regarding that which is the fruit of the fast .... The purpose of fasting is to fast from anyone who is not godly. ... When fasting, it behooveth the one who fasteth to take heed lest he be veiled from the good pleasure of God, so that, during his fast, should the Tree of Truth shine forth, and command the breaking of the fast, he would unhesitatingly obey. ... Guard thyself from drinking; eating; intercourse; contention, even in words; injustice, even to the slightest extent; and pronouncing judgment against God ....*[2]

> *... whosoever pronounceth judgment against the Point hath pronounced judgment against God, which rendereth his fasting null.*[3]

Learning the Word of God by heart

> *We verily have sent down unto Thee, in addition to this Book, the Hidden Epistle, that the people may recite its supplications in the daytime and in the night season, and learn from its sublime verses the paths of their servitude to God, in the path of this Most Great Gate (Báb). This, verily, is a mighty testimony from God unto the truth of the Most Great Remembrance. Learn ye by heart that which ye can from this Snow-white Book, and that Crimson-*

---

1 The Báb, *Selections*, p. 78.
2 The Báb in Nader Saiedi, *Gate of the Heart*, p. 331.
3 The Báb in Nader Saiedi, *Gate of the Heart*, p. 331.

coloured Epistle, for God hath, in very truth, guaranteed for those who learn the former by heart and recite from the latter, in the path of the Báb, a heavenly paradise.[1]

Manifesting God's attributes

O My beloved friends! ... It behoves each one of you to manifest the attributes of God, and to exemplify by your deeds and words the signs of His righteousness, His power and glory. The very members of your body must bear witness to the loftiness of your purpose, the integrity of your life, the reality of your faith, and the exalted character of your devotion.[2]

Marriage

The law of marriage is ordained thus that all may abide beneath the bounty of God's grace and mercy, and fix their eyes upon that which is the basis of the lawfulness of marriage, which is naught but the words 'for God,' that haply in the Day of the Revelation of Him Whom God will make manifest they will not deviate from the supreme Mirror of these words, the One Who testifieth unto God.[3]

Punishment for committing a misdeed

For those who commit a grievous act, no fire hath ever been, nor will ever be, more tormenting than their very own action, even as for the faithful no paradise hath ever been, nor will ever be, more mighty than their own recognition and faith.[4]

Recording and monitoring one's own actions

Let each one write his name and what he hath done of good and otherwise from the beginning of the Manifestation of the Matter until the day of its decline: and let his executors preserve it, until the day wherein the Tree of Truth [Bahá'u'lláh] *shall be manifest.*[5]

---

1 The Báb in Nader Saiedi, *Gate of the Heart*, p. 187.

2 The Báb in Nabíl-i-A'ẓam, *The Dawn-Breakers*, p. 92.

3 The Báb in Nader Saiedi, *Gate of the Heart*, p. 313.

4 The Báb in Nader Saiedi, *Gate of the Heart*, p. 312.

5 The Báb in Moojan Momen, *Selections from the Writings*, p. 372. In relation to writing a will and testament the *Kitáb-i-Aqdas* stipulates: "*Unto everyone hath been enjoined the writing of a will. The testator should head this document with the adornment of the Most Great Name, bear witness therein unto the oneness of God in the Dayspring of His Revelation, and make mention, as he may wish, of that which is praiseworthy, so that it may be a testimony for him in the kingdoms of Revelation and Creation and a treasure with his Lord, the Supreme Protector, the Faithful*" (para. 109, p. 59). "*His Holiness, the blessed Báb,*" 'Abdu'l-Bahá said, "*mentions in his book that every one must consider at the end of each day what have been his actions.*" (*Star of the West*, Vol. IX, No. 8, 1 August 1918), p. 96.)

Relying on God

Your faith must be immovable as the rock, must weather every storm and survive every calamity.[1]

Regard not the all-sufficing power of God as an idle fancy. It is that genuine faith which thou cherishest for the Manifestation of God in every Dispensation. It is such faith which sufficeth above all the things that exist on the earth, whereas no created thing on earth besides faith would suffice thee.[2]

Seeking God's good-pleasure

All that I beg of Thee, O my God, is to enable me, ere my soul departeth from my body, to attain Thy good-pleasure, even were it granted to me for a moment tinier than the infinitesimal fraction of a mustard seed. For if it departeth while Thou art pleased with me, then I shall be free from every concern or anxiety; but if it abandoneth me while Thou art displeased with me, then, even had I wrought every good deed, none would be of any avail, and had I earned every honor and glory, none would serve to exalt me.[3]

O My God, O my Lord, O my Master! I beg Thee to forgive me for seeking any pleasure save Thy love, or any comfort except Thy nearness, or any delight besides Thy good-pleasure, or any existence other than communion with Thee.[4]

Striving for perfection

[W]*hoever possesseth power over anything must elevate it to its uttermost perfection that it not be deprived of its own paradise. For example, the paradise of a sheet of paper on which a few excellent lines are inscribed is that it be refined with patterns of gold illumination, adornment, and excellence that are customary for the most exalted parchment scrolls. Then the possessor of that paper hath elevated it to its utmost degree of glory. Should he know of a higher degree of refinement and fail to manifest it upon that paper, he would deprive it of its paradise, and he would be held accountable, for why hast thou, despite the possession of the means, withheld the effusion of grace and favour?*[5]

1 The Báb in Nabíl-i-A'ẓam, *The Dawn-Breakers*, p. 87.

2 The Báb, *Selections*, p. 193.

3 The Báb, *Selections*, pp. 187–188.

4 The Báb, *Selections*, p. 216.

5 The Báb in Nader Saiedi, *Gate of the Heart*, p. 255.

Other individual ordinances

Cleanliness

The Báb places great emphasis on cleanliness. *"Naught in the Bayán and in the sight of God is more loved than purity and immaculate cleanliness,"*[1] said the Báb. The Bayán specifically mentions Christians as an example of cleanliness compared to the Muslim world,[2] some of whose members, particularly the Shí'a Muslims, paradoxically consider Christians as ritually "unclean" or "impure" because of their contact with what is "*ḥarám*" (forbidden) in Islam. For example, many Christians eat pork and drink wine, which is banned in Islam; and, nowadays, there are no specific requirements for the Christian laity regarding ablutions before prayer or for the congregation attending church.

It is important to realize that the reference to "ritual" impurity in Islam has stronger connotations than mere uncleanliness or lack of personal hygiene; it implies physical avoidance of any kind of contact, and a distancing that, throughout history, has been, and is still, used to justify segregation and discrimination. All such discrimination has been eliminated in the Bahá'í Faith.

Whereas the emphasis in Islám is for ritual purity before devotions, the emphasis of the Báb is on maintaining cleanliness and tidiness of one's person and dress at all times. The Báb prescribes that nails should be cut every four days and people should bathe at least every four days and pluck off their body hairs every 8 or 14 days. Even a speck of dirt on a person's clothes must be rectified. Believers are encouraged to care for their cleanliness and appearance by looking at themselves in a mirror morning and evening.[3] Public baths should be built in every village but, contrary to the Persian custom, the tank waters should be constantly changed. The Báb prefers that people bathe by pouring clean water on their bodies rather than submerging their bodies in water, especially if it is dirty and stagnant.[4] Bahá'u'lláh said in the Kitáb-i-Aqdas: *"It hath been enjoined upon you to pare your nails, to bathe yourselves each week in water that covereth your bodies, and to clean yourselves with whatsoever ye have formerly employed*

Bahá'u'lláh ratified these practices and principles in the *Kitáb-i-Aqdas*:

> *God hath enjoined upon you to observe the utmost cleanliness, to the extent of washing what is soiled with dust, let alone with hardened dirt and similar defilement. Fear Him, and be of those who are pure. Should the garb of anyone be visibly sullied, his prayers shall not ascend to God, and the celestial Concourse will turn away from him. Make use of rose water, and of pure perfume; this, indeed, is that which God hath loved from the beginning that hath no beginning, in order that there may be diffused from you what your Lord, the Incomparable, the All-Wise, desireth.*[5]

---

1 The Báb, *Selections*, p. 80.
2 The Báb, Persian Bayán 6:2.
3 The Báb, Persian Bayán 8:6.
4 The Báb, Persian Bayán 6:2.
5 Bahá'u'lláh, *The Kitáb-i-Aqdas*, para. 76, p. 47.

Further, Bahá'u'lláh prescribes that feet be washed "*once every day in summer, and once every three days during winter.*" Confirming many of the teachings of the Báb on cleanliness, Bahá'u'lláh wrote in the Kitáb-i-Aqdas:

> *Immerse yourselves in clean water; it is not permissible to bathe yourselves in water that hath already been used. See that ye approach not the public pools of Persian baths; whoso maketh his way toward such baths will smell their fetid odour ere he entereth therein. Shun them, O people, and be not of those who ignominiously accept such vileness. In truth, they are as sinks of foulness and contamination, if ye be of them that apprehend. Avoid ye likewise the malodorous pools in the courtyards of Persian homes, and be ye of the pure and sanctified. Truly, We desire to behold you as manifestations of paradise on earth, that there may be diffused from you such fragrance as shall rejoice the hearts of the favoured of God. If the bather, instead of entering the water, wash himself by pouring it upon his body, it shall be better for him and shall absolve him of the need for bodily immersion. The Lord, verily, hath willed, as a bounty from His presence, to make life easier for you that ye may be of those who are truly thankful.*[1]

Reading the Words of God every day

The Báb wrote in the Bayán:

> *Everyone must read 700 of the verses of the Bayán, night and day. And if he be not able, let him mention God 700 times by saying 'Alláh-u-Azhar' (God is most manifest).*[2]

In the Kitáb-i-Aqdas Bahá'u'lláh modified this requirement by taking away the number of verses to be read:

> *Recite ye the verses of God every morn and eventide. Whoso faileth to recite them hath not been faithful to the Covenant of God and His Testament, and whoso turneth away from these holy verses in this Day is of those who throughout eternity have turned away from God. Fear ye God, O My servants, one and all. Pride not yourselves on much reading of the verses or on a multitude of pious acts by night and day; for were a man to read a single verse with joy and radiance it would be better for him than to read with lassitude all the Holy Books of God, the Help in Peril, the Self-Subsisting. Read ye the sacred verses in such measure that ye be not overcome by languor and despondency. Lay not upon your souls that which will weary them and weigh them down, but rather what will lighten and uplift them, so that they may soar on the wings of the Divine verses towards the Dawning-place of His manifest signs; this will draw you nearer to God, did ye but comprehend.*[3]

---

1 Bahá'u'lláh, *The Kitáb-i-Aqdas*, para. 106, pp. 57–58.

2 The Báb in Momen, *Selections from the Writings of E. G. Browne*, p. 373.

3 Bahá'u'lláh, *Kitáb-i-Aqdas*, para. 149, pp. 73–74.

Renewing home furnishings every 19 years

The Báb exhorts believers **to renew their home furnishings every 19 years**, if possible.[1] Bahá'u'lláh confirms this exhortation in the *Kitáb-i-Aqdas*: *"Ye have been enjoined to renew the furnishings of your homes after the passing of each nineteen years .... Whoso findeth that his means are insufficient to this purpose hath been excused by God, the Ever-Forgiving, the Most Bounteous."*[2]

Exhortations in relation to others

Avoiding causing fear

> *The substance of this gate is that things which may cause a soul to become frightened by another are not beloved before God. ... It behooveth the servant to be ever watchful that nothing he doeth can cause fear to any soul, that haply in the Day of Resurrection all shall abide in the temple of humanity with all its befitting characteristics.*[3]

Avoid criticizing others

> *They may not refute each other, since whoever enters the Bayán is a believer. Whatever stage (maqám) he might have reached, it is good (khúb ast). Should one of the* [people of the] *Bayán refute another of the* [people of the] *Bayán, he shall be obliged to pay 95 mithqáls of* gold .... *The purpose of God in [prescribing] this provision is that none in the Bayán shall dare to refute anyone by calling* [him a] *non-believer."*[4]

Avoid quarrels

> *For quarrels are forbidden at all times and under any condition, and the ways of the faithful have never been, nor will ever be, aught but forbearance, patience,* [sense of] *shame, and tranquility. Verily, the House of God hath no need of such people!*[5]

Avoid saddening another person

> *It is ordained in this religion to design the doors of each place to allow a tall man to enter through them without bending his head. It behooveth them, each day, to build all the places in the utmost manner of exaltation possible at that time, so that haply in the Day of the Revelation of God, nothing that causeth grief may be witnessed in His kingdom.*[6]

---

1 The Báb, Arabic Bayán 9:14.

2 Bahá'u'lláh, *The Kitáb-i-Aqdas*, para. 151 p. 74.

3 The Báb in Nader Saiedi, *Gate of the Heart*, p. 324.

4 The Báb in Eschraghi, "Undermining the Foundations of Orthodoxy", p. 237. The plural of mithqál (a unit of weight) is matháqíl (mithqals is used in English). Quantities of gold and silver are used as a reference value that can be paid as its equivalent in any currency.

5 The Báb in Nader Saiedi, *Gate of the Heart*, pp. 324.

6 The Báb in Nader Saiedi, *Gate of the Heart*, p. 317.

Guard yourselves, that ye may not in any way be the cause of sadness to another soul, inasmuch as the hearts of the faithful are nearer to God than the House made out of clay ....[1]

God hath, at all times and under all conditions, been wholly independent of His creatures. He hath cherished and will ever cherish the desire that all men may attain His gardens of Paradise with utmost love, that no one should sadden another, not even for a moment, and that all should dwell within His cradle of protection and security until the Day of Resurrection which marketh the dayspring of the Revelation of Him Whom God will make manifest.[2]

Avoid striking people

It is illicit for you to torment men, even if this is only in striking them with the hand upon the elbow ... when you wish to remonstrate with someone, write your arguments and your proofs with prudence and with the most complete politeness.[3]

Bringing joy

In the Bayán no act of worship is nearer unto His acceptance than bringing joy to the hearts of the believers, and none more remote than inflicting sorrow upon them.[4]

Resolving rumours

If any bad man come unto you with news, clear up the matter at once, lest through ignorance ye harm others, and be speedily constrained to repent of what ye have done.[5]

Exercising restraint when punishing children

The substance of this gate is that God never wisheth that any soul should be saddened, how much less that he should be afflicted with harm. Thus, He hath prohibited all from punishing a child who hath not yet reached the age five, save by words, and He hath prohibited causing him any grief. And after reaching the age of five, more than five light strikes, not to the flesh but to a protecting cover, is not permitted, and should not be inflicted in a disrespectful and discourteous manner, as is customary in these days.[6]

---

1 The Báb in Nader Saiedi, *Gate of the Heart*, p. 324.
2 The Báb, *Selections*, p. 86.
3 The Báb in Muḥammad Afnán, "The Role of the Bahá'í Scholar", pp. 3–4.
4 Ali-Akbar Furutan, *The Story of my Heart*, p. 199.
5 The Báb in Nabíl-i-A'ẓam, *The Dawn-Breakers*, p. 150.
6 The Báb in Nader Saiedi, *Gate of the Heart*, pp. 324–325.

Guiding and teaching others

Even as the cloud that rains its bounty upon the earth, traverse the land from end to end, and shower upon its people the blessings which the Almighty, in His mercy, has deigned to confer upon you.[1]

It is better to guide one soul than to possess all that is on earth, for as long as that guided soul is under the shadow of the Tree of Divine Unity, he and the one who hath guided him will both be recipients of God's tender mercy, whereas possession of earthly things will cease at the time of death.[2]

Helping the poor

If ye find in your midst one who is hungry, send him, in truth and to the extent of your power, food in such a way that his heart will not be saddened, and if ye find one who has no clothes, provide him with clothes in the most dignified manner, to the extent possible for you.[3]

Look at spiritual things

Look not, O people, at the things ye possess. Look rather at the things God hath sent down unto you. This, surely, will be better for you than the whole of creation, could ye but perceive it.[4]

Responding to requests and correspondence

He is a man endued with vision who answereth the call of God in all worlds and stations, whether in writing, through utterance, or action, which is the most mighty means of response. And it is by virtue of the blessings accruing from the act of answering of such a soul that all are enjoined to respond to each other. So much so, that if an infant cry, it is a duty to respond to him through appropriate means.[5]

...it is enjoined in this Revelation that should anyone receive a letter from any other, it is his duty to write him back... Likewise, should one's condition silently call upon others, it is the duty of men of discernment to answer his call. In like manner should one's place of residence call for answer, or any other manifestation discernible to men of vision, it is binding upon them to reply, that at no time, no one may witness that which would cause him grief.[6]

Resolving arguments

Thus these two would dispute: This one sayeth, 'Thou art an extremist,' and the other one sayeth, 'Thou art intolerant.' This one adduceth evidence from a word of God, and that one reasoneth by another word of God. But I affirm

1 The Báb in Nabíl-i-A'ẓam, *The Dawn-Breakers*, p. 85.
2 The Báb, *Selections*, p. 77.
3 The Báb in Nader Saiedi, *Gate of the Heart*, p. 323.
4 Bahá'u'lláh, *Gleanings*, p. 146.
5 The Báb in Nader Saiedi, *Gate of the Heart*, pp. 321–322.
6 The Báb in Nader Saiedi, "The Worldview of the Báb", pp. 96–97.

unto them: Ye both are true and right, on the condition that thou not say unto him, 'He is an extremist,' and he not say unto thee, 'Thou art intolerant.' As to thee who art in the lower station, thou verily art created by this verse, and thus thou wouldst not comprehend above it. As to thee who art in the highest station, thou art fashioned by that verse and thou canst understand the station beneath thine existence .... Thus, wert thou to acquire wisdom, thou wouldst not reject anyone because of his limitation, but must foster the growth of all in the palm of thy mercy. Shouldst thou succeed in elevating him to the realm of glory, great would be his blessings from thee; and should he fail to ascend to thy height, thou shouldst train him within his own rank of existence. For verily he too is a creation of thy Lord; God loveth him and he loveth God ....[1]

Respecting women

Therefore, in the Bayán there is no act of obedience that ensureth greater nearness to God than bringing joy to the hearts of the faithful, even as naught yieldeth more remoteness than causing them grief. This law is doubly binding in dealing with the possessors of circles (women), whether in causing them joy or grief. However, man must always be watchful that even if he fail to bring joy to a human being, at least he should refrain from causing him grief.[2]

Conduct yourselves with your women in the most loving manner. Believing women are like the leaves of the heavenly camphor tree. Do not mistreat (mayázár) them even for a blink of an eye, because were you to do so, you shall be veiled from the command of God for that very blink of an eye.[3]

God attributes both to Himself that haply neither men exalt themselves over women, nor women exalt themselves over men.[4]

Obedience to parents and remembrance of them in prayer

After the right of thy faithful brothers, it is thy duty to submit in acquiescence unto thy parents, even though they should wrong thee. Utter no word of contempt to them, and repulse them not. Obey their wishes before they ask thee. For verily thine obedience to them is more beloved in My sight than thy heart's delight in refreshing, cool ice on a burning hot day.

Were either of them, for any reason, to be wrathful to thee, thou must reveal, in return, thy satisfaction even with their wrath, that no sorrow, even to the extent of a mustard seed, may ever cross their heart from thee. Verily the command of thy parents is mightier, in the sight of God, than all good deeds, unless it calleth thee to sin against the Lord. Seek thou their satisfaction with

---

1 The Báb in Nader Saiedi, *Gate of the Heart*, pp. 175–176.
2 The Báb in Nader Saiedi, *Gate of the Heart*, p. 322.
3 The Báb in Eschraghi, "Undermining the Foundations of Orthodoxy", p. 232.
4 The Báb in Saiedi, *Reconstruction of the Concept of the Human Being*, p. 4.

thee, for their pleasure is naught but the good pleasure of the Lord, exalted be His sanctity."[1]

It is seemly that the servant should, after each prayer, supplicate God to bestow mercy and forgiveness upon his parents. Thereupon God's call will be raised: "Thousand upon thousand of what thou hast asked for thy parents shall be thy recompense!" Blessed is he who remembereth his parents when communing with God. There is, verily, no God but Him, the Mighty, the Well-Beloved.[2]

Regard for the human body

As this physical frame is the throne of the inner temple, whatever occurs to the former is felt by the latter. In reality that which takes delight in joy or is saddened by pain is the inner temple of the body, not the body itself. Since this physical body is the throne whereon the inner temple is established, God hath ordained that the body be preserved to the extent possible, so that nothing that causeth repugnance may be experienced. The inner temple beholdeth its physical frame, which is its throne. Thus, if the latter is accorded respect, it is as if the former is the recipient. The converse is likewise true.

Therefore, it hath been ordained that the dead body should be treated with the utmost honor and respect.[3]

Other precepts from the Bayán are to visit the sick,[4] not to raise one's voice[5] and to earn a livelihood.[6] Interestingly, in regard to health and healing, according to 'Abdu'l-Bahá, "*The Báb hath said that the people of Bahá* [Bahá'ís] *must develop the science of medicine to such a high degree that they will heal illnesses by means of food.*"[7]

Some prohibitions

There were some prohibitions introduced in the Bábí Faith that were confirmed by Bahá'u'lláh: carrying arms, gambling, use of opium or any other intoxicating substances, theft, and entering a house without the owner's permission.

1 The Báb in Nader Saiedi, *Gate of the Heart*, p. 306.
2 The Báb, *Selections*, p. 94.
3 The Báb, *Selections*, p. 95.
4 The Báb, *Arabic* Bayán 9:2.
5 The Báb, *Arabic* Bayán 6:16.
6 The Báb, *Arabic* Bayán 8:17.
7 'Abdu'l-Bahá, *Selections from the Writings of 'Abdu'l-Bahá*, pp. 153–154.

Carrying arms

In the *Kitáb-i-Aqdas* is written *"It hath been forbidden you to carry arms unless essential"*.[1] This prohibition has its root in the Persian and Arabic Bayán,[2] but there is an exemption for essential purposes, as elucidated by the Universal House of Justice:

> With regard to circumstances under which the bearing of arms might be "essential" for an individual, 'Abdu'l-Bahá gives permission to a believer for self-protection in a dangerous environment. Shoghi Effendi in a letter written on his behalf has also indicated that, in an emergency, when there is no legal force at hand to appeal to, a Bahá'í is justified in defending his life. There are a number of other situations in which weapons are needed and can be legitimately used; for instance, in countries where people hunt for their food and clothing, and in such sports as archery, marksmanship, and fencing.[3]

Entering a house without the owner's permission

The Báb explicitly forbids **entering a house in the absence of the owner** or making anyone leave their home without their agreement. As a punishment, the transgressor was to be fined 19 mithqals of gold (or its equivalent in assets), and his wife was to be forbidden to visit him for 19 months.

Bahá'u'lláh confirms the general tenor of the above injunction in the *Kitáb-i-Aqdas*:

> *Take heed that ye enter no house in the absence of its owner, except with his permission. Comport yourselves with propriety under all conditions, and be not numbered with the wayward.*[4]

Bahá'u'lláh also states:

> *They that spread disorder in the land, and lay hands on the property of others, and enter a house without leave of its owner, We, verily, are clear of them, unless they repent and return unto God, the Ever-Forgiving, the Most Merciful.*[5]

Gambling and the use of opium and any other intoxicating substance

The Persian Bayán strictly forbids **gambling and the use of opium and any other substance** that provokes stupor and sluggishness[6] including wine because their consumption turns people away from God. The prohibition of opium is the only law mentioned twice in the *Kitáb-i-Aqdas*, and is highlighted in the very last

---

1 Bahá'u'lláh, *The Kitáb-i-Aqdas*, para. 159, p. 76.
2 The Báb, Persian Bayán 7:6 and Arabic Bayán 7:6.
3 *The Kitáb-i-Aqdas*, Note 173, pp. 240–1.
4 Bahá'u'lláh, *The Kitáb-i-Aqdas*, para. 145, p. 72.
5 Bahá'u'lláh, *Epistle to the Son of the Wolf*, p. 23.
6 The Báb, *Persian* Bayán 9:8.

verse. The Báb makes an exception for medical cases as opium was used in 19th century Persia for pain relief. In the *Kitáb-i-Aqdas*, Bahá'u'lláh states:

> *It is inadmissible that man, who hath been endowed with reason, should consume that which stealeth it away. Nay, rather it behoveth him to comport himself in a manner worthy of the human station, and not in accordance with the misdeeds of every heedless and wavering soul.*[1]

> *Gambling and the use of opium have been forbidden unto you. Eschew them both, O people, and be not of those who transgress. Beware of using any substance that induceth sluggishness and torpor in the human temple and inflicteth harm upon the body. We, verily, desire for you naught save what shall profit you, and to this bear witness all created things, had ye but ears to hear.*[2]

In this chapter, we have studied a number of exhortations and prohibitions of the Báb addressed to His followers as individuals and as a society. In these divinely revealed verses, we find the practices enjoined upon us, starting with what we owe to God, as well as what we owe to ourselves, to our families and to the community. These are the foundations and the pillars upon which will be raised the edifice of the new spiritual society—the "new creation" prophesied in the Qur'án (50:15). The essence of these ordinances was later modified or confirmed by Bahá'u'lláh.

1 Bahá'u'lláh, *The Kitáb-i-Aqdas*, para. 119, p. 62.
2 Bahá'u'lláh, *The Kitáb-i-Aqdas*, para. 155, p. 75.

12
Societal organization

The Báb introduced several provisions and arrangements to re-organize social and community interactions in terms of a new mindset and a new society.

According to Iranologist Mangol Bayat, in the Báb's social vision: "... the relationship of humans to the conditions of their existence is complex and subject to change; that a distinction must be made between conditions that are unchangeable and those that one can alter; and above all, that religious evolution has to accompany human social and intellectual evolution."[1]

In this chapter, the nature and structure of social engagements are discussed under two broad themes:

- Exhortations pertaining to community life and social development
- The new Badí' calendar and the Nineteen Day Feast.

Exhortations pertaining to community life and social development

Arts

> *Thus, just as today the letters of the Gospel* [Christians] *are distinguished amongst other communities in the art of ornament, the believers in the Bayán should likewise reflect in their handiwork naught but perfection within the limits of each endeavour, in such wise that a faithful believer in the Bayán in the East of the earth should be beloved in his station on account of his beauty and the beauty of all that he possesseth. And this is the most mighty path for attracting the people of other religions to the true Cause of the all-merciful God. However, these are all binding to the extent that one possesseth the means to do so, not to inflict pain on oneself toward perfecting things.*[2]

Education

> *Educate then, O my God, the people of the Bayán in such wise that no product may be found amongst them but that the very utmost perfection of industry shall be manifest therein .... For verily Thou hast desired, by this law, to build the earth anew by virtue of Thy glorious handiwork through the hands of Thy servants.*[3]

Equality

> *Say! God verily cultivateth on earth as He pleaseth, at His bidding. Will ye not behold? Think ye that ye are the sowers? Say! Glorified be God! We are, verily, the Cultivators. Say! Gaze ye then upon all even as ye behold the most*

---

1 Mangol Bayat, *Mysticism and dissent*, p. 107.

2 The Báb in Nader Saiedi, *Gate of the Heart*, pp. 317–318.

3 The Báb in Nader Saiedi, *Gate of the Heart*, p. 316.

exalted of the renowned amongst you. Verily, that which is shared by both the rulers and those who farm the lands is one thing: they all abide by the bidding of God. Say! We verily sow through Our verses in the soil of your hearts, spirits, souls, and bodies ....[1]

Fairness and honesty in business

I who am your example have been a merchant by profession. It behoves you in all your transactions to follow in My way. You must neither defraud your neighbour nor allow him to defraud you. Such was the way of your Master. The shrewdest and ablest of men were unable to deceive Him, nor did He on His part choose to act ungenerously towards the meanest and most helpless of creatures.[2]

Praise your Lord for sending down the blessing of the Heaven and Earth and in between, to those who are engaged in trade. O God! raise those who are fair in their dealings, and love those inferior to them as they love their own souls and give them respect and prosperity. You are the Omnipotent! Say! Whoever trades for the sake of God, and is honest in his business, God will guarantee him against fraud. Thereby, those of you who established your trade on the path of God, and thus [are partners] with the manifestation of God, are truthful in your trade.[3]

Handicrafts and industries

Say! We verily have perfected Our handiwork in the creation of the heavens, earth, whatever lieth between them, and in all things; will ye not then behold? ... Perfect ye then your own handiwork in all that ye produce with your hands working through the handiwork of God. Then would this indeed be a handiwork of God, the Help in Peril, the Self-Subsisting. Waste ye not that which God createth with your hands through your handiwork; rather, make manifest in them the perfection of industry or craft, be it a large and mass product or a small and retail one. For verily one who perfecteth his handiwork indeed attaineth certitude in the perfection of the handiwork of God within his own being.[4]

Interfaith tolerance

Should anyone lay claim unto a Revelation, and fail to produce any proof, do not protest, and sadden Him not.[5]

Should any one make a statement, and fail to support it by any proof, reject him not.[6]

---

1 The Báb in Nader Saiedi, *Gate of the Heart*, pp. 80–81.

2 The Báb in Nabíl-i-A'ẓam, *The Dawn-Breakers*, p. 303.

3 The Báb in Abbas Amanat, *Resurrection and Renewal*, pp. 129–130.

4 The Báb in Nader Saiedi, *Gate of the Heart*, p. 316.

5 The Báb; cited in Bahá'u'lláh's *Epistle to the Son of the Wolf*, pp. 159–160.

6 Bahá'u'lláh, *Epistle to the Son of the Wolf*, p. 165.

The path to guidance is one of love and compassion, not of force and coercion. This hath been God's method in the past, and shall continue to be in the future! He causeth him whom He pleaseth to enter the shadow of His Mercy. Verily, He is the Supreme Protector, the All-Generous.[1]

Relatives and family life

The Persian Bayán contains beautiful teachings about the family.[2] Parents must show the utmost love and kindness to their children. Children are encouraged to play with toys.[3] Also children must always treat with great politeness and love their parents, siblings and other relatives so that no sadness may reach their hearts.[4] This love should be a reflection of the love for *Him Whom God shall make Manifest.*[5] Armin Eschraghi writes that, in the Persian Bayán (4:19), "The greatest means to achieve nearness to God is showing utmost love and kindness to one's wife and children."[6]

Seeking knowledge

The Báb encourages His believers **to seek knowledge abroad** because their knowledge should encompass all of what is on earth—including countries, religions and governments.[7] He praises Christian Europeans for using the telescope to explore the universe.[8] He exhorts His followers to learn from Christians: *"... perfect then all your handiwork and industries, and seek to learn* [in that regard] *from the letters of the Gospel* [Christians]".[9]

Verily, whenever I have gazed upon the diversity of Thy creation upon the earth, I have seen none to resemble the people of Gospel in the creativity of their handiwork and the wonders of their products.[10]

Badí' Calendar

The new Badí' ("unique", "wonderful") Calendar inaugurated by the Báb is a distinctive feature of His Revelation that was ratified, adopted and further developed by Bahá'u'lláh. It is a calendar of 19 months each consisting of 19 days, that is, 361 days in total. This new calendar was instituted in *the Persian* Bayán[11] and the Kitáb-i-Asmá' (Book of Divine Names). In order to ensure the number of days of the Bahá'í year matched the number of days it takes the earth to circle the

---

1 The Báb, *Selections*, p. 77.
2 The Báb, Arabic Bayán 4:19.
3 The Báb, Persian Bayán 6:11.
4 Peter Terry, *A Thematic Analysis and Summary of the Persian Bayán*, p. 34.
5 Moojan Momen, *Selections from the Writings of E. G. Browne*, p. 345.
6 Armin Eschraghi, "Undermining the Foundations of Orthodoxy", p. 232.
7 The Báb, Arabic Bayán 11:15.
8 The Báb, Persian Bayán 6:3.
9 The Báb in Nader Saiedi, *Gate of the Heart*, p. 319.
10 The Báb in Nader Saiedi, *Gate of the Heart*, p. 319.
11 The Báb, Persian Bayán 5:3.

sun, Bahá'u'lláh later added four days in ordinary years or five days in leap years as intercalary days. These days are situated between the eighteenth and nineteenth months. According to the Báb:

> *The substance of this gate is that the Lord of the universe hath fashioned all types of years by His behest, and hath ordained that from the inception of the Bayán, each year should equal the numerical value of the words "all things" (kullu-shay')* [19 × 19 = 361], *to consist of nineteen months, where each month equalleth nineteen days, that from the moment of the rising of the sun in the vernal equinox—corresponding to the first sign of the Zodiac, the sign of Aries—till the end of its voyage at the end of winter—corresponding to the last sign of the Zodiac, the sign of Pisces—all beings may traverse through all the nineteen stages of the Letters of Unity.*[1]

A distinctive feature of the Badí' calendar is that each month bears the name of one of God's attributes, thus spiritualizing time and the civilization that grows within it. The Báb took the names of the months from a prayer (the *Du'á' al-Bahá'*) ascribed to Muḥammad al-Báqir, the fifth Imám, and used in Shí'a Islam during the Ramaḍán month of fasting. According to Bahá'í author, Adib Taherzadeh:

> There are nineteen invocations in this prayer and each revolves around one of His [God's] names, the first being Bahá (Glory). The Báb has taken these names in the same order and given them to the nineteen months of His calendar ....[2]

The Badí' calendar year starts on Naw-Rúz which is astronomically fixed at the March equinox. Years in the Badí' calendar are counted from the Naw-Rúz of the Bahá'í year in which the Báb made His Declaration to Mullá Ḥusayn, the first believer. Thus, the beginning of the Bahá'í Era (BE) is counted from Thursday 21 March 1844 (1 Rabí' al-Awwal 1260).[3] In the Bábí-Bahá'í Faith a new day starts after sunset. Therefore, year 1 BE began at sundown on 20 March 1844. The first month of the Bahá'í year carries the name of Bahá on behalf of *Him Whom God shall make Manifest*, and is followed by other months named after divine attributes. The Báb writes:

> *Thus, He hath destined each day to be the springtime of one of His laws, that the inmates of this paradise may partake of divine delights in the utmost joy possible within the realm of creation. Therefore, during the first three months (Splendour, Glory, Beauty)—the months of glorification—the fire of the hearts of existent beings is kindled. During the next four months (Grandeur, Light, Mercy, Words)—the months of the celebration of praise—the spirits of the contingent beings are created, during which time they are*

1 The Báb in Nader Saiedi, *Gate of the Heart*, p. 327.

2 Adib Taherzadeh, *The Revelation of Bahá'u'lláh*, vol. 1, p. 116.

3 The Universal House of Justice determined in 2014 that the date of Naw-Rúz each year would be based on the occurrence of the vernal equinox in Ṭihrán. Thus Naw-Rúz could fall between 20 and 22 March of the Gregorian calendar.

> *provided for. In the subsequent six months (Perfection, Names, Might, Will, Knowledge, Power)—the months of the exaltation of unity—God causeth the beings to expire, not as a physical death, but the death of negation and life in affirmation. Finally, in the last six months (Speech, Questions, Honour, Sovereignty, Dominion, Loftiness)—which are the months of magnification—the Lord of the universe, glorified and exalted be He, quickeneth those souls who have died to the love of anyone other than Him and have remained steadfast in His love.*[1]

The Báb created the institution of the *Nineteen Day Feast* based on provisions in the Arabic Bayán that a believer should invite nineteen believers every nineteen days and offer them hospitality, even if only water is served.[2] Bahá'u'lláh states:

> *Verily, it is enjoined upon you to offer a feast, once in every month, though only water be served; for God hath purposed to bind hearts together, albeit through both earthly and heavenly means.*[3]

This chapter covered some institutions established by the Báb concerning the organization and interactions of His community of followers that were designed to foster love and unity between its members. In instituting the Nineteen Day Feast during which the believers could gather together to celebrate the start of each month, the Báb created the ideal condition for enhancing the solidarity of the community.

The Báb marked the start of the new religious era with His Badí' calendar of 19 months of 19 days based on the solar year. There is nothing unusual about inaugurating a new religious dispensation in this way. There are still calendars in use from ancient times, though some may have undergone regional or sectarian changes. The earliest known is the *Saptarsi* calendar of Hinduism, which originated in 6676 BCE. According to tradition, the Hebrew calendar started at the time of Creation, placed at 3761 BCE; the Zoroastrian calendar starts from 1738 BCE, the year of Divine revelation; while the Buddhist calendar uses as its starting point the date of the Buddha's passing to *parinirvana* c. 544 BCE.

Where the Badí' calendar is unique is that, unlike the others, the Bahá'í "month" is not allied to the lunar cycle. Instead of the usual 30 days (plus or minus a day), the month in the calendar of the Báb is based on the mystic number 19—the *Vaḥíd* or "unity". Furthermore, every day of the week, and every month, carries the name of an attribute of God. Thus, time itself has become a "*remembrance of God*".

---

1 The Báb in Nader Saiedi, *Gate of the Heart*, p. 328.

2 The Báb, Arabic Bayán 9:17.

3 Bahá'u'lláh, *The Kitáb-i-Aqdas*, para. 57, p. 40.

13
Some prayers and invocations

The devotional nature of the teachings of the Báb should be emphasized. Communion with God and inner growth are central to His revelation—this was reviewed in chapter 9. The following are the main spiritual development themes of the Bábí-Bahá'í Faith discussed in this chapter:

- Devotions and worship
- Prayers
- Invocations

Devotions and worship

The Báb provides spiritual guidance in the Persian Bayán as to how devotions and worship should be practised to reach a state of purity:

> *The reason why privacy hath been enjoined in moments of devotion is this, that thou mayest give thy best attention to the remembrance of God, that thy heart may at all times be animated with His Spirit, and not be shut out as by a veil from thy Best-Beloved.*[1]
>
> *Worship thou God in such wise that if thy worship lead thee to the fire, no alteration in thine adoration would be produced, and so likewise if thy recompense should be paradise. Thus and thus alone should be the worship which befitteth the one True God. Shouldst thou worship Him because of fear, this would be unseemly in the sanctified Court of His presence, and could not be regarded as an act by thee dedicated to the Oneness of His Being. Or if thy gaze should be on paradise, and thou shouldst worship Him while cherishing such a hope, thou wouldst make God's creation a partner with Him, notwithstanding the fact that paradise is desired by men.*[2]
>
> *Let not thy tongue pay lip service in praise of God while thy heart be not attuned to the exalted Summit of Glory, and the Focal Point of communion. Thus if haply thou dost live in the Day of Resurrection, the mirror of thy heart will be set towards Him Who is the Day-Star of Truth ....*[3]

Prayers

Prayers—so indispensable for an individual's spiritual growth—are a vital element of the teachings of the Báb: "... *when the servant reciteth divine prayers, fixing his gaze utterly upon God, he will be drawn unto the court of nearness, in such*

1 The Báb, *Selections*, pp. 93–94.
2 The Báb, *Selections*, pp. 77–78.
3 The Báb, *Selections*, pp. 93–94.

wise as none can comprehend save he whom God willeth."[1] The Báb also affirmed the conditions and requirement for praying:

> *... its prolongation hath not been and is not beloved by God. The more detached and the purer the prayer, the more acceptable is it in the presence of God.*[2]
>
> *Know thou that it is incumbent upon one who engageth in prayer, first recognition of his Lord, then recognition of His attributes, then recognition of the names of His Self, then of his object of search, then of his end .... When thou hast attained these stations it is irrevocable that God shall grant thy prayer.*[3]

The Báb revealed supplications, devotions and orisons that are fathomless in their depth, mysticism and sheer volume. *Selections of the Writings of the Báb* is the current primary source of these inspiring communions. The compilation was produced in the hope that the believers would increase "their longing to draw nearer to the glorious spirit of Him Who was not only the Herald of the Faith but the bearer of an independent Revelation [the Báb] ...."[4]

At times, the written entreaties of the Báb convey His longings to be closer to God, praising and glorifying the Creator and revealing humility, awe and self-effacement toward the Divinity:

> *Vouchsafe unto me, O my God, the full measure of Thy love and Thy good-pleasure, and through the attractions of Thy resplendent light enrapture our hearts, O Thou Who art the Supreme Evidence and the All-Glorified. Send down upon me, as a token of Thy grace, Thy vitalizing breezes, throughout the daytime and in the night season, O Lord of bounty.*[5]

Some other prayers, revealed for the believers' individual use, are included in Bahá'í prayer books. There are prayers available for general use, for the removal of difficulties, for protection, detachment, families, forgiveness, nearness to God, parents, spiritual growth, steadfastness, for dealing with tests, for the triumph of the Cause, etc.

The Báb also revealed a number of important prayers specific to the Bábí dispensation, such as a "*prayer on the day of 'arafah* [the day before the Feast of Sacrifices], and a morning prayer and prayers for the days of the week",[6] for the

---

1 The Báb in Nader Saiedi, *Tafsír-i-Súriy-i-Kawthar.*

2 The Báb, *Selections*, p. 78.

3 The Báb in Nader Saiedi, "Phenomenology of Occultation and Prayer", p. 205.

4 Research Department of the Universal House of Justice, Preface, *Selections from the Writings of the Báb*, p. v.

5 *Bahá'í Prayers*, p. 149.

6 Behmardi & McCants, "A Stylistic Analysis of the Báb's Writings", p. 121.

new-born,[1] etc. These observance-oriented prayers were not mandated in the Kitáb-i-Aqdas or elsewhere by Bahá'u'lláh. Therefore, they are not in current use.

The Báb recommended in the Persian Bayán and the Dalá'il-i-Sab'ih ("The Seven Proofs") that the following, well-known prayer should be repeated 314 times[2]:

> *Rid thou thyself of all attachments to aught except God, enrich thyself in God by dispensing with all else besides Him, and recite this prayer:*
>
> *Say: God sufficeth all things above all things, and nothing in the heavens or in the earth or in whatever lieth between them but God, thy Lord, sufficeth. Verily, He is in Himself the Knower, the Sustainer, the Omnipotent.*
>
> *Regard not the all-sufficing power of God as an idle fancy. It is that genuine faith which thou cherishest for the Manifestation of God in every Dispensation. It is such faith which sufficeth above all the things that exist on the earth, whereas no created thing on earth besides faith would suffice thee. If thou art not a believer, the Tree of divine Truth would condemn thee to extinction. If thou art a believer, thy faith shall be sufficient for thee above all things that exist on earth, even though thou possess nothing.*[3]

Equally celebrated is another prayer of the Báb: *"Is there any Remover of difficulties save God? Say: Praised be God! He is God! All are His servants, and all abide by His bidding!"*[4][5] Bahá'u'lláh Himself used to repeat this prayer. Commenting on the moral decline that a large number of Bábís were experiencing after the martyrdom of the Báb, Bahá'u'lláh instructed a believer to "*Tell them* [Bábís] *to repeat it* [the prayer] *five hundred times, nay, a thousand times, by day and night, sleeping and waking, that haply the Countenance of Glory may be unveiled to their eyes, and tiers of light descend upon them.*"[6]

The following short prayer was revealed by the Báb for His wife Khadíjih Bagum to read in times of difficulties.[7] According to Nabíl:

> He entrusted her with a special prayer, revealed and written by Himself, the reading of which, He assured her, would remove her difficulties and lighten the burden of her woes. *"In the hour of your perplexity,"* He directed her, *"recite this prayer ere you go to sleep. I Myself will appear to you and will banish your anxiety."* Faithful to His advice, every time she turned to

1 The Báb, Arabic Bayán 5:11.

2 The Báb, Persian Bayán 9:6; Muhájir, *Dr Muhajir*, p. 674; & *Bahá'í Prayers*, p. 28.

3 The Báb, *Selections*, p. 123.

4 *Bahá'í Prayers*, p. 29.

5 Muhammad Afnan, The Invocation "Is There Any Remover of Difficulties Save God..." (trans. Adib Masumian), 2006.

6 Bahá'u'lláh in Shoghi Effendi. *God Pass By*, p. 119.

7 Wendi Momen, *A Basic Bahá'í Dictionary*, p. 127.

Him in prayer, the light of His unfailing guidance illumined her path and resolved her problems.[1]

Invocations

It is noteworthy that the Arabic invocation "*Yá Alláhu'l-Mustagháth*" ("O Thou God Who art invoked") was revealed by the Báb to be recited in times of distress, emergencies or difficulties.[2] It was used and recommended by 'Abdu'l-Bahá and Shoghi Effendi.[3] According to Florence Khan "... this was the prayer repeated over and over by the Master, as He paced His garden when the Turkish ship was coming to take Him away."[4] The following is another account of the use of "*Yá Alláhu'l-Mustagháth*" by 'Abdu'l-Bahá when he was 11 years old:

> *It had happened when Bahá'u'lláh had been gone from Baghdád. For some two years. At that time no one knew where He was and all hearts were sick with the fear that they never would see Him again. At this time Abdu'l-Bahá was a small boy, and the continued absence of His Beloved Father had become unendurable. So, one night, all night long, the little boy (whom, even then, Bahá'u'lláh referred to as The Master) paced restlessly up and down saying, shouting, beseeching, "Yá Alláhu'l-Mustagháth" "Yá Alláhu'l-Mustagháth" all night long. And in the morning, when dawn was breaking, a messenger came to the door to say that a stranger was at the city gate and had sent word to the Family that He wished them to bring to Him fresh raiment and water to bathe in .... So 'Abdu'l-Bahá knew His beloved Father had returned.*[5]

Another popular invocation of the Báb is "*O God, my God, my Beloved, my heart's Desire*".[6] When visiting the shrine of the Imám Ḥusayn, the Báb uttered this invocation with such "frequency and ardour that those of the visiting pilgrims who were near enough to hear Him instinctively interrupted the course of their devotions, and marvelled at the evidences of piety and veneration which that youthful countenance evinced".[7]

Concerning the use of this invocation, the Universal House of Justice has explained:

> While the invocation is prescribed in the Writings of the Báb to be repeated 2098 times during occasions of great need, 'Abdu'l-Bahá in one Tablet states that this verse is to be repeated 95 times and, in another Tablet, 81 times. Letters from the Guardian concerning this invocation, as well as

---

1 Nabíl-i-A'ẓam, *The Dawn-Breakers*, p. 192. Author's emphasis.

2 Letter of the Universal House of Justice, 25 November 1999.

3 Marzieh Gail, *Arches of the Years*, p. 310.

4 Florence Khan in Marzieh Gail, *Arches of the Years*, p. 312.

5 Muriel Newhall, *Mother's Stories*, p. 6.

6 The Báb in Balyuzi, *The Báb*, p. 45.

7 Nabíl-i-A'ẓam, *The Dawn-Breakers*, p. 30.

other prayers, indicate that repetition is a matter of individual choice. In a postscript added in his own handwriting to a letter to an individual he stated:

"There is no objection to saying "Yá Ilaha'l-Mustaghath" any time you like and as often as you like."[1]

Many prayers are petitionary: for instance, we pray for healing, for protection, for strength and for steadfastness. One may supplicate God's mercy and forgiveness for oneself or for the soul of a departed one. Some prayers may have a special intention, such as the success of a teaching project. Then there are prayers of thanksgiving, or prayers purely in praise of God.

In the Bábí-Bahá'í Faith, we have been blessed with a multitude of prayers and invocations for general or specific purposes. Hence, these prayers have a particular potency. However, whatever the prayer, the ultimate motivation is "*remembrance of God*" for the sake of the love of God. And however seemingly insignificant the supplication may be, the benefits that flow from the whole-hearted and fervent "*remembrance of God*" are all-embracing.

1 Letter from the Universal House of Justice, 28 December 2001; & 25 November 1999.

14
Messages of the Báb for His family

In several passages of His writings, the Báb refers to the members of His family in exalted and tender terms as presented below.

The Báb married <u>Kh</u>adíjih Bagum in 1842. Their only son died stillborn or possibly in very early infancy. Shoghi Effendi (1897–1957), the Guardian of the Bahá'í Faith, was the great-grandson of Ḥájí Mírzá Abu'l-Qásim, an elder brother to the wife of the Báb. Shoghi Effendi was also the great-grandson of Bahá'u'lláh.

The members of the family of the Báb, both men and women, are known as Afnán ("Twigs" in Arabic) of the sacred Lotus Tree. *"By 'Afnán',"* Bahá'u'lláh affirmed, *"it is meant the kinsmen of the Primal Point, may the spirit of all be a sacrifice unto Him."*[1] The Lotus tree represents the Manifestation of God and concurrently the boundary between the human and the divine beyond which there is no passing (Qur'án, 53:14)[2] On the other hand, the male descendants of Bahá'u'lláh are called A<u>gh</u>ṣán ("Branches"). A female descendant of the families of the Báb or Bahá'u'lláh is referred to as Waraqah ("Leaf").[3]

The Báb once affirmed, *"Our kinsmen have been reckoned among the 'Letters of the Exalted.' But not because they were deserving, nay, because of Our love for them."*[4]

To His male relatives

> *O ye kinsmen of the Most Great Remembrance! This Tree of Holiness, dyed crimson with the oil of servitude, hath verily sprung forth out of your own soil in the midst of the Burning Bush, yet ye comprehend nothing whatever thereof, neither of His true, heavenly attributes, nor of the actual circumstances of His earthly life, nor of the evidences of His powerful and unblemished behavior. Actuated by your own fancies, you consider Him to be alien to the sovereign Truth, while in the estimation of God He is none other than the Promised One Himself, invested with the power of the sovereign Truth, and verily He is, as decreed in the Mother Book, held answerable in the midst of the Burning Bush ....*[5]

---

1 Bahá'u'lláh in Rabbani, "The Conversion of the Great-Uncle of the Báb", p. 29.

2 Christopher Buck, *Symbol and Secret*, p. 3.

3 Baharieh Ma'ani, *Leaves of the Twin Divine Trees*, p. xix.

4 The Báb in Rabbani, "The Conversion of the Great-Uncle of the Báb", p. 29.

5 The Báb, *Selections*, p. 52.

To His female relatives

O Qurratu'l-'Ayn![1] *Deliver the summons of the most exalted Word unto the handmaids among Thy kindred, caution them against the Most Great Fire and announce unto them the joyful tidings that following this mighty covenant there shall be everlasting reunion with God in the Paradise of His good-pleasure, nigh unto the Seat of Holiness. Verily God, the Lord of creation, is potent over all things.*[2]

His mother, Fáṭimih Bagum

The Báb wrote to His mother, Fáṭimih Bagum (1800 – d. 1881 in 'Iráq):[3]

O Thou Mother of the Remembrance! May the peace and salutation of God rest upon thee. Indeed thou hast endured patiently in Him Who is the sublime Self of God. Recognize then the station of thy Son Who is none other than the mighty Word of God. He hath verily pledged Himself to be answerable for thee both in thy grave and on the Judgment Day, while thou hast, in the Preserved Tablet of God, been immortalized as the "Mother of the Faithful" by the Pen of His Remembrance.[4]

His wife, Khadíjih Bagum

The Báb wrote to His wife, Khadíjih Bagum (1822 – d. 1882 in Shíráz):[5] [6]

O thou who art the chosen one among women! He is God; glorified is the splendor of His light. The verses in this Tablet are revealed for the one who hath believed in the signs of her Lord and is reckoned among such as are wholly devoted unto Him. Bear thou witness that verily no God is there but Him, Who is both my Lord and thine, and that no other God besides Him

---

1 *Qurratu'l-'Ayn* ("Solace of the Eyes") is one of the titles of the Báb.

2 The Báb, *Selections,* p. 52.

3 "This is that which hath been now sent down from the Highest Realm of Glory: O people! Know ye that We have singled out for special favour the mother of the Primal Point, who hath been mentioned before the Throne as the most virtuous of all handmaids [Khayru'n Nisá']." From a Tablet revealed by Bahá'u'lláh to Fáṭimih Bagum (Baharieh Rouhani Ma'ani, *Leaves of the Twin Divine Trees,* p. 24).

4 The Báb, *Selections,* pp. 52–53.

5 Baharieh Ma'ani, *Leaves of the Twin Divine Trees,* p. 29.

6 "...calamities have always been and will continue to be the lot of God's chosen ones. Therefore, blessed is the one who is satisfied with and thankful for all that hath visited him. For nothing from God touches a person except what is best for him of all that hath been created between the heavens and the earth. Since people are unaware of this mystery and its secrets, they are saddened when calamity strikes. God willing, thou wilt be always seated upon the seat of assurance and nourished with the fruits of understanding. Verily, He is the best of all providers and protectors." From a Tablet revealed by Bahá'u'lláh to Khadíjih Bagum (Baharieh Rouhani Ma'ani, *Leaves of the Twin Divine Trees,* p.44).

existeth. He is the Bountiful, the Almighty. Yield thee thanks unto God, for He hath graciously aided thee in this Day, revealed for thee the clear verses of this Tablet, and hath numbered thee among such women as have believed in the signs of God, have taken Him as their guardian and are of the grateful. Verily God shall soon reward thee and those who have believed in His signs with an excellent reward from His presence. Assuredly no God is there other than Him, the All-Possessing, the Most Generous. The revelations of His bounty pervade all created things; He is the Merciful, the Compassionate.[1]

O concourse of Light! Hear My call from the point of Fire in this ocean of snow-white water on this crimson earth. Verily, I am God, besides Whom there is no other God. On the exalted throne a beloved noble woman, bearing the same name [Khadíjih] *as the beloved of the First Friend* [the Prophet Muḥammad], *was wedded to this Great Remembrance. And verily I caused the angels of Heaven and the denizens of Paradise, on the day of the Covenant, to bear witness, in truth, to God's Remembrance.*[2]

My sweet love, may God preserve thee. God is my witness that since the time of separation sorrow has been so intense that it cannot be described.[3]

His father, Siyyid Muḥammad Riḍá

A prayer of the Báb for His father, Siyyid Muḥammad Riḍá (1787 – d. 1828 in Shíráz):[4]

O Lord our God! Verily, my father hath died, having never beheld me invested with the Greatest Word. Impart my Cause unto him, O my Lord, as he dwelleth with the angels of the heavenly Throne. Make him steadfast in the greatest word by your grace, and inscribe his name with such are deemed praiseworthy in the estimation of the Remembrance (qustas al-zikr) in the vicinity of the Báb.[5]

Regarding His son, Aḥmad

Messages of comfort to His wife for the loss of their son, Aḥmad (d. 1843 in Shíráz)

O well-beloved![6] *Value highly the grace of the Great Remembrance, for it cometh from God, the Loved One. Thou shalt not be a woman, like other women, if thou obeyest God in the Cause of Truth, the greatest Truth. Know thou the great bounty conferred upon thee by the Ancient of Days, and take*

---

1 The Báb, *Selections*, p. 63.

2 The Báb in Baharieh Ma'ani, *Leaves of the Twin Divine Trees*, p. 32.

3 H.M. Balyuzi, *Khadíjih Bagum: The Wife of the Báb*, p. 36.

4 Dates provided by Amanat in *Resurrection and Renewal*, pp. 110–111.

5 The Báb in Fereydun Vahman, "The Báb", p. 7.

6 The Báb is addressing His wife.

pride in being the consort of the Well-Beloved, Who is loved by God, the Greatest. Sufficient unto thee is this glory which cometh unto thee from God, the All-Wise, the All-Praised. Be patient in all that God hath ordained concerning the Báb and His Family. Verily, thy son, Aḥmad, is with Fáṭimih,[1] *the Sublime, in the sanctified Paradise.*[2]

O thou who art loved by the Supreme Beloved of My Lover! Thou art unique amongst women. ... Verily thy son Aḥmad is, in very truth, with the exalted Fáṭimih, nurtured by knowledge in the heaven of holiness.[3]

Prayers for His son, Aḥmad

All praise be to God Who bestowed upon the Solace of the Eyes [The Báb], *in His youth, Aḥmad. We did verily raise him up unto God...O Solace of the Eyes! Be patient in what thy God hath ordained for thee. Verily he doeth whatsoever He willeth. He is the All-Wise in the exercise of His justice. He is thy Lord, the Ancient of Days, and praised be He in whatever He ordereth.*[4]

O God, my God! Would that a thousand Ishmaels were given Me, this Abraham of Thine, that I might have offered them, each and all, as a loving sacrifice unto Thee. O my Beloved, my heart's Desire! The sacrifice of this Aḥmad whom Thy servant 'Alí-Muḥammad hath offered up on the altar of Thy love can never suffice to quench the flame of longing in His heart. Not until He immolates His own heart at Thy feet, not until His whole body falls a victim to the cruelest tyranny in Thy path, not until His breast is made a target for countless darts for Thy sake, will the tumult of His soul be stilled. O my God, my only Desire! Grant that the sacrifice of My son, My only son, may be acceptable unto Thee. Grant that it be a prelude to the sacrifice of My own, My entire self, in the path of Thy good pleasure. Endue with Thy grace My life-blood which I yearn to shed in Thy path. Cause it to water and nourish the seed of Thy Faith. Endow it with Thy celestial potency, that this infant seed of God may soon germinate in the hearts of men, that it may thrive and prosper, that it may grow to become a mighty tree, beneath the shadow of which all the peoples and kindreds of the earth may gather. Answer Thou My prayer, O God, and fulfil My most cherished desire. Thou art, verily, the Almighty, the All-Bountiful.[5]

The Afnán as celebrated by Bahá'u'lláh

Verily, in this Dispensation, all have been summoned to the Most Exalted Horizon and guided to the Most Great Ocean. At the beginning of Our Days, a special prayer was revealed for the Afnán, which ordained that they would be faithful to the Manifestation of God and recognize Him. God willing, they

---

1 The daughter of the Prophet Muḥammad.

2 The Báb in Baharieh Ma'ani, *Leaves of the Twin Divine Trees*, p. 32.

3 The Báb in Nader Saiedi, *Gate of the Heart*, p. 153.

4 The Báb in Balyuzi, *The Báb*, p. 47.

5 The Báb in Nabíl-i-A'ẓam, *The Dawn-Breakers*, pp. 76–77.

> *will arise to fulfil what hath been decreed for them and will remain firm and steadfast in the Cause of God. Blessed are those whom We have called by this name, Afnán. Verily, the sweet fragrance of the All-Merciful hath been wafted from them. Moreover, We have established them as twigs of Our own Tree. Verily, this is Our favor upon them. We beseech God to protect them from the traces of the pen and the veils of knowledge. We have bestowed this gift on some in the Book, the contents of which are concealed from all save the Lord of Creation. Soon what hath been ordained for them by the Almighty, the All-knowing, will appear.*[1]

Of all the quotations from the Writings of the Báb presented in this volume, the ones cited in the present chapter show the Báb at His most tender. Indeed, all those who have been addressed, have been exalted through no merit of their own but simply because of the profound love that the Báb bore for them.

---

1 Bahá'u'lláh in Mírzá Afnán, *The Genesis of the Bábí-Bahá'í Faiths*, p. 296.

Part III
The Bábí and Bahá'í Revelations

15

He Whom God shall make Manifest: His station and influence

This chapter continues the discussion commenced in chapter 6 about *Him Whom God shall make Manifest* as elaborated on mainly in the Bayán.

In the Writings of the Báb, the expression *"He/Him Whom God shall make Manifest"* refers to Bahá'u'lláh.

The Figure of *"Man Yuẓhiruhu'lláh"*[1] provides for the continuation and extension of the Faith of the Báb towards its own fulfilment. The main part of the mission of the Báb, in the words of the Hand of the Cause A. Q. Faizi, was to plant "the seeds of love and obedience to the Promised One in the hearts of the Bábís."[2] This Figure was first mentioned in the second year of the Revelation of the Báb in a Tablet specifically addressed to *"... the All Glorious Lord—He Who hath been aforetime and will be hereafter made manifest."*[3]

The Báb referred to *Him Whom God shall make Manifest* explicitly as *Bahá* ("Glory", "Splendor" or "Light"), and addressed Bahá'u'lláh with that name.[4] The given name of Bahá'u'lláh was Mírzá Ḥusayn 'Alí. In the Persian Bayán, the Báb refers to the future "Order of Bahá'u'lláh".[5] Likewise, the Báb wrote in the Qayyúmu'l-Asmá' about the relationship of His Inner essence with the *"Spirit of Bahá"*:

> *By the righteousness of the One true God, I am the Maid of Heaven begotten by the Spirit of Bahá, abiding within the Mansion hewn out of a mass of ruby, tender and vibrant ....*[6]

"Between Bahá'u'lláh and the Báb there was communication privately." 'Abdu'l-Bahá said, *"The Báb wrote a letter to Him in which the name Bahá'u'lláh was incorporated 360 times."*[7] The Hand of the Cause A. Q. Faizí, wrote in this regard that, "The Báb adored the name 'Bahá' and used it profusely in all His Writings. He even made many derivatives from this one word and wrote them out in a Tablet which had the form of a five-pointed star, symbolizing the human

---

1 *Man Yuẓhiruhu'lláh* (من يظهره الله), "Him Whom God shall make manifest".

2 Faizi, *Penned by A. Q. Faizi*, pp. 236–237.

3 The Báb, *Selections*, p. 4.

4 Nabíl-i-A'ẓam, *The Dawn-Breakers*, p. 293.

5 Shoghi Effendi, *The World Order of Bahá'u'lláh*, pp. 146–147.

6 The Báb, *Selections*, p. 54.

7 'Abdu'l-Bahá in *Star of the West*, III:9, 20 August 1912, p. 3.

temple."[1] Bahá'u'lláh was the recipient of that Tablet.[2] Bahá'u'lláh and the Báb never met physically.[3]

The concurrence of the Báb and Bahá'u'lláh led to their joint designation as the "Twin Manifestations of God". This title links to the visions referred to by Zecharias as the "Two Anointed" (4:14)[4] and by John the Evangelist in his *Apocalypse* as the two "woes" (Revelation 9:12), the "Two Witnesses", the "Two Olive Trees" and the "Two Candlesticks" (Revelation 11:3–5) that would appear in the *last days*.[5] Similarly, in the Zoroastrian religion two figures were expected, U<u>sh</u>idár-Máh and the <u>Sh</u>áh Bahram.[6]

Muḥammad made a similar prophecy: "Verily I say, after the *Qá'im* ["He Who shall arise"] the *Qayyúm* ["the Self-Subsisting"] will be made manifest."[7] In the *Qur'án* He told of the Day when two Divine Messengers would appear. Prophet Muhammad had said:

> And there was a blast on the trumpet, and all who are in the heavens and all who are in the earth expired, save those whom God permitted to live. Then was there sounded another blast, and, lo! arising, they gazed around them. And the earth shone with the light of her Lord, and the Book was set, and the Prophets were brought up, and the witnesses; and judgment was given between them with equity; and none was wronged.[8]

Similarly, an Islamic tradition cited by Bukhari affirms:
At the time of the end God shall manifest himself to all mankind with the attributes of divinity and majesty, but very few shall advance towards him .... Then again he will appear a second time manifesting all the qualities of servitude and the people will flock around him and believe in him and praise and laud his uncreated virtues.[9]

This chapter deals with the role of Bahá'u'lláh as "*Him Whom God shall make Manifest*", then, reflects upon the act of believing in Him and observing His exhortations. The act of believing in Him and observing His exhortations are then considered. In this chapter the name of Bahá'u'lláh is used interchangeably in the context of *Him Whom God shall make Manifest*.

---

1 Faizi, *Penned by A. Q. Faizi*, p. 34.
2 Hasan Balyuzi, *The Báb*, pp. 151–152.
3 Bahá'í World Centre, "Whether Bahá'u'lláh and the Báb Met".
4 William Sears, *Thief in the Night*, p. 93.
5 William Sears, *Thief in the Night*, p. 93.
6 William Sears, *Thief in the Night*, p. 92.
7 Nabíl-i-A'ẓam, *The Dawn-Breakers*, p. 41. Author's emphasis.
8 Qur'án 39:60, cited in Nabíl-i-A'ẓam, *The Dawn-Breakers*, p. 41.
9 William Sears, *Thief in the Night*, p. 92.

The Báb counselled the people of His time about how to approach and interact with *Him Whom God shall make Manifest* at the time of His appearance.

The themes in this chapter are arranged in the following order:

- Greatness of Him Whom God shall make Manifest (Bahá'u'lláh)
- Writings of Bahá'u'lláh compared to the Bayán
- The station of Bahá'u'lláh
- Proof and testimony of Him Whom God shall make Manifest
- Praise for the station of Him Whom God shall make Manifest
- Period between the Revelations of the Báb and Bahá'u'lláh
- Believing in Him Whom God shall make Manifest
- Greatness of *Him Whom God shall make Manifest* (Bahá'u'lláh)

Greatness of *Him Whom God shall make Manifest*

The Writings of the Báb consistently explained the exalted position of the upcoming Messenger of God. In 1844 He directed Mullá Ḥusayn to Tehran and advised him that the city *"enshrines a Mystery of such transcendent holiness as … Shíráz* (His own birthplace) *cannot hope to rival."*[1]

"[*A*]*ny reference, revealed by God,"* the Báb wrote, *"to meeting God or attaining the presence of the Lord intendeth naught but Him Whom God shall make Manifest."*[2] Moreover, the Báb exhorted, *"Do not desire for Him Whose presence is none other than My Own presence that which ye would not wish for yourselves."*[3]

Bahá'u'lláh is referred to in the Writings of the Báb in the most superlative terms. For instance, in His first book, the Qayyúmu'l-Asmá', the Báb wrote:

> *Exalted art Thou, O my Lord the Omnipotent! How puny and contemptible my word and all that pertaineth unto me appear unless they be related to Thy great glory. Grant that through the assistance of Thy grace whatsoever pertaineth unto me may be acceptable in Thy sight.*[4]
>
> *And when the appointed hour hath struck, do Thou, by the leave of God, the All-Wise, reveal from the heights of the Most Lofty and Mystic Mount a faint, an infinitesimal glimmer of Thy impenetrable Mystery, that they who have recognized the radiance of the Sinaic Splendor may faint away and die as they catch a lightning glimpse of the fierce and crimson Light that envelops Thy Revelation.*[5]
>
> *Out of utter nothingness, O great and omnipotent Master Thou hast, through the celestial potency of Thy might, brought me forth and raised me up to proclaim this Revelation. I have made none other but Thee my trust; I have*

---

1 The Báb in Nabíl-i-A'ẓam, *The Dawn-Breakers,* p. 96.

2 The Báb in Nader Saiedi, *Gate of the Heart,* p. 354.

3 The Báb in Nader Saiedi, *Logos and Civilization,* p. 120.

4 The Báb in Shoghi Effendi, *The World Order of Bahá'u'lláh,* p. 101.

5 The Báb, *Selections,* p. 53.

clung to no will but Thy Will. Thou art, in truth, the All-Sufficing and behind Thee standeth the true God, He Who overshadoweth all things. Indeed sufficient unto Me is God, the Exalted, the Powerful, the Sustainer.[1]

The Báb asserts in His Writings that no one can fully understand the station of *Him Whom God shall make Manifest*:

No created thing comprehendeth Him, while He in truth comprehendeth all things. Even when it is said 'no created thing comprehendeth Him', this refers to the Mirror of His Revelation, that is Him Whom God shall make Manifest. Indeed too high and exalted is He for anyone to allude unto Him.[2]

In the Bayán, special divine powers are attributed to Bahá'u'lláh:

Blazes of hell-fire will God transform into light by Him Whom God shall make Manifest, and lights shall He transform into blazes of hell-fire by Him.[3]

The Báb compares the greatness of *Him Whom God shall make Manifest* with the Sun:

He resembleth the sun. Were it to shine forth infinite times from infinite horizons, it would be the same sun. Naught hath been created by God except for the sake of Him, for it is only through Him that anything reacheth up to God.[4]

The Báb declares Himself as the **First to believe in Him**:

He [the Báb] *is the First to believe in Him Whom God will make manifest, and He is the First Who hath believed in Him Who hath been manifested.*[5]

Verily, we have believed in Thee and in Thy signs ere the dawn of Thy Manifestation, and in Thee are we all well assured. Verily, we have believed in Thee and in Thy signs after the fulfillment of Thy Manifestation, and in Thee do we all believe. Verily, we have believed in Thee and in Thy signs at the hour of Thy Manifestation and bear witness that through Thine injunction "Be Thou" all things have been created.[6]

This recognition has been through Bahá'u'lláh *in the immortal realm*:

I have attained the recognition of Thee through Thine Own Self before the dwellers of the heavens and the earth, bearing witness that Thou art in truth the Almighty, the All-Praised.[7]

---

1 The Báb, *Selections*, p. 59.
2 The Báb, *Selections*, p. 113.
3 The Báb in Hasan Balyuzi, *Edward Granville Browne*, p. 84.
4 The Báb in Nader Saiedi, *Introduction to the Tablet to Báqir*, p. 10.
5 The Báb in Nader Saiedi, *Gate of the Heart*, p. 198.
6 The Báb, *Selections*, p. 4.
7 The Báb, *Selections*, pp. 4–5.

From all eternity I have indeed recognized Thee and unto all eternity will ever do so through Thine Own Self and not through anyone else besides Thee.[1]

The Báb **expresses His humility before** Bahá'u'lláh:

Thus, were I to find Him alone, in His transcendent unity, I would bow down, unhesitatingly, before Him, solely on account of His intrinsic supreme worth, inasmuch as that kneeling is naught but adoration for Thee in Thy oneness, for there is none other God but Thee.[2]

In truth I Myself am the first to bow down before God and to believe in Him... However, when the Tree of the Bayán attaineth its highest development, We shall bend it low as a token of adoration towards its Lord Who will appear in the person of Him Whom God will make manifest.[3]

Such is His devotion that the Báb also asks for forgiveness from *Him Whom God shall make Manifest*:

From everlasting I have besought and unto everlasting will beseech forgiveness for my limited understanding of Thee, aware as I am that there is no God but Thee, the All-Glorious, the Almighty.[4]

The Báb also offers **to lay down His life** for the sake of Bahá'u'lláh:

O Thou Remnant of God! I have sacrificed myself wholly for Thee; I have accepted curses for Thy sake, and have yearned for naught but martyrdom in the path of Thy love. Sufficient witness unto me is God, the Exalted, the Protector, the Ancient of Days.[5]

Writings of Bahá'u'lláh compared to the Bayán

Though the Báb magnifies *Him Whom God shall make Manifest* in His books and epistles, He also acknowledges that His words cannot do justice to the Writings of *Him Whom God shall make Manifest*:

Of all the tributes I have paid to Him Who is to come after Me, the greatest is this, My written confession, that no words of Mine can adequately describe Him, nor can any reference to Him in My Book, the Bayán, do justice to His Cause.[6]

1 The Báb, *Selections*, p. 4.
2 The Báb in Nader Saiedi, *Introduction to the Tablet to Báqir*, p. 3.
3 The Báb, *Selections*, p. 167.
4 The Báb, *Selections*, p. 4.
5 The Báb, *Selections*, p. 59.
6 The Báb in Bahá'u'lláh. *Gleanings from the Writings of Bahá'u'lláh*, p. 10.

15. *He Whom God shall make manifest*, Section I

For example, He says that "*a thousand perusals of the Bayán cannot equal the perusal of a single verse to be revealed by* Him Whom God shall make manifest[1] He further states:

> *Say, every favorable and praiseworthy designation in the Bayán is but an allusion to those who recognize Him Whom God will make manifest, and who believe with certainty in God and in His holy Writings, while every unfavorable designation therein is meant to refer to such as repudiate Him Whom God will make manifest, though they may act uprightly within the bounds laid down in the Bayán.*[2]
>
> *And should anyone inscribe with true faith but one letter of that Revelation* [Bahá'u'lláh], *his recompense would be greater than for inscribing all the heavenly Writings of the past and all that has been written during previous Dispensations.*[3]

The Báb states that "*the Revealer of the Bayán knoweth its beginning and end, which is none other than Him Whom God will make manifest.*[4] The fact that the Bayán emanated from Bahá'u'lláh[5] confers a sense of the importance of this Holy Book in the Bábí-Bahá'í dispensation. In this respect, Bahá'u'lláh stated:

> *In this Day the Bayán is conditioned and dependent upon the acceptance of this Most Great Revelation. We, verily, did send down unto My Herald that which caused the Books of God, the Help in Peril, the Self-Subsisting, to rejoice. We sent it unto Him and, when it reached Him and He perused it, He was so transported by the breaths of Revelation that with His whole being He soared into Mine atmosphere, and purposed to attain My presence and to stand before My face. Such was the vibrant influence of Our words upon Him as no tongue can ever tell, nor any pen recount. To this testifieth the Mother Book in this, the Day of Return. We, verily, concealed the root of the Cause in order to ensure its preservation—this in token of Our wisdom, and I, truly, am the All-Glorious, the Unconstrained.*[6]

The station of Bahá'u'lláh

The Writings of the Báb articulate the exalted position of Bahá'u'lláh as the Primal Will and the Messenger of God to appear on the Day of Resurrection. This section explores what the Báb wrote about Bahá'u'lláh's divine prerogatives as

---

1 The Báb, *Selections*, p. 104.

2 The Báb, *Selections*, p. 138.

3 The Báb, *Selections*, p. 91.

4 The Báb in Nader Saiedi, *Gate of the Heart*, p. 290.

5 The Báb. Persian Bayán 6:1; 6:16.

6 Bahá'u'lláh, *The Bahá'í Reference Library.* Available from: https://www.bahai.org/library/authoritative-texts/bahaullah/additional-tablets-extracts-from-tablets-revealed-bahaullah/additional-tablets-extracts-from-tablets-revealed-bahaullah.pdf?369f2267

the Supreme Manifestation of God for this age, and the relationship between the Báb and Bahá'u'lláh

As the Primal Will

The Báb refers to the manifest station of Bahá'u'lláh as the Primal Will:

> *All, according to their capacity, are enjoined to love Him and recognize Him and traverse the path of the Seas of Names and Attributes. Should it be beyond their power, however, God hath ordained for Him a different station and a lesser course, which is to recognize His manifest station, known also as the Sun of Truth, the Primal Creation, the Primal Will, the Eternal Sun. ... It is within this lesser station that after the utterance, 'There is none other God but God,' servitude and its association with the Manifestation of each divine Revelation have been mentioned.*[1]

As the Supreme Manifestation of God

The Báb states that all Manifestations of God have been generated by the actions of Bahá'u'lláh:

> *Every Manifestation is but a revelation of Thine Own Self, with each of Whom we have truly appeared and we bow down in adoration before Thee.*[2]

> *He it is Who, by a mere vibration of His eternal and Holy Tongue, createth, instantly, Whomsoever He willeth of Prophets, Vicegerents, Men of truth or Pure Ones. Inasmuch as all Guides and Messengers are His creation, and all are sent forth by Him, they all emphatically proclaimed: There is none other God but God. Await anxiously for the One Whose Countenance shall remind you of God. For, verily, but for attaining His presence ye would not have been created. He it is Who createth all things at His behest.*[3]

Furthermore, all previous revelations were created for the Revelation of Bahá'u'lláh, which is the consummation of all previous religions:

> *... and all [previous] Revelations and this Revelation and the Revelation of Him Whom God will make manifest were created for the Revelation of Him who shall come after Him Whom God will make manifest (ba'd man yuzhiruh Alláh). And all these Revelations [were] for the coming of the One after the One after Him Whom God will make manifest. And in this manner incessantly the Sun of Truth shines forth and sets, without beginning or end.*[4]

Divine prerogatives of Bahá'u'lláh

The Báb stated that *He Whom God shall make manifest* can appoint any person a Prophet:

---

1 Nader Saiedi, *Gate of the Heart*, p. 185.
2 The Báb, *Selections*, p. 4.
3 The Báb in Saiedi, Nader. *Introduction to the Tablet to Báqir*, p. 7.
4 The Báb in Eschraghi, "Undermining the Foundations of Orthodoxy", p. 227.

> *Were He to make of every one on earth a Prophet, all would, in very truth, be accounted as Prophets in the sight of God.*[1]

> *In the day of the revelation of Him Whom God will make manifest all that dwell on earth will be equal in His estimation. Whomsoever He ordaineth as a Prophet, he, verily, hath been a Prophet from the beginning that hath no beginning, and will thus remain until the end that hath no end, inasmuch as this is an act of God. And whosoever is made a Vicegerent by Him, shall be a Vicegerent in all the worlds, for this is an act of God.*[2]

Similarly, the Báb says that *Him Whom God shall make Manifest* **is effectively the Mouthpiece of God**:

> *The light of the people of the world is their knowledge and utterance; while the splendors shed from the glorious acts of Him Whom God will make manifest are His Words, through whose potency He rolleth up the whole world of existence, sets it under His Own authority by relating it unto Himself, then as the Mouthpiece of God, the Source of His divine light—exalted and glorified be He—proclaimeth: "Verily, verily, I am God, no God is there but Me; in truth all others except Me are My creatures. Say, O My creatures! Me alone, therefore, should ye fear."*[3]

Relationship between the Báb and Bahá'u'lláh

The Báb states that He was manifested because of *Him Whom God shall make Manifest*:

> *Cling thou to His Will, inasmuch as the Day of His Revelation is the life to come in relation to this life; and were it not for His Book, This Book would not have been revealed; and were it not for Him, God would not have revealed Me. I am verily, Him, and He verily, is Me.*[4]

The Báb also states that They comprise a single reality:

> *Therefore let not your recognition become fruitless, inasmuch as the Bayán, notwithstanding the sublimity of its station, beareth fealty to Him Whom God will make manifest, and it is He Who beseemeth most to be acclaimed as the Seat of divine Reality, though indeed He is I and I am He.*[5]

Such a unity will be evident on the day of the appearance of *Him Whom God shall make Manifest*:

---

1 The Báb in Bahá'u'lláh, *Epistle to the Son of the Wolf*, p. 155.
2 The Báb in Bahá'u'lláh, *Epistle to the Son of the Wolf*, p. 155.
3 The Báb, *Selections*, p. 98.
4 The Báb in Nader Saiedi, *Modernity in the Writings of the Báb*, p. 3.
5 The Báb, *Selections*, pp. 167–168.

All things return unto, and by, this Indivisible One Being. During the next Resurrection, this Indivisible One Being is naught but the very being of Him Whom God will make manifest ....[1]

Proof and testimony of *Him Whom God shall make Manifest*

The Báb states that the verses of Bahá'u'lláh will verify the divine truth of His Mission. He writes: *"Certitude itself is ashamed to be called upon to certify His truth ... and Testimony itself is ashamed to testify unto Him."*[2] Furthermore, as previously stated, in the Persian Bayán, the Báb made mention of a "*Living Book*", identifying it as *Him Whom God will make manifest* [Bahá'u'lláh].[3]

The Báb states that the testimony of Bahá'u'lláh's is like the sun:

> *If at the time of the appearance of Him Whom God will make manifest all the dwellers of the earth were to bear witness unto a thing whereunto He beareth witness differently, His testimony would be like unto the sun, while theirs would be even as a false image produced in a mirror which is not facing the sun. For had it been otherwise their testimony would have proved a faithful reflection of His testimony.*[4]

The Báb also states that the verses of Bahá'u'lláh are His ultimate proof:

> *Recognize Him by His verses. The greater your neglect in seeking to know Him, the more grievously will ye be veiled in fire.*[5]

> *His verses are, by themselves, sufficient proof of the radiant lights of the Sun of His Being, just as the powerlessness of all is the mighty evidence of the utter need and dependence of all upon Him.*[6]

Moreover, such a truth is so sublime that it is unmistakable in relation to any other writings:

> *On the Day of Resurrection when He Whom God will make manifest cometh unto you, invested with conclusive proofs, ye shall hold His Cause as being devoid of truth, whereas God hath apprised you in the Bayán that no similarity existeth between the Cause of Him Whom God will make manifest and the cause of others.*[7]

The Báb writes that one verse from Bahá'u'lláh is more magnificent than the entire world's literature:

---

1 The Báb in Nader Saiedi, *Gate of the Heart*, p. 266.
2 The Báb in Shoghi Effendi, *God Passes By*, p. 30.
3 The Báb in Bahá'u'lláh, *The Kitáb-i-Aqdas*, p. 231.
4 The Báb, *Selections*, p. 100.
5 The Báb in Bahá'u'lláh, *Epistle to the Son of the Wolf*, p. 159.
6 The Báb in Nader Saiedi, *Gate of the Heart*, p. 371.
7 The Báb, *Selections*, p. 134.

I swear by the most sacred Essence of God that but one line of the Words uttered by Him is more sublime than the words uttered by all that dwell on earth. Nay, I beg forgiveness for making this comparison. How could the reflections of the sun in the visible heaven compare with the wondrous rays of the sun in the visible heaven? The station of one is that of nothingness, while the station of the other, by the righteousness of God—hallowed and magnified be His Name—is that of the Reality of things ....[1]

The teachings of the "Twin Manifestations" reinforce each other. For example, the Báb explained that Bahá'u'lláh will come to perfect His own revelation as "*He is made manifest in order to gather the fruits of the trees He hath planted ....*[2] That is, the appearance of Bahá'u'lláh will vindicate the Cause of the Báb:

Say, He Whom God shall make manifest will surely redeem the rights of those who truly believe in God and in His signs, for they are the ones who merit reward from His presence .... Say, He shall vindicate the Cause through the potency of His command and shall bring to naught all perversion of truth by virtue of His behest. Verily God is potent over all things.[3]

Praise for the station of *Him Whom God shall make Manifest*

According to the Báb, *He Whom God shall make manifest* is like the sun, independent of all beneath it:

He—glorified be His mention—resembleth the sun. Were unnumbered mirrors to be placed before it, each would, according to its capacity, reflect the splendor of that sun, and were none to be placed before it, it would still continue to rise and set, and the mirrors alone would be veiled from its light.[4]

Praise be to God that He hath enabled us to become cognizant of Him Whom God will make manifest in the Day of Resurrection, so that we may derive benefit from the fruit of our existence and be not deprived of attaining the presence of God. For indeed this is the object of our creation and the sole purpose underlying every virtuous deed we may perform. Such is the bounty which God hath conferred upon us; verily He is the All-Bountiful, the Gracious.[5]

The glory of Him Whom God will make manifest is immeasurably above every other glory, and His majesty is far above every other majesty. His beauty excelleth every other embodiment of beauty, and His grandeur immensely exceedeth every other manifestation of grandeur. Every light paleth before the radiance of His light, and every other exponent of mercy falleth short before the tokens of His mercy. Every other perfection is as naught in face of His consummate perfection, and every other display of might is as nothing

1 The Báb, *Selections*, p. 100.
2 The Báb, *Selections*, pp. 107–108.
3 The Báb, *Selections*, p. 141.
4 The Báb, *Selections*, p. 156.
5 The Báb, *Selections*, p. 110.

before His absolute might. His names are superior to all other names. His good-pleasure taketh precedence over any other expression of good-pleasure. His preeminent exaltation is far above the reach of every other symbol of exaltation. The splendor of His appearance far surpasseth that of any other appearance. His divine concealment is far more profound than any other concealment. His loftiness is immeasurably above every other loftiness. His gracious favor is unequalled by any other evidence of favor. His power transcendeth every power. His sovereignty is invincible in the face of every other sovereignty. His celestial dominion is exalted far above every other dominion. His knowledge pervadeth all created things, and His consummate power extendeth over all beings.[1]

Period between the two Revelations

The Báb often referred in His Writings to the imminence of the appearance of Bahá'u'lláh, "*Verily, the Rising of the Sun to its zenith is at hand and yet do ye not recognise that Day.*"[2]

The Báb specified two periods to denote the length of time between the start of the two Revelations: namely, from His own declaration in 1844 to the first intimations of the mission of Bahá'u'lláh in the Síyáh-Chál in 1853 (nine years); and from His own declaration to the public declaration of Bahá'u'lláh in Baghdád in 1863 (nineteen years).

Year nine

In several passages, the Báb refers to the **year nine**, meaning the lapse of time since His revelation began in 1844. This prophecy was fulfilled with the first indications of the mission of Bahá'u'lláh, which were hidden from the community. Bahá'u'lláh attributes the following statements to the Báb:

> *"In the year nine ye will attain unto all good." "In the year nine ye will attain unto the Presence of God." "In the year nine ye shall attain unto all good." ... "In the year nine ye will attain unto the Presence of God."*[3]
>
> *Ere nine will have elapsed from the inception of this Cause, the realities of the created things will not be made manifest. All that thou hast as yet seen is but the stage from the moist germ until We clothed it with flesh. Be patient, until thou beholdest a new creation. Say: 'Blessed, therefore, be God, the most excellent of Makers!'*[4]
>
> *This, verily, is that which We promised thee, ere the moment We answered thy call. Wait thou until nine will have elapsed from the time of the Bayán. Then exclaim: 'Blessed be God, the most excellent of Makers!'*[5]

1 The Báb, *Selections*, pp. 156–157.
2 The Báb in Nader Saiedi, *Logos and Civilization*, p. 120.
3 The Báb cited in *Epistle to the Son of the Wolf*, p. 141.
4 The Báb cited in *Epistle to the Son of the Wolf*, p. 152.
5 The Báb cited in *Epistle to the Son of the Wolf*, p. 142.

The Báb also referred to the year AH 1268 (CE 1853): *"After Ḥín (68)*[1] *a Cause shall be given unto you which ye shall come to know."*[2]

Shoghi Effendi makes the following statement about the words of Bahá'u'lláh in reference to the *"year nine"*:

> *"Behold,"* Bahá'u'lláh further explains in the Kitáb-i-Badí', one of His works refuting the arguments of the people of the Bayán, *"behold, how immediately upon the completion of the ninth year of this wondrous, this most holy and merciful Dispensation, the requisite number of pure, of wholly consecrated and sanctified souls had been most secretly consummated."*[3]

Nineteen-year respite

In addition to the *"year nine"* prophecies, there are also references in the Writings of the Báb to a nineteen-year respite period. This is the duration of the Dispensation of the Báb.

> *... do Thou grant a respite of nineteen years as a token of Thy favor so that those who have embraced this Cause may be graciously rewarded by Thee.*[4]

This nineteen-year term was consummated in 1863 when Bahá'u'lláh declared His station to the Bábís gathered in the Garden of Riḍván in Baghdád. In this regard, the Báb warned His followers to *"be attentive from the inception of the Revelation till the number of Váḥid (19)"*,[5] because *"The Lord of the Day of reckoning"* would be *"manifested at the end of Váḥid (19) and the beginning of eighty (AH 1280)."*[6]

There is another reference to the number nineteen in the Persian Bayán:

> *As to the Revelation of Him Whom God will make manifest, God knoweth the age at which He maketh Him to become manifest. However, from the inception of the Revelation till nineteen years (the number of unity), take heed and be watchful, inasmuch as each year the faith of the believers will be manifested through the affirmation of a different Letter, after which they will not be able to manifest the fruits of the past Revelation except through the next Revelation.*[7]

The time of his appearance

In terms of the exact timing of His appearance, the Báb explains that nobody knows when *He Whom God shall make manifest* will appear:

---

1 Abjad value of *Ḥín.*

2 The Báb cited in *Epistle to the Son of the Wolf*, p. 152.

3 Bahá'u'lláh cited in *The World Order of Bahá'u'lláh*, p. 124.

4 The Báb, *Selections*, p. 7.

5 See the Báb in Shoghi Effendi, *God Passes By*, p. 29.

6 See the Báb in Shoghi Effendi, *God Passes By*, p. 29.

7 The Báb in Nader Saiedi, *Gate of the Heart*, p. 356.

For none knoweth the time of the Revelation except God. Whenever it appeareth, all must acknowledge the Point of Truth, and render thanks unto God.[1]

Whenever the people ask Thee of the appointed Hour say: Verily the knowledge of it is only with My Lord, Who is the Knower of the unseen.[2]

Thus in the Bayán and other Writings, the Báb **alerts the Bábís to be on guard** while awaiting Bahá'u'lláh:

At all times, await the beginning of the Revelation (awwal-i-ẓuhúr). Should you hesitate for less than a moment you will be counted among the 'new [*converts*]*' in the sight of God. Just as you call today those non-Muslims who enter Islam.*[3]

The allusion to 'new converts' (*jadíd al-Islámí*) in the above quotation refers to the Islamic tradition of according a lower status to Muslim converts—many of whom had been coerced by the sword—in comparison to believers who had been born into the faith or whose families had been Muslims for generations. However, in the teachings of the Báb, true believers are those who come to the Faith through their **own** search for truth, rather than by imitating the beliefs of their forebears, religious instructors or peers.

What is important in the context of the rest of this chapter of the Bayán, in which the Báb exalted the station of the 18 Letters of the Living beyond any of the apostles of old, is the emphasis He places on the **instant** recognition by His followers of *Him Whom God shall make Manifest*. For, if any of his most exalted followers—they who had immediately accepted His own revelation—should hesitate even for an instant before accepting Bahá'u'lláh, their station would be of no higher worth than any other convert to the Bahá'í Faith.[4]

He Whom God shall make manifest is among the believers

The Báb states in His Writings that *He Whom God shall make manifest* is like a normal human being:

Say, He Whom God shall make manifest is but one of you; He will make Himself known unto you on the Day of Resurrection. Ye shall know God when the Manifestation of His Own Self is made known unto you, that perchance ye may not stray far from His Path.[5]

---

1 The Báb in Bahá'u'lláh, *Epistle to the Son of the Wolf*, p. 157.

2 The Báb, *Selections*, p. 65.

3 Persian Bayán 6:13 (prov. tr.) in Armin Eschraghi, "Undermining the Foundations of Orthodoxy", p. 230.

4 With appreciation to Mr Nasser Saeedi, Australia, for his help in unravelling the significance of the above quotation.

5 The Báb, *Selections*, p. 144.

There are also indications that the interval between the Báb and Bahá'u'lláh would be a period of relative obscurity. For the Báb, purgatory is the period between two Manifestations of God rather than the Christian concept of being a place for suffering where people expiate their sins.[1] The Báb also used the term "*Days of Concealment*" for the period between Himself and Bahá'u'lláh.[2] The Báb anticipated a period of confusion between His passing and the advent of *Him Whom God shall make Manifest*:

> *The day will come when ye will earnestly desire to know that which would meet with the good-pleasure of God but, alas, ye shall find no path unto Him. Ye, even as camels that wander aimlessly, will not find a pasture wherein ye may gather and unite upon a Cause in which ye can assuredly believe. At that time God shall cause the Sun of Truth to shine forth and the oceans of His bounty and grace to surge, while ye will have chosen droplets of water as the object of your desire, and will have deprived yourselves of the plenteous waters in His oceans.*[3]

> *The people, during the absence of the Báb, re-enacted the episode of the Calf by setting up a blaring figure which embodied animal features in human form ....*[4]

However, the Báb reassures the Bábís **that they will be always guided** from the realms above even after His passing:

> *Today, from the inception of the Revelation of the Bayán until the advent of Him Whom God will make manifest, all attainment of exaltation by anyone is a token reflection of the exalted station of the Point of Unity and the Dayspring of the Morn of Eternity.*[5]

However, in order to be guided, the Bábís must *abide by the teachings* of the Bayán:

> *We have planted the Garden of the Bayán in the name of Him Whom God will make manifest, and have granted you permission to live therein until the time of His manifestation; then from the moment the Cause of Him Whom God will make manifest is inaugurated, We forbid you all the things ye hold as your own, unless ye may, by the leave of your Lord, be able to regain possession thereof.*[6]

In relation to the aforementioned unusually short interval of time between two consecutive Manifestations of God, Shoghi Effendi commented:

---

1 The Báb, Persian Bayán 2:8.

2 See Muḥammad Afnán, "Ayyám-i-Butún".

3 The Báb, *Selections*, p. 136.

4 The Báb, *Selections*, p. 65. The *Golden Calf* was an idol made and worshipped by the Jewish people during Moses's absence on Mount Sinai. (Exodus 32)

5 The Báb in Nader Saiedi, *Gate of the Heart*, p. 193.

6 The Báb, *Selections*, p. 135.

> The short duration of His Dispensation, the restricted range within which His laws and ordinances have been made to operate, supply no criterion whatever wherewith to judge its Divine origin and to evaluate the potency of its message. "That so brief a span," Bahá'u'lláh Himself explains, "should have separated this most mighty and wondrous Revelation from Mine own previous Manifestation, is a secret that no man can unravel and a mystery such as no mind can fathom. Its duration had been foreordained, and no man shall ever discover its reason unless and until he be informed of the contents of My Hidden Book."[1]

One of the most important points to be gleaned from the Writings of the Báb quoted in this chapter is that *He Whom God shall make manifest* was already present amongst the Bábís at the time—a Man amongst men. Yet, although physically the Manifestations of God are members of the human race—i.e. those whom science has classified as Homo sapiens—spiritually, the Manifestation belongs to a completely separate category of God's Creation.

He whom God shall make manifest is certainly a recurring and a central theme in the Writings of the Báb, particularly in the Persian Bayán. Shoghi stated that the Persian Bayán should be considered a tribute to the Promised One more than a code of laws. In this regard, Bahá'u'lláh wrote in the *Kitáb-i-Aqdas*:

> *God is My witness that the Bayán was sent down for no other purpose than to celebrate My praise, did ye but know. In it the pure in heart will find only the fragrance of My love, only My Name that overshadoweth all that seeth and is seen.*[2]

The Báb Himself stated that His laws were not permanent but were in force for a short time until the coming of Bahá'u'lláh. They had a transitory character like a bridge between the Islamic and the Bahá'í dispensations annulling under its span the religious laws from previous faiths and creeds facilitating thus the enunciation of new laws as it happened when Bahá'u'lláh revealed the Kitáb-i-Aqdas in 1873.

When the declaration of Bahá'u'lláh as the Supreme Manifestation of God occurred in the year 1863 as predicted, the way was paved; and great numbers of joyous Bábís were already prepared and waiting to accept the new divine summons.

It is noteworthy that many believers recognized Bahá'u'lláh's sublime station before the 1863 declaration. Ṭáhirih wrote the following tribute about Bahá'u'lláh:

---

1 Shoghi Effendi, *The World Order of Bahá'u'lláh*, pp. 123–124.

2 Bahá'u'lláh, *Kitáb-i-Aqdas*, para. 179, pp. 84–85

15. *He Whom God shall make manifest,* Section I

> The effulgence of the Abhá Beauty hath pierced the veil of night; behold the souls of His lovers dancing, moth-like, in the light that has flashed from His face![1]

The next chapter will explore various themes from the Writings of the Báb pertaining to the belief in and acceptance of Bahá'u'lláh as "*Him Whom God shall make Manifest*".

---

1 Ṭáhirih in *Dawn-Breakers*, p. 286.

Image Section 3

Figure 33: Tablet by the Báb in His own handwriting (1)

Figure 34: Tablet by the Báb in His own handwriting (2)

Figure 35: Tablet by the Báb in His own handwriting (3)

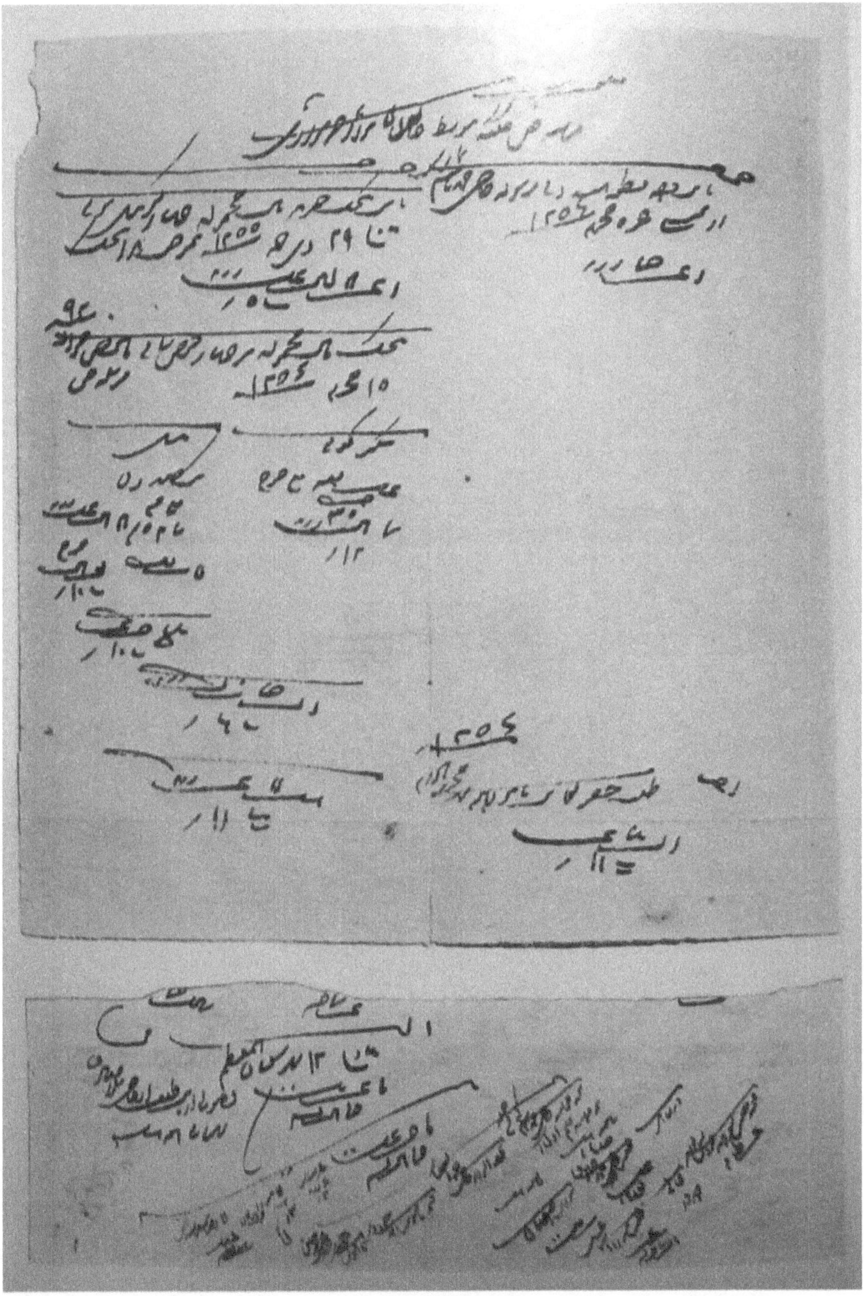

Figure 36: Trading accounts in the handwriting of the Báb, March 1840

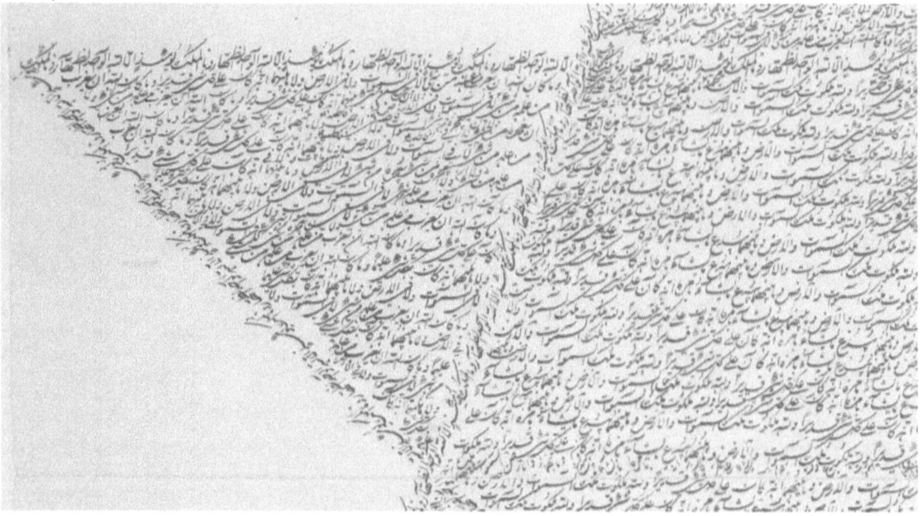

Figure 37: Tablet by the Báb in His own handwriting (4)

Figure 38: A printed version of the Persian Bayán (British Museum)

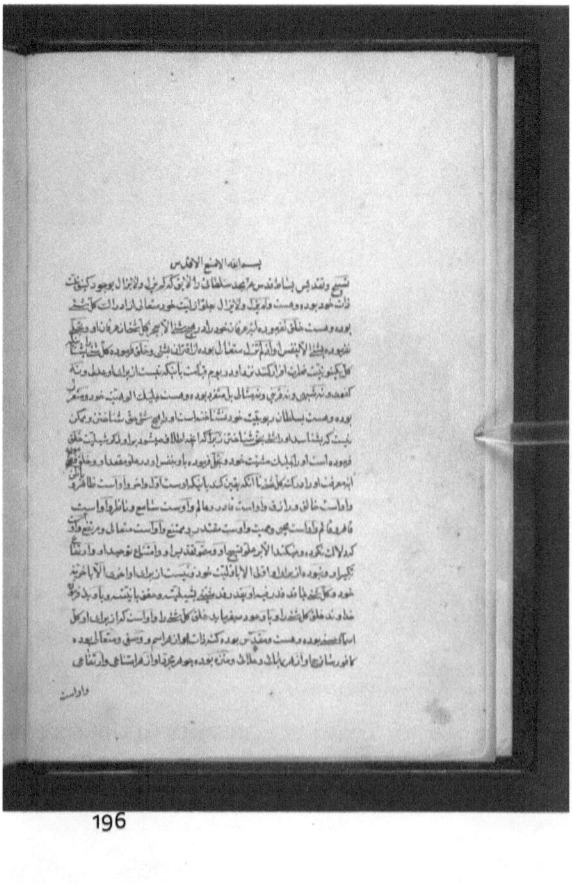

بسم الله الامنع الاقدس

Figure 39: Mírzá Taqí Khán, The Amír Kabír

Figure 40: Muḥammad Sháh

Figure 41: Ḥájí Mírzá Áqásí

Figure 42: Dr William Cormick (1822–1877) who once treated the Báb

Figure 43: Dress worn under the jubbih, worn by the Báb

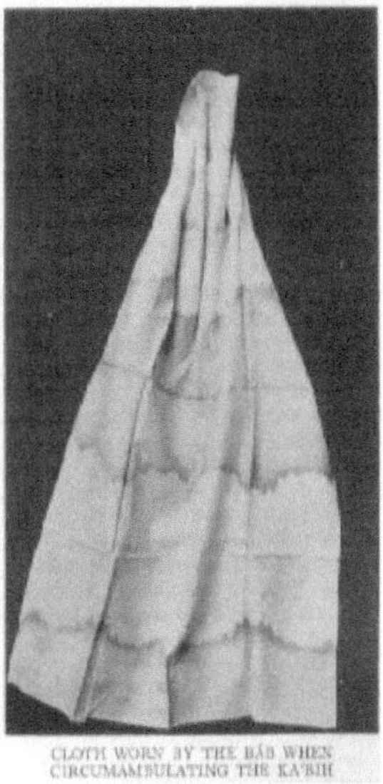

Figure 44: Cloth worn by the Báb when circumambulating the Ka'bih

Figure 45: Green silk robe worn by the Báb

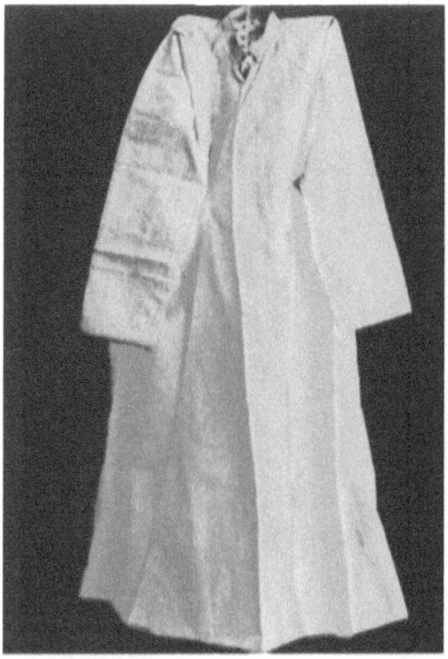

Figure 46: Robe of the Báb (1)

Figure 47: Robe of the Báb (2)

Figure 48: A coat of the Báb

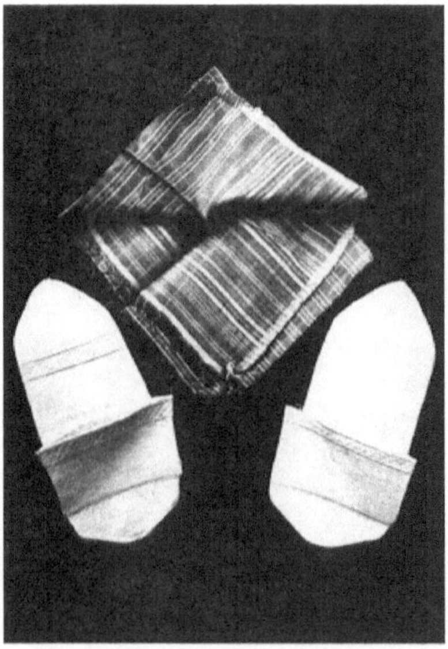

Figure 49: Sandals of the Báb

16

He Whom God shall make Manifest: Believing and accepting

There are many exhortations in Writings of the Báb warning people about the "veils" that could hinder their recognition of Bahá'u'lláh in the years after the passing of the Báb. He also gave special instructions as to how we should approach and treat *He Whom God Shall Make Manifest* when He appears.

This chapter discusses the following related themes:

- Believing in Him Whom God shall make Manifest
- Veils hindering recognition of Bahá'u'lláh
- Encouragement of certain predispositions toward *Him Whom God shall make Manifest*
- Discouragement of certain attitudes and behaviours towards *Him Whom God shall make Manifest*
- Promoting the Cause of Him Whom God shall make Manifest

Believing in *Him Whom God shall make Manifest*

En masse conversions were a distinctive feature of the Bábí dispensation. An estimate of the Bábí population by the late 1840s was one hundred thousand believers.[1] Bahá'u'lláh blessed these converts:

> *Bless, O my God those of the followers of the Bayán as have been numbered with the people of Bahá, who have entered within the Crimson Ark in Thy Name, the Most Exalted, the Most High. Thy might, verily, is equal to all things."*[2]

Referring to the effect of the declaration of Bahá'u'lláh in 1863 in Baghdád, historian Dr Peter Smith remarked that "... after a year or two the claims of an already popular leader were accepted by the vast majority of the Babis."[3] In Biblical terms, the Báb had been like the Gate for the Shepherd—Bahá'u'lláh—to lead the faithful through, just as Jesus had prophesised: "The one who enters by the Gate is the shepherd of the sheep. The Gatekeeper [God] opens the Gate for Him, and the sheep listen to His voice. He calls His own sheep by name and leads them out" (John 10:2). The Orientalist Mirza Alexander Kazem-Beg wrote that "Babism had many adepts in all classes of society, and many among them were of important standing; great lords, members of the clergy, military men and merchants had accepted this doctrine."[4]

---

1 Abbas Amanat, "The Shaping of the Babi Community", p. 145.

2 Bahá'u'lláh, *Prayers and Meditations*, pp. 44–45.

3 Peter Smith, *The Babí and Bahá'í Religions*, p. 67.

4 Mirza Kazem-Beg in the *Journal Asiatique*, 1866, tome 8, p. 251. Cited by Emily McBride Périgord, *Translation of French Foot-Notes*, p. 21.

Station of the believer accepting *Him Whom God shall make Manifest*

The Báb discloses the station of the believer in Bahá'u'lláh:

> *He who recogniseth Him is assuredly numbered amongst the letters of the sublime paradise, and he who faileth to recognise Him is registered in very truth amongst those of the nethermost region.*[1]
>
> *If ye wish to distinguish truth from error, consider those who believe in Him Whom God will make manifest and those who disbelieve Him at the time of His appearance. The former represents the essence of truth, as attested in the Book of God, while the latter the essence of error, as attested in that same Book.*[2]
>
> *Since that Day is a great Day it would be sorely trying for thee to identify thyself with the believers. For the believers of that Day are the inmates of Paradise, while the unbelievers are the inmates of the fire. And know thou of a certainty that by Paradise is meant recognition of and submission unto Him Whom God shall make Manifest, and by the fire the company of such souls as would fail to submit unto Him or to be resigned to His good-pleasure. On that Day thou wouldst regard thyself as the inmate of Paradise and as a true believer in Him, whereas in reality thou wouldst suffer thyself to be wrapt in veils and thy habitation would be the nethermost fire, though thou thyself wouldst not be cognizant thereof.*[3]

According to the Báb, accepting *Him Whom God shall make Manifest* is the cause of spiritual growth, while failure to recognize Him leads to perversity:

> *Say, God shall of a truth cause your hearts to be given to perversity if ye fail to recognize Him Whom God will make manifest; but if ye do recognize Him God shall banish perversity from your hearts ....*[4]

When a person accepts *Him Whom God shall make Manifest*, a special process of growth begins to occur in his or her heart:

> *Indeed the hearts of them that truly believe in Him Whom God will make manifest are vaster than the expanse of heaven and earth and whatever is between them. God hath left no hindrance in their hearts, were it but the size of a mustard seed. He will cheer their hearts, their spirits, their souls and their bodies and their days of prosperity or adversity, through the exaltation of the name of Him Who is the supreme Testimony of God and the promotion of the Word of Him Who is the Dayspring of the glory of their Creator. Verily, these are souls who take delight in the remembrance of God, Who dilates their hearts through the effulgence of the light of knowledge and wisdom. They seek naught but God and are oft engaged in giving praise unto Him.*

---

1 The Báb, *Tablet to Mullá Báqir*, p. 9, provisional translation, Nader Saiedi.

2 The Báb, *Selections*, p. 142.

3 The Báb, *Selections*, pp. 82–83.

4 The Báb, *Selections*, p. 148.

They desire naught except whatever He desireth and stand ready to do His bidding. Their hearts are mirrors reflecting whatsoever He Whom God shall make manifest willeth.[1]

Such is the spiritual ascendancy of the new believers that they "*prevail over all who dwell in heaven and earth and in whatever lieth between them.*"[2] The Báb continues:

> *Say, God hath, according to that which is revealed in the Book, taken upon Himself the task of ensuring the ascendancy of any one of the followers of the Truth, over and above one hundred other souls, and the supremacy of one hundred believers over one thousand nonbelievers and the domination of one thousand of the faithful over all the peoples and kindreds of the earth; inasmuch as God calleth into being whatsoever He willeth by virtue of His behest.*[3]

Recognizing *Him Whom God shall make Manifest*

In His *Epistle to the Son of the Wolf*, Bahá'u'lláh quotes the words of the Báb, giving advice on how humanity will recognize ***Him Whom God shall make Manifest***: "*the Primal Point* [the Báb] *saith: 'Behold ye Him* [Bahá'u'lláh] *with His own eyes. Were ye to behold Him with the eyes of another, ye would never recognize and know Him.'*"[4] Bahá'u'lláh cites the Báb further:

> *"Look not upon Him* [Bahá'u'lláh] *with any eye except His own. For whosoever looketh upon Him with His eye, will recognize Him; otherwise he will be veiled from Him. Shouldst thou seek God and His Presence, seek thou Him and gaze upon Him".*[5]

In the Tablet to Mullá Báqir, the Báb avers:

> *Bear thou witness that there is no cherished end besides God, that no one can gaze upon the Eternal Essence, and that what can be seen and is worthy such that God attributeth it unto Himself, is naught but Him, the exalted Countenance of Unity and the Face of Eternity.*[6]

Explaining that the new Manifestation of God should be recognized by His own attributes, the Báb wrote: "*who then can know Him through any one except Himself?*"[7] Likewise, He stated:

> *In like manner, should I find that all on earth bow their knees before Him, this in no wise would increase the awe of His majesty in my heart. Then, should I behold all the inhabitants of the world, the number of all things,*

---

1 The Báb, *Selections*, p. 145.
2 The Báb, *Selections*, p. 153.
3 The Báb, *Selections*, p. 153.
4 The Báb in Bahá'u'lláh, *Epistle to the Son of the Wolf*, p. 151.
5 The Báb in Bahá'u'lláh, *Epistle to the Son of the Wolf*, p. 153.
6 The Báb "Tablet to Mullá Báqir", p. 7, provisional translation, Nader Saiedi.
7 The Báb in Bahá'u'lláh, *Epistle to the Son of the Wolf*, p. 153.

> *kneel before Him when He proclaimeth, "Verily, I am the Lord God, none other God is there but Me, and all else besides Me are My creation. Say! O ye My creatures! Bow down before Me," I would recognize this on account of His intrinsic supreme worth, in such wise that the creation of all things would not alter my glorification and exaltation of Him. For recognizing Him by Him, and by the mere testimony of His own Self, is paradise, whose like hath not been created in Thy Knowledge. Were I to be altered by anything, I would neither praise Thy unity by virtue of Thine intrinsic worth, nor acknowledge Him by virtue of His intrinsic worth.*[1]

Writing of the effect of hearing the words of *Him Whom God shall make Manifest* the Báb states, "*Know thou that every ear which hearkeneth unto His Words with true faith shall be immune from the fire.*"[2] Believers are also advised that "*whenever thou makest mention of Him Whom God will make manifest, only then art thou making mention of God.*"[3]

Bábís converting to the Faith of *Him Whom God shall make Manifest*

The Writings of the Báb state that Bábís would be tested and not all would accept the Faith of Bahá'u'lláh. Regarding the allegiance of the Bábís, the Báb indicates that *He Whom God shall make manifest* can "*dismiss the entire company of the followers of the Bayán in the Day of the Latter Resurrection by a mere sign of* [His] *finger*"[4] if He so wishes. Since He can "*pronounce a pious and truthful follower of the Bayán as false, it is incumbent upon you to submit to His decree, as this hath been affirmed by God in the Bayán.*"[5]

Accepting the Faith of Bahá'u'lláh will be the test of being a true Bábí: "*No one believeth in the Bayán, the true meaning of faith, save those who will believe in Him.*"[6] The Báb warns the Bábís:

> *On that Day ye will continue to rove distraught, even as camels, seeking a drop of the water of life. God will cause oceans of living water to stream forth from the presence of Him Whom God will make manifest, while ye will refuse to quench your thirst therefrom, notwithstanding that ye regard yourselves as the God-fearing witnesses of your Faith ...Take good heed to yourselves, inasmuch as the Cause of God will come upon you at a time when you will all be entreating and tearfully imploring God for the advent of the Day of His Manifestation; yet when He cometh ye will tarry and will fail to be of those who are well-assured in His Faith.*[7]

---

1 The Báb "Tablet to Mullá Báqir", p. 3, provisional translation, Nader Saiedi.
2 The Báb, *Selections*, pp. 98–99.
3 The Báb, *Selections*, p. 80.
4 The Báb, *Selections*, p. 7.
5 The Báb, *Selections*, pp. 141–142.
6 The Báb "Tablet to Mullá Báqir", p. 9, provisional translation, Nader Saiedi.
7 The Báb, *Selections*, p. 141.

It is also clear that Bahá'u'lláh would be bitterly disappointed by many of the Bábís:

> *On that Day, the Daystar of Truth* [Bahá'u'lláh] *will address the people of the Bayán and will recite this Súrih of the Qur'án* [Súra 109]*: "Say: O ye unbelievers! I worship not that which ye worship, and ye do not worship that which I worship. I shall never worship that which ye worship, neither will ye worship that which I worship. To you be your religion, to Me My religion."*[1]

This disappointment is shared by the Báb Himself:

> *By the righteousness of Him Whose power causeth the seed to germinate and Who breatheth the spirit of life into all things, were I to be assured that in the day of His Manifestation thou wilt deny Him, I would unhesitatingly disown thee and repudiate thy faith*[2] *inasmuch as thou wert not created but to recognise Him.*[3] *If, on the other hand, I be told that a Christian, who beareth no allegiance to My Faith, will believe in Him, the same will I regard as the apple of Mine eye,*[4] *and accept as My believer, without making the slightest allusion against him. For should the Christian, in the Day of His manifestation, believe in Him, all his worlds would be turned into the light; but should the believer, in the day of His Revelation, be veiled from Him, all his worlds would be turned into fire.*[5]

An eventual decline in the Bábí community after the passing of the Báb would predispose some Bábís to absurdly assert that *He Whom God shall make manifest* is not a believer. In the words of the Báb, as cited by Bahá'u'lláh, "*They will even refuse unto that Tree, which is neither of the East nor of the West, the name believer, for were they so to name Him, they would fail to sadden Him.*"[6] One is tempted to say, such is human miserliness.

A warning for all mankind

Not only the Bábís would be tested—the whole of humanity would be tested irrespective of rank or riches: "*In the day of the revelation of Him Whom God will make manifest all that dwell on earth will be equal in His estimation*"[7] and "*the most distinguished among the learned and the lowliest of men shall both be judged*

---

1 Bahá'u'lláh, *Epistle to the Son of the Wolf*, p. 150.

2 The Báb "Tablet to Mullá Báqir" cited in Shoghi Effendi, *The World Order of Bahá'u'lláh*, pp. 62–63.

3 The Báb, "Tablet to Mullá Báqir", p. 9, provisional translation, Nader Saiedi.

4 The Báb, "Tablet to Mullá Báqir" cited in Shoghi Effendi, *The World Order of Bahá'u'lláh*, pp. 62–63.

5 The Báb "Tablet to Mullá Báqir", p. 9, provisional translation, Nader Saiedi.

6 The Báb in Bahá'u'lláh, *Epistle to the Son of the Wolf*, pp. 156–157.

7 The Báb, "Tablet to Mullá Báqir", p. 9, provisional translation, Nader Saiedi.

alike".[1] *"Those who disbelieve in the Most Great Remembrance of God,"* He further warns, *"neither their wealth nor their children will avail them ....*[2]

Referring to the power of Bahá'u'lláh the Báb averred that it was lawful for Him to accept a new believer, or *"to reject him who is greatest on earth, inasmuch as such a one is but a creature in His grasp ...."*[3]

Prominent people would reject the teachings of Bahá'u'lláh while, at the same time, simple souls would accept His claim as *Him Whom God shall make Manifest* as *"He will cause the abased to be exalted, and the exalted to be abased."*[4]

> *How many the fires which God converteth into light through Him Whom God will make manifest; and how numerous the lights which are turned into fire through Him! I behold His appearance even as the sun in the midmost heaven, and the disappearance of all even as that of the stars of the night by day.*[5]

The Báb also expresses His hope that Christians would accept the Faith of Bahá'u'lláh and prays: *"Raise up, then, amongst them, O My God, one who shall bring them into Thy Faith inasmuch as they follow Thy path and seek Thy way."*[6]

Veils hindering recognition of Bahá'u'lláh

In the *Epistle to the Son of the Wolf*, Bahá'u'lláh reminds the Bábís, nearly forty-five years after the martyrdom of the Báb, about a chapter of the Bayán[7] dealing specifically with the coming of *Him Whom God shall make Manifest*, and reminds them of the exhortation contained therein:

> *Once every nineteen days this Chapter should be read, that haply they may not be veiled, in the time of the revelation of Him Whom God will make manifest, by considerations foreign to the verses, which have been, and are still, the weightiest of all proofs and testimonies.*[8]

"Veils" are impediments that deprive people from recognizing divine truth. In this regard, the Báb states:

> *Hence God desireth that all men should be guided aright through the potency of the Words of Him Whom God will make manifest. However, such as are conceited will not suffer themselves to be guided. They will be debarred from the Truth, some by reason of their learning, others on account of their glory*

---

1 The Báb, *Selections*, p. 91.
2 The Báb in Todd Lawson, "The terms 'Remembrance' and 'Gate', p. 19.
3 The Báb in Bahá'u'lláh, *Epistle to the Son of the Wolf*, p. 152.
4 The Báb, *Selections*, p. 92.
5 The Báb in Bahá'u'lláh, *Epistle to the Son of the Wolf*, p. 173.
6 The Báb in Nader Saiedi, *Modernity in the Writings of the Báb*, p. 7.
7 The Báb, Persian Bayán 6:8.
8 The Báb in Bahá'u'lláh, *Epistle to the Son of the Wolf*, pp. 157–158.

> *and power, and still others due to reasons of their own, none of which shall be of any avail at the hour of death.*[1]

Among the "veils" that obscure human spiritual perception, the Báb mentions the following:

Selfish desires

> *Know thou, that thou wilt succeed in doing so if thou believest with undoubting faith. However, since thou canst not attain the state of undoubting faith, due to the intervening veils of thy selfish desires, therefore thou wilt tarry in the fire, though realizing it not.*[2]

Self-righteousness

> *How vast the number of people who will, on the Day of Resurrection, regard themselves to be in the right, while they shall be accounted as false through the dispensation of Providence, inasmuch as they will shut themselves out as by a veil from Him Whom God will make manifest and refuse to bow down in adoration before Him Who, as divinely ordained in the Book, is the Object of their creation.*[3]

Preoccupied in church ritual

> *If ye entertain any doubts in this matter consider the people unto whom the Gospel was given. Having no access to the apostles of Jesus, they sought the pleasure of the Lord in their churches, hoping to learn that which would be acceptable unto God, but they found therein no path unto Him.*[4]

The Bayán itself

> *And beware, beware that the words sent down in the Bayán shut thee not out as by a veil from Him.*[5]

> *Suffer not the Bayán and all that hath been revealed therein to withhold you from that Essence of Being and Lord of the visible and invisible.*[6]

Disunity amongst the believers

> *Regard ye not others save as ye regard your own selves, that no feeling of aversion may prevail amongst you so as to shut you out from Him Whom God will make manifest on the Day of Resurrection. It behooveth you all to be one indivisible people; thus should ye return unto Him Whom God will make manifest.*[7]

---

1 The Báb, *Selections*, p. 96.
2 The Báb, *Selections*, p. 110.
3 The Báb, *Selections*, p. 143.
4 The Báb, *Selections*, p. 137.
5 Bahá'u'lláh, *Epistle to the Son of the Wolf*, p. 153.
6 Bahá'u'lláh, *Epistle to the Son of the Wolf*, p. 171.
7 The Báb, *Selections*, p. 129.

Disdain

> *Perchance He will appear invested with the power of Truth while ye are fast asleep on your couches, or His messengers will bring glorious and resplendent Tablets from Him while ye turn away disdainfully from Him, pronounce sentence against Him—such sentence as ye would never pass on yourselves—and say, "This is not from God, the All-Subduing, the Self-Existent."*[1]

Material possessions

> *O peoples of the East and the West! Be ye fearful of God concerning the Cause of the true Joseph and barter Him not for a paltry price established by yourselves, or for a trifle of your earthly possessions, that ye may, in very truth, be praised by Him as those who are reckoned among the pious who stand nigh unto this Gate.*[2]

Self-delusion

> *On that Day thou wouldst regard thyself as the inmate of Paradise and as a true believer in Him, whereas in reality thou wouldst suffer thyself to be wrapt in veils and thy habitation would be the nethermost fire, though thou thyself wouldst not be cognizant thereof.*[3]

Position and rank

> *Among those to whom it will never occur that they might merit the displeasure of God, and whose pious deeds will be exemplary unto everyone, there will be many who will become the personification of the nethermost fire itself, when they fail to embrace His Cause; while among the lowly servants whom no one would imagine to be of any merit, how great the number who will be honored with true faith and on whom the Fountainhead of generosity will bestow the robe of authority.*[4]

The Báb stresses the fact that all believers, without exception, are merely mirrors who have no light of their own. They "*are not illumined by themselves .... All the mirrors abide by His bidding, return unto Him, utter His glory, and seek shelter beneath His shadow.*"[5]

While in the above quote the Báb was referring to all believers as "mirrors", He honoured certain worthy disciples with the title of "***Mirrors***". Other distinguished believers were referred to as "***Guides***" and "***Witnesses***". ***Witnesses***, or more correctly "*Witnesses of the Bayán*", were those persons who testified to the validity and authenticity of the Words of the blessed Báb until the

1 The Báb, *Selections*, p. 166.
2 The Báb, *Selections*, p. 48.
3 The Báb, *Selections*, pp. 82–83.
4 The Báb, *Selections*, 83–84.
5 The Báb in Nader Saiedi, *Gate of the Heart*, ch. 6, endnote 17, p. 393.

appearance of Bahá'u'lláh. Collectively, in addition to the **Letters of the Living,** the **Mirrors**, **Guides** and **Witnesses** constituted a hierarchy in the Bábí Revelation.[1]

To the "***Mirrors***" in particular, the Báb issued some warnings that are quoted by Bahá'u'lláh in the *Epistle to the Son of the Wolf* written over forty years later:

> *O Sun-like Mirrors! Look ye upon the Sun of Truth. Ye, verily, depend upon it, were ye to perceive it. Ye are all as fishes, moving in the waters of the sea, veiling yourselves therefrom, and yet asking what it is on which ye depend.*[2]
>
> *I complain unto thee, O Mirror of My generosity, against all the other Mirrors. All look upon Me through their own colors.*[3]
>
> *Beware, O Concourse of Mirrors, lest on that Day titles make you vainglorious. Know ye of a certainty that ye, together with all those who stand above you or below you, have been created for that Day.*[4]

As predicted by the Báb, a few Bábís rejected Bahá'u'lláh as *Him Whom God shall make Manifest*, despite the warning in the Bayán: "*Beware, beware lest the Váḥid of the Bayán*[5] *or that which hath been sent down in that Book shut thee out as by a veil from Him, inasmuch as it is but a creature in His sight.*"[6] The Báb also gave the following warning:

> *And shouldst Thou behold, O my God, any branch, leaf, or fruit upon Me that hath failed to bow down before Him, on the day of His Revelation, cut it off, O My God, from that Tree, for it is not of Me, nor shall it return unto Me.*[7]

'Abdu'l-Bahá explained the downfall of those believers:

> *And yet, behold to what vain imaginings the people of the Bayán are clinging. They cry out: "Where is the primary school of Him Whom God shall make Manifest?*[8] *Where are the kings of the Bayán? Where are its places of worship and its Witnesses?"* ...

---

1 See Shoghi Effendi, *God Passes By*, pp. 89–90.

2 The Báb in Bahá'u'lláh, *Epistle to the Son of the Wolf*, p. 160.

3 The Báb in Bahá'u'lláh, *Epistle to the Son of the Wolf*, p. 160.

4 The Báb, *Selections*, p. 164.

5 The Báb and the eighteen Letters of the Living.

6 'Abdu'l-Bahá. *Light of the World*, p. 150.

7 Bahá'u'lláh, *Epistle to the Son of the Wolf*, p. 162.

8 The Universal House of Justice explains that "Bahá'u'lláh confronts one of the reasons some of the Bábís rejected His claim to be the Promised One of the Bayán. Their rejection was based on a Tablet addressed by the Báb to "*Him Who will be made manifest*" on the reverse side of which the Báb had written: *"May the glances of Him Whom God shall make manifest illumine this letter at the primary school."* (*The Kitáb-i-Aqdas*, p. 246)

The statement "or that which hath been revealed in the Bayán" is indeed meant to caution the people of the Bayán not to say, "Where are the kings of the Bayán,[1] *and where is the school of Him Whom God shall make Manifest?" Great God! These people condition that Most Great Revelation upon His being admitted, like a child, into a primary school and regard this as the proof of the validity of His Cause.*[2]

Those Bábís, who rejected Bahá'u'lláh as *Him Whom God shall make Manifest*, were mostly followers of Mírzá Yaḥyá (1831–1912), a half-brother of Bahá'u'lláh. Mírzá Yaḥyá, who claimed to be the successor of the Báb and the leader of the Bábí community, had shown strong opposition to the mandate of Bahá'u'lláh. Those who followed Mírzá Yaḥyá became known as "Azalis", based on the title "Ṣubḥ-i-Azal", which Mírzá Yaḥyá had assumed. It is clear that Mírzá Yaḥyá was not appointed as the successor of the Báb but only as a figure-head of the Bábís until the appearance of *Him Whom God shall make Manifest.*[3]

The Blessed Beauty addressed the following words to the Bábís:

O people of the Bayán! Abandon your idle fancies and vain imaginings, then with the eye of fairness look at the Dayspring of His Revelation [Bahá'u'lláh] *and consider the things He hath manifested, the words He hath divinely revealed and the sufferings that have befallen Him at the hands of His enemies. He is the One Who hath willingly accepted every manner of tribulation for the proclamation of His Cause and the exaltation of His Word. At one time He suffered imprisonment in the land of Ṭá' (Ṭihrán), at another in the land of Mím (Mázindarán), then once again in the former land, for the sake of the Cause of God, the Maker of the heavens. In His love for the Cause of God, the Almighty, the All-Bountiful, He was subjected there to chains and fetters.*[4]

In the *Epistle to the Son of the Wolf*, Bahá'u'lláh likens these Bábís to the followers of John the Baptist who protested against Jesus: "*The dispensation of John hath not yet ended; wherefore hast thou come?*"[5]

Encouragement of certain predispositions toward *Him Whom God shall make Manifest*

A distinctive feature of the Bábí Revelation is that their Promised One is portrayed as a human being as distinct from prophecies of past religions in which the Messianic figure was referred to by the use of symbolic language. The

1 The Báb wrote about the establishment of a theocracy ruled by a Bábí king, but under the Báb's sovereignty. (Persian Bayán 4:5; Arabic Bayán 9:3)

2 'Abdu'l-Bahá, *Light of the World*, p. 152.

3 The title "Ṣubḥ-i-Azal" appears in an Islamic tradition, which was quoted by the Báb in "Dala'il-i-Sab'ih". Mírzá Yaḥyá took this term as a reference to himself. (See https://bahai-library.com/uhj_vasaya_mirza_yahya)

4 Bahá'u'lláh, *Tablets of Bahá'u'lláh*, p. 104.

5 Bahá'u'lláh, *Epistle to the Son of the Wolf*, p. 157.

Writings of the Báb make it clear that *He Whom God shall make manifest* is a person who lives, interacts and even dies as a normal human being.

The Writings of the Báb provide guidance as to how believers should approach Bahá'u'lláh. These include: to turn the mirror of the heart towards Him, to love Him, perform acts and deeds for His sake, to observe His precepts and to ask for His forgiveness. The Báb also encourages the Bábís to educate people in the teachings of the Bayán, and assist *Him Whom God shall make Manifest* in propagating His Cause. Among his exhortation are:

- To make of one's heart a mirror set towards *Him Whom God shall make Manifest*:

Thus if haply thou dost live in the Day of Resurrection, the mirror of thy heart will be set towards Him Who is the Daystar of Truth; and no sooner will His light shine forth than the splendor thereof shall forthwith be reflected in thy heart. For He is the Source of all goodness, and unto Him revert all things.[1]

- To listen to Him Whom God shall make Manifest:

At whatever time ye hear of Him, hasten ye towards Him, and cleave ye to whatsoever He may reveal unto you. Naught else besides Him can ever profit you, no, not though ye produce from first to last the testimonies of all those who were before you.[2]

- To show love towards Him Whom God shall make Manifest:

All, according to their capacity, are enjoined to love Him and recognize Him and traverse the path of the Seas of Names and Attributes ....[3]

- To observe the precepts of Him Whom God shall make Manifest:

The acts of Him Whom God will make manifest are like unto the sun, while the works of men, provided they conform to the good-pleasure of God, resemble the stars or the moon .... Thus, should the followers of the Bayán observe the precepts of Him Whom God will make manifest at the time of His appearance, and regard themselves and their own works as stars exposed to the light of the sun, then they will have gathered the fruits of their existence ....[4]

- To perform acts and deeds for the sake of *Him Whom God shall make Manifest*:

In like manner, the people who are now acting in accordance with the Bayán, and recite this verse, should they, in the day of the Revelation of Him Whom

1 The Báb, *Selections*, p. 94.

2 Bahá'u'lláh, *Gleanings from the Writings of Bahá'u'lláh*, p. 147.

3 The Báb in Nader Saiedi, *Gate of the Heart*, p. 185.

4 The Báb, *Selections*, p. 97.

God will make manifest, perform action for Him, they act for the sake of God, otherwise their action will come to naught, as if they had not done anything.[1]

- To ask Him Whom God shall make Manifest for forgiveness:

  If divine revelation ceaseth, thou shouldst write a petition to Him Whom God will make manifest, imploring that it be delivered into His presence. Therein thou must beg pardon of thy Lord, turn unto Him in repentance and be of them that are wholly devoted to Him. Perchance God will transform thy fire into light at the next Resurrection.[2]

- To assist Him Whom God shall make Manifest:

  I swear by the holy Essence of God, were all in the Bayán to unite in helping Him Whom God will make manifest in the days of His Revelation, not a single soul, nay, not a created thing would remain on earth that would not gain admittance into Paradise. Take good heed of yourselves, for the sum total of the religion of God is but to help Him, rather than to observe, in the time of His appearance, such deeds as are prescribed in the Bayán.[3]

- To attain the presence of Him Whom God shall make Manifest:

  Take ye heed, therefore, lest ye deprive yourselves of attaining the presence of Him Who is the Manifestation of God, notwithstanding that ye have been day and night praying to behold His countenance ....[4]

- To show respect in His presence:

  When the Daystar of Bahá will shine resplendent above the horizon of eternity it is incumbent upon you to present yourselves before His Throne. Beware lest ye be seated in His presence or ask questions without His leave. Fear ye God, O concourse of the Mirrors.

  Beg ye of Him the wondrous tokens of His favor that He may graciously reveal for you whatever He willeth and desireth, inasmuch as on that Day all the revelations of divine bounty shall circle around the Seat of His glory and emanate from His presence, could ye but understand it.

  It behooveth you to remain silent before His Throne, for indeed of all the things which have been created between heaven and earth nothing on that Day will be deemed more fitting than the observance of silence.[5]

Likewise, particular courtesies should be shown to Him:

- To listen to His words:

---

1 The Báb in Nader Saiedi, *Gate of the Heart*, p. 312.
2 The Báb, *Selections*, pp. 33–34.
3 The Báb, *Selections*, p. 85.
4 The Báb, *Selections*, p. 136.
5 The Báb, *Selections*, pp. 164–165.

Know thou that every ear which hearkeneth unto His Words with true faith shall be immune from the fire. Thus the believer, through his recognition of Him will appreciate the transcendent character of His heavenly Words, will wholeheartedly choose Him over others, and will refuse to incline his affections towards those who disbelieve in Him.[1]

- To leave a vacant chair for Him and the Letters of the Living:

... and in every assembly of glory which is formed, it is well that they should leave vacant places for the number of the Wáḥid [19], that if at that hour He whom God shall manifest were to appear with the [eighteen] Letters of the Living none should be in propinquity.[2]

Among other provisions are:

The Báb exhorts believers to stand when they hear a mention of *Him Whom God shall make Manifest* and the name of the Qá'im (the Báb). In both the Persian and Arabic Bayán, the Báb asks the believers to compose their will and testaments that are to be addressed to *Him Whom We shall make manifest*, and He indicates that by doing so they are writing to God.[3] Oaths are to be sworn by God or by *Him Whom God shall make Manifest.*[4]

In addition, there are two ordinances in the Bayán: one, forbidding the posing of questions to *Him Whom God shall make Manifest* except in writing; and the second, being an exhortation to offer Him priceless gifts. Both these points will be discussed in the last section of chapter 19.

Discouragement of certain attitudes and behaviours towards *Him Whom God shall make Manifest*

Just as the Báb taught people how to approach Bahá'u'lláh, He advised against certain actions in relation to *Him Whom God shall make Manifest.*

- To eschew vanities:

Turn not your religion into a means of material gain, spending your life on vanities, and inheriting thereby on the Day of Resurrection that which would displease Him Whom God will make manifest, while ye deem that what ye do is right.[5]

---

1 The Báb, *Selections*, pp. 98–99.

2 Moojan Momen, *Selections from the Writings of E. G. Browne*, p. 376. Adib Taherzadeh wrote: "In the same Book, the Báb makes a statement which reveals His sense of humour. He says that 'He Whom God shall make manifest' will also leave a seat of honour vacant in His own home, because the believers will not recognize Him! He will be inwardly amused by those who venerate His name while remaining veiled from Him at the time of His Revelation". (Taherzadeh, *The Covenant of Bahá'u'lláh*, p. 51)

3 The Báb, Persian Bayán, 5:13 & Arabic Bayán.5:13. See Bahá'u'lláh, *Kitáb-i-Aqdas*, para. 109, p. 59.

4 The Báb, Arabic Bayán 11:1.

5 The Báb, *Selections*, pp. 129–130.

- To refrain from passing judgement:

O ye who are invested with the Bayán! Should ye be apprised of a person laying claim to a Cause and revealing verses which to outward seeming are unlikely to have been revealed by anyone else save God, the Help in Peril, the Self-Subsisting, do not pass sentence against him, lest ye may inadvertently pass sentence against Him Whom God will make manifest.[1]

- To avoid argumentation:

Take heed to carefully consider the words of every soul, then hold fast to the proofs which attest the truth. If ye fail to discover truth in a person's words, make them not the object of contention, inasmuch as ye have been forbidden in the Bayán to enter into idle disputation and controversy, that perchance on the Day of Resurrection ye may not engage in argumentation, and dispute with Him Whom God will make manifest.[2]

- To refrain from being a cause of grief:

If thou attainest unto His Revelation, and obeyest Him, thou wilt have revealed the fruit of the Bayán; if not, thou art unworthy of mention before God. Take pity upon thyself. If thou aidest not Him Who is the Manifestation of the Lordship of God, be not, then, a cause of sadness unto Him.[3]

I beg of Thee, by Thy bounty, O my God, and by the outpourings of Thy mercy and bestowals, O my Lord, and by the evidences of Thy heavenly favors and grace, O my Best-Beloved, to watch over Him Whom God will make manifest that no trace of despondency may ever touch Him.[4]

Take good heed of yourselves, O people of the Bayán, lest ye perform such deeds as to weep sore for His sake night and day, to stand up at the mention of His Name, yet on this Day of fruition—a Day whereon ye should not only arise at His Name, but seek a path unto Him Who personifies that Name—ye shut yourselves out from Him as by a veil.[5]

Promoting the cause of *Him Whom God shall make Manifest*

Specific advice is given in the teachings of the Báb on how to promote the Faith of Bahá'u'lláh both on an individual level and as a community.

Individually, the Bábís were encouraged *to arise and teach the Cause of God:*

Therefore, manifest thou this attribute to the utmost of thine ability in the days of Him Whom God will make manifest. For indeed if thou dost open the

1 The Báb, *Selections*, p. 144.
2 The Báb, *Selections*, p. 134.
3 The Báb in Bahá'u'lláh, *Epistle to the Son of the Wolf*, p. 172.
4 The Báb, *Selections*, p. 172.
5 The Báb, *Selections*, pp. 84–85.

> *heart of a person for His sake, better will it be for thee than every virtuous deed; since deeds are secondary to faith in Him and certitude in His Reality.*[1]

Such a service should be carried out in a spirit of self-abnegation:

> *The station of light resembleth that of the lamp, which consumeth its own self in order to illumine others, for there remaineth no trace of identity in the light. Thus shouldst thou be alive, thou wouldst witness the lights of this Revelation who will relinquish, by their own will, their own being in order to render victorious the unity of God, and His ordinances and prohibitions.*[2]

The Báb also wrote that the act of bringing another soul into the Faith of Bahá'u'lláh **brings immense spiritual benefits***:*

> *Wert thou to open the heart of a single soul by helping him to embrace the Cause of Him Whom God will make manifest, thine inmost being would be filled with the inspirations of that august Name. It devolveth upon you, therefore, to perform this task in the Days of Resurrection, inasmuch as most people are helpless, and wert thou to open their hearts and dispel their doubts, they would gain admittance into the Faith of God.*[3]

Collectively, the Bábís were summoned to covenant with each other regarding Him Whom God shall make manifest:

> *Covenant with all those who acknowledge their faith, every single one that is known to thee, concerning His Mission, through their own written testimony. The whole of the Bayán is such a testimony of Mine, written by Me. Verily, whoso writeth such an acknowledgment, hath testified to his belief in Him ere His Manifestation. Therefore, seek thou testimony from all who can be sought, that they may register their testimony of faith in writing before the Day of His manifestation.*[4]

Four particular exhortations pertaining to advancing the Cause of *Him Whom God shall make Manifest.* One is the ordinance *to reply to letters and respond to others* to facilitate information about the arrival of Bahá'u'lláh "*for should all be assured that He is that same He Whom God shall make manifest whom the Point of the Bayán hath foretold, not one would turn aside.*"[5] The Báb explains further:

> *It is enjoined in this Revelation that should anyone receive a letter from someone, it is his duty to reply, by his own hand or that of another on his behalf; indeed, any delay is abhorred. In like manner, should one ask a question, it is incumbent upon the person asked, to give a guiding answer, that haply in the Day of the Revelation of God no one may be shut out as by a veil from Him. Hence, the question revealed by God, 'Am I not your Lord?'*

1 The Báb, *Selections*, p. 133.
2 The Báb in Nader Saiedi, *Gate of the Heart*, p. 78.
3 The Báb, *Selections*, p. 133.
4 The Báb, "Tablet to Mullá Báqir", p. 12, provisional translation, Nader Saiedi.
5 The Báb, *Selections*, pp. 110–112.

> *requireth all to answer, 'Yea.' Thus, the duty to reply is enjoined for this purpose, although its influence will last until the very last atom of existence.*[1]

Hence, the Báb instructs His followers *to develop a postal service:*

> *It is for this reason that such an ordinance is decreed, that haply in the Day of the Revelation of that Most Mighty Day-Star, the means to facilitate the attainment of the glory of guidance for His servants will be prepared. However, until such a system is made universal, its benefit will not reach those servants of the kingdom unless there come a time when it will be accessible to all the people. Although today the kings have their own special couriers, this is fruitless, for the poor are deprived of such a service.*[2]

Thirdly, a provision is made not to grieve anyone who in turn might grieve *Him Whom God shall make Manifest*:

> *Take ye good heed in your night lest ye be a cause of sadness to any soul, whether ye be able to discover proofs in him or not, that haply on the Day of Resurrection ye may not grieve Him within Whose grasp lieth every proof. And when ye do not discern God's testimony in a person, he will verily fail in manifesting the power of Truth; and God is sufficient to deal with him. Indeed on no account should ye sadden any person; surely God will put him to the proof and bring him to account. It behooveth you to cling to the testimony of your own Faith and to observe the ordinances laid down in the Bayán.*[3]

Mírzá Muḥammad Gulpáygání (1844–1914), to whom Bahá'u'lláh had given the title Abu'l-Faḍl ("Father of Virtue"), was a very knowledgeable and devoted believer, and an Apostle of Bahá'u'lláh. The following incident occurred during the first pilgrimage of Mírzá 'Alí Muḥammad (known as Varqá). Mírzá Abu'l-Faḍl writes regarding the instructions of the Báb to write books to advance the Cause of *Him Whom God shall make Manifest*:

> In the early years of my conversion, I refused to write books, supporting that in the days in which the Supreme Pen was moving, its sound would be heard in all regions. Therefore, I reasoned, it would be a great presumption for a man to attempt writing and composition. Finally in 1887, when in Á<u>dh</u>arbayján, I was favored with the privilege of meeting Varqá the Martyr, and he encouraged me to write and compose. He said: "During the days when I was at the brilliant city of 'Akká, and attained the honor of meeting the Blessed Perfection, the Blessed Tongue repeated the Command of the 'First Point,' which was that the believers should each one write books demonstrating the truth of 'He whom God shall manifest.' I inquired if He deemed it advisable to employ Mírzá Abu'l-Faḍl in this service. Then He said, "As the "First Point" has commanded it, such

1 The Báb in Nader Saiedi, *Gate of the Heart*, p. 321.

2 The Báb in Nader Saiedi, *Gate of the Heart*, p. 320.

3 The Báb, *Selections*, pp. 134–135.

persons should employ themselves in writing and propounding arguments."[1]

All religions of the past had a Lesser Covenant—a line of succession after the Messenger of God departs from this terrestrial life. Abraham designated Isaac; while Moses appointed Joshua; Jesus referred to Peter; and Muḥammad conferred that mantle upon 'Alí. However, the Báb did not designate a successor. He indicated clearly that there were no vicegerents in His Dispensation. According to Bahá'u'lláh:

> *In My previous Dispensation [the Báb], the matter of successorship was totally obliterated from the Book of God. As all are aware, all that was revealed from the Pen of the All-Merciful was confined to the Letters and the Mirrors of the Bayán. Also, the number of Mirrors was not fixed.*[2]

Shoghi Effendi explains how this vacuum was due to the imminence of *Him Whom God shall make Manifest*:

> A successor or vicegerent the Báb never named, an interpreter of His teachings He refrained from appointing. So transparently clear were His references to the Promised One, so brief was to be the duration of His own Dispensation, that neither the one nor the other was deemed necessary. All He did was, according to the testimony of 'Abdu'l-Bahá in *A Traveller's Narrative*, to nominate, on the advice of Bahá'u'lláh and of another disciple, Mírzá Yaḥyá, who would act solely as a figure-head pending the manifestation of the Promised One, thus enabling Bahá'u'lláh to promote, in relative security, the Cause so dear to His heart.[3]

It is noteworthy that the Báb designated Mullá Muḥammad 'Alí-i-Bárfurú<u>sh</u>í (c. 1820–1849), entitled *Quddús* (meaning "Holy"), as His foremost disciple. Quddús was chosen from among all the eighteen Letters of the Living to accompany the Báb on pilgrimage to Mecca in October 1844. In the Persian Bayán the Báb praised Quddús as the one on whose "*detachment and the sincerity of whose devotion to God's will God prideth Himself amidst the Concourse on high.*"[4] Similarly, Bahá'u'lláh identifies Quddús with the parable as one of the three "*Messengers* [falsely] *charged with imposture*" in Qur'án 36:13.[5] Despite the

---

1 Mírzá Abu'l-Faḍl, *Bahá'í Proofs*, p. 14.

2 Bahá'u'lláh, *The Bahá'í Reference Library.* Available from: https://www.bahai.org/library/authoritative-texts/bahaullah/additional-tablets-extracts-from-tablets-revealed-bahaullah/additional-tablets-extracts-from-tablets-revealed-bahaullah.pdf?369f2267

3 Shoghi Effendi. *God Passes By*, p. 28.

4 The Báb in Shoghi Effendi. *God Passes By*, p. 49.

5 Bahá'u'lláh in Shoghi Effendi. *God Passes By*, p. 49.

elevated position of Quddús, "he should by no means be considered [as] having had the station of a Prophet" nor as a Manifestation of God.[1]

The focus of the Báb' mission was on the appearance of the next Messenger of God in the form of *Him Whom God shall make Manifest*, namely, Bahá'u'lláh. The abundance of references that the Báb made to this heralded Figure bears witness to the care He took—particularly on the issue of "spiritual veils"—to prepare the world for that great spiritual phenomenon. No other Messenger of God has written as much as the Báb did concerning the signs and roles of the next Manifestation.

The Báb explained that He did not leave a successor because of the imminence of the new revelation:

> *Glorified art Thou, O My God! Bear Thou witness that, through this Book, I have covenanted with all created things concerning the Mission of Him Whom Thou shalt make manifest, ere the covenant concerning Mine own Mission had been established. Sufficient witness art Thou and they that have believed in Thy signs.*[2]

---

1 Letter titled "Letters of Living, Dawn-Breakers, Quddús, Terraces" written August 1975 on behalf of the Universal House of Justice. Available from https://bahai-library.com/uhj_letters_quddus_dawnbreakers.

2 The Báb in Bahá'u'lláh. *Epistle to the Son of the Wolf*, p. 160.

17
Progressive Revelation—Divine Laws

In chapter 2, we covered the topic of progressive revelation from the point of view of God revealing Himself to humanity through His Prophets in accordance with man's capacity to understand. Such a concept is not totally foreign to the followers of earlier religions though some Christians have preferred to use the term "progressive comprehension" or "theological evolution". For instance, regarding the relationship between Judaism and Christianity, Jesus said: "For had ye believed Moses, ye would have believed me: for he wrote of me. But if ye believe not his writings, how can ye believe my words?" (John 5:46)

Progressive revelation can also be inferred from the Holy Qur'án with its accounts of past Prophets Who are referred to as "Muslims", i.e. "those who submit to God". The Jews, Christians, Magians (Zoroastrians) and Sabians are recognized as the "*People of the Book*"; i.e., as believers in the One God and recipients of God's Revelation through His Prophets. The concept of progression is implied in several surahs, especially when considered together. Perhaps the most significant verse is in Qur'án 12:6, in which the story is told of how Jacob addressed the following words to his beloved son, Joseph:

> It is thus that thy Lord shall choose thee and will teach thee the interpretation of dark sayings, and will perfect his favours on thee and on the family of Jacob, as of old he perfected it on thy fathers Abraham and Isaac; verily thy Lord is Knowing, Wise!

Take particular note of the use of the word "*perfect*". If this was the only time it was used in the above passage, one might have taken it to mean that whatever was revealed to Joseph was the ultimate of all Revelation. Yet this perfection is likened to an earlier perfection of God's favours on Abraham and Isaac.

The Bahá'í Faith propounds a new and all-inclusive concept of Progressive Revelation. Though hinted at in the Scriptures of previous religions, the concept was not fully comprehended, and the lack of a clear definition allowed various misinterpretations to arise with the followers of each faith believing that their Prophet was unique and that there would be no further Revelation. Only in the Bahá'í Writings is there a precise explanation of the station of the Messengers (Manifestations) of God, and Their relationship to God and to each other.

Thus, the Bahá'í Faith brings clarity to these issues, explaining how God, the loving Creator, reveals His Law to man through this successive chain of Manifestations, each One of Them renewing and redefining the Revelation of the One Who came before, according to the growing understanding of humanity. Each Messenger has a particular Mission, bringing specific social laws that serve the needs of humanity for that Age. The fundamental spiritual teachings, i.e., virtues such as loving-kindness, courage, generosity, justice, steadfastness, truthfulness and trustworthiness remain; but they are raised to a higher level related to the advances in human spiritualization. 'Abdu'l-Bahá explains:

> *All sin is prompted by the dictates of nature. These dictates of nature, which are among the hallmarks of corporeal existence, are not sins with respect to the animal but are sins with regard to man. The animal is the source of imperfections such as anger, lust, envy, greed, cruelty, and pride. All these blameworthy qualities are found in the nature of the animal, and do not constitute sins with regard to the animal, whereas they are sins with regard to man.*[1]
>
> *"The good deeds of the righteous are the sins of the near ones"*[2]

As every new religious dispensation has dawned, it has re-established and upgraded the teachings of the older faith from which it sprung. In its heyday, the potency of the Revelation of the Word of God for that age has propelled civilization forward, both spiritually and materially. It is at such a time that advances and discoveries have been made in every field of human endeavour. A new paradigm is established for humanity, which becomes imbedded in the culture and traditions of the people although they may not recognize its source. Even the pagan philosophers of ancient times were influenced by the echoes of some otherwise forgotten Revelation of the past.

The following themes are covered in this chapter.

- Evolvement of religious laws from one dispensation to the next
- Evolvement of religious laws within each dispensation
- Messianic expectations about the Qá'im
- Implementation of the laws of the Báb
- Nature of religious laws in the Bábí-Bahá'í Faith
- Response of Bahá'u'lláh to the laws of the Bayán

Evolvement of religious laws from one dispensation to the next

One of the clearest examples of progressive revelation is found in the Gospels. According to the Gospel of Matthew, Jesus emphatically upheld the Law of God as revealed to mankind by Moses:

> Think not that I am come to destroy the law, or the prophets: I am not come to destroy, but to fulfil. For verily I say unto you, till heaven and earth pass, one jot or one tittle shall in no wise pass from the law, till all be fulfilled. Whosoever therefore shall break one of these least commandments, and shall teach men so, he shall be called the least in the kingdom of heaven: but whosoever shall do and teach them, the same shall be called great in the kingdom of heaven. For I say unto you, that except

---

1 'Abdu'l-Bahá, *Some Answered Questions*, p. 133.

2 'Abdu'l-Bahá, *Some Answered Questions*, p. 142.

> your righteousness shall exceed the righteousness of the scribes and Pharisees, ye shall in no case enter into the kingdom of heaven.[1]

The last statement in the above extract is of particular interest. It seems that Jesus was accusing the scribes and Pharisees of corruption, as He had done in some of His other statements: "Woe unto you, scribes and Pharisees, hypocrites! for ye are as graves which appear not, and the men that walk over them are not aware of them." (Luke 11:44). However, in the context of what follows, Jesus was redefining the law and upgrading how it should be observed: "Ye have heard that it was said of them of old time, Thou shalt not kill; and whosoever shall kill shall be in danger of the judgment: But I say unto you, That whosoever is angry with his brother without a cause shall be in danger of the judgment ...."[2]

Jesus did not change "**one jot or one tittle**" of the Sixth Commandment: but He raised man's response to a higher level. Likewise, Jesus refined the Seventh Commandment: "Ye have heard that it was said by them of old time, Thou shalt not commit adultery: But I say unto you, That whosoever looketh on a woman to lust after her hath committed adultery with her already in his heart."[3]

When Jesus healed the sick on the Sabbath, the Jews sought to kill Him for breaking the very specific statement of the Fourth Commandment. However, the Pharisees had substituted the spirit of the law for an array of petty and, in effect, ungodly rules. They knew that the Sabbath was intended for man to rest from his work in order to worship God, but they interpreted this in a very narrow way. They did not take into account that the worship of God also includes doing the work of God, such as the healing of the sick. Jesus brought back to the Sabbath the spirit of the law. He said: **"The Sabbath is made for man not man for the Sabbath."**[4] Jesus also refined the Old Testament teachings on the nature of God from a wrathful Avenger to a loving and forgiving Father: "Be ye therefore perfect, even as your Father which is in heaven is perfect." (Matthew 5:48)

The laws of Moses forbid the eating of various foods, including pork (Leviticus 11:7); whereas Jesus declared all foods clean (Mark 7:15). The day of rest for Jews is Saturday while most Christians observe it on Sunday, and all Muslims celebrate Friday. Capital punishment is prescribed for some offences in the Torah (Exodus 21:12), while Jesus demonstrated mercy for the "woman taken in adultery" by stipulating the innocence of the would-be executioners as a condition for casting the first stone (John 8:3–11). According to some hadiths (al-Bukhari, vol. 6, bk. 60, no. 79), capital punishment as set down in the Torah; was re-instated by Muḥammad in Medina, although not indicated in the Qur'án, in which killing the enemy was only allowed in time of war (Qur'án 5:33-34). Capital punishment was forbidden by the Báb, then reinstated by Bahá'u'lláh for murder and arson under certain conditions with the option of life imprisonment (*The Kitáb-i-Aqdas*, p. 41

1 Matthew 5:17–20, KJB

2 Matthew 5:21–4, KJB

3 Matthew 5:27–8, KJB

4 Mark 2:27, KJB

para 62). As discussed earlier, Moses allowed divorce, Jesus prohibited it, Muḥammad made provision for it, whereas the Báb and Bahá'u'lláh made it conditional on a year of waiting. 'Abdu'l-Bahá stated:

> *... in the time of Noah certain requirements made it necessary that all seafood be allowable or lawful. During the time of the Abrahamic Prophethood it was considered allowable, because of a certain exigency, that a man should marry his aunt, even as Sarah was the sister of Abraham's mother. During the cycle of Adam it was lawful and expedient for a man to marry his own sister, even as Abel, Cain and Seth, the sons of Adam, married their sisters. But in the law of the Pentateuch revealed by Moses these marriages were forbidden and their custom and sanction abrogated. Other laws formerly valid were annulled during the time of Moses. For example, it was lawful in Abraham's cycle to eat the flesh of the camel, but during the time of Jacob this was prohibited. Such changes and transformations in the teaching of religion are applicable to the ordinary conditions of life, but they are not important or essential. Moses lived in the wilderness of Sinai where crime necessitated direct punishment. There were no penitentiaries or penalties of imprisonment. Therefore, according to the exigency of the time and place it was a law of God that an eye should be given for an eye and a tooth for a tooth. It would not be practicable to enforce this law at the present time—for instance, to blind a man who accidentally blinded you. In the Torah there are many commands concerning the punishment of a murderer. It would not be allowable or possible to carry out these ordinances today. Human conditions and exigencies are such that even the question of capital punishment—the one penalty which most nations have continued to enforce for murder—is now under discussion by wise men who are debating its advisability. In fact, laws for the ordinary conditions of life are only valid temporarily. The exigencies of the time of Moses justified cutting off a man's hand for theft, but such a penalty is not allowable now. Time changes conditions, and laws change to suit conditions. We must remember that these changing laws are not the essentials; they are the accidentals of religion. The essential ordinances established by a Manifestation of God are spiritual; they concern moralities, the ethical development of man and faith in God. They are ideal and necessarily permanent—expressions of the one foundation and not amenable to change or transformation. Therefore, the fundamental basis of the revealed religion of God is immutable, unchanging throughout the centuries, not subject to the varying conditions of the human world.*[1]

Obedience to the Law of God for one's era is indisputable: but there is also the question of motivation. As we saw in chapters 10 and 13, the Báb set a higher standard of motive for the worship of God than what had previously been considered acceptable:

---

1 'Abdu'l-Bahá, *The Promulgation of Universal Peace*, pp. 365–6.

That which is worthy of His Essence is to worship Him for His sake, without fear of fire, or hope of paradise.[1]

Evolvement of religious laws within each Revelation

Religious laws evolve not only from one Dispensation to the next but also **throughout each Revelation** because societal requirements and conditions are different at each point in history. Even within a single revelation, ordinances and narratives change and evolve. "I was sent only to the lost sheep of Israel" [Matthew 15:22–24] Jesus told the apostles; but later He said: "... go and make disciples of all nations." (Matthew 28:18–20) Muḥammad and His followers initially prayed facing Jerusalem but later this changed to Mecca. (Qur'án 2:142) In Mecca, Muslims were still following the marriage practices of pre-Islamic times; but in Medina, the Prophet Muḥammad revealed Sura 4, detailing the laws that protected the rights of women, within and outside of marriage.

Likewise, the laws of the Báb were progressively revealed during His six-year Ministry. It can be seen that these laws evolved from mostly unobtrusive ordinances to more demanding ones. According to the Báb:

> *His first Book enjoined the observance of the laws of the Qur'án, so that the people might not be seized with perturbation by reason of a new Book and a new Revelation and might regard His Faith as similar to their own, perchance they would not turn away from the Truth and ignore the thing for which they had been called into being.*[2]

For the same wise reason, even the full rank of the Báb as the *Qá'im* ("He Who will arise"), the Promised One of Islam, was not overtly disclosed until mid-1848—chiefly through the dissemination of the Persian Bayán.[3] It was only later in His Ministry that the Báb openly proclaimed to be the *Qá'im*. At about the same time, the Báb was placed on trial by a religious court in Tabríz where He openly proclaimed:

> *I am, I am, I am, the promised One! I am the One whose name you have for a thousand years invoked, at whose mention you have risen, whose advent you have longed to witness, and the hour of whose Revelation you have prayed God to hasten. Verily I say, it is incumbent upon the peoples of both the East and the West to obey My word and to pledge allegiance to My person.*[4]

Armin Eschraghi writes:

> Appointment of Friday prayer leaders is a prerogative of the Hidden Imám [the Báb's messianic role] but for obvious pragmatic reasons this has been suspended. The Báb, in his earliest writings, declared all Friday prayers as

---

1 The Báb, *Selections*, p. 77.
2 The Báb, *Selections*, p. 119.
3 The Báb, Persian Bayán 1:15.
4 Nabíl-i-A'ẓam, *The Dawn-Breakers*, p. 316.

unlawful if they were conducted by a leader not appointed by him (*Kitáb al-Rúh*, sura 206). Later he abrogated congregational obligatory prayers altogether (*Persian Bayán*, 9:9)."[1]

In the Persian Bayán, the Báb explained that a new corpus of laws must precede any abrogation of prior law[2]; and therefore, at the beginning of His Ministry, He did not abrogate any major Islamic law. The new laws of the Báb in the Persian and Arabic Bayán were issued in Máh-Kú about four years after His Declaration in Shíráz. Following this, the Báb began openly acknowledging His identity as the Promised *Qá'im*. Gradually, the Bábís started to understand the scope and implications of the teachings they had embraced and began breaking away from Islamic laws.

The laws of the Bahá'í Faith were also revealed gradually. For example, after a few years Bahá'u'lláh substituted a single obligatory prayer referred to in the Kitáb-i-Aqdas with a choice of three obligatory prayers.[3]

Another example as to how religious laws evolved within a dispensation is the case of the pilgrimage rituals to the House of the Báb in Shíráz. Bahá'u'lláh prescribed the shaving of the head while, years later, in the Kitáb-i-Aqdas this practice was revoked:

> *All are charged with obedience to the Kitáb-i-Aqdas; whatsoever is revealed therein is the Law of God amid His servants. The injunction on pilgrims to the sacred House to shave the head hath been lifted.*[4]

Messianic expectations about the *Qá'im*

Most authors agree that the Iranian Shí'ah population expected the *Qá'im* to appear dramatically provisioned with armies, full sovereignty and encompassed by supernatural events. "He was not expected to be a man of compassion and grace," wrote Ruhu'llah Mehrabkhani. "He was to be a man of the sword who would declare war against all the inhabitants of the earth. The ensuing blood bath would be such that its wave is to reach up to the stirrup of his horse."[5] According to the same author:

> They believe that the first act the promised Qá'im shall perform will be to raise an army and wage war to avenge the sufferings and persecutions of the Shí'ihs—a war that will cause rivers of blood to flow in retribution for the wrongs done to the true believers [the early Shí'ihs killed by their Sunní opponents].[6]

---

1 Armin Eschraghi, "Undermining the Foundations of Orthodoxy", p. 236.

2 The Báb, Persian Bayán 6:12.

3 Baha'is are required to recite one of the three obligatory prayers (short, medium or long) on a daily basis.

4 Bahá'u'lláh, *The Kitáb-i-Aqdas,* Questions and Answers 10, p. 109.

5 Ruhu'llah Mehrabkhani, "Some Notes on Fundamental Principles", pp. 22–43, esp. 29–35.

6 Ruhu'llah Mehrabkhani, *Mulla Husayn*, p. 162.

The narrative around the Islamic *Qá'im* was similar to the expectations of the Jews about their Messiah in the light of Isaiah's visions. The Messiah from the *Old Testament* was to be a powerful king who would liberate them from their foreign yoke. It is for this reason that the inscription INRI was placed on the top of the cross of Jesus. INRI is an abbreviation for *Iesus Nazarenus, Rex Iudaeorum*, i.e. "Jesus of Nazareth, King of the Jews" (Matthew 2:2). Isaiah (66:14–16) describes the powers of the upcoming Messiah:

> When you see this, your heart will rejoice and you will flourish like grass;
>
> the hand of the Lord will be made known to his servants, but his fury will be shown to his foes.
>
> See, the Lord is coming with fire, and his chariots are like a whirlwind; he will bring down his anger with fury, and his rebuke with flames of fire. For with fire and with his sword the Lord will execute judgment on all people.

In like manner to the transition from Judaism to Christianity, it was difficult for most people in 19th century Iran to accept that the *Qá'im* would come to annul the laws of Islam and to replace them with new ones. As a point of fact, some argued that the Báb could not be the *Qá'im* because He did not take up the sword.[1]

Continuity rather than change has been the expectation of Islamic theologians. Permanency of the Islamic order, however, was not the Will of God. Instead, the Báb brought a totally different new order which seemed radical in relation to the old one. Shoghi Effendi writes:

> The severe laws and injunctions revealed by the Báb can be properly appreciated and understood only when interpreted in the light of His own statements regarding the nature, purpose and character of His own Dispensation. As these statements clearly reveal, the Bábí Dispensation was essentially in the nature of a religious and indeed social revolution, and its duration had therefore to be short, but full of tragic events, of sweeping and drastic reforms. Those drastic measures enforced by the Báb and His followers were taken with the view of undermining the very foundations of Shi'ih orthodoxy, and thus paving the way for the coming of Bahá'u'lláh. To assert the independence of the new Dispensation, and to prepare also the ground for the approaching Revelation of Bahá'u'lláh, the Báb had therefore to reveal very severe laws, even though most of them were never enforced. But the mere fact that He revealed them was in itself a proof of the independent character of His Dispensation and was sufficient to create such widespread agitation, and excite such opposition on the part of the clergy that led them to cause His eventual martyrdom.[2]

To propose, even in principle, the annulment of the old order was a defying endeavour that challenged the legitimacy of the Iranian theocracy of the time. It also constituted a serious theological provocation to the senior divines who

1 Armin Eschraghi, "From Bábí Movement to Bahá'í Faith", p. 398.
2 Shoghi Effendi, *Dawn of a New Day*, pp. 77–78.

considered themselves the gatekeepers of truth. Further, the new teaching appears simultaneously to openly assert the unlimited power of the Báb as an independent Manifestation of God and the proclamation of a New Day.

As the Báb proclaimed Himself to be the *Qá'im*, that is, the return of the 12th Hidden Imám,[1] in the Persian Bayán He likewise pronounced Mullá Ḥusayn and Mullá 'Alí Basṭámí, the first and second Letters of the Living, to be the return of the Prophet Muḥammad and Imám 'Alí[2] respectively.[3] Ṭáhirih was regarded by the Bábís as the incarnation of Fáṭima,[4] the Prophet Muḥammad's daughter, based on the assertion by the Báb that the latter had returned to earth.[5]

Implementation of the laws of the Báb

Most of the laws of the Báb mention, or are conditional upon, acceptance by *Him Whom God shall make Manifest.* These include laws of inheritance; obligatory prayer; the calendar; travelling; pilgrimage; Qibla (Qiblih) direction; Ḥuqúqu'lláh; marriage; and the use of ringstones and talismans, among others, all being a clear testimony of the purpose of the Revelation of the Báb:

> *But for the sole reason of His being [Him Whom God will make manifest] present amongst this people, We would have neither prescribed any law nor laid down any prohibition.*[6]

Much has been said about the harshness and inapplicability of the laws of the Báb in real-life.[7] Some believed that the burdensome nature of His laws was a sign that they would be short-lived.[8] The laws of the Báb were not fully enacted as such because of the short span of His Ministry, the restrictions on disseminating His writings created by a lack of access to printing presses, and ongoing persecutions.[9]

Inapplicability

Many of the individual laws were problematic when it came to implementation. For example, all the graves of the Bábís were to contain the dust from the "first and last [Bábí] believers",[10] and each believer was to mention God

---

1 According to the Shi'ih belief, the 12th Imám, a direct descendant of Muhammad, disappeared in 873–874 CE and was expected to come back in the Day of Judgement.

2 'Alí was the cousin and son-in-law of Muḥammad and is considered the first believer. See Bahá'u'lláh, *Tablets of Bahá'u'lláh*, p. 184.

3 The Báb, Persian Bayán 1:3.

4 Shoghi Effendi, *God Passes By*, p. 32.

5 The Báb, Persian Bayán 1:4.

6 The Báb, *Selections*, p. 149.

7 Armin Eschraghi, "From Bábí Movement to Bahá'í Faith", p. 390.

8 Hasan Balyuzi, *Eminent Bahá'ís in the Time of Bahá'u'lláh*, p. 132.

9 Christopher Buck, *Paradise and Paradigm*.

10 Names were not specified. The Báb, Persian Bayán 8:11.

four thousand times each day.[1] The Bayán prescribed turning towards *Him Whom God shall make Manifest* for the obligatory prayer although Bahá'u'lláh only revealed Himself many years later. The Báb also ordained that His House should be filled with diamonds from the ground to the roof, and be provisioned with 95 doors. In addition, it was ordained that the walls of those towns should be built of red rubies.[2]

There were other ordinances prescribed by the Báb that have been considered as idiosyncratic or eccentric. In those cases, the Báb was stipulating a law in direct opposition to an Islamic ordinance, which He was abrogating. For example, tattoos were forbidden in Islam but the Báb recommended them. Similarly, in defiance of Shariah law, the Báb allowed His followers to break eggs before cooking them, and permitted the eating of fertilized eggs ("eggs with blood")—unless it was abhorrent to the person.[3]

Harshness

For instance, in the Persian Bayán there is a prescription that the properties of non-believers should be transferred to the Bábís because the enjoyment of material things should be accompanied by belief in His revelation and an appreciation of God's munificence. However, two impossible conditions are given; firstly, the order must come from the sovereign and secondly, the procedure should not cause loss or sadness to anyone.[4] Likewise, only believers were to be allowed to live in five specific regions: namely, Fárs, Iraq, Á<u>dh</u>arbayján, <u>Kh</u>urásán and Mázindarán as people in those lands would be closer to God, and non-believers were not to be permitted in those areas.[5] This command was to stay in effect until the appearance of *Him Whom God shall make Manifest.*

Many of the laws of the Báb were difficult to implement and there were reasons for that. The Báb wrote about the establishment of a theocracy ruled by a Bábí king[6] but under the sovereignty of the Báb. The Bábí king ideally had the authority to run an army,[7] levy taxes[8] and appoint government ministers.[9] E.G. Browne remarked that: "the original Bábís ... aimed at a Babi theocracy and a reign of the saints on earth...... and were only interested for the most part in the triumph of their faith, not only in any projects of social or political reform"[10]

---

1 The Báb, Persian Bayán 8:19.

2 The Báb, Persian Bayán 6:4.

3 The Báb, Arabic Bayán 10:15.

4 The Báb, Persian Bayán 5:5; and Nader Saiedi, *Gate of the Heart,* p. 135.

5 Muḥammad Afnán, "The Báb's Bayán", pp. 7–16.

6 The Báb, Persian Bayán 4:5; 5:5; 7:16; & Arabic Bayán 9:3; 11:2; 11:13; 11:17.

7 The Báb, Arabic Bayán 5:6; 5:19; 4:9.

8 The Báb, Arabic Bayán 5:19.

9 The Báb, Arabic Bayán 11:2.

10 E.G. Browne. *Materials for the Study of the Bábí Religion,* p. xv.

Armin Eschraghi remarked that, "The main theological problem for the followers of the Báb was that a considerable portion of Bayanic laws appeared to presume the existence of a society where the population and its rulers would be Bábís."[1] Furthermore, the Báb permitted His followers to engage in religious wars and allowed future Bábí kings to conquer countries.[2] According to Mangol Bayat, "There is in the Bayán an implicit assumption that Iran would eventually adopt Babism as the state religion"[3].

If armies and harsh laws were proposed, they matched the Shí'a aggressive rhetoric associated with the expected prophecies about the *Qá'im*, which, according to the Kitáb-i-Íqán, should be allegorically interpreted. While the Báb was issuing ordinances, such as the previously mentioned transfer of properties from non-believers to believers,[4] He was simultaneously imposing impossible conditions for their practice.[5] For instance prohibitions against:

- causing sadness
- entering someone's house without permission
- coercive conversions to His Faith.

Leniency

The harshness of the laws of the Báb is juxtaposed against the leniency of the punishments. Chastisements for breaking a Bábí law consisted of paying fines or prohibition of intimate marital relations for a period of time. However, physical chastisement such as imprisonment or corporal punishment was not enjoined.[6]

The penalty for causing sadness was nineteen mithqals of gold, but only if the offender could afford it; whereas intentional murder was punished with the payment of one-thousand fold blood money, about a quarter of a current million dollars, as well as the loss of intimate marital relationships for nineteen years.

Nature of religious laws in the Bábí-Bahá'í Faith

The Báb observes that all the laws enshrined in the Persian Bayán have a spiritual foundation because they *"have been revealed on the basis of the recognition of God and divine mysteries."*[7] The Báb also wrote that *"there is no paradise more exalted than the very act of observing the ordinances of God."*[8] In a

---

1 Armin Eschraghi, "From Bábí Movement to Bahá'í Faith", p. 390.
2 The Báb, Persian Bayán 6:4.
3 Mangol Bayat, *Mysticism and dissent*, p. 106.
4 The Báb, Persian Bayán 5:5.
5 Muḥammad Afnán, "The Báb's Bayán".
6 See Nader Saiedi, *Gate of the Heart*, p. 368.
7 The Báb in Nader Saiedi, *Gate of the Heart*, p. 326.
8 The Báb in Nader Saiedi, *Gate of the Heart*, p. 312.

similar vein, Bahá'u'lláh has described His laws as *"the lamps of My loving providence among My servants"*[1] and *"the keys of My mercy for My creatures."*[2]

Since the early beginnings of the Bahá'í Faith, it has been understood that the Revelations of the Báb and Bahá'u'lláh would develop into a single and unique global Faith. The Báb and Bahá'u'lláh are referred to by Shoghi Effendi as the "twin Luminaries of the Bahá'í Revelation",[3] with the Báb being "the martyr Prophet and co-founder of their Faith".[4] Their teachings form one vast treasure trove of divine pearls and jewels for the benefit of humanity.

Shoghi Effendi said of the Báb that His "Dispensation in a sense will last as long as Bahá'u'lláh's lasts."[5] As a point of fact, out of the eleven holy days of the Badí' calendar, four of them are related to the Báb, namely, the birth, declaration and martyrdom of the Báb as well as the celebration of Naw-Rúz (New Year) established in the Bayán as the *Day of God*.[6] As the following letter states, both Dispensations form one global Faith with a continuing, all-encompassing goal:

> Shoghi Effendi feels that the unity of the Bahá'í Revelation as one complete whole embracing the Faith of the Báb should be emphasized ... The Faith of the Báb should not be divorced from that of Bahá'u'lláh. Though the teachings of the Bayán have been abrogated and superseded by the laws of the Aqdas, yet due to the fact that the Báb considered Himself as the Forerunner of Bahá'u'lláh, we would regard His Dispensation together with that of Bahá'u'lláh as forming one entity, the former being introductory to the advent of the latter.[7]

The Bayán was essentially superseded by the revelation of the Kitáb-i-Aqdas around 1873. Until then the Bayán remained as the central book. In the acclaimed Tablet of Aḥmad, revealed in 1865, Bahá'u'lláh affirms:

> *Say: O people be obedient to the ordinances of God, which have been enjoined in the Bayán by the Glorious, the Wise One. Verily He is the King of the Messengers and His book is the Mother Book did ye but know.*[8]

From His Writings, it seems the Báb expected that many of His laws would be abrogated by Bahá'u'lláh.

> *Better is it for a person to write down but one of His verses than to transcribe the whole of the Bayán and all the books which have been written in the*

1 Bahá'u'lláh, *The Kitáb-i-Aqdas*, p. 20.
2 Bahá'u'lláh, *The Kitáb-i-Aqdas*, p. 20.
3 Shoghi Effendi, *God Passes By*, p. 237.
4 Shoghi Effendi, *Unfolding Destiny*, p. 234.
5 Shoghi Effendi, *Dawn of a New Day*, p. 94.
6 The Báb, Persian Bayán 6:14.
7 Letter written on behalf of Shoghi Effendi included in Introduction to *The Kitáb-i-Aqdas*, p. 8.
8 *Bahá'í Prayers*, p. 210.

> *Dispensation of the Bayán. For everything shall be set aside except His Writings* [Bahá'u'lláh], *which will endure until the following Revelation.*[1]

The Kitáb-i-Aqdas[2] was revealed in 1872–1873, when, according to Bahá'u'lláh, the circumstances were deemed to be appropriate for the Cause and the believers.[3] After the revelation of the Kitáb-i-Aqdas, Bahá'u'lláh summarized His actions regarding the currency of the laws enunciated by the Báb, as follows:

> *Our Exalted Herald—may the life of all else besides Him be offered up for His sake—hath revealed certain laws. However, in the realm of His Revelation these laws were made subject to Our sanction, hence this Wronged One hath put some of them into effect by embodying them in the Kitáb-i-Aqdas in different words. Others We set aside. He holdeth in His hand the authority. He doeth what He willeth and He ordaineth whatsoever He pleaseth. He is the Almighty, the All-Praised. There are also ordinances newly revealed. Blessed are they that attain. Blessed are they that observe His precepts.*[4]

The Báb abrogated innumerable Islamic laws, from both the Qur'án and hadiths (oral traditions). He created His own religious legislature, thus freeing Bahá'u'lláh from this role. Bahá'u'lláh confirms this principle in *The Kitáb-i-Aqdas*:

> *Verily, He* [the Báb] *revealed certain laws so that, in this Dispensation, the Pen of the Most High might have no need to move in aught but the glorification of His own transcendent Station and His most effulgent Beauty. Since, however, We have wished to evidence Our bounty unto you, We have, through the power of truth, set forth these laws with clarity and mitigated what We desire you to observe. He, verily, is the Munificent, the Generous.*[5]

Response of Bahá'u'lláh to the laws of the Bayán

Several of the laws of the Báb were subject to clarification or repeal when Bahá'u'lláh revealed His own book of laws, the Kitáb-i-Aqdas, about twenty-five years after the Bayán. "The Báb states that His laws are provisional and depend upon the acceptance of the future Manifestation," Shoghi Effendi affirmed in a letter written on his behalf. "This is why in the Book of Aqdas Bahá'u'lláh sanctions some of the laws found in the Bayán, modifies others and sets aside many."[6] The Universal House of Justice states:

---

1 The Báb, *Selections*, p. 91.

2 The original document, al-Kitábu'l-Aqdas (in Arabic), was not translated in full into English until 1992 when it was published under the Persian form of the name, *The Kitáb-i-Aqdas.*

3 Adib Taherzadeh, *The Revelation of Bahá'u'lláh,* vol. 3, p. 279.

4 Bahá'u'lláh, *Tablets of Bahá'u'lláh*, p. 132.

5 Bahá'u'lláh, *The Kitáb-i-Aqdas*, p. 71.

6 Letter written on behalf of Shoghi Effendi included in Introduction to *The Kitáb-i-Aqdas*, p. 8.

> "*For a number of years*", Bahá'u'lláh states in one of His Tablets, "*petitions reached the Most Holy Presence from various lands begging for the laws of God, but We held back the Pen ere the appointed time had come.*"

Not until twenty years from the birth of His Prophetic Mission in the Síyáh-Chál of Ṭihrán had elapsed did Bahá'u'lláh reveal the Kitáb-i-Aqdas, the Repository of the laws of His Dispensation. Even after its revelation the Aqdas was withheld by Him for some time before it was sent to the friends in Persia. **This divinely purposed delay in the revelation of the basic laws of God for this age, and the subsequent gradual implementation of their provisions, illustrate the principle of progressive revelation which applies even within the ministry of each Prophet.**[1]

Shoghi Effendi has also explained:

> The formulation by Bahá'u'lláh, in His Kitáb-i-Aqdas, of the fundamental laws of His Dispensation was followed, as His Mission drew to a close, by the enunciation of certain precepts and principles which lie at the very core of His Faith, by the reaffirmation of truths He had previously proclaimed, by the elaboration and elucidation of some of the laws He had already laid down, by the revelation of further prophecies and warnings, and by the establishment of subsidiary ordinances designed to supplement the provisions of His Most Holy Book. These were recorded in unnumbered Tablets, which He continued to reveal until the last days of His earthly life....
>
> Concerning the implementation of the laws themselves Bahá'u'lláh wrote in one of His Tablets: "*Indeed the laws of God are like unto the ocean and the children of men as fish, did they but know it. However, in observing them one must exercise tact and wisdom.... Since most people are feeble and far-removed from the purpose of God, therefore one must observe tact and prudence under all conditions, so that nothing might happen that could cause disturbance and dissension or raise clamour among the heedless. Verily, His bounty hath surpassed the whole universe and His bestowals encompassed all that dwell on earth. One must guide mankind to the ocean of true understanding in a spirit of love and tolerance. The Kitáb-i-Aqdas itself beareth eloquent testimony to the loving providence of God.*"
>
> ... "*Know of a certainty that in every Dispensation the light of Divine Revelation hath been vouchsafed to men in direct proportion to their spiritual capacity. Consider the sun. How feeble its rays the moment it appeareth above the horizon. How gradually its warmth and potency increase as it approacheth its zenith, enabling meanwhile all created things to adapt themselves to the growing intensity of its light. How steadily it declineth until it reacheth its setting point. Were it all of a sudden to manifest the energies latent within it, it would no doubt cause injury to all created things. ... In like manner, if the Sun of Truth were suddenly to reveal,*

---

1 *The Kitáb-i-Aqdas*, Note 126, pp. 219–220.

> *at the earliest stages of its manifestation, the full measure of the potencies which the providence of the Almighty hath bestowed upon it, the earth of human understanding would waste away and be consumed; for men's hearts would neither sustain the intensity of its revelation, nor be able to mirror forth the radiance of its light. Dismayed and overpowered, they would cease to exist."*[1]

As mentioned a few pages previously, it is clear that the Báb expected that many of His laws would be abrogated by Bahá'u'lláh. One difference between the Bayán and the Kitáb-i-Aqdas is that the latter did not deal with a large number of specific individual or social regulations but made provisions for the creation in the future of a new institution, the Universal House of Justice, which would enact new laws according to the needs of the time. Furthermore, Bahá'u'lláh widened the scope of personal responsibility and individual conscience in implementing His laws.[2] In contrast to about 8,000 verses in the Persian Bayán, the Kitáb-i-Aqdas consists of 474 verses allotted between 190 paragraphs.[3]

While reviewing the continuity between the Bábí and Bahá'í dispensations in respect of their joint history, and the development of their teachings and ordinances to form a single entity, we have noted the evolutionary nature of the teachings of the Báb. Of particular importance is the statement of the Báb regarding the imminent and overarching revelation of *Him Whom God shall make Manifest*

> *Well is it with him who fixeth his gaze upon the Order of Bahá'u'lláh, and rendereth thanks unto his Lord. For He will assuredly be made manifest. God hath indeed irrevocably ordained it in the Bayán.*[4]

As to the role of the Kitáb-i-Aqdas, the Universal House of Justice writes that it "removes those elements of past religious codes that now constitute obstacles to the emerging unification of the world and the reconstruction of human society".[5] The Universal House of Justice remarks that its contents "constitute the kernel of a vast range of law that will arise in centuries to come."[6]

Shoghi Effendi, in his account of the first hundred years of the Bahá'í dispensation in *God Passes By*, gave the following description of the Kitáb-i-Aqdas:

> The laws and ordinances that constitute the major theme of this Book, Bahá'u'lláh, moreover, has specifically characterized as *"the breath of life unto all created things,"* as *"the mightiest stronghold,"* as the *"fruits"* of His

1 Shoghi Effendi, *Synopsis and Codification of the Kitáb-i-Aqdas*, pp. 4–5.
2 Roshan Danesh, *The Dimensions of Bahá'í Law.*
3 Muḥammad Afnán, "The Báb's Bayán", pp. 7–16.
4 The Báb in Shoghi Effendi, *The World Order of Bahá'u'lláh*, pp. 146–7.
5 Introduction to *The Kitáb-i-Aqdas*, p. 2.
6 Introduction to *The Kitáb-i-Aqdas*, p. 4.

"Tree," as *"the highest means for the maintenance of order in the world and the security of its peoples,"* as *"the lamps of His wisdom and loving-providence,"* as *"the sweet-smelling savor of His garment,"* and the *"keys"* of His *"mercy"* to His creatures. *"This Book,"* He Himself testifies, *"is a heaven which We have adorned with the stars of Our commandments and prohibitions."* *"Blessed the man,"* He, moreover, has stated, *"who will read it, and ponder the verses sent down in it by God, the Lord of Power, the Almighty. Say, O men! Take hold of it with the hand of resignation ... By My life! It hath been sent down in a manner that amazeth the minds of men. Verily, it is My weightiest testimony unto all people, and the proof of the All-Merciful unto all who are in heaven and all who are on earth."* And again: *"Blessed the palate that savoreth its sweetness, and the perceiving eye that recognizeth that which is treasured therein, and the understanding heart that comprehendeth its allusions and mysteries. By God! Such is the majesty of what hath been revealed therein, and so tremendous the revelation of its veiled allusions that the loins of utterance shake when attempting their description."* And finally: *"In such a manner hath the Kitáb-i-Aqdas been revealed that it attracteth and embraceth all the divinely appointed Dispensations. Blessed those who peruse it! Blessed those who apprehend it! Blessed those who meditate upon it! Blessed those who ponder its meaning! So vast is its range that it hath encompassed all men ere their recognition of it. Erelong will its sovereign power, its pervasive influence and the greatness of its might be manifested on earth."*[1]

1 Shoghi Effendi, *God Passes By*, pp. 215–216.

18
Transition from the Bábí to the Bahá'í Faith

Over a hundred and seventy years have now elapsed since the Báb was executed (1850) by a firing squad in Tabríz. Since that time, the process He started in 1844 has continued to unfold with great velocity, influence and success.

Renewed interest in Babism

We know that the Faith of the Báb expanded very quickly. It is noteworthy that Christianity took at least seventy decades to reach China[1] after the Jesus' crucifixion of Jesus while the Bábí Faith achieved the same milestone only a decade after the martyrdom of the Báb.[2]

Similarly, Christendom only arrived in England in CE 597, while the Faith of the Báb had been already mentioned by *The London Times* one year after its birth. In its regular edition of 1 November 1845, an article was published under the title "Persia" which described the journey of the Báb to Mecca, His return to Persia and the suffering of the Bábís in Shíráz. As predicted in the Bible, "... as the lightning comes from the east and shines as far as the west",[3] the new Gospel illuminated the Western world as well as the rest of the world where that famous international newspaper was read, announcing the Manifestation of the Báb.

In 2019, the 200th anniversary of His birth was celebrated across the globe[4]—a realization of the words revealed through the Báb at the start of His ministry: *"Be patient, O Apple of My eyes. Verily, God has pledged with Him Thy might in all the lands."*[5]

In recognition of the significance of this occasion, testimonials flowed from prominent dignitaries, including from formal sessions of the Australian Parliament and the California State Senate as well as members of the parliaments of New Zealand and the United Kingdom.

The President of Israel, Reuven Rivlin, visited the Shrine of the Báb to honour the occasion. Also, the President of India, Ram Nath Kovind, publicly paid homage to the Prophet-Martyr of the Bahá'í Faith with the following words:

> The Writings which He has left behind has continued to guide and inspire us, as they expressed profound eternal truths and summon the world to an exalted standard of conduct .... It is my hope that those gathered here

1 Daniel Bays, *A New History of Christianity in China.*

2 Ḥájí Mírzá Muḥammad 'Alí, a maternal cousin of the Báb lived in Shanghai (1862–1868) and then in Hong Kong (1870–1897). See Seow, *The Pure in Heart.*

3 Matthew 24:27.

4 The Universal House of Justice to the Bahá'ís of the world, 8 November 2019.

5 The Báb in Javidukht Khadem, *Zikrullah Khadem*, p. 274.

> today, along with every other Indian, strives to fulfill the vision of the Báb to arise to selfless and steadfast service and to make the welfare of humanity their common and collective aim.[1]

The interest in Babism continues. In recent decades, several Western scholars including Richard Losch,[2] Harsha Ram,[3] Jack Kalpakjan,[4] Tadd Fernée,[5] Nikki Keddie,[6] Jürgen Osterhammel,[7] and Geoffrey Nash[8] confirmed that the Báb was an influential religious, social, intellectual and moral reformer of nineteenth century Persia. In 2018, Christopher De Bellaigue wrote in his book *The Islamic Enlightenment* that "The Babi movement, which began in the 1840s, went on to become an important catalyst of social progressiveness in mid-nineteenth-century Iran, promoting interreligious peace, social equality between the sexes and revolutionary anti-monarchism."[9]

The Báb as a new force in human development

The Prophets of God stimulate human development both at the spiritual and at the intellectual level. Jesus Christ's revelation resulted in advances in the arts and sciences in the Western world and Muḥammad's revelation led to the emergence of the Islamic civilization which inspired the European Renaissance.[10] Bahá'u'lláh Himself confirms the influence of the Messengers of God on humanity's progress and specifically refers to the impact of Jesus Christ:

> *By sacrificing Himself, however, a fresh capacity was infused into all created things. Its evidences, as witnessed in all the peoples of the earth, are now manifest before thee. The deepest wisdom which the sages have uttered, the profoundest learning which any mind hath unfolded, the arts which the ablest hands have produced, the influence exerted by the most potent of rulers, are but manifestations of the quickening power released by His transcendent, His all-pervasive, and resplendent Spirit.*[11]

With respect to the Báb, the historian Nabíl noted His suffering during an agonizing sea journey to Mecca due to the primitive maritime technology of the time and prayed that the means of seafaring transportation would improve. As Nabíl wrote:

---

1 *Bahá'í World News Service*, 22 December 2019. Available from: https://news.bahai.org/story/1379/

2 Richard Losch, *The Many Faces of Faith*.

3 Harsha Ram, "Literature as World Revolution".

4 Jack Kalpakian, "Representing the Unpresentable".

5 Tadd Graham Fernée, "Modernity and Nation-making".

6 Keddie & Yann, "Continuity and Change Under the Qajars".

7 Jürgen Osterhammel, *The Transformation of the World*, p. 896.

8 Geoffrey Nash, "Aryan and Semite".

9 Christopher De Bellaigue, *The Islamic Enlightenment*, p. 96.

10 Hasan Balyuzi, *Muḥammad and the Course of Islám*.

11 Bahá'u'lláh, *Gleanings from the Writings of Bahá'u'lláh*, pp. 85–86.

Within a short space of time, since that prayer was offered, the evidences of a remarkable improvement in all forms of maritime transport have greatly multiplied, and the Persian Gulf, which in those days hardly possessed a single steam-driven vessel, now boasts a fleet of ocean liners that can, within the range of a few days and in the utmost comfort, carry the people of Fárs on their annual pilgrimage to Ḥijáz [Mecca and Medina].

The peoples of the West, among whom the first evidences of this great Industrial Revolution have appeared, are, alas, as yet wholly unaware of the Source whence this mighty stream, this great motive power, proceeds—a force that has revolutionised every aspect of their material life. Their own history testifies to the fact that in the year which witnessed the dawn of this glorious Revelation, there suddenly appeared evidences of an industrial and economic revolution that the people themselves declare to have been unprecedented in the history of mankind.[1]

In their book *The Báb o la Puerta a un Mundo Mejor,* José Enrique Ruiz-Domènec and Arash Arjomandi[2] argue that the Revelation of the Báb brought an unprecedented impetus to the development of scientific discovery in the nineteenth century. The authors cite the discovery of the telegraph in 1844, the development of the principles of thermodynamics in the 1840s, the industrial production of steel in 1855, the first oil refinery in 1856, the first transatlantic cable in 1858 and the invention of the phonautograph in 1858. Similarly, electromagnetism was discovered in 1859, the London metro opened in 1863 and dynamite was invented in 1867. Other new inventions of the time included the phonograph in 1877 and the electric light bulb in 1879. In addition, the first commercial automobile was sold in 1886, the discovery of the rabies vaccine by Pasteur occurred in 1885 and aspirin was patented in 1889. It was during this period (1859) that Charles Darwin established his theory of evolution. As 'Abdu'l-Bahá acknowledged:

The manifestation of such marvellous signs and mighty undertakings, the influence exerted upon the thoughts and minds of the people, the laying of the foundations of progress, and the establishment of the prerequisites of success and prosperity by a young merchant constitute the greatest proof that He [the Báb] *was a universal Educator—a fact that no fair-minded person would ever hesitate to acknowledge.*[3]

The Shrine of the Báb

A magnificent shrine erected on the slopes of Mount Carmel now guards the precious remains of the Báb. It is located close to the "Retreat of Elijah, Whose return the Báb Himself symbolizes."[4] The Shrine of the Báb, built on the spot

---

1 Nabíl-i-A'ẓam, *The Dawn-Breakers,* p. 131.

2 Ruiz-Domènec & Arjomandi, *The Báb o la Puerta a un Mundo Mejor.*

3 'Abdu'l-Bahá, *Some Answered Questions,* p. 31.

4 *The Bahá'í World,* Vol. XII, pp. 349–50.

designated by Bahá'u'lláh, was described by the Guardian as "the Queen of Carmel enthroned on God's Holy Mountain, crowned with glowing gold, robed in shimmering white and girdled with emerald green, a sight enchanting every eye, whether viewed from the air, the sea, the plain or the hill."[1]

Shoghi Effendi wrote of the Shrine of the Báb:

> Upon thee, O Queen of Carmel, be the purest, the most tender salutations, the fairest, the most gracious blessings! Glorified is He Whose footsteps have ennobled the spot whereon thou standest, Who ordained thy Seat, and Who extolled thee in His Tablet and Book. How great is the potency of thy might, a might which has bewildered the souls of the favored ones of God and His Messengers.
>
> Methinks I behold thee in my dreams established upon thy glorious throne, attired in thy white raiment, crowned with thy golden crown, resplendent with the lights shining within thee and around thee, calling aloud in ringing tones and raising thy voice between earth and heaven.
>
> Methinks I perceive the souls of the holy ones and of the dwellers of the realms above hastening toward thee with utmost joy, eagerness and ecstasy, pointing to thee, circling round thee, inhaling the perfume of thy flowers and roses, seeking blessing from the earth of thy precincts, bowing their foreheads to the ground before thee in recognition of the majesty and glory which surround the Holy Dust reposing within thee, the Pearl which is enshrined in thy bosom.
>
> Blessed, immeasurably blessed is the person who visits thee and circles around thee, who serves at thy threshold, waters thy flowers, inhales the fragrance of holiness from thy roses, celebrates thy praise and glorifies thy station for the love of God, thy Creator, in this hallowed and radiant, this great, august and wondrous age.[2]

'Abdu'l-Bahá, envisioned future sovereigns of the world disembarking in Haifa and *"... bareheaded and barefooted, and carrying on their shoulders vases studded with jewels, they advance toward the Shrine."*[3] In 2008, the UNESCO added the Shrine of the Báb to the UNESCO World Heritage list in recognition of its "Outstanding Universal Value" to the common heritage of humanity.[4]

A vast collection of the original Writings of the Báb, as well as many personal relics, are kept in the International Bahá'í Archives as a tangible remnant of His presence. Importantly, His painted portrait is preserved in that building, the

---

1 Rúḥíyyih Rabbání, *The Priceless Pearl*, p. 246.

2 Shoghi Effendi in Javidukht Khadem, *Zikrullah Khadem*, pp. 265–266.

3 'Abdu'l-Bahá in Javidukht Khadem, *Zikrullah Khadem*, 1990, p. 264.

4 See *UNESCO World Heritage Centre (2008-07-08).* Three New Sites Inscribed on UNESCO's World Heritage List. Last retrieved 15 April 2022 from https://whc.unesco.org/en/news/452

viewing of which is "... an inestimable privilege and blessing ... as past generations were denied a glimpse of the Face of the Manifestation, once He had passed on."[1]

Growth of the Bábí-Bahá'í Faith

Years after the martyrdom of the Báb in 1850, when the appearance of Bahá'u'lláh (*The Glory of God*, in Arabic) occurred, the assurances of the Báb regarding the coming of *Him Whom God shall make Manifest* were fully realized. Referring to the continuation between the Bábí and the Bahá'í religions, Bahá'u'lláh has stated that, "*They that have turned away from the latter Manifestation* [Bahá'u'lláh] *have indeed failed to recognize the former* [the Báb].[2]

Concurrently, with the acceptance of the Revelation of Bahá'u'lláh, about eight million believers[3] around the world have recognized the divine station of the Báb and learned to love Him in their hearts. The Faith of the Báb and Bahá'u'lláh has spread from its initial spark in one city, i.e., Shíráz, in 1844 to nearly 100,000 localities by 2020.[4] After Christianity, it is considered the world's second-most widespread religion[5] established in 218 countries, among 2,100 ethic and tribal minorities[6] and its literature has been translated to more than 700 language and dialects.[7] It all happened as per the promise revealed to the Báb, "... *God hath indeed pledged to establish Thy sovereignty throughout all countries and over the people that dwell therein.*"[8]

The life of Bahá'u'lláh

Bahá'u'lláh was a distinguished champion of the Cause of the Báb, and n Persian aristocrat whose family had served the crown with loyalty and honesty. Following the death of the Báb in 1850, Bahá'u'lláh was imprisoned and then banished to Baghdád in the neighbouring country of Iraq where, in 1863, He made the public declaration of His divine role as a Manifestation of God.

In the years after His declaration, the Muslim hierarchy and the Persian government ferociously opposed the teachings of Bahá'u'lláh for the same reasons as their execution of the Báb. As a result of those persecutions, thousands of Bahá'ís were martyred for their beliefs in the second half of the 19th century—repeating the tragedy of the Bábí believers.

---

1 Letter written on behalf of the Guardian 13 November 1944 to an individual believer. Cited in Helen Hornby, *Lights of Guidance*, p. 471.

2 Bahá'u'lláh in *Immortal Youth*, p. 28; *Days of Remembrance*, § 28.5.

3 Peter Smith, "The History of the Bábí and Bahá'í Faiths".

4 Peter Smith, "The History of the Bábí and Bahá'í Faiths".

5 *Encyclopædia Britannica*. "Worldwide Adherents of All Religions by Six Continental Areas, Mid-2002". *Encyclopædia Britannica*, 2002.

6 Barrett, et al, "World Summary".

7 Martin Douglas, "The Bahá'í Faith in its Second Century", pp. 61–66.

8 The Báb, *Selections*, p. 57.

Bahá'u'lláh was subsequently banished from Baghdád to the cities of Constantinople (present-day Istanbul) and then Adrianople (present-day Edirne), all of which were part of the Ottoman Empire. The final banishment of Bahá'u'lláh was to the penal colony of 'Akká in Palestine (present-day Israel) in 1868 and He remained there as a prisoner of the Ottoman Empire until his death on 29 May 1892, having endured about forty years of exile and imprisonment. The Bahá'ís consider the location of His sepulchre as the most sacred spot in the world.

Bahá'u'lláh states: *"Well nigh a hundred volumes of luminous verses and perspicuous words have already been sent down from the heaven of the will of Him Who is the Revealer of signs, and are available unto all."*[1]

These Holy Writings encompass metaphysical, doctrinal, ethical, mystical and social issues, including the principles of: independent investigation of truth; the elimination of religious, national or racial prejudices; the equality of rights between men and women; the essential harmony between science and religion; the elimination of extremes of poverty and wealth; the creation of an international tribunal of justice to safeguard world peace; and the espousal of an international auxiliary language to enable communication and understanding between the peoples of the planet.

Bahá'u'lláh issued bold and commanding epistles to the monarchs and rulers of the world. These included: Queen Victoria, Napoleon III, Pope Pius IX, the Czar Alexander II of Russia, the Emperor Franz Joseph of Austria, Kaiser Wilhelm I of Germany, the Sháh of Iran and the Sultan of the Ottoman Empire. The *"crowned heads"* were summoned to reconcile their differences and dwell as members of a united family. His Message was one of universal peace and amity. Bahá'u'lláh not only honoured the Message of the Báb but took it to new heights by spreading it all over the world.

Two years before His ascension, Bahá'u'lláh granted a unique interview to Professor Edward Granville Browne of Cambridge University, where He summarized the main purpose of His revelation:

> *We desire but the good of the world and the happiness of the nations; yet they deem us a stirrer up of strife and sedition worthy of bondage and banishment .... That all nations should become one in faith and all men as brothers; that the bonds of affection and unity between the sons of men should be strengthened; that diversity of religion should cease, and differences of race be annulled—what harm is there in this? ... Yet so it shall be; these fruitless strifes, these ruinous wars shall pass away, and the 'Most Great Peace' shall come .... Do not you in Europe need this also? Is this not what Christ foretold? ... Yet do we see your kings and rulers lavishing their treasures more freely on means for the destruction of the human race than on that which would conduce to the happiness of mankind .... These strifes*

1 Bahá'u'lláh, *Epistle to the Son of the Wolf*, p. 115.

and this bloodshed and discord must cease, and all men be as one kindred and one family .... Let not a man glory in this, that he loves his country; let him rather glory in this, that he loves his kind ....[1]

The relevance of the teachings of the Báb to a modern world

Nowadays, no one can dispute the increasing threat to the security of the world, foreshadowed by the gloomy clouds, which darkened the skies of the nineteenth century—a century fraught with "blights of war, imperialism, and slavery, and suffering the oppression of prejudice, growing materialism, and loss of faith"[2] . Over sixty major wars have been fought between 1844 and now for reasons involving national, racial and religious prejudices.[3] In a moribund world currently in turmoil and in accelerating disorder and destruction, the words of the blessed Báb to the "peoples of the West" are as relevant today as they were in 1844:

Become as true brethren in the one and indivisible religion of God, free from distinction, for verily God desireth that your hearts should become mirrors unto your brethren in the Faith, so that ye find yourselves reflected in them, and they in you.[4]

And again with these calls to peace and unity:

O peoples of the earth! Verily the resplendent Light of God hath appeared in your midst ... that ye may be guided aright to the ways of peace and, by the leave of God, step out of the darkness into the light and onto this far-extended Path of Truth.[5]

We have created you from one tree and have caused you to be as the leaves and fruit of the same tree, that haply ye may become a source of comfort to one another.[6]

At a time characterized by pessimism and cynicism, the message of the Báb resonates even more clearly today, bringing a message of joy, hope and mutual understanding to posterity as a new morning for humanity:

Yea, that promise hath indeed come true and the decree of God hath been accomplished as He hath ordained. Assuredly we are today living in the Days of God. These are the glorious days on the like of which the sun hath never risen in the past. These are the days which the people in bygone times

1 Bahá'u'lláh in John Esslemont, *Bahá'u'lláh and the New Era*, pp. 39–40.

2 Elham Afnan, "A Twofold Mission", p. 1.

3 *Britannica.* "Wars, Battles & Armed Conflicts". Last retrieved on 30 April 2022 from www.britannica.com/topic/list-of-wars-2031197

4 The Báb, *Selections*, p. 56.

5 The Báb, *Selections*, p. 61.

6 The Báb, *Selections*, p. 129.

> *eagerly expected. What hath then befallen you that ye are fast asleep? These are the days wherein God hath caused the Daystar of Truth to shine resplendent. What hath then caused you to keep your silence? These are the appointed days which ye have been yearningly awaiting in the past—the days of the advent of divine justice. Render ye thanks unto God, O ye concourse of believers.*[1]

In a talk given in America in 1912, 'Abdu'l-Bahá explains the significance of the life of the Báb for a Bahá'í believer:

> *Consider how the Báb endured difficulties and tribulations; how He gave His life in the Cause of God; how He was attracted to the love of the Blessed Beauty, Bahá'u'lláh; and how He announced the glad tidings of His manifestation. We must follow His heavenly example; we must be self-sacrificing and aglow with the fire of the love of God. We must partake of the bounty and grace of the Lord, for the Báb has admonished us to arise in service to the Cause of God, to be absolutely severed from all else save God during the day of the Blessed Perfection, Bahá'u'lláh, to be completely attracted by the love of Bahá'u'lláh, to love all humanity for His sake, to be lenient and merciful to all for Him and to upbuild the oneness of the world of humanity.*[2]

1 The Báb, *Selections*, p. 161.

2 'Abdu'l-Bahá, *The Promulgation of Universal Peace*, p. 139.

Part IV
The laws of the Báb

This section discusses the main laws of the Báb, beginning with a chapter covering the abrogation of Jewish, Christian and Islamic laws, whose annulment was confirmed by Bahá'u'lláh. This is followed by a discussion of the laws of the Báb abrogated by Bahá'u'lláh; and then, a chapter on Bábí laws modified and/or confirmed by Bahá'u'lláh. The final chapter focuses on some Bábí ordinances not discussed in the Kitáb-i-Aqdas.

19
Abrogation of Jewish, Christian and Islamic laws whose annulment is confirmed by Bahá'u'lláh

A number of Jewish, Christian and Islamic laws underwent transformation or were abrogated in the Bayán and in the *Kitáb-i-Aqdas*. As previously discussed, the Báb gave *Him Whom God shall make Manifest* full authority over His own and past revelations:

> *The tree of affirmation, by turning aside from Him, is accounted as the tree of denial, and the tree of denial, by turning towards Him, is accounted as the tree of affirmation.*[1]

Jewish laws

The following injunctions about Jewish religious laws are discussed in this section:

- Prohibition against the use of pulpits and exhortation to sit in chairs
- Prohibition of congregational prayers or rituals
- Abolition of the priesthood
- Semen is declared clean
- Dietary injunctions

Prohibition against use of pulpits and exhortation to sit in chairs

Pulpits are used by some religions. The Báb wrote in the Persian Bayán: *"It is not permitted to ascend into pulpits; and men are commanded to sit in chairs."*[2] The Persian Bayán also prescribes that children should sit on chairs in schools rather than on the floor as was the 19th century custom[3]

The prohibition against using pulpits was confirmed by Bahá'u'lláh in the Kitáb-i-Aqdas:

> *'Ye have been prohibited from making use of pulpits. Whoso wisheth to recite unto you the verses of his Lord, let him sit on a chair placed upon a dais, that he may make mention of God, his Lord, and the Lord of all mankind. It is pleasing to God that ye should seat yourselves on chairs and benches as a mark of honour for the love ye bear for Him and for the Manifestation of His glorious and resplendent Cause.*[4]

---

1 Bahá'u'lláh, *Epistle to the Son of the Wolf*, p. 159.

2 The Báb in Momen, *Selections from the Writings of E. G. Browne*, p. 365.

3 The Báb, Persian Bayán 6:11.

4 Bahá'u'lláh, *The Kitáb-i-Aqdas*, para. 154, p. 75.

Prohibition of congregational prayers or rituals

The Prayer for the Dead is the only obligatory prayer[1] to be recited in congregation. It is to be recited by one believer while all present stand in silence. Otherwise, the Bayán prohibited congregational prayers or community rituals. Believers were counselled to attend mosques but to pray individually rather than in a group led by a religious leader.[2] This provision was confirmed by Bahá'u'lláh in the Kitáb-i-Aqdas.[3]

Abolition of the priesthood

The Báb also prescribed that the official interpretation of the Word of God, as an important priesthood prerogative and fundamental element of religious jurisprudence (ijtihád), was to be abolished:

> *Indeed, We have sent down this Book with the truth from God to our servant and have made all the verses in it clear (muḥkamat), not ambiguous (mutashábihát). And none know their interpretation (ta'wíla-há) except God and whomsoever We desire from among the sincere servants of God. Therefore, ask the Remembrance their interpretation (ta'wíl). Indeed, as decreed in the Book, He has, through the bounty of God, knowledge of all its verses.*[4]

The priesthood, an ancient religious institution with Biblical roots,[5] has been abolished in the Kitáb-i-Aqdas[6] as a further development of the above removal of priestly roles. Likewise, the Báb forbade the practice of kissing the hands of clergymen.[7]

Semen is declared clean

In some religions such as Judaism[8] and in most Islamic schools of jurisprudence, semen was considered ritually impure. The Báb stated that semen is endowed with cleanliness since we are created therewith.[9] Bahá'u'lláh in the Kitáb-i-Aqdas confirms: *"God hath decreed, in token of His mercy unto His creatures, that semen is not unclean."*[10]

As aforementioned, in Islám, ritual impurity refers to a state of uncleanliness that invalidates prayer. In the Bahá'í Faith, semen is not deemed impure in

---

1 The daily obligatory prayers are to be recited in private.

2 The Báb, Arabic Bayán 9:9, and Persian Bayán 9.9.

3 Bahá'u'lláh, *The Kitáb-i-Aqdas*, para. 12, p. 23.

4 The Báb in Todd Lawson, "The terms 'Remembrance' and 'Gate'", p. 19.

5 Genesis 14:18–20.

6 The Universal House of Justice, *The Kitáb-i-Aqdas*, p. 14.

7 Armin Eschraghi. *From Bábí Movement to the Bahá'í Faith*, p. 381.

8 Leviticus 15:16–18, 32; Leviticus 22:4; Deuteronomy 23:10; & Numbers 5:13.

9 The Báb, Persian Bayán 5:15.

10 Bahá'u'lláh, *The Kitáb-i-Aqdas*, para. 74, p. 46.

essence, and contamination with semen does not invalidate prayer, which is a great blessing for believers.

Dietary injunctions

The prohibition about eating certain foods varies in each religion. Neither Jesus nor Bahá'u'lláh burdened the believers with such restrictions. Jesus said: "What goes into someone's mouth does not defile them, but what comes out of their mouth, that is what defiles them" (Matthew 15:11). Bahá'u'lláh allowed the consumption of any type of food:

> *Eat ye, O people, of the good things which God hath allowed you, and deprive not yourselves from His wondrous bounties.*[1]

Bahá'u'lláh explained these differences in terms of the time and environment where each revelation took place:

> *... were He to pronounce water itself to be unlawful, it would indeed become unlawful, and the converse holdeth equally true. For upon no thing hath it been inscribed 'this is lawful' or 'this is unlawful'; nay rather, whatsoever hath been or will be revealed is by virtue of the Word of God, exalted be His glory.*[2]

There are no major dietary prohibitions in the Bábí Faith. In the Arabic Bayán[3] the Báb allows fish to be eaten after removing the intestines and the scales, but this was most likely prescribed to counteract some previous religious prohibitions. There is no reason to believe the Báb forbade the consumption of any meat, such as pork, as the concept of "impure animals" disappeared in the Bábí Faith. The Bayán does not allow the mistreatment or overloading of animals and requires them to be treated with kindness, thus giving them specific rights.[4] It is noteworthy that in the Arabic Bayán, the Báb recommends a specific invocation before killing an animal.[5] The Báb also entreats the chastisement of God if an animal is mistreated on a journey by its owner.[6]

What is most evident is the affirmation by the Báb that, for the believers, all things have been immersed in the sea of purity except what is abhorrent **to them.**[7] By abhorrent is meant something disagreeable, that is, "food" that is physically contaminated, for example, being rotten, having a bad smell or an unappetizing appearance. There is no essential impurity but only empirical cleanliness on earth. Similarly, Bahá'u'lláh declared in the Kitáb-i-Aqdas:

---

1 Bahá'u'lláh, *Gleanings from the Writings of Bahá'u'lláh*, p. 60.

2 Bahá'u'lláh, *The Tabernacle of Unity*, p. 36.

3 The Báb, Arabic Bayán 9:19.

4 Nader Saiedi, *Gate of the Heart*, p. 325. In the Bayán the Báb forbids cows to be ridden or used for transportation. See Ma'ani & Ewing, *Laws of the Kitáb-i-Aqdas*, p. 180.

5 The Báb, Arabic Bayán 9:18.

6 The Báb, Persian Bayán 6:16.

7 The Báb, Arabic Bayán 10:5.

God hath, likewise, as a bounty from His presence, abolished the concept of "uncleanness," whereby divers things and peoples have been held to be impure. He, of a certainty, is the Ever-Forgiving, the Most Generous. Verily, all created things were immersed in the sea of purification when, on that first day of Riḍván ....[1]

Finally, Shoghi Effendi clarified that "[t]he eating of pork is not forbidden in the Bahá'í Teachings."[2]

Christian laws

Certain Christian traditions, such as baptism and confession, have been abrogated or not reaffirmed. Specifically, the Bayán[3] prohibits the confession of sins to other people: "*Repentance is not permitted except to God in the person of His Manifestation, when He is manifested; and if not, ask pardon of God secretly with yourselves.*"[4] The Kitáb-i-Aqdas confirms this new principle with these words: "*To none is it permitted to seek absolution from another soul; let repentance be between yourselves and God.*"[5] Also in this regard, Bahá'u'lláh says in the Tablet of Bis͟hárát:

When the sinner findeth himself wholly detached and freed from all save God, he should beg forgiveness and pardon from Him. Confession of sins and transgressions before human beings is not permissible, as it hath never been nor will ever be conducive to divine forgiveness. Moreover such confession before people results in one's humiliation and abasement, and God—exalted be His glory—wisheth not the humiliation of His servants. Verily He is the Compassionate, the Merciful.[6]

Islamic laws

The Báb abrogated several Islamic laws related to the individual and society. The following sub-sections discuss six of the Bayanic laws that were ratified by Bahá'u'lláh.

Penalties for adultery

Both the Báb and Bahá'u'lláh forbade and condemned immoral practices such as **adultery**.[7] The Islamic sentence of death by stoning[8]—or sentencing

---

1 Bahá'u'lláh, *The Kitáb-i-Aqdas*, para. 75, p. 47.

2 Letter written 27 March 1938 on behalf of Shoghi Effendi to an individual believer, quoted in *Lights of Guidance*, no. 1012.

3 The Báb, Persian Bayán 7: 14.

4 The Báb in Momen, *Selections from the Writings of E. G. Browne*, p. 367.

5 Bahá'u'lláh, *The Kitáb-i-Aqdas*, para. 34, p. 30.

6 Bahá'u'lláh, *Tablets of Bahá'u'lláh*, p. 24.

7 Denis MacEoin, *The Messiah of* S͟híráz, p. 181.

8 Stoning for adultery was prescribed in the Torah. There is no mention of capital punishment by stoning in the Qur'án.

perpetrators to death in general—was prohibited in the Bayán. In the Kitáb-i-Aqdas, Bahá'u'lláh states:

> *God hath imposed a fine on every adulterer and adulteress, to be paid to the House of Justice: nine mithqáls of gold, to be doubled if they should repeat the offence. Such is the penalty which He Who is the Lord of Names hath assigned them in this world; and in the world to come He hath ordained for them a humiliating torment. Should anyone be afflicted by a sin, it behoveth him to repent thereof and return unto his Lord. He, verily, granteth forgiveness unto whomsoever He willeth, and none may question that which it pleaseth Him to ordain. He is, in truth, the Ever-Forgiving, the Almighty, the All-Praised.*[1]

The Universal House of Justice clarifies:

> Although the term translated here as adultery refers, in its broadest sense, to unlawful sexual intercourse between either married or unmarried individuals ..., 'Abdu'l-Bahá has specified that the punishment here prescribed is for sexual intercourse between persons who are unmarried. He indicates that it remains for the Universal House of Justice to determine the penalty for adultery committed by a married individual.[2]

Penalties for murder

Like the Old Testament (Exodus 20:13) and New Testament (Matthew 5:21–22), the Báb prohibits *murder*, including ordering someone else's murder. In the Persian Bayán the Báb affirms Qur'án 5:32: "Whosever kills voluntarily, it is as if he has killed all men". Interestingly, Edward Browne wrote that the Báb also forbade "the use of drugs to produce abortion."[3]

The Báb forbade any type of *murder* and considered it the most heinous sin: A believer could be excommunicated for even thinking of murdering someone.[4] The Arabic Bayán extends this murder injunction to anyone playing any role in support of a murderer. The penalty for anyone involved in a murder in any way is a fine of 11,000 mithqals of gold to be paid to the heirs of the victim. Murder is a sin that God does not pardon, even in the afterlife.[5]

The above prescriptions do not apply to involuntary murder. In the case of an accidental fatality, the person responsible must convince the family of the victim that the death was unintentional. One should express one's deep remorse and ask forgiveness from them and from God. However, the Kitáb-i-Aqdas changed the injunction in the Arabic Bayán and prescribed the payment of a fine for involuntary murder:

---

1 Bahá'u'lláh, *The Kitáb-i-Aqdas*, para. 49, p. 37.
2 Bahá'u'lláh, *The Kitáb-i-Aqdas*, p. 200.
3 Edward Granville Browne, "The Bábís of Persia", p. 908.
4 The Báb, Persian Bayán 4:5.
5 The Báb, Arabic Bayán 11:16.

> *Should anyone unintentionally take another's life, it is incumbent upon him to render to the family of the deceased an indemnity of one hundred mithqáls of gold. Observe ye that which hath been enjoined upon you in this Tablet, and be not of those who overstep its limits.*[1]

Although, as seen earlier, Bahá'u'lláh approved the above prescriptions, death sentences may be permitted for homicide or arson. However, commutation of the death penalty for life imprisonment is an alternative.

Permission to use silk clothes and gold and silver dishes and cups

The Bayán says: "*Silk clothes are lawful under all circumstances. So also, is the use of gold and silver*".[2] This was not an injunction from the Qur'án but from Islamic traditions (hadiths). This injunction by the Báb was ratified by Bahá'u'lláh in The Kitáb-i-Aqdas: "*It hath been ... permitted you to attire yourselves in silk*"[3] and "*Whoso wisheth to make use of vessels of silver and gold is at liberty to do so.*"[4]

Permission to charge interest on loans

Usury, in the form of excessive interest, is condemned in the Qur'án (2:275–2:280) and in the Bible (Exodus 22:25–27). Several Islamic scholars argue that charging *any* interest on commercial transactions is morally unacceptable. The Báb categorically declared that purchasing and selling with interest is allowed provided that both parties are satisfied and there is a time is set to complete the loan.[5]

Bahá'u'lláh elaborates in the Kitáb-i-Aqdas on charging interest on loans:

> *Many people stand in need of this. Because if there were no prospect for gaining interest, the affairs of men would suffer collapse or dislocation. One can seldom find a person who would manifest such consideration towards his fellow-man, his countryman or towards his own brother and would show such tender solicitude for him as to be well-disposed to grant him a loan on benevolent terms. Therefore as a token of favour towards men We have prescribed that interest on money should be treated like other business transactions that are current amongst men. Thus, now that this lucid commandment hath descended from the heaven of the Will of God, it is lawful and proper to charge interest on money, that the people of the world may, in a spirit of amity and fellowship and with joy and gladness, devotedly engage themselves in magnifying the Name of Him Who is the Well-Beloved of all mankind. Verily He ordaineth according to His Own choosing. He hath now*

---

1 Bahá'u'lláh, *The Kitáb-i-Aqdas*, para. 188, pp. 87–88.
2 Moojan Momen, *Selections from the Writings of E. G. Browne*, p. 359.
3 Bahá'u'lláh, *Kitáb-i-Aqdas*, para. 159, pp. 76.
4 Bahá'u'lláh, *The Kitáb-i-Aqdas*, para. 46, p. 36.
5 The Báb, Arabic Bayán 5:18, and Persian Bayán 5:18.

> *made interest on money lawful, even as He had made it unlawful in the past. Within His grasp He holdeth the kingdom of authority.*[1]

Animal hair, sable and bones do not nullify one's prayers

In Judaism some objects—particularly those pertaining to animal cadavers—are considered unclean and require ritual ablution by immersion in order to validate prayer. The eating of any part of an animal that was not ritually slaughtered and bled is considered particularly abhorrent. The first Christians were Jews, and they continued to observe these Jewish prohibitions. Although later non-Jewish converts to Christianity considered that Jesus had abrogated Judaism's dietary restrictions, some Christian "reform" or orthodox churches returned to the Jewish prohibitions against unclean meat, and developed methods of ablution to remove "ritual impurity". Likewise, Shí'a Islam formulated restrictions regarding some animal products. "This is not a teaching of the Qur'án," Baharieh Rouhani Ma'ani and Sovaida Ma'ani Ewing wrote, "but one that evolved later as a result of the pronouncements of the 'ulama who imposed certain restrictions regarding the manners of clothing ...."[2] In this regard, the Báb wrote that neither animal hair nor their body components invalidate an individual's prayers.[3]

The Kitáb-i-Aqdas confirms:

> *Hair doth not invalidate your prayer, nor aught from which the spirit hath departed, such as bones and the like. Ye are free to wear the fur of the sable as ye would that of the beaver, the squirrel, and other animals; the prohibition of its use hath stemmed, not from the Qur'án, but from the misconceptions of the divines. He, verily, is the All-Glorious, the All-Knowing.*[4]

Prohibition on amputation of limbs for crimes

The Bayán explicitly forbids the Islamic practice of killing a criminal or even of amputating a criminal's limbs for any offence or crime, including theft.[5]

Instead of amputation for criminals, the Kitáb-i-Aqdas instructs the following for thieves:

> *Exile and imprisonment are decreed for the thief, and, on the third offense, place ye a mark upon his brow so that, thus identified, he may not be accepted in the cities of God and His countries.*[6]

---

1 Bahá'u'lláh, *Tablets of Bahá'u'lláh*, p. 132.
2 Ma'ani & Ewing, *Laws of the Kitáb-i-Aqdas*, p. 41.
3 The Báb, Arabic Bayán 9:12.
4 Bahá'u'lláh, *The Kitáb-i-Aqdas*, para. 9, p. 22.
5 The Báb, Arabic Bayán 11:16.
6 Bahá'u'lláh, *The Kitáb-i-Aqdas*, para. 45, pp. 35–36.

Theft offenses are penalized with nineteen months of prohibition of marital relationships.[1] It is noteworthy that the specification of the levels of penalties for such crimes as adultery, sodomy and theft will be decided in future by the Universal House of Justice.[2]

Prohibition of reciting the names of God in public

Dhikr (ذِكر, "recollection, remembrance, commemoration, praising or glorification of God") is the Islamic practice of reciting and repeating daily the names and attributes of God. This practice was changed in the Bayán. Instead of being spoken aloud and in public, privacy is enjoined in its observance.[3] The Islamic practice was misused to feign devoutness. A. L. M. Nicolas commented:

> The Báb wants to prevent the abuses that everyone witnesses in the streets of Tehran: the ostentation of piety. It is thus that a mullá [Muslim priest] that one meets constantly moves his lips to make [us] believe that he is busy glorifying God.[4]

Bahá'u'lláh reiterated this Bayanic principle in the Kitáb-i-Aqdas:

> *To none is it permitted to mutter sacred verses before the public gaze as he walketh in the street or marketplace.*[5]

Bahá'u'lláh does not prescribe a specific number of verses. However, He provides the following guidance about the obligation of reading the divine verses twice a day:

> *Pride not yourselves on much reading of the verses or on a multitude of pious acts by night and day; for were a man to read a single verse with joy and radiance it would be better for him than to read with lassitude all the Holy Books of God, the Help in Peril, the Self-Subsisting. Read ye the sacred verses in such measure that ye be not overcome by languor and despondency. Lay not upon your souls that which will weary them and weigh them down, but rather what will lighten and uplift them, so that they may soar on the wings of the Divine verses towards the Dawning-place of His manifest signs; this will draw you nearer to God, did ye but comprehend.*[6]

Prohibition on marrying one's divorced wife

The Islamic proscription of marrying one's divorced wife is another law abrogated in the Bayán.[7] According to the Qur'án: "... if he has divorced her (the third time), then she is not lawful unto him thereafter until she has married another husband" (Qur'án 2:230).

---

1 The Báb, Persian Bayán 16:6.

2 *The Kitáb-i-Aqdas*, Questions and Answers 49, p. 121.

3 The Báb, Persian Bayán 9:4.

4 A. L. M. Nicolas, *Le Béyan Persan*, fn. 1, p. 150. (Author's translation)

5 Bahá'u'lláh, *The Kitáb-i-Aqdas*, para. 135, p. 225.

6 Bahá'u'lláh. *The Kitáb-i-Aqdas*, para. 68, p. 44.

7 The Báb, Persian Bayán 6:12.

Bahá'u'lláh ratified the abrogation by the Báb of this Islamic injunction in the Kitáb-i-Aqdas:

> *The Lord hath prohibited, in a Tablet inscribed by the Pen of His command, the practice to which ye formerly had recourse when thrice ye had divorced a woman. This He hath done as a favor on His part, that ye may be accounted among the thankful. He who hath divorced his wife may choose, upon the passing of each month, to remarry her when there is mutual affection and consent, so long as she hath not taken another husband. Should she have wed again, then, by this other union, the separation is confirmed and the matter is concluded unless, clearly, her circumstances change.*[1]

Music

Various schools of Islamic thought forbade the use of musical instruments and singing although there is no explicit prohibition in the Qur'án. In the Bayán, music is only allowed on Naw-Rúz (New Year's Day), which is the day of *Him Whom God shall make Manifest* and when "permission is given at that time to use all musical instruments and luxuries which at other times are not permitted."[2] The following is Nader Saiedi's comment on the *Risálah Fi'l-Ghiná'* (Treatise on Singing) by the Báb:

> Instead of offering a traditional discussion of the Islamic law related to singing and music, however, the Báb defines the philosophical conditions of moral or immoral action by discussing the dual station of the human being as possessing both an aspect of divine revelation (existence) and an aspect of specific determination (essence). Like every other human action, singing becomes moral or immoral depending on the intention of the actor and the function of the act.[3]

In the Kitáb-i-Aqdas, Bahá'u'lláh altered the restrictions of the Báb and allowed the use of music subject to the exercise of propriety and decorum:

> *We have made it lawful for you to listen to music and singing. Take heed, however, lest listening thereto should cause you to overstep the bounds of propriety and dignity. Let your joy be the joy born of My Most Great Name, a Name that bringeth rapture to the heart, and filleth with ecstasy the minds of all who have drawn nigh unto God. We, verily, have made music as a ladder for your souls, a means whereby they may be lifted up unto the realm on high; make it not, therefore, as wings to self and passion. Truly, We are loath to see you numbered with the foolish.*[4]

---

1 Bahá'u'lláh, *The Kitáb-i-Aqdas*, para. 68, p. 43.
2 Moojan Momen, *Selections from the Writings of E. G. Browne*, p. 361.
3 Nader Saiedi, *Gate of the Heart*, pp. 34–35.
4 Bahá'u'lláh, *The Kitáb-i-Aqdas*, para. 51, p. 38.

The Báb brought a fresh set of laws and, in that process, religious regulations had to be rewritten according to the exigencies of the New Day of God. Three Abrahamic religions, Judaism, Christianity and Islam, were particularly affected by the Bábí Faith. To the priests and ministers of those religions, the Báb asserted in the Qayyúmu'l-Asmá': *"Follow ye the Book which His Remembrance hath revealed in praise of God, the True One"*[1] meaning the time has come for a new revelation and new laws.

1 The Báb, *Selections*, p. 44.

Image Section 4

Figure 50: Relics of the Báb (beads)

Figure 51: Relics of the Báb—the Qur'án

Figure 52: A ring belonging to the Báb

Figure 53: The Báb's brazier and samovar

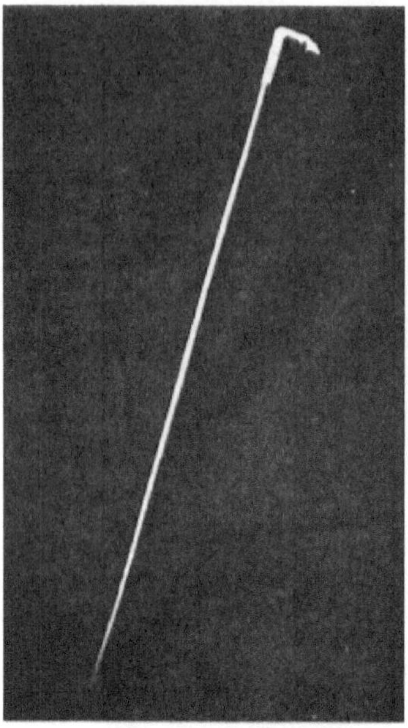

Figure 54: Some Relics of the Báb (1)

Figure 55: Some Relics of the Báb (2)

Figure 56: Some relics of the Báb (3)

Figure 57: Cap worn by the Báb

Figure 58: A signet ring of the Báb

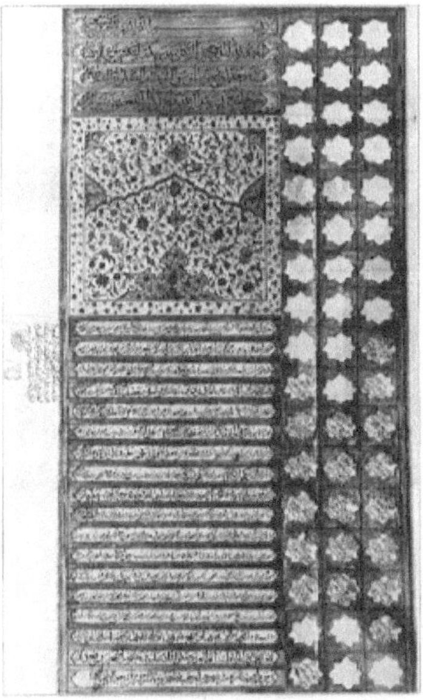

Figure 59: The Marriage Certificate of the Báb

Figure 60: A crystal Persian tea glass and china saucer with rose luster flowers belonging to the Báb

Figure 61 A small wool money purse which belonged to the Báb

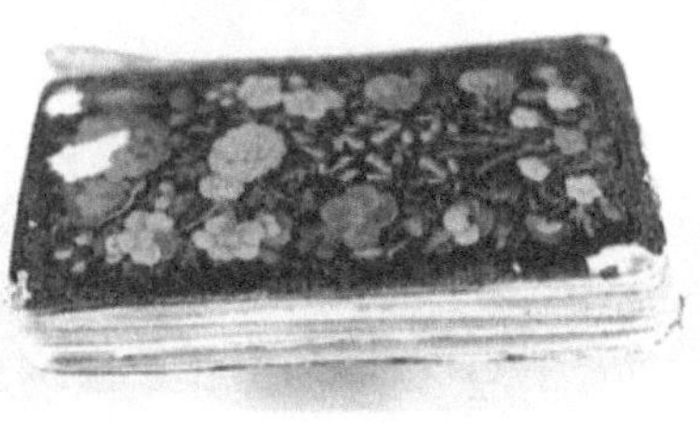

Figure 62: Pocket Qur'án of the Báb

Figure 63: Shrine of the Báb in Mount Carmel

20
Bábí laws abrogated by Bahá'u'lláh

Bahá'u'lláh had full authority to change the laws of the Báb given their transitory character. "*The Bayán deriveth all its glory* from *Him Whom God shall make Manifest*," the Báb stated[1] and that the "*whole of the Bayán is only a leaf amongst the leaves of His Paradise*."[2]

This chapter discusses those Bábí Laws abrogated by Bahá'u'lláh in the Kitáb-i-Aqdas or in His other books and epistles. "*Throughout the Bayán*," 'Abdu'l-Bahá stated, "*He* [the Báb] *openly and unambiguously declared that the object of all the Scriptures and sacred Books was none other than the Most Great Light*."[3]

Bahá'u'lláh abrogated several other Bábí laws. This section discusses ten of such injunctions as outlined below:

- Death penalty
- Payment of a fine for causing sadness
- Travel restrictions
- Destruction of books
- Shaving of heads
- Waging of holy war abolished
- Abolition of the prohibition on reading certain books
- Abolishing religious shrines
- Prostrations for obligatory prayer
- Laws regarding Him Whom God shall make Manifest

Death penalty

According to Qur'án 5:33–34, the penalty for those who waged war against Islám and devastated the land was death, amputations or banishment. Those enemies who repented before they were caught were to be forgiven. However, under Shariah Law, the death penalty is prescribed for apostasy and adultery, neither of which appear in the Qur'án. The Bible (Leviticus 20:10) also prescribes the death penalty for adultery.

The Báb prohibited the issuing of the death penalty,[4] particularly on religious grounds, when the injunction was used as a justification for killing infidels by Islamic religious authorities:[5]

---

1 The Báb in Shoghi Effendi, *God Passes By*, p. 30.
2 The Báb in Bahá'u'lláh, *Epistle to the Son of the Wolf*, p. 158.
3 'Abdu'l-Bahá, *Light of the World*, p. 18.
4 The Báb, Arabic Bayán 11:16.
5 The Báb, Persian Bayán 4:5.

> *No one is to be slain for unbelief, for the slaying of a soul is outside the religion of God ... and if anyone commands it, he is not and has not been of the Bayán, and no sin can be greater for him than this.*[1]
>
> *In case there should arise differences in questions of the* [religious] *sciences, God has not given permission for anyone in the Bayán to issue a death warrant (fatwá-yi qatl) against anyone, at any time, under any circumstances and under any condition. Moreover, it is God who judges and commands. How does it behove you, O wayward people, to issue a death warrant against anyone?*[2]

In the Kitáb-i-Aqdas the death penalty applies only to those individuals who "intentionally destroy a house by fire"[3] and for those who "deliberately take another's life."[4] However, Bahá'u'lláh affirms that: *"Should ye condemn the arsonist and the murderer to life imprisonment, it would be permissible according to the provisions of the Book."*[5] The Universal House of Justice clarifies that

> The details of the Bahá'í law of punishment for murder and arson, a law designed for a future state of society, were not specified by Bahá'u'lláh. The various details of the law, such as degrees of offense, whether extenuating circumstances are to be considered, and which of the two prescribed punishments is to be the norm are left to the Universal House of Justice to decide considering prevailing conditions when the law is to be in operation. The way the punishment is to be carried out is also left to the Universal House of Justice to decide.[6]

Payment of a fine for causing sadness

There are penalties in the Persian Bayán for causing sadness: "... *he who knowingly causeth grief to any soul must pay a fine of nineteen mithqáls of gold, should it be in his power to do so.*"[7] This injunction was changed in *The Kitáb-i-Aqdas*:

> *A fine of nineteen mithqáls of gold had formerly been prescribed by Him Who is the Lord of all* ***mankind for anyone who was the cause of sadness to another; in this Dispensation****, however, He hath absolved you thereof and exhorteth you to show forth righteousness and piety. Such is the commandment which He hath enjoined upon you in this resplendent Tablet. Wish not for others what ye wish not for yourselves ....*[8]

---

1 The Báb, "The Bayán". See *Journal of the Royal Asiatic Society*, Oct. 1889, art. 12, pp. 927–8; also cited in *The Dawn-Breakers*, p. 330.

2 Armin Eschraghi, "Undermining the Foundations of Orthodoxy", p. 237.

3 Bahá'u'lláh, *The Kitáb-i-Aqdas*, para. 62, p. 41.

4 Bahá'u'lláh, *The Kitáb-i-Aqdas*, para. 62, p. 41.

5 Bahá'u'lláh, *The Kitáb-i-Aqdas*, para. 62, p. 41.

6 Bahá'u'lláh, *The Kitáb-i-Aqdas*, pp. 204–205.

7 The Báb in Nader Saiedi, *Gate of the Heart*, p. 322.

8 Bahá'u'lláh, *The Kitáb-i-Aqdas*, para. 148, p. 73. Author's emphasis.

Travel restrictions

Regarding travel, the Bayán prescribes, "*It is not lawful to anyone to travel unless he means to go to the House of God or the house of the Nuqṭa* [The Point, e.g., the Báb]."[1] This restriction was valid till the appearance of *Him Whom God shall make Manifest* when the believers would be ready to attain His presence. In the Kitáb-i-Aqdas Bahá'u'lláh wrote: "*God hath removed the restrictions on travel that had been imposed in the Bayán.*"[2]

Destruction of books

Regarding the destruction of books, the Báb wrote in the Bayán:

> *Concerning the renewal of all books after 202 years have passed over them; and the destruction of what was written before, or its bestowal on someone. God wishes all things to become new in this Manifestation; therefore every 202 years everyone must renew his books, either cast them into fresh water, or give them to some one.*[3]

This command is abrogated in the Kitáb-i-Aqdas:

> *God hath relieved you of the ordinance laid down in the Bayán concerning the destruction of books. We have permitted you to read such sciences as are profitable unto you, not such as end in idle disputation; better is this for you, if ye be of them that comprehend.*[4]

Ruhollah Mehrabkhani explains that those disciplines that Bahá'u'lláh refers to are sciences that "*begin with words and end with words*"[5] rather than those that "*can profit the peoples of the earth*".[6] According to Ruhollah Mehrabkhani:

> The subjects of their [Islamic theologians] study were mostly superstitious and pointless arguments. They held endless discussions on the proper way to wash the different parts of the body before prayer; on the various acts and objects that might nullify one's prayers, and so on. Heated debates might arise over such questions as whether the urine of the holy Imam was ritually clean, or whether the Prophet Mohammad had a shadow. Could He be in 40 places at the same time? Could the Imam travel long distances in the twinkling of an eye? Such subjects kept them occupied for months, or even years.[7]

---

1 The Báb in Momen, *Selections from the Writings of E. G. Browne*, p. 362.
2 Bahá'u'lláh, *The Kitáb-i-Aqdas*, para. 131, p. 66.
3 The Báb in Momen, *Selections from the Writings of E. G. Browne*, p. 365.
4 Bahá'u'lláh, *The Kitáb-i-Aqdas*, para. 77, p. 48.
5 Bahá'u'lláh, *Tablets of Bahá'u'lláh*, p. 52.
6 Bahá'u'lláh, *Tablets of Bahá'u'lláh Revealed*, p. 52.
7 Ruhu'llah Mehrabkhani, *Mulla Husayn*, pp. 5–6.

Shaving of heads

The Bayán gives "*Permission to shave the hair on the head and remove the hair of the face ....*[1] In the Kitáb-i-Aqdas it is written:

> *Shave not your heads; God hath adorned them with hair, and in this there are signs from the Lord of creation to those who reflect upon the requirements of nature. He, verily, is the God of strength and wisdom. Notwithstanding, it is not seemly to let the hair pass beyond the limit of the ears. Thus hath it been decreed by Him Who is the Lord of all worlds.*[2]

By contrast, there is a Quranic injunction instructing men to shave their head during the pilgrimage to Mecca (Qur'án, 2:217) and some Hindu religious schools encourage the practice.

Waging of holy war

The principle of waging holy war is established in several books of the *Old Testament* (for example, Deuteronomy 20 specifies some regulations), as well as in the Qur'án. In the latter, holy war could be waged for defence purposes only (2:90). Despite the religious wars waged during the Christian dispensation, holy war was not prescribed by Jesus. When Jesus said "Think not that I am come to send peace on earth: I came not to send peace, but a sword" (Matthew 10:34), this was not a call to war. Rather, it can be interpreted to mean that belief in Him severs the righteous from the unrighteous, and thus His teachings are like a sword.

The Báb neither abrogated holy war nor did He command its use. In some of His Writings[3] the Báb appears to allow the waging of holy war against unbelievers. This was an injunction that was impossible to fulfil for several reasons as, according to the Báb, "*this law is confined to the sovereign Bábí kings and does not apply to everyone.*"[4] Additionally, the decisions of Bábí kings were subject to the Báb's approval Who, in fact, never gave permission to anyone to use any type of violence.[5] The Báb discouraged the use of force, prohibited the use of weapons and prescribed fines for saddening another person. The Persian Bayán also says that conquering new lands for His Faith should be done without causing any sorrow[6] and that "*not a single hair on anybody's head would be harmed.*"[7]

As Nader Saiedi points out, the Báb placed an additional restriction by leaving such a decision to the exaltation of His Cause, which meant the appearance of *Him Whom God shall make Manifest.* According to Nader Saiedi:

---

1 The Báb in Momen, *Selections from the Writings of E. G. Browne*, p. 372.
2 Bahá'u'lláh, *The Kitáb-i-Aqdas*, para. 44, p. 35.
3 The Báb, Persian Bayán 5:5.
4 The Báb in Nader Saiedi, *Gate of the Heart*, p. 363.
5 The Báb, Persian Bayán 6:16.
6 The Báb, Persian Bayán 4:5.
7 The Báb in Armin Eschraghi, "Promised One".

> The exaltation of the Promised One [Bahá'u'lláh] will precede the exaltation of His own Cause. In other words, the exaltation of the Cause of the Báb means the Revelation of the Promised One. Putting this law into effect is thus deferred until the advent of *Him Whom God shall make Manifest*. Yet after His advent, the laws of the Bayán would no longer be binding, unless the Promised One chose to confirm them, and in this case He did not. The conditions set by the Báb make it clear that He made His law of the sword impossible to carry out.[1]

Hence, the Báb implies that the sovereignty of the *Qá'im* is spiritual rather than temporal or military.[2] This is the explanation given by Bahá'u'lláh:

> *Nay, by sovereignty is meant that sovereignty which in every dispensation resideth within, and is exercised by, the person of the Manifestation, the Daystar of Truth. That sovereignty is the spiritual ascendancy which He exerciseth to the fullest degree over all that is in heaven and on earth, and which in due time revealeth itself to the world in direct proportion to its capacity and spiritual receptiveness ....*[3]

Further, Siyamak Zabihi-Moghaddam observes:

> References to Bábí kings in the Persian Bayán seem to anticipate the appearance of some form of a Bábí state (or states). The laws of the Bayán regarding holy war, however, are given as instructions to Bábí kings, implying that a Bábí king must be in power before offensive jihad can be carried out. There are no provisions here for rank-and-file Bábís to declare offensive jihad without a Bábí king. Neither are there provisions for the Bábís to wage a jihad in order to put a Bábí king into power.[4]

Bahá'u'lláh totally abrogated the use of the sword as a religious injunction. At the public declaration of His Mission in the Garden of Riḍván in 1863, His first command was "*... in this Revelation the use of sword is prohibited*"[5] and in the Tablet of Bis͟hárát He also stated that "*the law of holy war hath been blotted out from the Book.*"[6]

In general, the Báb's position on the matter of holy war is overruled by His more frequent statements on "*love and compassion*" rather than "*force and coercion*" to guide people unto His Faith,[7] the prohibition to engage in religious controversies,[8] the statement that slaying a soul for unbelief is considered the

---

1 Nader Saiedi, *Gate of the Heart*, p. 364.
2 Nader Saiedi, *Gate of the Heart*, p. 87.
3 Bahá'u'lláh, *The Kitáb-i-Íqán*, pp. 107–108.
4 Zabihi-Moghaddam, "The Babi-state conflict at Shaykh Tabarsi", p. 101.
5 The Báb in Nader Saiedi, *Logos and Civilization*, p. 242.
6 Bahá'u'lláh, *Tablets of Bahá'u'lláh*, p. 21.
7 The Báb, *Selections*, p. 77.
8 The Báb, *Selections*, p. 134.

greatest of all sins,[1] and the assertion that conversion is only possible through "*evidence and proof, and testimony, and certitude.*"[2]

Prohibition against "reading certain books"

The Persian Bayán prescribes that Bábís should not teach, write or read books other than the Bayán unless they are somehow related to "*scholastic philosophy.*"[3] Books associated with religious logic, jurisprudence and philosophy, as well as dead languages, were not allowed. Further, the study of Arabic grammar and syntax are permitted only if the reader is learning to read the Bayán. This injunction was valid until the appearance of *Him Whom God shall make Manifest.*

Believers should only own up to 19 books—the first must be the Bayán and the other eighteen must be related to it. Any excess is punishable with a fine.[4] In this regard, the Bayán indicates that in the days of *Him Whom God shall make Manifest* nothing should be written except His words.[5]

These radical injunctions were aimed in part at discouraging reading about anachronistic Islamic sciences that, upon the appearance of the Revelation of the Báb, had become obsolete. The Báb refers to the futility of engaging in useless disciplines that are mostly based on obscure Islamic interpretations. He encourages alignment with the teachings of the Bayán.[6]

In the Tablet of Bishárát ("Glad-Tidings"), Bahá'u'lláh wrote that "*In former religions such ordinances ... as the destruction of books, the ban on association and companionship with other peoples or on reading certain books had been laid down and affirmed according to the exigencies of the time*"[7]. The annulment by Bahá'u'lláh of laws concerning the burning of books also implies the abrogation of the Bayán's prohibition against reading certain books. More specifically, Bahá'u'lláh stated:

> *The unbelievers and the faithless have set their minds on four things: first, the shedding of blood; second, the burning of books; third, the shunning of the followers of other religions; fourth, the extermination of other communities and groups. Now however, through the strengthening grace and potency of the Word of God these four barriers have been demolished, these clear injunctions have been obliterated from the Tablet and brutal dispositions have been transmuted into spiritual attributes.*[8]

---

1 The Báb, The Bayán. *cf. Journal of the Royal Asiatic Society*, Oct. 1889, art.12, pp. 927–8; also cited in *The Dawn-Breakers*, p. 330.

2 The Báb in Nader Saiedi, *Gate of the Heart*, p. 368.

3 The Báb, Persian Bayán 4:10.

4 The Báb, Arabic Bayán 11:7.

5 The Báb, Persian Bayán 7.1.

6 The Báb, Arabic Bayán 4:10.

7 Bahá'u'lláh, *Tablets of Bahá'u'lláh*, p. 28.

8 *Tablets of Bahá'u'lláh*, p. 91

Religious shrines

Another example of Bábí laws preparing for the advent of *Him Whom Him God shall make manifest* is the ordinance by the Báb to abolish the practice of pilgrimage to "*tombs of prophets and patriarchs*" so that people would not be veiled from the new revelation because of their attachments to the past. Instead, new shrines were to be built in their place.[1]

The Báb explains that Jews visit Jerusalem, while the Muslims go to Mecca to see the Ka'bah with the Shí'a believers also making their pilgrimage to the shrines of the Imams—direct descendants of Muḥammad—in Iraq. In turn, Christians visit their own holy places located in various parts of the world. In a passage of the Persian Bayán, the Báb laments His isolation in the mountain of Máh-Kú while the faithful of other religions are oblivious of Him and spend their time worshipping in shrines and other places on pilgrimages:

> *In this day no less than seventy thousand people make pilgrimage every year to the Holy House of God in compliance with the bidding of the Apostle of God; while He Himself Who ordained this ordinance took refuge for seven years in the mountains of Mecca. And this notwithstanding that the One Who enjoined this commandment is far greater than the commandment itself. Hence all this people who at this time go on pilgrimage do not do so with true understanding, otherwise in this Day of His Return which is mightier than His former Dispensation, they would have followed His commandment. But now behold what hath happened. People who profess belief in His former religion, who in the daytime and in the night season bow down in worship in His Name, have assigned Him to a dwelling place in a mountain, while each one of them would regard attaining recognition of Him as an honor.*[2]

Writing about the proper use of places of worship, Bahá'u'lláh stated in the *Kitáb-i-Aqdas* that any holy place should be used purely for the worship of God:

> *Whatever hath been constructed for the worship of the one true God, such as mosques, chapels and temples, must not be used for any purpose other than the commemoration of His Name. This is an ordinance of God, and he who violateth it is verily of those who have transgressed. No harm attacheth to the builder, for he hath performed his deed for the sake of God, and hath received and will continue to receive his just reward.*[3]

Prostrations for obligatory prayer

Another example of a Bayanic law, whose purpose was solely to abrogate a Shí'a ordinance, was the exhortation of the Báb that His followers should prostrate during obligatory prayers on a crystal box containing the dust of the

---

1 The Báb, Persian Bayán 4:12.

2 The Báb, *Selections*, p. 93.

3 Bahá'u'lláh, *The Kitáb-i-Aqdas*, Questions and Answers 4, pp. 134–135.

first and the last Bábí believer.[1] This ordinance was abrogating the Shí'a practice of prostrating upon a small box with dust from the holy shrine of Imám Ḥusayn in Karbilá, Iraq. There is an element of provocation and a challenge to the ecclesiastical establishment embedded in this law.[2] However, Bahá'u'lláh repealed this command in the Kitáb-i-Aqdas:

> *God hath granted you leave to prostrate yourselves on any surface that is clean, for We have removed in this regard the limitation that had been laid down in the Book; God, indeed, hath knowledge of that whereof ye know naught.*[3]

Laws regarding *Him Whom God shall make Manifest*

There are two provisions in the Bayán regarding *Him Whom God shall make Manifest* that Bahá'u'lláh abrogated in the Kitáb-i-Aqdas about twenty-five years later. The first is the Báb's prohibition on asking questions of *Him Whom God shall make Manifest* and the second is the exhortation to offer priceless gifts to Him.

Prohibition of asking questions of *Him Whom God shall make Manifest*

> *It is not permissible to ask questions from Him Whom God will make manifest, except that which well beseemeth Him. For His station is that of the Essence of divine Revelation .... Whatever evidence of bounty is witnessed in the world, is but an image of His bounty; and every thing owes its existence to His Being .... Should anyone desire to ask questions, he is allowed to do so only in writing, that he may derive ample understanding from His written reply and that it may serve as a sign from his Beloved. However, let no one ask aught that may prove unworthy of His lofty station. For instance, were a person to inquire the price of straw from a merchant of rubies, how ignorant would he be and how unacceptable. Similarly unacceptable would be the questions of the highest-ranking people of the world in His presence, except such words as He Himself would utter about Himself in the Day of His manifestation.*[4]

The Báb explains the wisdom of this injunction:

> *Methinks I visualize those who would, prompted by their own deluded conceptions, write to Him and ask Him questions about that which hath been revealed in the Bayán, and He would answer them with words not of His Own, but divinely inspired, saying: "Verily, verily, I am God; no God is there but Me. I have called into being all the created things, I have raised up divine Messengers in the past and have sent down Books unto Them. Take heed not to worship anyone but God, He Who is My Lord and your Lord. This indeed is the undoubted truth. However, alike shall it be to Me; if ye believe in Me,*

---

1 The Báb, Arabic Bayán 10:8.

2 Moojan Momen, "The Trial of Mullá 'Alá Basṭámí", pp. 113–143.

3 Bahá'u'lláh, *The Kitáb-i-Aqdas*, para. 10, p. 23.

4 The Báb, *Selections*, p. 101.

> *ye will provide good for your own souls, and if ye believe not in Me, nor in that which God hath revealed unto Me, ye will suffer yourselves to be shut out as by a veil. For verily I have been independent of you heretofore, and shall remain independent hereafter. Therefore it behooveth you, O creatures of God, to help your own selves and to believe in the Verses revealed by Me ....*"[1]

However, Bahá'u'lláh annulled the injunction in the Kitáb-i-Aqdas:

> *In the Bayán it had been forbidden you to ask Us questions. The Lord hath now relieved you of this prohibition, that ye may be free to ask what you need to ask, but not such idle questions as those on which the men of former times were wont to dwell. Fear God, and be ye of the righteous! Ask ye that which shall be of profit to you in the Cause of God and His dominion, for the portals of His tender compassion have been opened before all who dwell in heaven and on earth.*[2]

Exhortation to offer priceless gifts to *Him Whom God shall make Manifest*

The ordinance to offer gifts to *Him Whom God shall make Manifest* was rescinded in the Kitáb-i-Aqdas. The Bayán stipulated that:

> *If there be anything which is peerless of its kind, none shall possess it but the Nuqṭa-i-Bayán. But, if the Sun hath set, then let them keep it for its rising-place* [*He Whom God shall make manifest*][3]

Also, for those who are able, *He Whom God shall make manifest* and the Letters of the Living[4] on the day of His manifestation should be presented with three diamonds, four yellow amethysts, six emeralds, and six rubies.[5] Bahá'u'lláh changed those provisions in the Kitáb-i-Aqdas:

> *God had formerly laid upon each one of the believers the duty of offering before Our throne priceless gifts from among his possessions. Now, in token of Our gracious favour, We have absolved them of this obligation.*[6]

The Báb abolished many precepts of Islam and proclaimed new laws in overthrowing the decadent old order. In His book of Laws, the Persian Bayán (Exposition), revealed in the Máh-Kú fortress, the Báb annulled many ordinances established in the Qur'án and the Sharí'a, and substituted them with fresh ordinances. Some of these ordinances referred to *Him Whom God shall make Manifest*.

---

1 The Báb, *Selections*, pp. 101–2.
2 Bahá'u'lláh, *The Kitáb-i-Aqdas*, para. 126, p. 64.
3 The Báb in Momen, *Selections from the Writings of E. G. Browne*, pp. 348–349.
4 The "Letters of the Living" were the first 18 believers in the Báb. See *Dawn-Breakers*, pp. 80–82.
5 The Báb, Persian Bayán 8:5.
6 Bahá'u'lláh, *The Kitáb-i-Aqdas*, para. 114, p. 60.

Following the same principle of religious renewal, Bábí laws were abolished, modified or confirmed by Bahá'u'lláh in the Kitáb-i-Aqdas. 'Abdu'l-Bahá wrote that "*The Book to which the Bahá'ís turn is the Kitáb-i-Aqdas, not the Bayán*".[1]

As discussed earlier, the laws of the Persian Bayán were not permanent but were in force for a short time until "*He Whom God would make manifest*" would appear.

The next chapter will explore the laws of the Báb that were modified and/or confirmed by Bahá'u'lláh in the Kitáb-i-Aqdas.

---

1 'Abdu'l-Bahá, *Additional Tablets*, p. 5.

21
Bábí laws modified and/or confirmed by Bahá'u'lláh

There was a group of Bábí laws that entered the Bahá'í Faith with no or only some modification. However, 'Abdu'l-Bahá remarked that "*The Bayán hath been superseded by the Kitáb-i-Aqdas, except in respect of such laws as have been confirmed and mentioned in the Kitáb-i-Aqdas.*"[1]

Previously in Part III some ordinances have been discussed such as, prohibition from begging, changing furniture every 19 years, writing a will, monitoring one's actions, and others. Many of these laws had an Islamic background such as ordinances related to marriage, divorce, prayer, tithes and alms, fasting, inheritance and several other personal observances and prohibitions. This chapter presents some of those injunctions that were enunciated in the Bayán and later confirmed or amended by Bahá'u'lláh:

- Major spiritual laws
- Laws of personal status
- Other individual ordinances

Major spiritual laws

As explored below, these fundamental laws are: obligatory prayer and fasting as well as reciting "*Alláh-u-Abhá*" ninety-five times a day:

Obligatory prayer

Provisions pertaining to obligatory prayers include guidelines for how to conduct the prayers as well as how to replace a missed obligatory prayer. The Báb prescribed the observance of **obligatory prayer**, saying that those reciting the prayer should turn towards *Him Whom God shall make Manifest.* In the Bayán, the obligatory prayer period starts at noon. The total number of *rak'ah*[2] sets required in Islam was changed to 19 in the Bayán.

In the first three *rak'át*, the believer focuses on the unity of the divine essence. In the following four sets, the worshipper declares the unity of the divine attributes, while in the next six sets, the emphasis is on the unity of God's acts. The final six sets are about the unity of His worship. The Báb affirms that in all these steps the believer should only see God as the Unique One.[3] In a way, these nineteen steps resemble a journey of spiritual discovery. However, the Báb does not indicate as to what should be recited during these prostrations, leaving the presumption that each believer is free to pray according to their inspiration

1 'Abdu'l-Bahá, *Additional Tablets extracts and Talks*, 2019, p. 5.

2 Each *rak'ah* (ركعة plural - ركعات *rak'át*) consists of a set of prescribed movements and supplications performed by Muslims as part of the prescribed obligatory prayer known as Ṣaláh (صَلاة).

3 The Báb, Persian Bayán 7:19.

based on the nineteen stages and wait until the appearance of *Him Whom God shall make Manifest* for guidance on which direction to turn.

Bahá'u'lláh initially developed an obligatory prayer involving nine *ra'kát*. However, this was subsequently abrogated and replaced by the aforementioned currently binding choice of three obligatory prayers distinguished from each other by their duration, frequency and use of ablutions. These prayers are to be recited facing the Shrine of Bahá'u'lláh in 'Akká, Israel, a point that is called the Qibla ("Point of Adoration").

The Bayán prescribes a verse that should be said eighteen times in the event that the obligatory prayer cannot be recited while travelling.[1] In the Kitáb-i-Aqdas, Bahá'u'lláh changed this verse for unsaid obligatory prayers:

> *When travelling, if ye should stop and rest in some safe spot, perform ye—men and women alike—a single prostration in place of each unsaid Obligatory Prayer, and while prostrating say "Glorified be God, the Lord of Might and Majesty, of Grace and Bounty". Whoso is unable to do this, let him say only "Glorified be God"; this shall assuredly suffice him. He is, of a truth, the all-sufficing, the ever-abiding, the forgiving, compassionate God. Upon completing your prostrations, seat yourselves cross-legged—men and women alike—and eighteen times repeat "Glorified be God, the Lord of the kingdoms of earth and heaven". Thus doth the Lord make plain the ways of truth and guidance, ways that lead to one way, which is this Straight Path. Render thanks unto God for this most gracious favour; offer praise unto Him for this bounty that hath encompassed the heavens and the earth; extol Him for this mercy that hath pervaded all creation.*[2]

Likewise, the Bayán exempts women in their courses from performing the obligatory prayer if they recite a specific verse 95 times a day.[3] Such an exemption is ratified in the Kitáb-i-Aqdas and the verse "*Glorified be God, the Lord of Splendours and Beauty*" is prescribed.[4]

Fasting

The Báb taught that fasting should be observed during the month of 'Alá' (Loftiness), which is the last month of the Badí' calendar, followed immediately by Naw-Rúz (New Year's Day). Fasting was only prescribed for believers between 11 and 42 years of age. Beyond those ages, fasting was not acceptable. Fasting was to involve abstention from drinking, eating, sexual intercourse, and disputes even if these are of a scientific nature. The Báb is said to have fasted most of His life.[5]

---

1 The Báb, Arabic Bayán 8:10.

2 Bahá'u'lláh, *The Kitáb-i-Aqdas*, para. 14, p. 24.

3 Ma'ani & Ewing, *Laws of the Kitáb-i-Aqdas*, p. 35.

4 Bahá'u'lláh, *The Kitáb-i-Aqdas*, para. 13, pp. 23–24.

5 Ma'ani & Ewing, *Laws of the Kitáb-i-Aqdas*, p. 61.

In the Kitáb-i-Aqdas, Bahá'u'lláh reaffirms the law of fasting during the month of 'Alá' and makes it compulsory between 15 and 70 years of age:

> *O Pen of the Most High! Say: O people of the world! We have enjoined upon you fasting during a brief period, and at its close have designated for you Naw-Rúz as a feast. Thus hath the Day-Star of Utterance shone forth above the horizon of the Book as decreed by Him Who is the Lord of the beginning and the end. Let the days in excess of the months be placed before the month of fasting. We have ordained that these, amid all nights and days, shall be the manifestations of the letter Há,*[1] *and thus they have not been bounded by the limits of the year and its months. It behoveth the people of Bahá, throughout these days, to provide good cheer for themselves, their kindred and, beyond them, the poor and needy, and with joy and exultation to hail and glorify their Lord, to sing His praise and magnify His Name; and when they end—these days of giving that precede the season of restraint—let them enter upon the Fast. Thus hath it been ordained by Him Who is the Lord of all mankind. The traveller, the ailing, those who are with child or giving suck, are not bound by the Fast; they have been exempted by God as a token of His grace. He, verily, is the Almighty, the Most Generous.*[2]

Repeating Alláh-u-Abhá 95 times every day

In the Kitáb-i-Aqdas Bahá'u'lláh wrote about reciting the *Most Great Name* (*Alláh-u-Abhá*,[3] "God is the Most Glorious"):

> *It hath been ordained that every believer in God, the Lord of Judgement, shall, each day, having washed his hands and then his face, seat himself and, turning unto God, repeat "Alláh'u'Abhá" ninety-five times.*[4]

This prescription had its roots in the Bayán[5] in which Bábís were required to recite a name of God daily 95 times. This was a form of dhikr (ذِكْر, "recollection, remembrance"), meaning praise of God through the mention of His names. In the Bayán, this was a complex practice performed in cycles of 19 days, starting with *Alláhu Abhá* ("God is Most Glorious") and followed by a range of other names including *Alláhu 'A'ẓam* ("God is Most Mighty"), *Alláhu Aẓhar* ("God is Most Manifest"), *Alláhu Anwar* ("God is Most Luminous"), *Alláhu Akbar* ("God is Most Great"), and concluding with *Alláhu Aqdam* ("God is the Pre-Existent").

---

1 Bahá'ís celebrate *Ayyám-i-Há* (that is, days for hospitality) in the intercalary days prior to the Fast.

2 Bahá'u'lláh, *The Kitáb-i-Aqdas*, para. 16, pp. 24–25.

3 "*Alláh-u-Abhá*" should in fact be Romanised as "*Alláhu Abhá*". However, in the Bahá'í Faith, Arabic words, names, and phrases are often spelled as though they were Persian; for example, Kitáb-i-Aqdas instead of Kitábu'l-Aqdas. Shoghi Effendi spoke Persian with an Iṣfahání accent learned from his grandmother Munírih Khánum.

4 Bahá'u'lláh, *The Kitáb-i-Aqdas*, para. 18, p. 26.

5 The Báb, Persian Bayán 5:17.

Bahá'u'lláh simplified the practice, requiring the 95-fold repetition of only the one invocation of *"Alláh'u'Abhá"*.

Laws of personal status

Personal status laws provide guidelines regarding marriage, divorce and inheritance.

Marriage (dowry)

Marriage guidelines cover the marriage ceremony and dowries. In the Bayán it is written: *"**It is obligatory on each one to take a wife,**[1] that a soul may remain after him to [testify to the unity of] God, its Lord ...."*[2] Hence, the Islamic law limitation of four wives is reduced to one.[3]

At the ceremony, the bride and groom must recite a sentence indicating their contentment with the will of God and to place their seals on a nuptial document. Witnesses are required whom both parties naturally must agree upon. The sentence from the Persian Bayán[4] is cited below.

> *Verily I abide by the will of God [I am for God], the Lord of the heavens, the Lord of the earth, the Lord of all things, the Lord of that which is visible and that which is unseen, the Lord of all the worlds.*[5]

The sentence specified in the Arabic Bayán has been replaced by words specified by Bahá'u'lláh, "We will all, verily, abide by the Will of God" for men and "We will all, verily, abide by the Will of God" for women.[6][7]

The Báb also wrote that the purpose of the couple's wedding vows is *"that haply in the Day of the Revelation of Him Whom God shall make Manifest they will not deviate from the supreme Mirror of these words, the One Who testifieth unto God."*[8]

---

1 The Universal House of Justice advised that: "It is apparent from the Guardian's writings that where Bahá'u'lláh has expressed a law as between a man and a woman it applies, *mutatis mutandis*, between a woman and a man unless the context should make it impossible ...." (Letter dated 24 April 1974 to an individual believer. *A Compilation on Women*, p. 14.)

2 The Báb in Momen, *Selections from the Writings of E. G. Browne*, p. 373. Present author's emphasis.

3 Peter Smith, *The Bábí and Bahá'í Religions*, p. 34.

4 The Báb, Persian Bayán 6:7.

5 The Báb in Nader Saiedi, *Gate of the Heart*, p. 313.

6 Bahá'u'lláh, *The Kitáb-i-Aqdas*, Q&A 3, p. 102.

7 In the Kitáb-i-Aqdas the two verses are different because Arabic is gender specific. Shoghi Effendi instructed that the sentence in English should be read as "We will all, verily, abide by the will of God" by both genders.

8 The Báb in Nader Saiedi, *Gate of the Heart*, p. 313.

In the Kitáb-i-Aqdas marriage is recommended as *"fortress for well-being"*[1] although it is not compulsory. According to Shoghi Effendi

> ... Of course, under normal circumstances, every person should consider it his moral duty to marry. And this is what Bahá'u'lláh has encouraged the believers to do. But marriage is by no means an obligation. In the last resort it is for the individual to decide whether he wishes to lead a family life or live in a state of celibacy.[2]

In addition, as aforementioned, the Báb indicates that Bábís can only marry Bábís but postpones the time that the restriction takes effect to the time when *Him Whom God shall make Manifest* appears. In the Bayán we find:

> *It is unlawful to enter into marriage save with a believer in the Bayán. Should only one party to a marriage embrace this Cause, his or her possessions will become unlawful to the other, until such time as the latter hath converted. This law, however, will only take effect after the exaltation of the Cause of Him Whom We shall manifest in truth, or of that which hath already been made manifest in justice. Ere this, ye are at liberty to enter into wedlock as ye wish, that haply by this means ye may exalt the Cause of God.*[3]

Bahá'u'lláh changed the above injunction and allowed marriage with followers from other religions.[4] In the Kitáb-i-Aqdas, Bahá'u'lláh explained "*Both taking and giving in marriage are permissible* [to non-believers]; *thus did the Lord decree when He ascended the throne of bounteousness and grace.*"[5]

The Báb states in the Bayán that if either the husband or the wife is unable to procreate then the fertile partner may, with the permission of the spouse, choose another. However, the Báb banned the Islamic practice of *ṣíg͟ha* (i.e. temporary marriage).[6]

The Universal House of Justice explains the permitted number of wives in the Bahá'í Faith:

> While the text of the *Kitáb-i-Aqdas* appears to permit bigamy, Bahá'u'lláh counsels that tranquillity and contentment derive from monogamy. In another Tablet, He underlines the importance of the individual's acting in such a way as to "bring comfort to himself and to his partner." 'Abdu'l-Bahá, the authorized Interpreter of the Bahá'í Writings, states that in the text of the Aqdas monogamy is in effect enjoined. He elaborates this theme in a number of Tablets, including the following:

1 Bahá'u'lláh, *The Kitáb-i-Aqdas*, Note 88, p. 205.
2 *Messages from the Universal House of Justice, 1968–1973*, pp. 109–110.
3 The Báb in *The Kitáb-i-Aqdas*, para. 139, pp. 69–70.
4 Universal House of Justice, *The Kitáb-i-Aqdas*, p. 150.
5 Bahá'u'lláh, *The Kitáb-i-Aqdas*, Questions and Answers 84, p. 131.
6 Muḥammad Afnán, "The Báb's Bayán", pp. 7–16.

"Know thou that polygamy is not permitted under the law of God, for contentment with one wife hath been clearly stipulated. Taking a second wife is made dependent upon equity and justice being upheld between the two wives, under all conditions. However, observance of justice and equity towards two wives is utterly impossible. The fact that bigamy has been made dependent upon an impossible condition is clear proof of its absolute prohibition. Therefore it is not permissible for a man to have more than one wife."[1]

According to the Bayán, marriage is conditioned upon the *payment of a dowry* by the groom to the bride. The dowry is negotiated between 19 and 95 mithqals[2] of gold for city-dwellers, or silver for village dwellers, the place being that of the residence of the groom's parents.[3] Bahá'u'lláh confirmed this law in *the* Kitáb-i-Aqdas:

No marriage may be contracted without payment of a dowry, which hath been fixed for city-dwellers at nineteen mithqals of pure gold, and for village-dwellers at the same amount in silver. Whoso wisheth to increase this sum, it is forbidden him to exceed the limit of ninety-five mithqáls. Thus hath the command been writ in majesty and power. If he content himself, however, with a payment of the lowest level, it shall be better for him according to the Book. God, verily, enricheth whomsoever He willeth through both heavenly and earthly means, and He, in truth, hath power over all things.[4]

It should be noted that at the time of writing some of the laws of the Kitáb-i-Aqdas are not currently universally enforced, such as the dowry. The Universal House of Justice will decide in the future when the laws are to be implemented.

Divorce and year of waiting

"Formerly in Persia divorce was very easily obtained," said 'Abdu'l-Bahá. *"Among the people of the past* [Islamic] *Dispensation a trifling matter would cause divorce."*[5] A form of Islamic divorce is called *ṭaláq* ("repudiation") where the husband pronounces that word to the wife three times in order to immediately dissolve the marriage. In this regard, the Bayán discourages but permits divorce after a year of waiting and patience in an effort to renew affection and love.[6]

There is also an allowance in the Bayán for a divorced couple to marry again.[7] The *Kitáb-i-Aqdas* confirms these provisions:

---

1 Bahá'u'lláh, *The Kitáb-i-Aqdas*, pp. 205–206.

2 A *mithqál* is about 3.64 g. Nineteen matháqíl (mithqals) of gold had a value of about $US4,000 in August 2021.

3 The Báb, Persian Bayán 6:7.

4 Bahá'u'lláh, *The Kitáb-i-Aqdas*, para. 66, p. 42.

5 'Abdu'l-Bahá in *Lights of Guidance*, section 1306, p. 391.

6 The Báb, Persian and Arabic Bayán 6:12.

7 The Báb, Persian Bayán 6:12.

> *Should resentment or antipathy arise between husband and wife, he*[1] *is not to divorce her but to bide in patience throughout the course of one whole year, that perchance the fragrance of affection may be renewed between them. If, upon the completion of this period, their love hath not returned, it is permissible for divorce to take place. God's wisdom, verily, hath encompassed all things. The Lord hath prohibited, in a Tablet inscribed by the Pen of His command, the practice to which ye formerly had recourse when thrice ye had divorced a woman. This He hath done as a favour on His part, that ye may be accounted among the thankful. He who hath divorced his wife may choose, upon the passing of each month, to remarry her when there is mutual affection and consent, so long as she hath not taken another husband. Should she have wed again, then, by this other union, the separation is confirmed and the matter is concluded unless, clearly, her circumstances change. Thus hath the decree been inscribed with majesty in this glorious Tablet by Him Who is the Dawning-place of Beauty.*[2]

According to Peter Smith, the new regulations on matrimony by the Báb "contrasts with the Shi'i practice of the time in which child marriage, polygamy, concubinage, and instant divorce by the husband were common."[3]

Division of inheritance

The Bayán divides a deceased's state into seven categories: (1) the children, (2) the spouse, (3) the father, (4) the mother, (5) the brother, (6) the sister and the (7) teacher, meaning "teachers of the "sciences of the Bayán",[4] in decreasing portions, following an order of proximity to the deceased.[5] Children receive the greatest allocation in the ratio of 9 parts.

As mentioned earlier, it is obligatory for Bahá'ís to leave a will and they are free to decide howsoever they would like to distribute their estate. In cases of intestacy, Bahá'u'lláh confirms in the Kitáb-i-Aqdas the above arrangement but allocates double the portion to the children because "*He 'heard the clamour of the children as yet unborn.*'"[6] The additional children's portion is deducted from the portions of the other recipients. The following table shows the various inheritance ratios.

---

1 The Universal House of Justice clarification regarding gender laws: "In general, the laws of the *Kitáb-i-Aqdas* are stated succinctly. An example of this conciseness can be seen in the fact that many are expressed only as they apply to a man, but it is apparent from the Guardian's writings that, where Bahá'u'lláh has given a law as between a man and a woman, it applies *mutatis mutandis* between a woman and a man unless the context makes this impossible." (*The Kitáb-i-Aqdas*, p. 7)

2 Bahá'u'lláh, *The Kitáb-i-Aqdas*, para. 68, pp. 43–44.

3 Peter Smith, *The Babí and Bahá'í Religions*, pp. 34–35.

4 Peter Terry, *Translation into English of A. L. M. Nicolas' French.*

5 The Báb, Persian Bayán 8:16.

6 Bahá'u'lláh, *The Kitáb-i-Aqdas*, para. 20, p. 26; & note 38, p. 184.

Category	Ar. Bayán shares	%	Kitáb-i-Aqdas shares	%
Children	9 × 60 = 540	21	18 × 60 = 1080	43
Spouse	8 × 60 = 480	19	6.5 × 60 = 390	15
Father	7 × 60 = 420	17	5.5 × 60 = 330	13
Mother	6 × 60 = 360	14	4.4 × 60 = 270	11
Brother	5 × 60 = 300	12	3.5 × 60 = 210	8
Sister	4 × 60 = 240	10	2.5 × 60 = 150	6
Teacher	3 × 60 = 180	7	1.5 × 60 = 90	4
	Total 2,520		Total 2,520	

Table of inheritance ratios

The Universal House of Justice has provided the following comment on the wisdom of this law:

> In the Arabic Bayán the Báb described His inheritance law as being "in accordance with a hidden knowledge in the Book of God—a knowledge that shall never change or be replaced." He also stated that the numbers by which the division of the inheritance was expressed had been invested with a significance intended to aid in the recognition of Him Whom God will make manifest.
>
> The "nine" mentioned here is represented in the Arabic text by the letter "Tá'", which is its equivalent in the abjad notation [see Glossary]. It is the first element of the Báb's division of inheritance, where He designates "nine parts" as the share of the children. The significance of nine lies in its being the numerical equivalent of the Greatest Name "Bahá," alluded to in the next part of this verse as "the concealed and manifest, the inviolable and unapproachably exalted Name."[1]

The Universal House of Justice explains the intestacy arrangements provided for in the Kitáb-i-Aqdas:

> It is worth noting that the Bahá'í laws of inheritance apply only when the individual dies without making a will. Indeed, one of 'Abdu'l-Bahá's Tablets seems to indicate that the very provisions of the Bahá'í law of intestacy are intended as an incentive to individuals not to neglect the duty of making a will early in life.[2]

---

1 Bahá'u'lláh. *The Kitáb-i-Aqdas*, Note 48, p. 188.

2 Letter 1 July 1996 from the Universal House of Justice to an individual.

Age of maturity

The age of maturity for girls in Islam is 9 lunar years, which is when puberty sometimes occurs following first menstruation.[1] The Báb raises this minimum age requirement for marriage and fasting to eleven.[2]

In 19th century Persia marriages were arranged at a very early age and very often were not consummated until many years later. The Kitáb-i-Aqdas states that the *"age of maturity is fifteen for both men and women."*[3]

Burial, Ḥuqúqu'lláh and pilgrimage

The following discussion pertains to burials, Ḥuqúqu'lláh, cleanliness and pilgrimage.

Burial

This section deals with burial guidelines and the prayer for the dead. In Islam the deceased are wrapped in fabric. Burial in coffins is frowned upon and Muslims follow the practise of the time of Muḥammad. Innovation is not allowed.

According to the Bayán, the deceased should be buried in a coffin made of crystal, or carved and polished stone. The body should be wrapped in five sheets of silk or cotton and a ring should be placed upon the person's right hand.[4] These burial provisions were confirmed by Bahá'u'lláh with the exception of the words inscribed on the ring.

In the Bayán the inscription on the ring for men was: *"Unto God belongeth all that is in the heavens and on the earth and whatsoever is between them, and He, in truth, hath knowledge of all things"* and for women *"Unto God belongeth the dominion of the heavens and the earth and whatsoever is between them, and He, in truth, is potent over all things."*[5] These verses were replaced in the Kitáb-i-Aqdas by a single verse for both men and women: *"I came forth from God, and return unto Him, detached from all save Him, holding fast to His Name, the Merciful, the Compassionate."*[6]

In the Kitáb-i-Aqdas, Bahá'u'lláh also adds good quality wood as a suitable material for a coffin:

> *The Lord hath decreed that the dead should be interred in coffins made of crystal, of hard, resistant stone, or of wood that is both fine and durable, and that graven rings should be placed upon their fingers.*[7]

---

1 Baharieh Rouhani Ma'ani, *Leaves of the Twin Divine Trees*, p. 4.
2 The Báb, Persian and Arabic Bayán 8:15.
3 Bahá'u'lláh, *The Kitáb-i-Aqdas*, Questions and Answers 20, p. 113.
4 The Báb, Persian Bayán 8:11.
5 Bahá'u'lláh, *The Kitáb-i-Aqdas*, para, 19, pp. 64–65.
6 Bahá'u'lláh, *The Kitáb-i-Aqdas*, para, 19, pp. 64–65.
7 Bahá'u'lláh, *The Kitáb-i-Aqdas*, para, 129, p. 64.

The *Prayer for the Dead* is **the only obligatory, congregational** prayer stipulated by the Báb. This means that it must be recited by one person while the others stand listening in silence. However, the reader has no special religious rank.

The Prayer for the Dead revealed by the Báb in the Arabic Bayán(5:11) consists of six invocations, each of which is recited 19 times. These six invocations were later confirmed by Bahá'u'lláh in the Kitáb-i-Aqdas with an additional preceding prayer. Bahá'u'lláh provides the following instruction:

> *In the Prayer for the Dead six specific passages have been sent down by God, the Revealer of Verses. Let one who is able to read recite that which hath been revealed to precede these passages; and as for him who is unable, God hath relieved him of this requirement. He, of a truth, is the Mighty, the Pardoner.*[1]

Apart from reiterating the six verses revealed by the Báb, Bahá'u'lláh added an invocation:[2]

> *Let him, then, repeat six times the greeting "Alláh-u-Abhá," and then repeat nineteen times each of the following verses:*
>
> *We all, verily, worship God.*
> *We all, verily, bow down before God.*
> *We all, verily, are devoted unto God.*
> *We all, verily, give praise unto God.*
> *We all, verily, yield thanks unto God.*
> *We all, verily, are patient in God.*[3]

The Universal House of Justice explains the structure of the Prayer for the Dead in the Bahá'í Faith:

> The passages that form part of the Prayer for the Dead comprise the repetition of the greeting "Alláh-u-Abhá" (God is the All-Glorious) six times, each followed by nineteen repetitions of one of six specifically revealed verses. These verses are identical with those in the Prayer for the Dead revealed by the Báb in the Bayán. Bahá'u'lláh added a supplication to precede these passages.[4]

Transporting the deceased remains to a distant shrine is forbidden in the Persian Bayán.[5] There is also an injunction in the Kitáb-i-Aqdas to bury the dead within one hour's journey from the place of death.[6]

---

1 Bahá'u'lláh, *The Kitáb-i-Aqdas*, para. 8, p. 22.

2 Bahá'u'lláh, *The Kitáb-i-Aqdas*, p. 170.

3 Bahá'u'lláh, *The Kitáb-i-Aqdas*, pp. 101–102.

4 Bahá'u'lláh, *The Kitáb-i-Aqdas*, p. 170.

5 See the Persian Bayán 14:18; & Browne, "Introduction to Nuqṭat al-Káf", p. 51.

6 Bahá'u'lláh, *The Kitáb-i-Aqdas*, p. 66.

The Báb counsels mourning in moderation for a relative's passing—avoiding practices such as tearing one's clothes or beating one's own body.[1] The Báb also counsels the parents of a dead child not to approach the body in order to avoid further pain.[2] In this regard, Bahá'u'lláh writes:

> *Lament not in your hours of trial, neither rejoice therein; seek ye the Middle Way which is the remembrance of Me in your afflictions and reflection over that which may befall you in future. Thus informeth you He Who is the Omniscient, He Who is aware.*[3]

In the aforementioned passage, Shoghi Effendi translated *maṣá'ib*[4] as "*hours of trial*" to characterize the loss of a loved one.

Payment of Ḥuqúqu'lláh

The payment of Ḥuqúqu'lláh ("Right of God") is an ordinance enunciated by Bahá'u'lláh in the Kitáb-i-Aqdas. It is a voluntary payment offered to the Head of the Bahá'í Faith. The funds are used to advance the Cause of God, for socio-economic projects or for philanthropic purposes.[5]

The law of Ḥuqúqu'lláh has its roots in the Bayán. The Bayán prescribes that whenever the value of a person's newly acquired possessions exceed 100 mithqals of gold they must give 19 mithqals of gold (or its equivalent) to the Báb. The Báb retains one mithqál of gold and gives one mithqál of gold to each of the eighteen Letters of the Living—some of which can be used to support their spouses and their children). What is not used by the Báb of His share is preserved for *Him Whom God shall make Manifest* when He appears.[6]

It is noteworthy that, the Báb created a wealth tax on each believer of 95 out of every 6,005 (about 16%) mithqals of newly acquired gold or its equivalent, the proceeds of which ultimately must be passed to *Him Whom God shall make Manifest.*[7] Bahá'u'lláh once wrote: *"The Primal Point hath said that they should pay Ḥuqúqu'lláh on the value of whatsoever they possess, but notwithstanding, We have in this greatest Dispensation exempted the residence and household furnishings, that is, such furnishings as are needful."*[8]

---

1 The Báb, Arabic Bayán 9:18.

2 The Báb, Arabic Bayán 10:12.

3 Bahá'u'lláh, *The Kitáb-i-Aqdas*, para. 43, p. 35.

4 Muṣíba, plural Muṣíbát, Maṣá'ib ("misfortune, calamity, disaster")

5 Allan Waters. *Ḥuqúqu'lláh, the Right of God*, pp. 7-10.

6 Moojan Momen, *Selections from the Writings of E. G. Browne*, p. 373.

7 The Báb, Persian Bayán 8:17.

8 Bahá'u'lláh, *The Bahá'í Reference Library.* Available from: https://www.bahai.org/library/authoritative-texts/bahaullah/additional-tablets-extracts-from-tablets-revealed-bahaullah/additional-tablets-extracts-from-tablets-revealed-bahaullah.pdf?369f2267

In the Kitáb-i-Aqdas, Bahá'u'lláh formalizes the law of Ḥuqúqu'lláh in the following terms:

> *Should anyone acquire one hundred mithqáls of gold, nineteen mithqáls thereof are God's and to be rendered unto Him, the Fashioner of earth and heaven. Take heed, O people, lest ye deprive yourselves of so great a bounty. This We have commanded you, though We are well able to dispense with you and with all who are in the heavens and on earth; in it there are benefits and wisdoms beyond the ken of anyone but God, the Omniscient, the All-Informed. Say: By this means He hath desired to purify what ye possess and to enable you to draw nigh unto such stations as none can comprehend save those whom God hath willed.*[1]
>
> *The basic sum on which Ḥuqúqu'lláh is payable is nineteen mithqáls of gold. In other words, when money to the value of this sum hath been acquired, a payment of Ḥuqúq falleth due. Likewise Ḥuqúq is payable when the value, not the number, of other forms of property reacheth the prescribed amount. Ḥuqúqu'lláh is payable no more than once. A person, for instance, who acquireth a thousand mithqáls of gold, and payeth the Ḥuqúq, is not liable to make a further such payment on this sum, but only on what accrueth to it through commerce, business and the like. When this increase, namely the profit realized, reacheth the prescribed sum, one must carry out what God hath decreed. Only when the principal changeth hands is it once more subject to payment of Ḥuqúq, as it was the first time. The Primal Point* [the Báb] *hath directed that Ḥuqúqu'lláh must be paid on the value of whatsoever one possesseth; yet, in this Most Mighty Dispensation, We have exempted the household furnishings, that is such furnishings as are needed, and the residence itself.*[2]

The Ḥuqúqu'lláh payment is to be offered to the Head of the Bahá'í Faith, according to the provisions of the Will and Testament of 'Abdu'l-Bahá. The Head of the Bahá'í Faith is now the Universal House of Justice.

Pilgrimage and the Qibla

The Báb designated a new *Qibla* (*Qiblih* in Persian) for the believers, this being the direction towards which one turns in prayer, as well as the destination of pilgrimage. Thus, the Báb replaced the *Qibla* of the Muslims, which is the *Ka'bah* in Mecca, mentioned in the Qur'án (2:127; 3:96) as *al-Bayt*, meaning "the House [of God]". In regards to the "*House*", the Báb explained that

> *... there hath never been, nor will ever be, a material dwelling-place for God, but that during each Revelation of the Will, it is the earth that He hath attributed to Himself that hath become His House and the seat around which the angels of heaven and the people of the earth revolve. Nay, rather, all circle round His Command which is manifested in that realm of dust. If this*

---

1 Bahá'u'lláh, *The Kitáb-i-Aqdas*, para. 97, p. 55.

2 Bahá'u'lláh, *The Kitáb-i-Aqdas*, Questions and Answers 8, pp. 108–109.

sanctity were intrinsic to the dust itself, there would have been no change in the House of God in the past, and likewise no change in the future.[1]

The sacredness of the *Ka'bah* is not inherent in its physical foundation but in the Word of God, which is identical with the Revealer, this now being the Báb. Thus, the Báb referred to Himself as the House of God—i.e. the new *Qibla*, which was to be the true "turning" point of adoration until the appearance of *Him Whom God shall make Manifest.*

The Báb also describes His living corporeal body and His mortal remains, as a point of veneration; and, in the Qayyúmu'l-Asmá', He designated His remains as a future place of pilgrimage. The site of His martyrdom was also to be a place of pilgrimage,[2] and the Báb permitted the believers to recite 95 verses for the anniversary of His birth and passing.[3]

> *God, besides Whom there is none other true God, saith: Indeed, whoso visiteth the Remembrance of God after His passing, it is as though he hath attained the presence of the Lord, seated upon His mighty Throne. Verily this is the Way of God, the Most Exalted, which hath been irrevocably decreed in the Mother Book ....*[4]

Bahá'u'lláh Himself selected the spot on Mount Carmel upon which the sepulchre of the Báb was to be built, effectively designating it as a place of pilgrimage. The Tomb of the Báb was acclaimed by 'Abdu'l-Bahá *"as the Spot round which the Concourse on high circle in adoration."*[5]

While the Báb was the *Qibla* or "House of God" for His dispensation, thereafter, the *Qibla* would be the physical presence of *Him Whom God shall make Manifest,* wherever that might be. Bahá'u'lláh confirms the *Qibla* chosen by the Báb:

> *O people of the Bayán! Fear ye the Most Merciful and consider what He hath revealed in another passage. He* [The Báb] *said: "The Qiblih is indeed He Whom God will make manifest; whenever He moveth, it moveth, until He shall come to rest."*[6] *Thus was it set down by the Supreme Ordainer when He desired to make mention of this Most Great Beauty. Meditate on this, O people, and be not of them that wander distraught in the wilderness of error. If ye reject Him at the bidding of your idle fancies, where then is the Qiblih to which ye will turn, O assemblage of the heedless? Ponder ye this verse, and judge equitably before God, that haply ye may glean the pearls of mysteries from the ocean that surgeth in My Name, the All-Glorious, the Most High.*[7]

---

1 The Báb, Persian Bayán 4:16; Provisional translation in Nader Saiedi, *Gate of the Heart,* p. 279.

2 The Báb, Persian Bayán 8:12.

3 The Báb, Persian Bayán 8:13.

4 The Báb, *Selections,* p. 64.

5 'Abdu'l-Bahá in *God Passes By,* p. 277.

6 The Báb, Arabic Bayán 8:7.

7 Bahá'u'lláh, *The Kitáb-i-Aqdas,* para. 137, p. 68.

Furthermore, the Báb prescribed pilgrimage to the resting place of the corporal body of Bahá'u'lláh after His passing, which is where the *Qibla* would come to rest. The Báb has given the following explanation regarding the importance of the remains of Bahá'u'lláh:

> *He* [Bahá'u'lláh] *is the Sun of Truth, the Face of Unity, the Countenance of Lordship, the Inmost Reality of Divinity, and the Self of Eternity.*
>
> *Should He repose upon the dust, all its atoms would call aloud proudly: Verily This is the Throne which the All-Merciful hath mounted! When even the dust, by virtue of this honour, glorieth in being the Throne of His Lord, how much more doth it behove men of insight to glory in their Incomparable, All-Compelling God, and to seek illumination from their Peerless, All-Victorious Lord!*[1]

In the Persian Bayán[2] "the new Ka'ba or House of God was to be the house of the Báb in Shiraz",[3] which is now designated as a place for pilgrimage.[4] Except for a prescription for circumambulating His House, the Báb did not provide any major pilgrimage ritual. This observance was not compulsory for women if it was difficult for them to travel.

Years later, in the Kitáb-i-Aqdas, Bahá'u'lláh formally prescribed pilgrimage to the House of the Báb in Shíráz[5] and the House of Bahá'u'lláh in Baghdád[6] for those who are able, although women are exempted from this requirement.[7]

> *The Lord hath ordained that those of you who are able shall make pilgrimage to the sacred House, and from this He hath exempted women as a mercy on His part. He, of a truth, is the All-Bountiful, the Most Generous.*[8]

Furthermore, before the revelation of the Kitáb-i-Aqdas, Bahá'u'lláh revealed two Tablets of the Pilgrimage, referred to in Persian as Súriy-i-Ḥajj (Sura of the Pilgrimage) I and II. It is said that Nabíl[9] fulfilled with utmost devotion the performance of the rites. The ceremony specific for the House of the Báb begins from outside the city and continues along the path that leads to the House and then within the House. It is said that when people saw Nabíl wandering through the streets wholly absorbed in the fulfilment of this extensive rite, they thought that he may have lost his mind.[10] Shoghi Effendi writes:

---

1 The Báb in Nader Saiedi, *Introduction to the Tablet to Báqir*, pp. 7–8.

2 The Báb, Persian Bayán 4:16.

3 Armin Eschraghi, "Undermining the Foundations of Orthodoxy", p. 231.

4 Denis MacEoin, *Rituals in Babism and Baha'ism*, p. 25.

5 The House of the Báb in Shíráz was demolished in 1979 by orders of the Iranian government.

6 The House of Bahá'u'lláh in Baghdád was demolished in 2013 by adversaries of the Bahá'í Faith.

7 Bahá'u'lláh, *The Kitáb-i-Aqdas*, para. 137, p. 68.

8 Bahá'u'lláh, *The Kitáb-i-Aqdas*, para. 32, p. 30 .

9 Nabíl-i-A'ẓam, Apostle of Bahá'u'lláh and author of *The Dawn-Breakers.*

10 Adib Taherzadeh, *The Revelation of Bahá'u'lláh*, Vol. 2, p. 240..

> It was during those days that Nabíl, recently honored with the title of Nabíl-i-A'ẓam, in a Tablet specifically addressed to him, in which he was bidden to "deliver the Message" of his Lord "to East and West," arose, despite intermittent persecutions, to tear asunder the "most grievous veil," to implant the love of an adored Master in the hearts of His countrymen, and to champion the Cause which his Beloved had, under such tragic conditions, proclaimed. It was during those same days that Bahá'u'lláh instructed this same Nabíl to recite on His behalf the two newly revealed Tablets of the Pilgrimage, and to perform, in His stead, the rites prescribed in them, when visiting the Báb's House in Shíráz and the Most Great House in Baghdád—an act that marks the inception of one of the holiest observances, which, in a later period, the Kitáb-i-Aqdas was to formally establish.[1]

The review of the laws introduced by the Báb and Bahá'u'lláh in chapters 18, 19, 20 & 21 was set mainly in the context of the Persian Bayán and the Kitáb-i-Aqdas. The discussion revealed the close association and smooth progression from the dispensation of the Báb to the dispensation of Bahá'u'lláh. The laws of the Báb provided a transition between Islam and the Bahá'í Faith. Within a six-year period, the laws of the Báb radically changed the religious landscape, allowing *Him Whom God shall manifest* to create a new framework without the need to refer to Jewish, Christian and Islamic conventions. The Writings of Bahá'u'lláh focused on creating an even more progressive religious system that is destined to last at least one thousand years.

The next chapter focuses on Bábí ordinances not discussed by Bahá'u'lláh in the Kitáb-i-Aqdas.

1 Shoghi Effendi, *God Passes By*, pp. 176–177.

22
Some Bábí ordinances not discussed in the Kitáb-i-Aqdas

The laws of the Bayán that were not confirmed in the Kitáb-i-Aqdas are considered to have been abrogated. In the same way, any laws of Islam not mentioned by the Báb, such as circumcision,[1] were abrogated with the coming of the Báb. However, some Bábí practices were addressed by 'Abdu'l-Bahá, Shoghi Effendi and the Universal House of Justice. Five of those practices are outlined below:

Notwithstanding this, some Bábí practices still found their way into the individual and social life of Bahá'ís, and were subsequently dealt with by 'Abdu'l-Bahá, Shoghi Effendi or the Universal House of Justice.

- Use of ringstones
- Prohibition on use of tobacco
- New personal salutations
- Tattoos
- Facing the sun and moon

Use of ringstones

In the Bayán, the Báb advised believers to wear a ring made of red cornelian containing certain verses,[2] the purpose of which was to enable the person wearing the ring to recognize *Him Whom God shall manifest* at the time of His appearance. Shoghi Effendi indicated that wearing a Bahá'í ring is not obligatory.[3] 'Abdu'l-Bahá mentioned that ringstones with the Greatest Name should be worn on the small finger of the right hand[4] which is similar to Islamic practices.[5]

---

1 Circumcision is not mentioned in the Qur'án. On the contrary, the Qur'án forbids harming oneself or others (See Qur'án 7:33 & 6:120). The practice of circumcision is an ancient tradition, which is followed in Shariah Law on the basis of hadiths. Shoghi Effendi wrote that "with regard to the practice of circumcision; the Teachings bear no reference to this matter, and it is therefore not enjoined upon the believers." (Shoghi Effendi, *Dawn of a New Day*, p. 86)

2 The Báb, Persian Bayán 6:10.

3 Letter 22 February 1956 written on behalf of Shoghi Effendi to an individual believer.

4 'Abdu'l-Bahá, *Tablets of Abdul-Baha Abbas*, vol. 1, p. 178.

5 Abu'l-Qasim Faizi, "Explanation", p. 11.

Talismans and gematria

Engagement with talismans and gematria remained important in the Revelation of the Báb.[1] These practices were common in Shí'í Islam.[2] In particular, talismatics was part of the Islamic pseudo-sciences and a subject of study in religious seminars along with the study of the Qur'án, the hadiths and other topics. The later included theology, Arabic grammar and pronunciation, and elements of Islamic philosophy and logic, all of which the *Persian* Bayán (4:10) described as useless knowledge and sometimes harmful.[3]

Gematria is the technique of assigning a numerical value to letters and words in order to represent mystical statements or meanings. For example, using the *abjad* code system, the words Bahá' and the Báb, have a numerical value of nine and five, respectively.[4] Shoghi Effendi advised that, "This practice is no more in use but during the time of Bahá'u'lláh and the Báb it was quite in vogue among the educated classes, and we find it very much used in the Bayán."[5]

"This method [of numerical values] was used a great deal by the Báb," the Hand of the Cause Abu'l-Qásim Faizí wrote. "He very often gave people and places surnames which had the same numerical value as the original names. For example, He called Máh-Kú, *Básiṭ* (open). Máh-Kú and Básiṭ have the same numerical value of 72. He called Chihríq *Shadíd* (Grievous). Both of these have an abjad numerical value of 318. Likewise, the author of the *Dawn-Breakers* was named Muḥammad, but surnamed Nabíl; both names have a numerical value of 92."[6]

In turn, talismans constituted graphical and artistic representations of mystical principles on objects or paper.[7] Believers were advised to wear talismans round their necks with inscriptions related to divine names. The design of such talismans was to be taught to children from eleven years, which was the age of maturity identified by the Báb.[8] Bahá'u'lláh and 'Abdu'l-Bahá did not value these practices and there is no mention of them in the Kitáb-i-Aqdas.

Elaborating on the use of talismans in the Bábí Faith, Moojan Momen wrote:

> The Báb did not prohibit such practices but rather wanted to educate his followers gradually away from them. He saw their function more as a spiritual protection rather than a physical one ... the purpose of this is not

---

1 The Báb, Persian Bayán 3:16.
2 Peter Smith, *The Babí and Bahá'í Religions.*
3 A. L. M. Nicolas, *Le Beyan Arabe*, pp. 31–32.
4 Abu'l-Qásim Faizí, "Explanation", p.16.
5 Letter written 28 July 1936 on behalf of the Shoghi Effendi to an individual believer. Cited in Helen Hornby, *Lights of Guidance*, section 1372, p. 414.
6 Naysan and Zohre Faizi, *Penned by A. Q. Faizi*, pp. 41–42.
7 Nader Saiedi, *Gate of the Heart*, p. 329.
8 Denis MacEoin, *Rituals in Babism and Baha'ism*, p. 19.

> to achieve some magical effect but rather that what is written on the paper should appear in the soul of that person[1] ... [The Báb's] intention in asking his followers to carry these pentagrams and circles is that by having their attention constantly turned towards God, his followers will, in the day when the next Manifestation of God [Bahá'u'lláh] appears, immediately turn to him.[2]

Bahá'u'lláh elevated the concept of talisman from a physical to a human dimension asserting in a metaphor that: *"Man is the supreme Talisman. Lack of a proper education hath, however, deprived him of that which he doth inherently possess."*[3]

As with gematria, Bahá'u'lláh made it a secondary issue and scarcely used it whereas 'Abdu'l-Bahá engaged with that tradition though only minimally. None of those practices were considered in *the Kitáb-i-Aqdas.*

Tobacco

The prohibition against smoking tobacco[4] is an example of a law of the Báb that was not confirmed in the Kitáb-i-Aqdas. The practice was, however, strongly discouraged by 'Abdu'l-Bahá because of its impurity and effects as a "deadly poison".[5] The prohibition against smoking tobacco (likewise due to its impurity) by the Báb is accompanied with a similar ban on using *asafoetida* (Arabic حلتيت, ḥiltít, Persian انگژه, anguzha), a spice with a strong pungent smell and a bitter taste that is used in some foods in Afghanistan, India and Iran.

New personal salutations

The Báb changed the traditional Muslim greeting of "as-Salámu 'alaykum" ("Peace be upon you") whose reply is "wa 'alaykumu's-salám ("And upon you be peace") for men and women.

The Báb states that men should greet each other with "Alláhu Akbar" ("God is Most Great") and reply with "Alláhu A'ẓam" ("God is Most Mighty"), whereas women should salute with "Alláhu Abhá" ("God is Most Glorious") and respond with "Alláhu Ajmal" ("God is the Most Beauteous"). These were more an invocation to God than a regular salutary greeting.[6]

---

1 The Báb, Persian Bayán 4:5.

2 Moojan Momen, *The Star Tablet of the Báb.*

3 Bahá'u'lláh, *Gleanings of the Writings of Bahá'u'lláh,* pp. 259–260.

4 The Báb, Persian Bayán 9:7.

5 'Abdu'l-Bahá, *Selections*, pp. 147–148.

6 The invocations are here given as transcripted Arabic forms. For example, the Persian form of Alláhu Abhár is Alláh-u-Abhár (sometimes given as Alláh'u'Abhá).

Shoghi Effendi wrote that when Bahá'u'lláh was in Adrianople (Edirne), *Alláh-u-Abhá* was adopted as a new salutation among the Bahá'ís.[1] At that time, the believers were using the Islamic greeting of *Alláh'u'Akbar.*

Tattoos

According to the *Merriam-Webster Dictionary*, a tattoo is "a mark, figure, design, or word intentionally fixed or placed on the skin."[2] Tattoos can be delible or indelible.

The Islamic prohibition on tattoos was replaced by the exhortation by the Báb for both men and women to tattoo their chests with *"O Thou My God"* (*Alláhumma*) and *"the Most Gracious"* (*ar-Raḥmán*), respectively, in beautiful calligraphy.[3]

On this matter, the Universal House of Justice advised an individual believer as follows:

> In reply to your enquiry, nothing at all has been found in the Holy Texts on the matter of tattooing. There is, of course, the following general counsel given by Bahá'u'lláh:
>
> *Let there be naught in your demeanour of which sound and upright minds would disapprove, and make not yourselves the playthings of the ignorant. Well is it with him who hath adorned himself with the vesture of seemly conduct and a praiseworthy character.* (The Kitáb-i-Aqdas, para. 159)
>
> Generally, what is appropriate in such matters will clearly vary from culture to culture.[4]

Further, on the matter of using the "Greatest Name" on tattoos, the Universal House of Justice recommends:

> While the House of Justice is reluctant to issue a list of the specific uses of the Greatest Name which should be avoided, the principal thing is for the friends to realize the great sacredness of this symbol, and to use it in ways which are dignified and appropriate ....[5]

---

1 Shoghi Effendi, *God Passes By,* p. 176.

2 *Merriam-Webster Dictionary* (online). Available from: www.merriam-webster.com/dictionary/tattoo

3 Nader Saiedi, *Gate of the Heart,* p. 329.

4 Letter 19 August 2003 from the Universal House of Justice. Available online from: https://bahai-library.com/uhj_permissibility_tattoos

5 Letter written 3 June 1987 on behalf of the Universal House of Justice to the National Spiritual Assembly of the Hawaiian Islands. Cited in Helen Hornby, *Lights of Guidance,* p. 267.

Facing the sun and moon

There were some provisions by the Báb that, although controversial from a Quranic perspective, can be better understood in the light of the coming of Bahá'u'lláh. For example, the Báb exhorts believers to recite a verse every Friday facing the sun in honour of the Sun of Truth[1]—*Him Whom God shall make Manifest.* The verse was, "*The Brightness* [Bahá] *on thine aspect is only from God, O rising Sun, and bear witness unto that Which God hath witnessed concerning Himself, that there is no God but Him, the Precious, the Beloved.*"[2] There is also a verse to be recited facing the moon once a month.[3] In the Qayyúmu'l-Asmá': the Báb called Himself "*this Radiant Moon.*"[4]

Some authors[5] consider these practices to be similar to practices of the Zoroastrian religion.[6] Whether this was His intention or not, the adoption by the Báb of the millenary Zoroastrian Naw-Rúz (New Year) celebration[7] and its subsequent ratification by Bahá'u'lláh represent the most prominent intersection of these three Persian-born religions. Both the Zoroastrian and Badí' calendars were solar, contrary to the Islamic one, which was lunar, with the names of the month reflecting attributes of God, and it began with the vernal equinox. Nevertheless, the Bábí devotions involving turning to the sun and moon were not ratified by Bahá'u'lláh.

The above remarks warrant a broader elaboration on the influence and bond between Zoroastrianism and the five Abrahamic religions, namely, Judaism, Christianity, Islam, and the Bábí and Bahá'í Faith.

Historical data about Zoroaster, the Prophet founder of Zoroastrianism, is somewhat unclear. According to the Universal House of Justice, "Regarding the beginning of the Zoroastrian era, in one of His Tablets 'Abdu'l-Bahá states that Zoroaster lived about 750 years after Moses; in a letter to an individual believer the Guardian's secretary wrote on his behalf: 'Zoroaster lived about a thousand years before Christ. There is no exact date in the teachings regarding the beginning of His Dispensation.'"[8]

There were two messianic figures expected in the Zoroastrian religion, namely, U<u>sh</u>idár-Máh ("Grand Promoter of Righteousness") and the <u>Sh</u>áh Bahram

---

1 The Báb, *Persian Bayan*, 7:17.

2 Edward Granville Browne, "The Bábís of Persia", p. 929.

3 Nader Saiedi, *Gate of the Heart*, p. 929–930.

4 Nader Saiedi, *Gate of the Heart*, p. 134.

5 Edward Browne, "The Bábís of Persia", p. 908; Abbas Amanat, *Resurrection and Renewal*, p. 133; Vahman, "The Conversion of Zoroastrians", p. 38.

6 Boyce & Grenet, *History of Zoroastrianism*, p. 114.

7 Sadri & Ferdowsi, *Shahnameh*, p. 21.

8 On behalf of Shoghi Effendi in *Lights of Guidance*, para. 1691, p. 502.

("King Victorious")[1] meaning the Báb and Bahá'u'lláh, respectively. Bahá'u'lláh Himself was a descendant of Zoroaster.[2]

According to the Hand of the Cause Zikrullah Khadem:

> The Parsis were long awaiting the fulfillment of their prophecies that, 'After the victory of the Arabs and the decline of the Zoroastrians I (God) will raise a great man in Iran from the dynasty of the Kings, who will gather the people of the world from the east and the west to the worship of God." "He (the Promised One), then (at that time) will make the whole universe anew."[3]

"A great Bahá'í scholar, Mírzá Abu'l-Faḍl (Fazl)," Adib Taherzadeh wrote, "through extensive historical research has verified that Bahá'u'lláh was descended from Zoroaster and the Sasaniyan kings of Persia, thereby fulfilling certain traditions that the great Redeemer of mankind would be of pure Persian lineage."[4]

'Abdu'l-Bahá affirmed that in the land of Israel, Zoroaster "held converse with some of the Prophets of Israel"[5] and Bahá'u'lláh refers to Him as "*He Who is the Spirit of Purity*"[6] and wrote that "*... the fire-temples of the world stand as eloquent testimony to this truth. In their time they summoned, with burning zeal, all the inhabitants of the earth* [to him]."[7] About Zoroaster, Bahá'u'lláh wrote:

> *A divine Manifestation Who hath extolled and magnified the one true God, exalted be His glory, Who hath borne witness to His knowledge and confessed that His Essence is sanctified above all things and exalted beyond every comparison—such a Manifestation hath been called at various times a worshipper of the sun or a fire-worshipper. How numerous are those sublime Manifestations and Revealers of the Divine of Whose stations the people remain wholly unaware, of Whose grace they are utterly deprived, nay, God forbid, Whom they curse and revile!*[8]

Other striking parallels among them is their strong emphasis in ethics, the showing of kindness to animals, cleanliness, importance of agriculture, the value of social peace and tranquillity, contentment under all circumstances and the outstanding similarity between the ancient Persian calendar and the new (Bábí-Bahá'í) Badí' calendar.[9]

---

1 William Sears, *Thief in the Night*, p. 92.
2 Shoghi Effendi, *God Passes By*, p. 94.
3 Javidukht Khadem, *Zikrullah Khadem*, p. 289.
4 Adib Taherzadeh, *The Revelation of Bahá'u'lláh*, Vol. 1, p. 7.
5 Shoghi Effendi, *God Passes By*, p. 193.
6 Bahá'u'lláh, *The Tabernacle of Unity*, p. 6.
7 Bahá'u'lláh, *The Tabernacle of Unity*, p. 43.
8 Bahá'u'lláh, *The Tabernacle of Unity*, pp. 32–33.
9 Fereydun Vahman, "The Conversion of Zoroastrians", p. 38.

During the time of the Báb, Zoroastrians constituted the largest religious minority group in Persia and were discriminated against as "impure" alongside any other non-Muslim communities such as the Bábís. As a result, there were Zoroastrians who accepted the Faith of the Báb after watching a Bábí being paraded in a cruel manner, as described in *A Traveller's Narrative*:

> Thus they relate that the possessions of a certain Bábí in Káshán were plundered, and his household scattered and dispersed. They stripped him naked and scourged him, defiled his beard, mounted him face backwards on an ass, and paraded him through the streets and bazaars with the utmost cruelty, to the sound of drums, trumpets, guitars, and tambourines. A certain *gabr* [a Zoroastrian follower] who knew absolutely naught of the world or its denizens chanced to be seated apart in a corner of a caravansary. When the clamor of the people rose high he hastened into the street, and, becoming cognizant of the offence and the offender, and the cause of his public disgrace and punishment in full detail, he fell to making search, and that very day entered the society of the Bábís, saying, "This very ill-usage and public humiliation is a proof of truth and the very best of arguments. Had it not been thus it might have been that a thousand years would have passed ere one like me became informed."[1]

The Zoroastrian Faith was one of the most widespread religions in the ancient world. It was forcibly displaced as the state religion by Islam in around CE 650. The Bible does not mention the name of this religion but there are favourable comments about Zoroastrian kings in various sections of the Old Testament (II Chronicles 1, 26; 1; 8:1; Nehemiah, 2:1; Esther 1:3; 10:2; Isaiah 44:28; 45:1; Daniel, 9:1; 10:1; 11:1; Haggai 1:1; 1:10). For example, the Zoroastrian king Cyrus the Great is referred to as "His Messiah" (Isaiah 45:1) and "My Shepherd" (Isaiah 44:28), titles that the Bible usually uses for Jesus (John 1:41; 4:25) or God Himself (Psalm 23:1) respectively. In another passage we read that Cyrus the Great is "the man who executes my counsel, from a far country" (Isaiah 46:11). All those references coming from a Hebrew prophet of such a stance like Isaiah confirm the strong spiritual link between both religions.

Such tributes were in recognition to the fact that Cyrus the Great, after conquering Babylonia in 539 BCE, allowed the 70,000 captives from the Jewish nation[2] to return to Jerusalem and even helped them to rebuild their temple upon their arrival. As a result of such a cultural and historical encounter between Jewish and Persians, the Jewish scripture experienced a theological transformation incorporating motifs from the Zoroastrian religion such as the concept of angels and demons, the advent of a Saviour, Heaven as a place for reward and Hell as a space for chastisement, the notion of a final resurrection and latter days or Day of Judgement. Religious terms have come to European languages from the old Persian vocabulary of that time, such as *Paradise*

---

1 E. G. Browne, *A Traveller's Narrative*, p. 21.

2 'Abdu'l-Bahá in *Star of the West*, III:13, 4 November 1912, p. 5.

("Paridaeza"), *Satan* ("Shaitin") and *Devil* ("Daeva"). The above theological concepts subsequently found their way into Christianity and Islám,[1] and from there into the Bábí-Bahá'í Faith.

For Zoroastrians, fire is a natural, purifying element, which symbolizes God's light and wisdom. For this reason, they have continuously burning flames in their temples. A tradition says that the fires were extinguished in all their temples the day Muḥammad was born. The Qur'án does not make mention of Zoroaster directly but identifies Him with those dwelling at *ar-Rass* (Qur'án 25:38 & 50:12), the place where Zoroaster used to preach in the region near the Araxes river and the region to the east of the castles of Máh-Kú and Chihríq.[2] The Zoroastrians are also mentioned as "*al-Majús*" (the Magians) in Qur'án 22:17 alongside the Jews, the Sabians and the Christians.

'Abdu'l-Bahá commented on an important prophecy about the status of Muḥammad, the Báb and Bahá'u'lláh in the Zoroastrian scriptures:

> *Thou hadst written that in the sacred texts of the followers of Zoroaster it is written that in the latter days, in three separate dispensations, the sun must needs be brought to a standstill. In the first dispensation, it is predicted, the sun will remain motionless for ten days; in the second for twice that time; in the third for no less than one whole month. The interpretation of this prophecy is this: the first Dispensation to which it refers is the Muḥammadan Dispensation during which the Sun of Truth stood still for ten days. Each day is reckoned as one century. The Muḥammadan Dispensation must have, therefore, lasted no less than one thousand years, which is precisely the period that has elapsed from the setting of the star of the Imamate to the advent of the Dispensation proclaimed by the Báb . The second Dispensation referred to in this prophecy is the one inaugurated by the Báb Himself, which began in the year 1260 A.H. and was brought to a close in the year 1280 A.H. As to the third Dispensation—the Revelation proclaimed by Bahá'u'lláh—inasmuch as the Sun of Truth when attaining that station shineth in the plenitude of its meridian splendor its duration hath been fixed for a period of one whole month, which is the maximum time taken by the sun to pass through a sign of the Zodiac. From this thou canst imagine the magnitude of the Bahá'í cycle—a cycle that must extend over a period of at least five hundred thousand years.*[3]

As expected, some practices of the Báb were not accepted into the Bahá'í dispensation. However, some practices remain in use in the Bahá'í community although they are not binding and are subject to certain changes established by 'Abdu'l-Bahá, Shoghi Effendi and the Universal House of Justice.

---

1 Robert Hume, *The World's Living Religions*, p. 114.

2 Marzieh Gail, *Six Lessons on Islam*, p. 14; & Abbas Amanat, *Resurrection and Renewal*, p. 99n.

3 Shoghi Effendi, *The World Order of Bahá'u'lláh*, pp. 101–102.

In this chapter, we also reflected upon the spiritual link between six world religions—i.e., Zoroastrianism, Judaism, Christianity, Islam and the Bábí and Bahá'í Faith. In the context of God's progressive revelation, such a theological bond is also expressed in the legislative sphere, each time augmenting and redefining God's purpose for humanity, and strengthening the theological connection between the previous dispensations.

As the Báb once revealed about God's progressive revelation:

> *The process of the rise and setting of the Sun of Truth will thus indefinitely continue—a process that hath had no beginning and will have no end.*
>
> [1]

---

1 The Báb, *Selections*, pp. 105–106.

Appendix: Best-known works of the Báb

Work	Place	≈ Time
The Persian Bayán	Máh-Kú	1847–1848
The Arabic Bayán	Máh-Kú	1847–1848
The Qayyúmu'l-Asmá'—The Name of the Self-Subsistent, Commentary on the Súra of Joseph	Shíráz	1844
The Ṣaḥífatu'l-Ḥaramayn—The Epistle between the Two Shrines (Mecca and Medina)	Between Mecca and Medina	January 1845
The Dalá'il-i-Sab'a—The Seven Proofs	Máh-Kú	1848–1849
Commentary on the Súra of Kawthar—Commentary on the Sura of the Abundance	Shíráz	May 1846
Commentary on the Súra of Va'l-'Aṣr—Commentary on the Sura of the Afternoon	Iṣfahán	Fall of 1846
The Kitáb-i-Asmá'—The Book of Divine Names	Máh-Kú—Chihríq	1848–1849
Ṣaḥífiy-i-Makhzúmíyyih—The Hidden Treasured Epistle	Shíráz	Jan 1844–Jan 1846
Ṣaḥífiy-i-Ja'faríyyih—Epistle to Ja'far	Shíráz	January 1846
Zíyarát-i-Sháh-'Abdu'l-'Aẓím—Tablet of Visitation to the Shrine of Sháh 'Abdu'l-'Aẓím	Unknown	Unknown
Kitáb-i-Panj-Sha'n—The Book of Five Modes or Five Grades	Chihríq	19 March–4 April 1950
Ṣaḥífiy-i-Raḍavíyyih—Treatise on Paradise	Unknown	Before Jan 1846
Risáliy-i-'Adlíyyih—Treatise on Justice	Shíráz	Before January 1846
Risáliy-i-Fiqhíyyih—Treatise on Jurisprudence	Búshihr	When the Báb was 19 years old.
Risáliy-i-Dhahabíyyih—The Golden Treatise	Shíráz	1846
Kitábu'r-Rúḥ—The Book of the Spirit	On way back to Búshihr	1845
Súriy-i-Tawḥíd—Sura of the Unity of God	Shíráz	June 1845–September 1846
Lawḥ-i-Ḥurúfát—Tablet of the Letters	Chihríq	19 March–4 April 1950

Work	Place	≈ Time
Tafsír-i-Nubuwat-i-Kháṣṣih—Treatise on the Prophethood of Muḥammad	Iṣfahán	Late 1846
Risáliy-i-Furú'-i-'Adlíyyih—Treatise on Aspects of Jurisprudence	Shíráz	Early to mid 1846
Khaṣá'il-i-Sab'ih—The Seven Qualifications or Directives	Probably in Búshihr	1845
Epistle to Muḥammad Sháh (I) (in the Qayyúmu'l-Asmá') delivered by Mullá Ḥusayn	Shíráz	1844
Epistle to Muḥammad Sháh (II)	Búshihr	May–June 1845
Epistle to Muḥammad Sháh (II)	Síyáh-Dihán, Qazvín (on way to Máh-Kú)	April–May 1847
Epistle to Muḥammad Sháh (III)	Máh-Kú	About 1848
Epistles to Muḥammad Sháh (IV and V) before and after the trial in Tabríz (July 1848)	Chihríq	April 1848–September 1848
Message to Ḥájí Mírzá Áqásí (I) (in the Qayyúmu'l-Asmá') taken by Mullá Ḥusayn (I)	Shíráz	1844
Epistle to Ḥájí Mírzá Áqásí II	Búshihr	May–June 1845.
Epistle to Ḥájí Mírzá Áqásí II	Síyáh-Dihán, Qazvín April-May 1847	
Epistle to Ḥájí Mírzá Áqásí III (Khuṭbiy-i-Qahríyyih—Sermon of Wrath)	Chihríq	About August 1858
Epistle to Sulṭán 'Abdu'l-Majíd	Muscat (Oman)	Early 1845

Bibliography

'Abdu'l-Bahá. *'Abdu'l-Bahá in London.* Bahá'í Publishing Trust, London. 1982.

________. *Additional Tablets, Extracts and Talks.* Bahá'í World Centre, Haifa. 2019. Last retrieved 30 June 2022 at www.bahai.org/library/authoritative-texts/abdul-baha/additional-tablets-extracts-talks/456128820/1#228370274

________. *Foundations of World Unity.* Bahá'í Publishing Trust, Wilmette, Ill. 1979.

________. *Light of the World: Selected Tablets of 'Abdu'l-Bahá.* Bahá'í Publications Australia, Sydney. 2021.

________. *The Promulgation of Universal Peace.* Bahá'í Publishing Trust, Wilmette, Ill. 1982.

________. *Selections from the Writings of 'Abdu'l-Bahá.* Compiled by the Research Department of the Universal House of Justice. Bahá'í World Centre, Haifa. 1978.

________. *Some Answered Questions.* 2nd ed. Bahá'í World Centre, Haifa. 2014. Also www.Baháí.org/library/authoritative-texts/abdul-Bahá/some-answer ed-questions/

________. *Tablets of Abdul-Baha Abbas.* Vols 1–3. Bahá'í Publishing Committee, Chicago. 1909, 1919 & 1916.

________. *A Traveller's Narrative.* Bahá'í Publishing Trust, Wilmette, Ill. 1980.

________. *The Will and Testament of 'Abdu'l-Bahá.* Bahá'í Publishing Trust, Wilmette, Ill. 1990.

'Abdullah Yúsuf 'Alí. *The Meaning of the Holy Qur'án.* Amana Corp., Maryland, USA. 1989.

Abu'l-Faḍl Gulpáygání, Mírzá. *Bahá'í Proofs.* J. W. Pratt & Co, New York. 1902. Also https://bahai-library.com/gulpaygani_bahai_proofs

________. *Miracles and Metaphors.* Kalimát Press, Los Angeles. 1981.

Afnan, Elham. 'A Twofold Mission: Some Distinctive Characteristics of the Person and Teachings of the Báb'. *The Bahá'í World,* November 2019. Available at https://bahaiworld.bahai.org/wp-content/uploads/2020/10/ twofold-mission.pdf

Afnán, Mírzá Ḥabíbu'lláh. *The Genesis of the Bábí-Bahá'í Faiths in Shíráz and Fárs.* Tr. Ahang Rabbani. Brill, 2008. Last retrieved 30 June 2022 at https://bahai-library.com/pdf/a/afnan_rabbani_genesis_faiths.pdf

Afnán, Muḥammad. 'Ayyám-i-Butún' (The Days of Concealment). *Pazhúheshnámeh* 2(1):3–38, 1997.

________. 'The Báb's Bayán: An Analytical Survey'. *World Order,* 31:4, pp. 7–16. 2000

________. 'The Role of the Bahá'í Scholar in Defending the Faith'. *Associate.* Association for Bahá'í Studies English-Speaking Europe, London. 2001 Winter/Spring. Last accessed 30 September 2021 https://Baháí-library.com/afnan_scholar_defending_faith

________. The Invocation "Is There Any Remover of Difficulties Save God..." (trans. Adib Masumian). *Safíniy-i-'Irfán, vol. 9 (2006), pp. 263–64.* Available at: https://bahai-library.com/pdf/a/afnan_masumian_remover_difficulties.pdf

Amanat, Abbas. 'The Persian Bayan and the Shaping of the Babi Renewal'. *Religious Texts in Iranian Languages* (eds F. Vahman & C. V. Pedersen), pp. 337–50. Det Kgl. Danske Videnskabemes Selskab, Copenhagen. 2007.

________. *Resurrection and Renewal: The Making of the Bábí Movement in Iran, 1844–1850.* Cornell University Press, 1989.

________. 'The Shaping of the Babi Community: Merchants, Artisans, and Others'. In *The Báb and the Bábí Community of Iran* (ed. Fereydun Vahman), pp. 101–150. OneWorld Academic. 2020.

Arnold, Matthew. 'A Persian Passion Play'. *The Cornhill Magazine,* vol. 24, p. 668. London. 1871.

The Báb. *Selections from the Writings of the Báb.* Bahá'í World Centre. 1982.

Bahá'í Prayers: A Selection of Prayers Revealed by Bahá'u'lláh, the Báb, and 'Abdu'l-Bahá. Bahá'í Publishing Trust, Wilmette, Ill. 1991.

The Bahá'í World, An International Record, vol. XIII (1954–1963). Haifa, Bahá'í World Center, Haifa. 1970.

Bahá'í World Faith: Selected Writings of Bahá'u'lláh and 'Abdu'l-Bahá. Bahá'í Publishing Trust, Wilmette, Ill. 1976.

Bahá'u'lláh. *Days of Remembrance: Selections from the Writings of Bahá'u'lláh for Bahá'í Holy Days.* www.bahai.org/library/authoritative-texts/ bahaullah/days-remembrance. 2017.

________. *Epistle to the Son of the Wolf.* Bahá'í Publishing Trust, Wilmette, Ill. 1988.

________. *Gleanings from the Writings of Bahá'u'lláh.* Bahá'í Publishing Trust, Wilmette, Ill. 1990.

________. *Kitáb-i-Badí'.* Bahá'í-Verlag, 2008. (Provisional tr. by Necati Alkan & Adib Masumian.)

________. *The Kitáb-i-Aqdas.* Bahá'í World Centre, Haifa. 1992.

________. *The Kitáb-i-Íqán.* Bahá'í Publishing Trust, Wilmette, Ill. 1989.

________. *Prayers and Meditations.* Bahá'í Publishing Trust, Wilmette, Ill. 1987.

________. *The Summons of the Lord of Hosts.* Bahá'í World Centre, 2002.

________. *The Tabernacle of Unity. Bahá'í World Centre.* 2006.

________. *Tablets of Bahá'u'lláh Revealed After the Kitáb-i-Aqdas.* Bahá'í Publishing Trust, Wilmette, Ill. 1988.

Balyuzi, H. M. *The Báb: The Herald of the Day of Days.* George Ronald, Oxford. 1973.

________. *Edward Granville Browne and the Bahá'í Faith.* George Ronald, Oxford. 1970.

________. *Eminent Bahá'ís in the Time of Bahá'u'lláh.* George Ronald, Oxford. 1986.

________. Muḥammad *and the Course of Islam.* George Ronald, Oxford. 1976.

________. Khadíjih Bagum: The Wife of the Báb. Oxford: George Ronald. 1981.

Barney, Laura Clifford. *God's Heroes: A Drama in Five Acts.* Kegan Paul, London. 1910.

Barrett, David B., Kurian, George T. & Johnson, Todd M. (2001). 'World Summary'. In *World Christian Encyclopedia: A comparative survey of churches and religions in the modern world* (2nd ed.). Oxford University Press, New York. 2001.

Bays, Daniel H. *A New History of Christianity in China.* John Wiley & Sons. 2011.

Behmardi, Vahid & McCants, William. 'A Stylistic Analysis of the Báb's Writings'. *Online Journal of Bahá'í Studies,* 114(1), pp. 114–136. 2007. Available from https://bahai-library.com/pdf/b/behmardi_stylistic_ analysis.pdf

Berger, Peter L. *From Sect to Church: A Sociological Interpretation of the Baha'i Movement.* PhD dissertation, Faculty of Political and Social Science of the New School for Social Research (New York City). 1954.

Bloomfield, Lady Sara. *The Chosen Highway.* Bahá'í Publishing Trust, Wilmette, Ill. 1940.

Bois, Jules. 'The New Religions of America, vol. III: Babism and Bahaism'. *The Forum* (Concord, N.H.), vol. 74 (1 July 1925), pp. 1–10.

Boyce, Mary & Grenet, F. *A History of Zoroastrianism: Zoroastrianism under Macedonian and Roman Rule.* Brill. 2015.

Browne, E. G. 'The Bábís of Persia. Vol. II: Their Literature and Doctrines'. *The Journal of the Royal Asiatic Society of Great Britain and Ireland, New Series,* Vol. 21, No. 4 (October 1889), pp. 881–1009. Cambridge University. Last retrieved: 30 June 2022: https://www.jstor.org/stable/25208956

________. 'Introduction to Nuqtat-al-Kaf, and Index and Concordance to the Persian Bayán'. In *Kitab-i Nuqtat al-Kaf: Being the Earliest History of the Babis.* E. J. Brill, Leiden. 1910.

________. *Materials for the Study of the Bábí Religion.* Cambridge University Press. 1918.

________. *New History (Tarikh-i-Jadid) of Mirza Ali Muhammad the Bab.* Philo Press, Amsterdam. 1893.

________. *A Traveller's Narrative.* Bahá'í Publishing Committee, New York. 1980.

Brown, Kevin. *Creation: The Nature of God and the Creation of the Universe in Bahá'í*

Cosmology, 2003. Last retrieved at: https://bahai-library.com/brown_creation_encyclopedia

________. *Selections from the Bahá'í Writings and from Shaykh Aḥmad on the Seven Stages of Creation* (provisional trs). Last retrieved 30 July 2022 at https://bahai-library.com/pdf/b/brown_seven_stages_creation.pdf

Buck, Cristopher. 'The Identity of the Ṣábi'ún: An Historical Quest'. *The Muslim World,* July/Oct. 1984, pp. 172–186. https://bahai-library.com/buck_ identity_sabiuns.

________. *Paradise and Paradigm: Key Symbols in Persian Christianity and the Bahá'í Faith.* State University of New York Press. 1999.

________. *Symbol and Secret: Qur'an Commentary in Bahá'u'lláh's Kitáb-i-Íqán.* Vol. 7. Kalimát Press, Los Angeles. 1995.

Bultmann, Rudolf. *The Gospel of John: A Commentary.* Westminster Press, Philadelphia. 1971.

Carpenter, Joseph Estlin. *Comparative Religion.* London: Williams and Norgate. Home University Library of Modern Knowledge. 1910.

Cheyne, T. K. & Black, J. S. (eds). *Encyclopaedia Biblica: A Critical Dictionary of the Literary, Political and Religious History, the Archaeology, Geography and Natural History of the Bible.* Adam and Charles Black, London. 1899.

Cheyne, Thomas Kelly. *The Reconciliation of Races and Religions.* Adam and Charles Black, London. 1914.

The Compilation of Compilations. Vol. II. Bahá'í Publications Australia, Maryborough, Victoria. 2000.

A Compilation on Women. Compiled by the Research Department of the Universal House of Justice. January 1986.

Cortés, Julio. *El Corán.* Editorial Nacional, Madrid. 1980.

Curzon, George N. *Persia and the Persian Question.* Frank Cass, London. 1966.

Danesh, Roshan. *The Dimensions of Bahá'í Law.* Bahá'í Publishing Trust, Wilmette, Ill. 2019.

Day, Michael V. *Journey to a Mountain: The Story of the Shrine of the Báb.* George Ronald, Oxford. 2017.

De Bellaigue, Christopher. *The Islamic Enlightenment: The Modern Struggle between Faith and Reason.* Liveright-Vintage. 2018.

Douglas, Martin. 'The Bahá'í Faith in its Second Century'. In *The Bahá'í Faith and Islam* (ed. Heshmat Moayyad), proceedings of a symposium, McGill University, 23–25 March 1984, pp. 57–72.

Encyclopædia Britannica. Worldwide Adherents of All Religions by Six Continental Areas, Mid-2002. Encyclopædia Britannica. 2002.

Eschraghi, Armin. 'From Bábí Movement to Bahá'í Faith: Some Observations About the Evolution of a New Religion'. In *The Báb and the Bábí Community of Iran,* pp. 326–406 (ed. Fereydun Vahman), OneWorld Academic. 2020.

________. 'Promised One (maw'ūd) or Imaginary One (mawhūm)? Some Notes on Twelver Shīʿī Mahdī Doctrine and its Discussion in Writings of Bahāʾ Allāh'. In *Unity in Diversity,* pp. 111–135 (ed. Orkhan Mir-Kasimov), Brill. 2014.

________. 'Undermining the Foundations of Orthodoxy: Some Notes on the Báb's Sharia Law (Sacred Law)'. In *A Most Noble Pattern* (eds Todd Lawson & Omid Ghaemmaghami), pp. 223–247. George Ronald, Oxford. 2012.

Esslemont, John. *Bahá'u'lláh and the New Era.* Bahá'í Publishing Trust, Wilmette, Ill. 1980.

Faizi, Abu'l-Qasim. 'Explanation of the Symbol of the Greatest Name'. In *Conqueror of Hearts.* Bahá'í Publishing Trust, New Delhi, India. 1968. There is also a booklet with the same title, BPT, India, nd.

Faizi, Naysan & Zohre. *Penned by A. Q. Faizi.* George Ronald, Oxford. 2021.

Fáḍil Mázandarání, Asadu'lláh. 'The Life of the Báb'. *Star of the West,* 14:7, 1938, pp. 193–202.

Faláhi-Skuce, Houri. *A Radiant Gem: A Biography of Jináb-i-Fáḍil-i-Shirází.* Trafford. 2004.

Fernée, Tadd Graham. 'Modernity and Nation-making in India, Turkey and Iran'. *International Journal of Asian Studies,* 9(1), 2012, pp. 71–97.

Fox, Carolyn Sparey. *Seeking a State of Heaven.* George Ronald, Oxford. 2018.

Furutan, Ali-Akbar. *The story of my heart.* George Ronald Publisher,.1984.

Giachery, Ugo. *Shoghi Effendi: Recollections.* George Ronald, Oxford. 1973.

Gail, Marzieh. *Arches of the years.* George Ronald, Oxford. 1991.

________. *Six Lessons on Islám.* Bahá'í Publishing Trust, Wilmette, IL. 1973.

Ghaemmaghami, Omid. "The Hand of God is not Chained up". In *The Báb and the Bábí Community of Iran* (ed. Fereydun Vahman), pp. 406–421. OneWorld Academic. 2020.

Hamadání, Mírzá Ḥuseyn. *The Táríkh-i-Jadíd or New History of Mírzá 'Alí Muḥammad the Báb.* Tr. E. G. Browne. Cambridge University Press. 1893. Last retrieved 30 September 2021: https://Bahái-library.com/hamadani_ browne_tarikh_jadid

Handal, Boris. *El Concurso en Lo Alto.* Editorial PROPACEB, Lima, 1985.

________. 'Finding the Lamp: My Bahá'í Experience'. In *Catholics and Catholicism in contemporary Australia: challenges and achievements* (ed. Abe Ata). David Lovell Publishing. 2021.

________. *A Trilogy of Consecration: The Courier, the Historian and the Missionary.* IngramSpark. 2020.

________. *Varqá and Rúḥu'lláh: 101 Stories of Bravery on the Move.* IngramSpark. 2020.

________. *The Khamsis: A Cradle of True Gold.* IngramSpark. 2020.

________. Muḥammad, *Profeta de Dios.* Editorial Bahá'í del Peru. 2020.

Hatcher, John S. *The Purpose of Physical Reality.* Bahá'í Publishing Trust, Wilmette, Ill. 2005.

Hatcher, John S. and Hemmat, Amrollah. *The Poetry of Ṭáhirih.* George Ronald, Oxford. 2002.

Ḥaydar 'Alí Uskú'í. *Ḥaji Mírzá. Monsieur Nicolas—the French: Extracts from Tarikh-i Azarbeyijan,* p. 102. Tr. Sepehr Manuchehri. 1950. Last retrieved 30 June 2022 at https://bahai-library.com/manuchehri_tarikh_azarbeyijan_ nicolas

Hornby, Helen. *Lights of Guidance.* Bahá'í Publishing Trust, India. 1988.

Hume, Robert. *The World's Living Religions.* Prentice Hall, Texas. 1978.

Immortal Youth: A Tribute to the Life and Station of the Báb. Bahá'í Publishing Trust, Wilmette, Ill. Also a Kindle Edition. 2019.

Kalpakian, Jack. 'Representing the Unpresentable: Historical Images of National Reform—From the Qajars to the Islamic Republic of Iran'. In *Digest of Middle East Studies,* vol. 17, no. 2, pp. 162–166. Fall 2008.

Kazemi, Farshid. 'Mysteries of Alast: The Realm of Subtle Entities ('Ālam-i dharr) and the Primordial Covenant in the Babi-Baha'i Writings'. *Bahá'í Studies Review,* 15, 2009, pp. 39–66.

Keddie, Nikki R. & Yann, Richard. 'Continuity and Change Under the Qajars: 1796–1890'. In *Modern Iran: Roots and Results of Revolution,* pp. 37–57. Yale University Press, 2006. www.jstor.org/stable/j.ctt5vkwwc.9.

Khadem, Javidukht. *Zikrullah Khadem: The Itinerant Hand of the Cause of God.* Champion Builder Books, Wilmette, Ill. 1990.

Khávári, Ishráq. *Má'ida-yi Ásmání,* vol 2, p. 16–7. (ed. 'Abd al-Hamíd). Tehran. BE 129/1972–1973.

Lambden, Stephen N. 'An Episode in the Childhood of Sayyid Alí Muḥammad the Báb'. *In Iran: Studies in Bábí and Bahá'í History,* vol. 3 (ed. Peter Smith), pp. 1–32. Kalimát Press, Los Angeles. 1986.

________. 'From a Primal Point to an Archetypical Book: Literary Trajectories through

Selected Writings of the Bab (1819–1850)'. In *The Báb and the Bábí Community of Iran*, pp. 151–234 (ed. Fereydun Vahman). OneWorld Academic. 2020.

________. 'The Messianic Roots of Babi-Bahá'í Globalism'. In *Bahá'í and Globalisation*, pp. 17–34 (ed. Margit Warburg). Aarhus University Press, Denmark. 2005.

________. 'The Sinaitic Mysteries: Notes on Moses/Sinai Motifs in Bábí and Bahá'í Scripture'. In *Studies in the Bábí and Bahá'í Religions,* vol. 5, pp. 65–184 (ed. Moojan Momen). George Ronald, Oxford. 1982.

________. *Some Aspects of Isrá'íliyyát and the Emergence of the Bábí-Bahá'í Interpretation of the Bible.* PhD dissertation. University of Newcastle upon Tyne. 2002.

Losch, R.R. *The many faces of faith: A guide to world religions and Christian traditions*. Wm. B. Eerdmans Publishing, 2002.

Lawson, Todd. *Gnostic apocalypse and Islam: Qur'an, exegesis, messianism and the literary origins of the Babi religion*. Routledge. 2012.

________. 'Interpretation as Revelation: The Qur'án Commentary of the Báb, Sayyid 'Alí Muḥammad Shírází (1819–1850)'. In *The Báb and the Bábí Community of Iran* (ed. Fereydun Vahman), pp. 235–274. OneWorld Academic, 2020.

________. 'The terms 'Remembrance' (dhikr) and 'Gate' (báb) in the Báb's Commentary on the Sura of Joseph'. In *Studies in Honour of the Late Hasan M. Balyuzi* (ed. Moojan Momen), pp. 1–64. Kalimat Press, Los Angeles. 1988.

Ma'ani, Baharieh Rouhani & Ewing, Sovaida Ma'ani. *Laws of the Kitáb-i-Aqdas—The Laws of Bahá'u'lláh Placed in Their Historical Context.* George Ronald, Oxford. 2004.

Ma'ani, Baharieh Rouhani. *Leaves of the Twin Divine Trees.* George Ronald, Oxford. 2008.

MacEoin, Denis. *The Messiah of Shíráz: Studies in Early and Middle Babism*. Vol. 3. Brill. 2009.

________. *Rituals in Babism and Baha'ism*. British Academy Press. 1994.

________. *The Sources for Early Bábí Doctrine and History: A Survey.* E. J. Brill, Leiden. 1992.

McLean, Jack. *John the Baptist and Bahá'í Prophetic Categories: An Atypical Paradigm*, 2012. Last retrieved 24 July 2022: https://bahai-library.com/mclean_john_baptist

Mangol, Bayat. *Mysticism and dissent: socioreligious thought in Qajar Iran.* Syracuse University Press. 2000.

Marouti, Andreh. 'Infrastructure for Trade Routes in Western Azerbaijan, Iran: Caravanserais, Bridges, and Fortresses'. In *Architectural Heritage in the Western Azerbaijan Province of Iran*, pp. 229–258. Eds Maurizio Boriani, Mariacristina Giambruno. Springer, Cham, Switzerland. 2021.

Marques, José Luis. *Cartas a un Buen Católico.* Editorial Bahá'í de España, Madrid. 1987

Mehrabkhani, Ruhu'llah. *Mulla Husayn: Disciple at Dawn.* Kalimát Press, Los Angeles. 1987.

________. 'Some Notes on Fundamental Principles: Western Scholarship and the Religion of the Báb'. *Bahá'í Studies Bulletin,* vol. 2, No. 4 (March 1984), pp. 22–43.

Mihrshahi, Robin. *A Wondrous New Day: The Numerology of Creation and 'All Things' in the Badí' calendar,* 2013. Last retrieved: https://bahai-library.com/mihrshahi_wondrous_new_day

Moayyad, Heshmat. 'The historical relationship between the Bahá'í Faith and Islam'. In *The Bahá'í Faith and Islam,* pp. 73–92 (ed. Heshmat Moayyad), proceedings of a symposium, McGill University, 23–25 March 1984.

Mohammadhosseini, Nosratollah. *The Báb as a Primary Source of Bahá'u'lláh's Teachings,* 2020. Last retrieved 30 September 2021: https:// Baháiteachings.org/the-Báb-primary-source-of-Baháullahs-teachings/

________. 'The Commentary on the Sura of Joseph'. In *A Most Noble Pattern* (eds Todd Lawson & Omid Ghaemmaghami). George Ronald, Oxford. 2012.

Momen, Moojan. *The Bábí and Bahá'í Religions, 1844–1944: Some Contemporary Western Accounts.* George Ronald, Oxford. 1981.

________. 'The God of Bahá'u'lláh'. In *The Bahá'í Faith and the World's Religions* (ed. Moojan Momen). George Ronald, 2005, pp. 1–38. Last retrieved 30 July 2022 at: https://bahai-library.com/momen_god_bahaullah

________. 'Relativism: A Basis for Bahá'í Metaphysics'. In *Studies in Honor of the Late Hasan M. Balyuzi* (ed. M. Momen). Kalimát Press, 1988.

________. *Selections from the Writings of E. G. Browne on the Bábí and Bahá'í Religions.* George Ronald, Oxford. 1987.

________. *The Star Tablet of the Báb.* British Library, 2019. Last retrieved 30 June 2022 at: https://blogs.bl.uk/asian-and-african/2019/10/the-star-tablet-of-the-bab.html#_edn3

________. 'The Trial of Mullá 'Alá Basṭámí: A Combined Sunní-Shí'í Fatwá Against the Báb'. *Iran* 20 (1), 1982, pp. 113–143.

Momen, Wendi (ed.). *A Basic Bahá'í Dictionary.* Oxford, George Ronald, Oxford. 1989.

Muhájir, I. F. *Dr Muhajir: Hand of the Cause of God, Knight of Bahá'u'lláh.* Bahá'í Publishing Trust, London. 1992.

Muḥammad-'Alíy-i-Salmání, Ustád. *My Memories of Bahá'u'lláh.* Tr. Marzieh Gail. Kalimát Press, Los Angeles. 1982.

Mohammadhosseini, Nosratollah. "The Commentary on the Sura of Joseph". In *A Most Noble Pattern*, pp. 6–27. Eds Todd Lawson & Omid Ghaemmaghami. George Ronald, Oxford. 2012.

Nabíl-i-A'ẓam. *The Dawn-Breakers: Nabíl's Narrative of the Early Days of the Bahá'í Revelation.* Wilmette, Ill., Bahá'í Publishing Trust. 1970.

Nash, Geoffrey. 'Aryan and Semite in Ernest Renan's and Matthew Arnold's Quest for the Religion of Modernity'. *Religion & Literature*, pp. 25–50. 2014.

Necati, Alkan. *Dissent and Heterodoxy in the Late Ottoman Empire.* Gorgias Press. 2010.

Newhall, Muriel Ives Barrow. *Mother's Stories: Recollections of 'Abdu'l-Bahá*, p. 6. 1970. Last retrieved 30 June 2022 at https://bahai-library.com/ives/ stories/MSTORIES.PDF

Nicolas, A. L. M. *Le Beyan Arabe. Le Livre Sacre du Babysme.* Ernest Leroux, Paris. 1905.

________. *Le Béyan Persan.* 4 vols. Librairie Paul Geuthner, Paris. 1911–1914.

________. *Le Livre des Sept Preuves de la Mission du Bab* ['The Book of Seven Proofs of the Mission of the Bab'], Paris, 1902. A translation of the Dalá'il-i-Sab'ih ("The Seven Proofs") by the Báb.

________. *Siyyèd Ali-Mohammed, dit le Bâb.* Dujarric, Paris. 1905.

Osterhammel, Jürgen. *The Transformation of the World. A Global History of the Nineteenth Century.* Princeton University Press. 2014.

Périgord, Emily McBride. *Translation of French Foot-Notes of the Dawn-Breakers.* Bahá'í Publishing Trust, Wilmette, Ill. 1939.

Phelps, Steven. *A Partial Inventory of the Works of the Central Figures of the Bahá'í Faith.* Version 2.02, 3 November 2020. Last retrieved 2 September 2022, http://blog.loomofreality.org/.

Quinn, Sholeh. 'Muhammad Shah Qajar in Four Early Writings of the Bab'. In *A Most Noble Pattern*, pp. 160–174 (eds Todd Lawson & Omid Ghaemmaghami). George Ronald, Oxford. 2012.

Rabbani, Ahang. *Witness to Shaykh Tabarsí: The Narrative of Hájí Nasír Qazviní*, 2007. Available at https://bahai-library.com/pdf/r/rabbani_narrative_haji_ qazvini.pdf

________. 'The Conversion of the Great-Uncle of the Báb'. *World Order*, Vol. 20, No, 3, 1999, pp. 19–38.

Rafati, Vahid. 'The Development of Shaykhí Thought in Shi'i Islam'. In *The Bahá'í Faith and Islam*, pp. 93–110 (ed. H. Moayyad). Proceedings of a Symposium at McGill University (23–25 March 1984. Bahá'í Studies Publications, Ottawa. 1990.

Ram, Harsha. 'Literature as World Revolution: Velimir Khlebnikov's Zangezi and the Utopian Geopoetics of the Russian Avant-garde'. In Glaser, Amelia M. & Lee, Steven S.

(eds). *Comintern Aesthetics*, pp. 31–80. University of Toronto Press. 2020.

Renan, Ernest. *The History of the Origins of Christianity.* Book II. Grand Rapids, MI. Christian Classics Ethereal Library. 1890.

Ruhe-Schoen, Janet. *Rejoice in My Gladness: The Life of Ṭáhirih.* Bahá'í Publishing Trust, London. 2011.

Ruiz-Domènec, José Enrique & Arjomandi, Arash. *The Báb o la Puerta a un Mundo Mejor.* Editorial Bahá'í de España. 2019.

Sadri, Ahmad & Ferdowsi, Abolqasem. *Shahnameh: The Epic of the Persian Kings.* Tr. Hamid Rahmanian. Quantuck Lane Press. 2013.

Saiedi, Nader. *Gate of the Heart: Understanding the Writings of the Báb.* Association for Bahá'í Studies and Wilfrid Laurier UP. 2008.

________. *Introduction to the Tablet to Báqir.* Last retrieved 30 September 2021 at https://user-hrqc9mo.cld.bz/Tablet-to-Mullá-Baqir-Translation

________. *Logos and Civilization.* University Press of Maryland. 2000.

________. *Modernity in the Writings of the Báb.* Last retrieved 30 September 2021 at https://user-hrqc9mo.cld.bz/Modernity-in-the-Writings-of-the-Báb/1

________. 'Phenomenology of Occultation and Prayer in the Báb's Ṣaḥífiy-i-Ja'faríyyih'. In *A Most Noble Pattern* (eds Todd Lawson and Omid Ghaemmaghami), pp. 212–213. George Ronald, Oxford. 2012.

________. *Reconstruction of the Concept of the Human Being in the Writings of the* Báb, p. 4. 2019. Available at https://user-hrqc9mo.cld.bz/Human-Being-in-the-Writings-of-the-Báb

________. *Tafsír-i-Súriy-i-Kaw<u>th</u>ar (Commentary on the Súrih of Abundance).* (Provisional tr. Nader Saiedi.). Last retrieved 20 September 2021 at https://user-hrqc9mo.cld.bz/Translation-Commentary-Surih-of-Kawthar

________. 'The Worldview of the Báb: The Reconstruction of Religion and Society'. In *The Báb and the Bábí Community of Iran* (ed. Fereydun Vahman), pp. 79–100. OneWorld Academic. 2021.

Sears, William. *Thief in the Night.* George Ronald, Oxford. 1961.

Seow, J. E. H. *The Pure in Heart: Historical Development of the Bahá'í Faith in China, Southeast Asia, and Far East.* Bahá'í Publications, Australia. 1991.

Sharon, Moshe. *Notes and Observations on some of the Writings of the Báb.* The Hebrew University of Jerusalem. 2013. Posted at web.archive.org/web/ 20170315235354 and www.hum.huji.ac.il/english/units.php?cat=3666&incat =3479

Shoghi Effendi. *Bahá'í Administration.* Bahá'í Publishing Trust, Wilmette, Ill. 1974.

________. *Citadel of Faith.* Bahá'í Publishing Trust, Wilmette, Ill. 1980.

________. *Dawn of a New Day.* Bahá'í Publishing Trust, New Delhi. 1970.

________. *Directives from the Guardian.* India & Hawaii. 1973.

________. *God Passes By.* Bahá'í Publishing Trust, Wilmette, Ill. 1979.

________. *Messages of Shoghi Effendi to the Indian Subcontinent: 1923–1957.* Bahá'í Publication Trust, New Delhi. 1970.

________. *The World Order of Bahá'u'lláh.* Bahá'í Publishing Trust, Wilmette, Ill. 1974.

________. *Unfolding Destiny.* Bahá'í Publishing Trust, London. 1981.

Smith, Peter. *The Bábí and Bahá'í Religions: from Messianic Shi'ism to a World Religion.* Cambridge University Press. 1987.

________. 'The History of the Bábí and Bahá'í Faiths'. In *The World of the Bahá'í Faith* (Robert Stockman, ed.), pp. 501–512. Routledge, Oxfordshire, UK. 2022.

Star of the West. US Bahá'í newsletter, 1910–1935. Reprinted in 8 vols, George Ronald, Oxford. 1978. See https://bahai.works/Star_of_the_West

Taherzadeh, Adib. *The Revelation of Bahá'u'lláh. Vol. 1: 'Akká 1853–63.* George Ronald, Oxford. 1974.

________. *The Revelation of Bahá'u'lláh.* Vol. 2: Adrianople 1863–68. George Ronald,

Oxford. 1977.

________. *The Revelation of Bahá'u'lláh.* Vol. 3: 'Akká 1868–77. George Ronald, Oxford. 1987.

________. *The Covenant of Bahá'u'lláh.* George Ronald, Oxford. 1992.

Terry, Peter. *Translation into English of A.L.M. Nicolas' French translation and notes of Mírzá Siyyid 'Alí Muḥammad Shírází, The Báb's Bayán Arabe originally written in Arabic,* 1980. Last retrieved 30 September 2021:
https://Bahái-library.com/pdf/b/Báb_Bayán_arabic_terry.pdf

________. *A Prophet in Modern Times.* Lulu Publications. 2008.

________. *A Thematic Analysis and Summary of the Persian Bayán.* 2015. Last retrieved 30 June 2022 at https://bahai-library.com/pdf/t/terry_analysis_ summary_bayan.pdf

Tillyer, D. B. *Union with God: The Teaching of St. John of the Cross.* Mowbray, London. 1984.

Townshend, George. *Christ and Bahá'u'lláh.* George Ronald, Oxford. 1957.

The Universal House of Justice. *A Compilation on Women.* The Research Department, Haifa. 1986.

________. *Messages from the Universal House of Justice, 1968–1973.* Bahá'í Publishing Trust, Wilmette, Ill. 1976.

________. *The Kitáb-i-Aqdas.* Bahá'í World Centre, Haifa. 1992.

________. 'Whether Bahá'u'lláh and the Báb Met, Indications in the Writings and Historical Records Relative to the Question', 1985. *'Andalíb Magazine,* 1985, vol. V, no. 17, pp. 20–21. Prepared by the Research Department and later translated into English. Last retrieved 3 September 2022 at https://bahai-library.com/uhj_meeting_bab_bahaullah

Younghusband, Francis. *The Gleam.* John Murray, London. 1923.

Van Voorst, Robert. *Jesus Outside the New Testament: An Introduction to the Ancient Evidence.* Wm. B. Eerdmans Publishing. 2000.

Vahman, Fereydun. 'The Báb: A Sun in a Night not Followed by Dawn'. In *The Báb and the Bábí Community of Iran* (ed. Fereydun Vahman), pp. 1–78. OneWorld Academic. 2020.

________. 'The Conversion of Zoroastrians to the Bahá'í Faith'. In *The Bahá'ís of Iran: Socio Historical-Studies,* pp. 44–62 (eds Dominic Parviz Brookshaw and Seena B. Fazel). Routledge. 2012.

Waters, Allan. *Ḥuqúqu'lláh, the Right of God.* Victoria, Australia: Bahá'í Publications Australia, 2012.

Weinberg, Robert. *The Primal Point.* George Ronald, Oxford. 2019.

Zabihi-Moghaddam, Siyamak. 'The Babi-state conflict at Shaykh Tabarsi'. *Iranian Studies,* 35:1–3, pp. 87–112. 2002. Last retrieved 30 October 2021 from https://bahai-library.com/pdf/z/zabihi-moghaddam_babi_conflict_ article.pdf

Index

Abjad, xix, 189
Abraham, xxviii, 1, 12, 36, 39, 48, 65, 175, 217, 219, 222
Á<u>dh</u>arbayján, 60, 92, 93, 216, 227
Afnán, xiii, 54, 83, 84, 90, 156, 172, 175, 176, 227, 228, 232, 271, 293
Aḥmad son of the Báb, xiii, xxi, 6, 26, 54, 62, 174, 175, 229, 295
Arabic Bayán, 6, 7, 8, 16, 83, 84, 86, 89, 155, 159, 160, 164, 166, 169, 210, 213, 224, 227, 244, 245, 247, 248, 249, 257, 262, 264, 268, 270, 272, 274, 275, 276, 279, 291
Báb The. Spiritual and mystical teachings
- Acceptance of deeds depend on God, 135
- Avoid criticizing others, 155
- Being and doing, 127
- Blessing on homes of the believers, 135
- Cleanliness, 128, 153
- Consideration, 128
- Contentment, 128
- Debts of faith, 135
- Deeds are to be done for the sake of God, 135
- Destiny and free choice, 136
- Discernment, 128
- Education, 162, 305
- Equality, 162
- Essence of knowledge, 136
- Essence of knowledge and faith, 136
- Faith, xi, xii, xiii, xiv, xix, xxi, xxiii, xxiv, xxvii, xxx, xxxi, 2, 5, 6, 8, 9, 10, 11, 13, 14, 16, 18, 29, 43, 44, 49, 74, 77, 83, 87, 90, 95, 96, 98, 99, 101, 102, 103, 105, 109, 111, 112, 117, 118, 119, 120, 121, 122, 123, 124, 125, 127, 129, 135, 142, 150, 153, 159, 165, 167, 168, 171, 172, 175, 178, 190, 204, 205, 206, 214, 215, 216, 219, 220, 223, 224, 225, 226, 228, 229, 231, 234, 235, 238, 240, 244, 245, 252, 260, 261, 267, 269, 271, 276, 277, 278, 280, 281, 283, 286, 288, 289, 290, 293, 294, 295, 297, 298, 299, 300, 305
- Family, 4, 170, 175
- Fasting, 150, 268
- Fear of God, 129
- Firmness, 129, 137
- Firmness in the Covenant, 137
- Forgiveness, 130
- Fruit of science is recognition, 137
- God is the Most Generous, 137
- Good character, 130
- Guiding and teaching others, 157
- Harmony, 130
- Heart of the true believer, 137
- Humility, 130
- Inner being, 138
- Joy and radiance, 130
- Kindness, 131
- Kindness to animals, 131
- Learning the Word of God by heart, 150
- Marriage, xviii, xxi, 151, 270
- Martyrs, 64, 139
- Miracles, 69, 139, 293
- Moderation, 131
- Obedience, 131, 158, 222
- Paradise and hell, 139
- Parents, 164
- Patience, 131
- Peace, xxvii, 1, 47, 132, 222, 239, 241, 284, 293
- Perfection, 132, 166, 216, 241
- Personal speech, 132
- Piety, 132
- Poetry, 8, 139, 296
- Potentialities of the new Day of God, 139
- Prayer for the believers, 140
- Purity, 132, 287
- Refinement, 133
- Relying on God, 152
- Responding to requests and correspondence, 157
- Reward and punishment, 140
- Riches should not be a barrier, 140
- Righteousness, 286
- Rumours, 74
- Seeking knowledge, 164

Servitude, 133, 141
Spiritual blindness and deafness, 141
Steadfastness, 133
Submission to the Will of God, 141
Tests from God, 141
True immortality, 142
Trust in God, 134
Unity, 11, 19, 24, 92, 101, 118, 135, 142, 157, 165, 191, 203, 245, 279, 287, 291, 293, 294, 295
Women, 270, 295, 300
Worship, 134, 167
Bada<u>sh</u>t, xxi, 13, 90
Bú<u>sh</u>ihr, xvii, xxi, 30, 58, 62, 291, 292
Calendar, xiii, 164
<u>Ch</u>ihríq, xvii, xxi, xxii, 13, 60, 76, 92, 93, 110, 283, 289, 291, 292
China, 234, 294, 299
Christ, xix, xxiii, 1, 5, 6, 11, 44, 45, 48, 52, 54, 63, 97, 102, 110, 117, 123, 235, 239, 286, 300
Christians, 6, 11, 44, 50, 52, 61, 104, 106, 117, 123, 153, 162, 164, 206, 219, 221, 249, 263, 289
Elijah, xxviii, xxix, 5, 236
Fárs, 227, 236, 293
Fáṭimih Bagum mother of the Báb, xiii, 173
Gobineau Arthur Comte de, 2, 3, 57
Hadi<u>th</u>s, 127
Haifa, xxiv, xxviii, 237, 293, 294, 300
Ḥájí Mírzá Áqásí, xii, 80, 110, 292
He/Him Whom God shall make Manifest, xiii, xiv, xix, xxxii, 15, 18, 36, 76, 87, 88, 89, 90, 94, 103, 164, 165, 178, 179, 180, 181, 182, 185, 186, 187, 190, 191, 193, 201, 202, 203, 204, 206, 209, 210, 211, 212, 213, 214, 215, 216, 217, 226, 227, 232, 238, 243, 251, 257, 259, 260, 261, 262, 264, 265, 267, 268, 270, 271, 277, 279, 286
He/HIm Whom God shall make manifest, xxiii, 15, 87, 184, 187, 189, 190, 192, 203, 204, 205, 211, 213, 215, 265
House of the Báb, xvii, 280
Imám Ḥusayn, 59, 63, 81, 170, 264
India, 1, 4, 112, 234, 284, 295, 296, 299
Iraq, xxii, xxviii, 59, 81, 111, 227, 238, 263, 264
Iṣfahán, xxi, 60, 61, 76, 118, 291, 292
Islam, xii, xxvii, xxix, 3, 4, 5, 8, 24, 28, 45, 58, 70, 80, 104, 112, 117, 122, 153, 165, 190, 223, 225, 227, 249, 252, 265, 267, 274, 275, 281, 282, 283, 286, 288, 289, 290, 294, 295, 297, 298
Jerusalem, xxvii, xxviii, 13, 97, 223, 263, 288, 299
Jesus, xi, xxvii, xxviii, xxix, xxx, 1, 5, 6, 9, 11, 12, 36, 37, 38, 39, 44, 46, 49, 50, 51, 52, 53, 54, 55, 56, 63, 70, 71, 76, 102, 117, 123, 127, 201, 207, 210, 217, 219, 220, 221, 223, 225, 234, 235, 245, 249, 260, 288, 300
John the Baptist, xi, xxvii, xxviii, xxix, 5, 49, 51, 52, 53, 54, 56, 210, 297
Judaism, 8, 219, 225, 244, 249, 252, 286, 290
Karbilá, xxi, 59, 62, 81, 264
<u>Kh</u>adíjih Bagum wife of the Báb, xiii, xxi, xxii, 169, 172, 173, 174, 294
<u>Kh</u>urásán, 227
Kitáb-i-Aqdas, xiv, xxxii, 14, 74, 77, 79, 85, 86, 87, 131, 151, 153, 154, 155, 160, 161, 166, 169, 186, 192, 209, 213, 221, 224, 229, 230, 231, 232, 233, 242, 243, 244, 245, 246, 247, 248, 249, 250, 251, 257, 258, 259, 260, 263, 264, 265, 266, 267, 268, 269, 270, 271,272, 273, 274, 275, 276, 277, 278, 279, 280, 281, 282, 283, 284, 285, 294, 297, 300
Kitáb-i-Asmá', 93, 164, 291
Kitáb-i-Íqán, 6, 10, 11, 16, 18, 50, 51, 64, 90, 99, 100, 101, 104, 123, 228, 261, 294, 295
Kitáb-i-Panj Sha'n, 93
Kulayn, xxi
Laws Bábí-Bahá'í
Age of maturity, 274
Badí' calendar, xxiv, 15, 162, 165, 166, 229, 268, 286, 287, 297
Burial, xiv, 275
Confession of sins, 246
Congregational prayers, 8
Death penalty, xiv, 257
Dietary injunctions, 243, 245
Fasting, 150, 268
Gambling, 160, 161
Naw-Rúz, 165, 229, 251, 268, 269, 286
Pilgrimage, 278, 280, 281
Prayer for the Dead, 244, 275, 276
Pulpits, 243
Qibla, 226, 268, 278, 279

Talismans, xv, 283
Tattoos, xv, 282, 285
Theft, 250
Tobacco, xv, 284
Women, 270, 295, 300
Laws, Bábí-Bahá'í
Prohibition to ask questions to *Him Whom God shall make manifest*, 213
Lebanon, xxviii
Letters of the Living, xxi, 55, 66, 86, 88, 92, 97, 190, 209, 213, 217, 226, 265, 277
Máh-Kú, ix, xii, xxi, 13, 60, 76, 79, 83, 90, 91, 92, 108, 110, 224, 263, 265, 283, 289, 291, 292
Mázindarán, 210, 227
Mecca, xix, xx, xxi, 8, 50, 60, 97, 104, 120, 217, 223, 234, 235, 236, 260, 263, 278, 291
Millerites, 5
Miracles, 69, 139, 293
Mírzá Abu'l-Faḍl, 69, 74, 216, 217, 287
Mírzá Yaḥyá, xix, 210, 217
Moses, xxiii, xxviii, 1, 6, 7, 9, 36, 38, 46, 48, 65, 70, 76, 115, 123, 191, 217, 219, 220, 221, 222, 286, 297
Mount Carmel, xviii, xxviii, 56, 236, 279
Muḥammad, 2, xii, xix, xx, xxi, xxiii, xxvii, 1, 4, 6, 9, 10, 11, 23, 36, 38, 43, 44, 45, 46, 48, 50, 52, 54, 56, 58, 61, 63, 64, 70, 71, 72, 73, 74, 76, 80, 81, 82, 83, 84, 90, 96, 100, 104, 105, 106, 107, 109, 110, 112, 116, 117, 120, 122, 123, 127, 156, 165, 174, 175, 179, 191, 216, 217, 221, 223, 226, 227, 228, 232, 234, 235, 263, 271, 275, 283, 289, 292, 293, 294, 296, 297, 298, 300, 305
Muḥammad Sháh, xii, xxi, 11, 23, 64, 80, 90, 96, 104, 105, 106, 107, 109, 110, 116, 292
Mullá Ḥusayn, xxi, 55, 59, 72, 77, 79, 80, 165, 180, 226, 292
Muslims, xii, xxiii, 5, 44, 59, 70, 104, 113, 117, 122, 153, 190, 219, 221, 223, 263, 267, 275, 278
Naw-Rúz, 165, 229, 251, 268, 269, 286
New Testament, xxxii, 8, 18, 45, 48, 75, 103, 247, 300
Old Testament, 6, 15, 102, 127, 221, 225, 247, 260, 288
Ottoman Empire, 1, 104, 239, 298
Palestine, xxvii, xxviii, 239
Persian Bayán, xii, xviii, xxxii, 3, 5, 6, 7, 10, 15, 16, 46, 64, 66, 71, 72, 77, 79, 83, 84, 86, 89, 92, 94, 118, 125, 127, 131, 153, 160, 164, 167, 169, 178, 183, 186, 189, 190, 191, 192, 206, 210, 213, 217, 223, 224, 226, 227, 228, 229, 232, 243, 244, 245, 246, 247,248, 250, 257, 258, 260, 261, 262, 263, 265, 266, 267, 269, 270, 272, 273, 275, 276, 277, 278, 279, 280, 281, 282, 283, 284, 291, 294, 300
Qayyúm, 179
Quddús, xxi, 217, 218
Russia, 1, 2, 4, 239
Salmán, xi, 49, 50
Seven Martyrs of Tehran The, xxi
Sháh Bahram, 179, 286
Shaykh Aḥmad-i-Aḥsá'í, xxi, 25, 54
Shaykh Ṭabarsí upheaval, xxi, 60
Shí'a, xx, xxiii, 59, 81, 101, 112, 125, 165, 224, 228, 249, 263
Shí'í, xx, 5, 104, 283, 298
Shí'í Muslim, 104
Shíráz, xxi, xxii, xxvii, xxxi, 1, 2, 3, 57, 62, 73, 76, 90, 95, 101, 173, 174, 180, 224, 234, 238, 246, 280, 291, 292, 293, 297
Shoghi Effendi, xii, xxiv, xxviii, xxix, xxxii, 2, 4, 5, 6, 8, 10, 14, 15, 16, 18, 44, 49, 51, 52, 53, 63, 70, 76, 79, 80, 81, 83, 84, 86, 87, 88, 90, 93, 94, 95, 99, 100, 101, 102, 103, 104, 107, 110, 117, 118, 125, 160, 169, 170, 172, 178, 180, 186, 189, 191, 192, 205, 209, 217, 218, 225, 226, 229, 230, 231, 232, 233, 237, 246, 257, 269, 270, 271, 277, 280, 281, 282, 283, 285, 286, 287, 289, 296, 299
Siyyid Ḥusayn, 84, 92
Siyyid Káẓim, xxi, 54
Siyyid Muḥammad Riḍá father of the Báb, xiii, xxi, 174
Sulṭán of the Ottoman Empire, 105, 111
Syria, xxviii
Tabríz, xxi, xxii, xxvii, 8, 11, 54, 60, 124, 223, 234, 292
Ṭáhirih, 7, 8, 55, 192, 193, 226, 296, 299
Tehran, xxi, 8, 63, 109, 180, 250, 296
Torah, 221, 222, 246
Universal House of Justice The, ix, xxix, xxxi, 2, 15, 16, 51, 75, 76, 86, 160, 165, 168, 170, 171, 209, 218, 230, 232, 234, 244, 247, 250, 258, 270, 271, 272, 273,

About the Author

Boris Handal is a Full Professor of Education at the University of Notre Dame Australia. He is the author of "Varqá and Rúḥu'lláh," "Eve Nicklin, She of the Brave Heart," "The Khamsis, a Cradle of True Gold" and "A Trilogy of Consecration". His books in Spanish include *El Concurso en Lo Alto* and *Muḥammad Profeta de Dios*. He has also written *Mírzá Mihdí, The Purest Branch* which has been translated to three languages. Dr Handal has published about thirty books and articles about the Bahá'í Faith and over a hundred educational academic articles.

www.ingramcontent.com/pod-product-compliance
Lightning Source LLC
Chambersburg PA
CBHW020314010526
44107CB00054B/1840